timesaver. It offers in a single, readily available work all those materials which might otherwise have to be sought out, one by one, in official publications and specialized libraries. The documents selected are also fully cross-referenced to the narrative discussion in THE UNITED STATES IN WORLD AFFAIRS.

This latest volume in a series which has provided almost a quarter-century of service to interested readers presents the documentary roots of American foreign policy in a year highlighted by President Johnson's landslide victory over Barry Goldwater; America's role in the post-Kennedy era; the Atlantic Alliance under the pressure of rising national tensions; the effects of Krushchev's ouster on Western policy; the significance of the Communist Chinese atom bomb on the Sino-Soviet rift; Latin America in search of a destiny; the growing pains of the reborn African continent; and the difficulties of the United Nations as it tries to bring order to an uneasy world and solve its financial problems.

Event by event, this volume provides a uniquely valuable guide to the development of America's relations with the other countries of the world.

DOCUMENTS ON AMERICAN FOREIGN RELATIONS 1964

DOCUMENTS ON AMERICAN FOREIGN RELATIONS 1964

EDITED BY JULES DAVIDS
WITH THE ASSISTANCE OF
ELAINE P. ADAM

Published for the
COUNCIL ON FOREIGN RELATIONS
by
HARPER & ROW, Publishers
NEW YORK *and* EVANSTON
1965

The Council on Foreign Relations is a non-profit institution devoted to the study of political, economic, and strategic problems as related to American foreign policy. It takes no stand, expressed or implied, on American policy.

The authors of books published under the auspices of the Council are responsible for their statements of fact and expressions of opinion. The Council is responsible only for determining that they should be presented to the public.

For a list of Council publications see pages 458-460.

DOCUMENTS ON AMERICAN FOREIGN RELATIONS, 1964

For information, address Council on Foreign Relations,
58 East 68th Street, New York, N.Y., 10021

FIRST EDITION

Quinn & Boden Company, Inc., Rahway, N.J.

Library of Congress catalog card number: LC 39-28987

Published by Harper & Row, Publishers, Incorporated

PREFACE

This book continues the series of annual documentary volumes initiated by the World Peace Foundation in 1939 and carried forward since 1952 by the Council on Foreign Relations. Its purpose is to provide in convenient reference form important available documentary materials concerning the foreign relations of the United States for the current year. It also serves as a companion volume to *The United States in World Affairs, 1964* (New York and Evanston: Harper & Row, for the Council on Foreign Relations, 1965), which presents a comprehensive, narrative account of the year's international developments, to which cross-references have been noted.

In the selection of documents, the editors have been guided by two considerations: first, to include those items which seem most likely to be permanently useful, e.g., treaties, agreements, significant communiqués, and resolutions of the United Nations and the Organization of American States; second, to make available relevant statements and excerpts from major speeches and addresses which enunciate the principles and objectives of American foreign policy and provide a historical background on key issues. Among the issues prominent in 1964 were the debate over the creation of a NATO multilateral force, East-West trade, the Cyprus dispute, and the crises in Southeast Asia, Panama, Cuba, and the Congo. Attention has also been directed to significant changes on the world scene, such as the deposing of Soviet Chairman Nikita S. Khrushchev and Communist China's explosion of a nuclear device. Other important items concern the Alliance for Progress, the Kennedy Round, disarmament, and the United Nations Conference on Trade and Development. The inclusion of a given document does not signify either approval or disapproval of its contents; it is intended primarily to aid in an understanding of policy positions adopted by the United States and to provide a documentary record of major events. Editorial treatment of the documents has been limited in most instances to the correction of obvious typographic or stenographic errors and the insertion within italicized brackets of any supplementary information deemed essential to full comprehension.

Like all the publications of the Council on Foreign Relations, this volume reflects a cooperative effort involving the talents of a number of people. Especially valued has been the expert assistance of John C. Campbell, Senior Research Fellow; Donald Wasson, Librarian, Janet Rigney, Assistant Librarian, Janis Kreslins, and others of the library staff; Grace Darling, Production and Promotion Manager; Robert W. Valkenier, Editor; Mary D'Agata, Photocopyist; and Alice E. Fine, Proofreader. The press offices of the White House, the Department of State, the French Embassy in the United States, the Soviet Embassy in London, and the United Nations have all been most helpful in making available their published materials, and we are much indebted to *The New York Times* for permission to reprint texts or excerpts of documents that appeared in its pages. The editors themselves are wholly responsible for the choice of documents and for the manner in which they are presented.

J. D.
E. P. A.

May 1965

CONTENTS

II. THE ATLANTIC ALLIANCE IN THE MID-SIXTIES

A. The United States and NATO

B. The North Atlantic Treaty Organization

C. Exchange of Atomic Information

D. France, the United States, and the European Community

E. Germany, the U.S.S.R., and the West

F. United States–United Kingdom Relations

III. PROBLEMS WITHIN THE WESTERN COMMUNITY

A. The Cyprus Crisis

VII. INTER-AMERICAN AFFAIRS

A. The Alliance for Progress

B. Cuba

C. The Ninth Meeting of Consultation of Ministers of Foreign Affairs of the American States, Washington, July 21-26, 1964

D. The Panama Crisis

E. United States–Mexican Relations

F. The Problem of Overthrow of Elected Governments

VIII. THE MIDDLE EAST AND SOUTH ASIA

A. The United States and the Middle East

B. Yemen

C. Jordan

D. Israel

B. The United Nations Crisis

C. The United Nations Conference on Trade and Development (UNCTAD), Geneva, March 23-June 16, 1964

D. The Third United Nations International Conference on the Peaceful Uses of Atomic Energy, Geneva, August 31-September 9, 1964

DOCUMENTS ON AMERICAN FOREIGN RELATIONS 1964

CHAPTER ONE

ISSUES AND GOALS OF U.S. FOREIGN POLICY

A. Charting America's Course.

(1) *The State of the Union: Message of President Lyndon B. Johnson, Delivered to the Congress, January 8, 1964.*[1]

(Excerpts)

MR. SPEAKER, MR. PRESIDENT, MEMBERS OF THE HOUSE AND SENATE, MY FELLOW AMERICANS:

I will be brief, for our time is necessarily short and our agenda is already long.

Last year's congressional session was the longest in peacetime history. With that foundation, let us work together to make this year's session the best in the Nation's history.

Let this session of Congress be known as the session which did more for civil rights than the last hundred sessions combined; as the session which enacted the most far-reaching tax cut of our time; as the session which declared all out war on human poverty and unemployment in these United States; as the session which finally recognized the health needs of all of our older citizens; as the session which reformed our tangled transportation and transit policies; as the session which achieved the most effective, efficient foreign aid program ever; and as the session which helped to build more homes, and more schools, and more libraries, and more hospitals than any single session of Congress in the history of our Republic. All this and more can and must be done.

* * *

Let us carry forward the plans and programs of John Fitzgerald Kennedy—not because of our sorrow or sympathy, but because they are right.

[1] House Document 1, 88th Cong., 1st sess. For brief discussion see *The United States in World Affairs, 1964,* pp. 5-6.

In his memory today, I especially ask all members of my own political faith, in this election year, to put your country ahead of your party, and to always debate principles—never debate personalities.

For my part, I pledge a progressive administration which is efficient, and honest, and frugal.

The budget to be submitted to the Congress shortly is in full accord with this pledge.[2] It will cut our deficit in half, from $10 billion to $4.9 billion. It will be, in proportion to our national output, the smallest budget since 1951. It will call for a substantial reduction in Federal employment, a feat accomplished only once before in the last 10 years. While maintaining the full strength of our combat defenses, it will call for the lowest number of civilian personnel in the Department of Defense since 1950.

It will call for total expenditures of $97.9 billion—compared to $98.4 for the current year, a reduction of more than $500 million. It will call for new obligational authority of $103.8 billion—a reduction of more than $4 billion below last year's request of $107.9 billion.

* * *

This administration today here and now declares unconditional war on poverty in America. I urge this Congress and all Americans to join with me in that effort.

It will not be a short or easy struggle—no single weapon or strategy will suffice—but we shall not rest until that war is won. The richest nation on earth can afford to win it. We cannot afford to lose it; $1,000 invested in salvaging an unemployable youth today can return $40,000 or more in his lifetime. Poverty is a national problem, requiring improved national organization and support. But this attack, to be effective, must also be organized at the State and local level and must be supported and directed by State and local efforts.

For the war against poverty will not be won here in Washington. It must be won in the field—in every private home, in every public office, from the courthouse to the White House.

* * *

Above all, we must release $11 billion of tax reduction into the private spending stream to create new jobs and new markets in every area of this land.[3]

* * *

[2] Document 2.
[3] Public Law 88-272, approved February 26, 1964.

Let me make one principle of this administration abundantly clear: All of these increased opportunities—in employment, in education, in housing, and in every field—must be open to Americans of every color. As far as the writ of Federal law will run, we must abolish not some but all racial discrimination.

For this is not merely an economic issue—or a social, political, or international issue. It is a moral issue; and it must be met by the passage this session of the bill now pending in the House.[4]

All members of the public should have equal access to facilities open to the public. All members of the public should be equally eligible for Federal benefits that are financed by the public. All members of the public should have an equal chance to vote for public officials, and to send their children to good public schools, and to contribute their talents to the public good.

Today Americans of all races stand side by side in Berlin and in Vietnam. They died side by side in Korea. Surely they can work and eat and travel side by side in their own country.

* * *

We must advance toward this goal in 1964 in at least 10 different ways, not as partisans but as patriots.

First, we must maintain—and our reduced defense budget will maintain—that margin of military safety and superiority obtained through 3 years of steadily increasing both the quality and the quantity of our strategic, our conventional, and our antiguerrilla forces. In 1964 we will be better prepared than ever before to defend the cause of freedom—whether it is threatened by outright aggression or by the infiltration practiced by those in Hanoi and Havana who ship arms and men across international borders to foment insurrection. And we must continue to use that strength, as John Kennedy used it in the Cuban crisis and for the test ban treaty,[5] to demonstrate both the futility of nuclear war and the possibilities of lasting peace.

Second, we must take new steps—and we shall make new proposals at Geneva—toward the control and the eventual abolition of arms.[6] Even in the absence of agreement we must not stockpile arms beyond our needs or seek an excess of military power that could be provocative as well as wasteful. And it is in this spirit that in this fiscal year we are cutting back our production of enriched uranium by 25 percent. We are shutting down four

[4] The Civil Rights Act of 1964 (Public Law 88-352, approved July 2, 1964).
[5] Text of treaty in *Documents, 1963*, pp. 130-132.
[6] Document 36.

plutonium piles. We are closing many nonessential military installations. And it is in this spirit that we today call on our adversaries to do the same.

Third, we must make increased use of our food as an instrument of peace, making it available—by sale, or trade, or loan, or donation—to hungry people in all nations which tell us of their needs and accept proper conditions of distribution.

Fourth, we must assure our preeminence in the peaceful exploration of outer space, focusing on an expedition to the moon in this decade—in cooperation with other powers if possible, alone if necessary.

Fifth, we must expand world trade. Having recognized in the act of 1962 [7] that we must buy as well as sell, we now expect our trading partners to recognize that we must sell as well as buy. We are willing to give them competitive access to our market—asking only that they do the same for us.

Sixth, we must continue, through such measures as the interest equalization tax [8] as well as the cooperation of other nations, our recent progress toward balancing our international accounts.

This administration must and will preserve the present gold value of the dollar.

Seventh, we must become better neighbors with the free states of the Americas—working with the councils of the OAS [*Organization of American States*], with a stronger Alliance for Progress, and with all the men and women of this hemisphere who really believe in liberty and justice for all.

Eighth, we must strengthen the ability of free nations everywhere to develop their independence and raise their standard of living—and thereby frustrate those who prey on poverty and chaos. To do this, the rich must help the poor—and we must do our part. We must achieve a more rigorous administration of our development assistance, with larger roles for private investors, for other industrialized nations, for international agencies, and for the recipient nations themselves.

Ninth, we must strengthen our Atlantic and Pacific partnerships, maintain our alliances, and make the United Nations a more effective instrument for national independence and international order.

Tenth, and finally, we must develop with our allies new means of bridging the gap between the East and the West, facing danger

[7] Trade Expansion Act of 1962; summary in *Documents, 1962,* pp. 496-508.
[8] Public Law 88-563, approved September 2, 1964.

boldly wherever danger exists, but being equally bold in our search for new agreements which can enlarge the hopes of all while violating the interests of none.

In short, I would say to the Congress that we must be constantly prepared for the worst and constantly acting for the best. We must be strong enough to win any war, and we must be wise enough to prevent one.

We shall neither act as aggressors nor tolerate acts of aggression. We intend to bury no one—and we do not intend to be buried. We can fight, if we must, as we have fought before—but we pray that we will never have to fight again.

My good friends and my fellow Americans, in these last 7 sorrowful weeks we have learned anew that nothing is so enduring as faith and nothing is so degrading as hate.

John Kennedy was a victim of hate, but he was also a great builder of faith—faith in our fellow Americans, whatever their creed or their color or their station in life; and faith in the future of man, whatever his divisions and differences.

This faith was echoed in all parts of the world. On every continent and in every land to which Mrs. Johnson and I traveled, we found faith and hope and love toward this land of America and toward our people.

So I ask you now, in the Congress and in the country, to join with me in expressing and fulfilling that faith, in working for a nation—a nation that is free from want and a world that is free from hate—a world of peace and justice, and freedom and abundance, for our time and for all time to come.

(2) *The Budget for Fiscal Year 1965: Message of President Johnson to the Congress, January 21, 1964.*[9]

(Excerpts)

To the Congress of the United States:

This is the budget of the United States Government for 1965.

The preparation of this budget was the first major task to confront me as President, and it has been a heavy one. Many decisions of great importance have had to be made in a brief span of weeks.

* * *

My proposals call for administrative budget expenditures in 1965 of $97.9 billion—$900 million less than was requested in

[9] House Document 265, Part I, 88th Cong., 2d sess.

the 1964 budget and $500 million less than I now estimate will be spent in 1964.

* * *

THE ECONOMY AND TAX REDUCTION

The Federal budget is a detailed plan for managing the business of Government, but it is more than that: In setting the relationship between Government expenditures and taxation, the budget is also a powerful economic force which can help or hamper our efforts to achieve stable prosperity and steady growth.

The expenditure proposals in this budget are ample to satisfy our most pressing needs for governmental services, but the broad economic stimulus needed to carry our economy to new high ground in production, income, and employment will not come principally from Government outlays. I believe—as did President Kennedy—that the primary impetus needed to move our economy ahead should come, in present circumstances, from an expansion of the private sector rather than the public sector. Therefore, the earliest possible enactment of the tax reduction bill now before the Congress [10] is an integral and vital part of my budgetary proposals.

* * *

With prompt enactment of the tax program, economic expansion in 1964 should proceed briskly. Reflecting the effects of the first stage of the tax reduction, the gross national product in calendar year 1964 should rise to about $623 billion, plus or minus $5 billion. This is substantially higher than the GNP which could be expected in the absence of prompt enactment of the tax legislation. In fact, since expectations of a tax reduction have been incorporated into the forward planning of many business firms, the effect on the economy of failure to pass the legislation swiftly might be deeply disturbing.

* * *

GOVERNMENT EXPENDITURES AND PROGRAMS

* * *

National defense.—To preserve freedom and protect our vital national interests in these recent years of uneasy peace, this Na-

[10] Same as note 3 to Document 1.

tion has invested heavily in the improvement of its defenses. We have chosen not to concede [*to*] our opponents supremacy in any type of potential conflict, be it nuclear war, conventional warfare, or guerrilla conflict. We have now increased the strength of our forces so that, faced with any threat of aggression, we can make a response which is appropriate to the situation. With present forces and those now planned, we will continue to maintain this vital military capability.

During the past 3 years, we have achieved notable increases in military readiness, including:

- A 100% increase in the number of nuclear weapons available in the strategic alert forces.
- A 60% increase in the tactical nuclear forces deployed in Western Europe.
- A 45% increase in the number of combat-ready Army divisions.
- A 35% increase in the number of tactical fighter squadrons.
- A 75% increase in airlift capability to improve mobility.

These rapid gains result from an increase in cash payments for military purposes from $47.7 billion in 1961 to $56.0 billion in 1964. Along with the high level of preparedness we have now achieved, vigorous efforts to promote economies in the management of our Armed Forces have been producing significant savings. We are therefore able to propose a decrease of $800 million in cash outlays ($1.3 billion in the administrative budget) for national defense in fiscal year 1965 while maintaining our position of strength.

Nevertheless, national defense expenditures will remain high. These payments, estimated at $55.2 billion ($54.0 billion in the administrative budget) in 1965, will provide for all essential military purposes, including substantial improvements in our present and planned military capabilities. For example, the 1965 budget provides for additional Minuteman missiles, further improvements in our air, land, and sea tactical forces, procurement of additional airlift aircraft, and continued research and development to ensure our ability to counter new threats.

To reinforce the total defense effort, the Congress should authorize funds for fallout shelters in public buildings, schools, hospitals, and other nonprofit institutions.

Although we continue to seek a relaxation of tensions, we cannot relax our guard. While the nuclear test ban treaty is a hopeful sign,[11] neither that treaty nor other developments to date

[11] Same as note 5 to Document 1.

have, by themselves, reduced our defense requirements. We will continue underground nuclear testing, maintain our above ground test facilities in ready condition, maintain strong weapons laboratories, and continue the development of detection devices. However, because of the nuclear strength we have achieved, it will be possible to cut production of enriched uranium by 25% and to shut down four plutonium piles.

Our inventories of strategic and critical materials are being reviewed to assure that they are necessary for current civil and military defense requirements. I recommend that the Congress enact legislation to improve the management of these materials and simplify the disposal of those no longer needed.

International affairs and finance.—The less-developed nations are engaged in a critical struggle for political independence and economic betterment. This struggle takes many forms, from combating armed aggression and subversion in Vietnam to advancing national efforts to reduce poverty and illiteracy in South Asia, Latin America, and other areas. Upon the outcome of this struggle will depend the stability and security of much of the world. Through our programs of foreign assistance, we provide aid to these free peoples and thereby advance our own vital interests. It is essential that we continue, with a small portion of our great resources and technical knowledge, to promote in the emerging nations hope and orderly progress, replacing misery, hostility, and violence.

The $2.4 billion of new obligational authority recommended for 1965 in this budget for the programs of the Agency for International Development is $1.1 billion less than originally requested for 1964. It will make the total 1965 obligational availability for the program equivalent to the amount provided by the Congress for 1964 including unobligated funds carried forward from the prior year. The 1965 recommendation represents a prudent assessment of the funds required to fulfill the obligations we have undertaken and the opportunities we seek in a changing and challenging world.

The amount requested reflects a continuing effort to increase the effectiveness and efficiency of our assistance programs. We are reducing AID staffing by several hundred employees, proportionately one of the largest reductions of any agency in Government. We are stressing the necessity for recipient countries to take adequate self-help measures. The 1965 request reflects the successes we have had in reducing the dependence of some nations upon the low-cost foreign aid loans made by the Agency for

International Development; by 1965 a number of countries will have turned to other sources and types of loans more consistent with their increasing economic strength.

On the other hand, the 1965 budget does not allow for sudden opportunities that sometimes present themselves in international economic affairs. We must be able to take quick advantage of situations in which resolute and decisive actions can turn threats to the free world into constructive evidence of our determination to preserve the peace. We must also be able to take advantage of opportunities in which swift action can advance us dramatically along the road to free world cooperation and prosperity. Should such opportunities arise, I will request prompt action by the Congress to provide any additional funds needed to meet emerging requirements.

Our partners in the Alliance for Progress will continue to receive our most determined support and generous cooperation. Recent improvements in the organization of the Alliance should permit an acceleration of this program and foster ever greater hemispheric unity. I am therefore proposing an expanded bilateral program for the Alliance in 1965. Upon completion of negotiations and arrangements with other member countries, legislation will also be proposed to provide additional funds for long-term, low-interest loans by the Inter-American Development Bank.

The sincerity of our purpose overseas is exemplified by the highly successful work of the Peace Corps. As a result of this record and the gratifying flood of requests for the services of the Corps, funds are requested in 1965 for 14,000 volunteers, as compared with 10,500 in 1964.

Space research and technology.—Our plan to place a man on the moon in this decade remains unchanged. It is an ambitious and important goal. In addition to providing great scientific benefits, it will demonstrate that our capability in space is second to no other nation's. However, it is clear that no matter how brilliant our scientists and engineers, how farsighted our planners and managers, or how frugal our administrators and contracting personnel, we cannot reach this goal without sufficient funds. There is no second-class ticket to space.

* * *

For 1965, I am requesting appropriations of $5.3 billion, $63 million above the 1964 amount, including the proposed supplemental appropriation. The 1964 and 1965 recommendations represent the minimum amount needed to achieve our goals in space. The estimated increase of $590 million in expenditures in 1965 is due principally to payments required by commitments made in 1964 and earlier years. With the leveling off of appropriations, annual outlays should remain relatively stable in subsequent years.

In addition to the manned space flight program, though related to it, funds are included to support unmanned space flights for lunar exploration and supporting research and development. Funds are also included for scientific satellites, planetary probes, and experiments with meteorological and communications satellites.

* * *

SPECIAL ASPECTS OF THE GOVERNMENT PROGRAM

Certain additional elements of the proposed 1965 Government program deserve special note.

Federal expenditures and the balance of payments.—The recent improvement in the U.S. balance of international payments represents progress toward eliminating our persistent payments deficit. Preliminary estimates indicate that the gross balance-of-payments deficit in the second half of calendar year 1963 was roughly one-third that of the first half. For the year as a whole, these estimates show the deficit to be the lowest since 1957.

Three factors in particular have contributed to the improvement during the past year: the continued price stability of U.S. products, a proposed interest equalization tax on foreign securities,[12] which would be effective as of July 1963, and an increase in short-term interest rates. Anticipation of the proposed tax, which is intended only as a temporary measure, has already had a favorable effect. To insure continuing benefits from the tax during the critical period ahead, I urge its speedy enactment by the Congress. Enactment of the tax reduction legislation now before Congress will also help the balance of payments by making U.S. firms more competitive in world markets and by promoting the kind of economy which will be more attractive to U.S. and foreign investors.

During the past one and a half years, all Federal Government activities affecting the balance of payments have been under continuing scrutiny for the purpose of finding savings—large

[12] Same as note 8 to Document 1.

and small—which can be made in payments abroad. In some cases, purchases or activities formerly conducted overseas have been restricted to the United States. In others, they have been eliminated. Over 80% of the current obligations by the Agency for International Development for loans and grants to developing countries now must be spent for goods and services produced in the United States. In addition, defense offset agreements with certain of our European allies, the prepayment of funds previously loaned to foreign governments, and the sale of special nonmarketable, medium-term Treasury bonds to foreign central banks have been particularly helpful to our balance of payments.

As a result of the reviews and actions undertaken, the net annual outflow from Federal Government programs—payments less regular receipts—is estimated to drop by $800 million between 1963 and 1965. This excludes special receipts of a nonrecurring nature, such as prepayments of loans, sales of nonmarketable medium-term securities, and advances received on military exports.

* * *

(3) *Monetary Policy and Balance of Payments: Economic Report of President Johnson to the Congress, January 20, 1964.*[13]

(Excerpt)

* * *

MONETARY POLICY AND BALANCE-OF-PAYMENTS MEASURES

A strong upswing in the economy after the tax cut need not bring tight money or high interest rates, especially when

—our balance of payments is improving so sharply in response to measures begun in 1961 and reinforced last July; [14]
—the budget for fiscal year 1965 [15] will cut the Federal deficit in half and ease pressures on interest rates from Treasury borrowing.

It would be self-defeating to cancel the stimulus of tax reduction by tightening money. Monetary and debt policy should be

[13] House Document 278, 88th Cong., 2d sess. Text from *Department of State Bulletin,* February 10, 1964, pp. 222-223.
[14] Text of President Kennedy's messages on balance of payments in *Documents, 1961,* pp. 26-38; same, *1962,* pp. 54-68.
[15] Document 2.

directed toward maintaining interest rates and credit conditions that encourage private investment.

But monetary policy must remain flexible, so that:

—It can quickly shift to the defense if, unexpectedly, inflation threatens or the balance of payments worsens.
—When monetary measures are not needed as defensive shock troops, they can reinforce fiscal policy in promoting domestic expansion.

Our balance of payments will continue to benefit from the special program launched last July. This requires

—early enactment of the *interest equalization tax,*[16] designed to raise the costs of foreign borrowing in our capital market without forcing up domestic interest rates,
—*further economies in dollar outflows* from Government programs, without compromising our efforts to maintain the strength of the free world,
—*continued price stability and export promotion* to maintain or improve the competitive position of our exports.

TRADE EXPANSION AND DEVELOPMENT ASSISTANCE

1. *The Kennedy Round.*[17] The United States' 30-year campaign to reduce barriers to world trade—and the intensified pursuit of that goal signalled by the passage of the Trade Expansion Act of 1962 [18]—will reach a climax in 1964.

U.S. industry and agriculture are in excellent condition to seize the new opportunities offered by trade liberalization and to weather the adjustments that may be required.

Our goal is a more prosperous America in a more prosperous world.

2. *The developing countries.* Reduced trade barriers will expand exports and help an increasing number of developing countries to become self-supporting.

But for most poorer countries full self-support is still some distance off. We must help them find a path to development through freedom—and freedom through development.

Our development assistance effort must and will be more sharply focused and rigorously administered. We shall encourage others to share more of its burden and seek a larger role for

[16] Same as note 8 to Document 1.
[17] Document 28.
[18] Same as note 7 to Document 1.

private investment. But a strong development assistance program continues to be vital to our pursuit of peace and stability in the free world.

* * *

(4) *The Foreign Aid Program for Fiscal Year 1965: Message of President Johnson to the Congress, March 19, 1964.*[19]

To the Congress of the United States:

The most important ingredient in the development of a nation is neither the amount nor the nature of foreign assistance. It is the will and commitment of the government and people directly involved.

To those nations which do commit themselves to progress under freedom, help from us and from others can provide the margin of difference between failure and success.

This is the heart of the matter.

The proposals contained in this message express our self-interest at the same time that they proclaim our national ideals. We will be laying up a harvest of woe for us and our children if we shrink from the task of grappling in the world community with poverty and ignorance. These are the grim recruiting sergeants of communism. They flourish wherever we falter. If we default on our obligations, communism will expand its ambitions.

That is the stern equation which dominates our age, and from which there can be no escape in logic or in honor.

NO WASTE, NO RETREAT

It is against our national interest to tolerate waste or inefficiency or extravagance in any of these programs. But it is equally repugnant to our national interest to retreat from our obligations and commitments while freedom remains under siege.

We recognize that the United States cannot and should not sustain the burden of these programs alone.

Other nations are needed in this enterprise of mutual help. Encouraging signs exist that the process of sharing the burden is steadily growing.

The best way for the United States to stimulate this growth and to broaden this partnership in freedom is to make our own example an incentive to our friends and allies.

[19] House Document 250, 88th Cong., 2d sess. For discussion see *The United States in World Affairs, 1964*, pp. 9-11.

We need the assurance of stability and progress in a world restless with many dangers and anxieties.

PRUDENT AND RESPONSIBLE PROGRAMS

In this program we do not seek to cover the whole world. Aid on a worldwide scale is no part of our purpose. We seek instead, through prudent and responsible programs, to help carefully selected countries whose survival in freedom is essential, and whose collapse would bring new opportunities for Communist expansion.

There are no easy victories in this campaign. But there can be sudden disasters. We cannot ask for a reprieve from responsibility while freedom is in danger. The vital interests of the United States require us to stay in the battle. We dare not desert.

Economic and military assistance, used at the right time and in the right way, can provide indispensable help to our foreign policy in enabling the United States to influence events instead of merely reacting to them. By committing a small part of our resources before crises actually occur, we reduce the danger and frequency of those crises.

Our foresight becomes a shield against misfortune.

The recommendations contained in this program for fiscal year 1965 are designed to move the aid program in that direction. They reflect views and experience of the Congress, of the executive branch, and of informed private citizens.

FIVE FUNDAMENTAL CONCEPTS FOR A SUCCESSFUL PROGRAM

First: The request for funds must be realistic.

For economic assistance, new authorizations of $917 million for fiscal 1965 are recommended. Specifically, I recommend $335 million for supporting assistance, $225 million for technical cooperation, $134 million for contributions to international organizations, $150 million for the President's contingency fund, and $73 million for administrative and miscellaneous expenses.

For military assistance, I recommend that the Congress provide a continuing authorization, subject to an annual review of each year's proposals by the authorizing committees in both Houses.

For fiscal 1965, I recommend no additional authorizations for the Alliance for Progress or for development lending assistance in Asia or Africa. Existing authorizations for these programs are adequate.

The appropriations recommended for fiscal 1965 total $1 billion for military assistance and $2.4 billion for economic assistance. In fiscal 1964, the initial request was $4.9 billion, later reduced to $4.5 billion.

This fiscal year, the request of $3.4 billion is $1.1 billion less than last year's request, although about the same as was available last year, taking into consideration the unexpended balance from the year before. Moreover, more than 80 percent of aid funds will be spent in the United States. The impact of the program on our balance of payments will be less than ever before.

INSURANCE TO AVOID COMMITTING AMERICAN MEN TO WAR

These requests reflect a determination to continue to improve the aid program both in concept and administration. The overall request represents a great deal of money—but it is an amount which we should, in all prudence, provide to serve essential U.S. interests and commitments throughout the world.

More than 1 million American men in uniform are now stationed outside the United States. As insurance to avoid involving them and the Nation in a major conflict, we propose to spend through aid programs less than 4 cents out of every tax dollar.

If there is any alternative insurance against war, it might be found in an increase in the defense budget. But that would require not only many times more than $3.4 billion, for a military budget which already takes more than 50 cents out of every tax dollar, but also a severalfold increase in our own military manpower.

The foreign assistance requested will provide—

the crucial assistance we have promised the people of Latin America who are committed to programs of economic and social progress;

continued economic development in India, Pakistan, and Turkey under the major international aid consortia to which we are a party;

the U.S. share of voluntary contributions to the United Nations technical cooperation programs and to such special international programs as the work of the United Nations Children's Fund, and the development of the Indus Basin; and

funds to meet our commitments to the freedom of the people of South Vietnam, Korea, and for the other obligations we have undertaken in Asia and Africa.

Second: The funds I am requesting will be concentrated where they will produce the best results, and speed the transition from U.S. assistance to self-support wherever possible.

Two-thirds of the proposed military assistance will go to 11 nations along the periphery of the Sino-Soviet bloc, from Greece and Turkey through Thailand and Vietnam to the Republic of China and Korea. These funds are a key to the maintenance of over 3.5 million men under arms, raised and supported in large measure by the countries receiving the assistance.

The need for supporting assistance—funds used primarily in countries facing defense or security emergencies—will continue to be reduced. Fourteen countries which received supporting assistance 3 years ago will receive none in fiscal year 1965. Four-fifths of the present request will go to four countries: Korea, Vietnam, Laos, and Jordan. Two-thirds of the development lending proposed for fiscal 1965 (including Alliance for Progress lending) will be concentrated in six countries: Chile, Colombia, Nigeria, Turkey, Pakistan, and India.

Funds for educational and technical cooperation—to help start schools, health centers, agricultural experiment stations, credit services, and dozens of other institutions—are not concentrated in a few countries. But they will be used for selected projects to raise the ability of less fortunate peoples to meet their own needs. To carry out these projects we are seeking the best personnel available in the United States—in private agencies, in universities, in State and local governments, and throughout the Federal Government. Wherever possible, we will speed up the transition from reliance on aid to self-support.

In 17 nations, the transition has been completed and economic aid has ended. Fourteen countries are approaching the point where soft economic loans and grants will no longer be needed. New funds for military equipment grants are being requested for seven fewer countries for fiscal 1965 than for the present year.

Third: We must do more to utilize private initiative in the United States—and in the developing countries—to promote economic development abroad.

During the past year—

The first new houses financed by U.S. private funds protected by aid guarantees were completed in Lima, Peru;

The first rural electrification surveys, conducted by the National Rural Electric Cooperative Association under contract to AID, were completed and the first rural electrification loan—in Nicaragua—was approved; and

The first arrangement linking the public and private resources of one of our States to a developing country was established, between California and Chile.

This effort must be expanded.

Accordingly, we are encouraging the establishment of an Executive Service Corps. It will provide American businessmen with an opportunity to furnish, on request, technical and managerial advice to businessmen in developing countries.

During the present year, the possibilities for mobilizing increased private resources for the development task will be developed by the Advisory Committee on Private Enterprise in Foreign Aid established under the Foreign Assistance Act of 1963.[20]

In this connection, two specific legislative steps are recommended:

One, legislation to provide a special tax credit for private investment by U.S. businessmen in less-developed countries.

Two, additional authority for a final installment of the pilot program of guaranteeing private U.S. housing investments in Latin America.

Fourth: We will continue to seek greater international participation in aid.

Other free world industrial countries have increased their aid commitments since the early 1950's. There are indications that further increases are in store. Canada recently announced that it expects to increase its aid expenditures by 50 percent next year. A 1963 British white paper and a French official report published in January 1964 point in the same direction. Other nations have reduced interest rates and extended maturities on loans to developing countries.

Of major importance in this effort are the operations of the International Development Association. Under the agreement for replenishing the resources of this Association, which is now before the Congress[21] for approval, other countries will put up more than $1.40 for every dollar the United States provides to finance on easy terms development projects certified as sound by the World Bank—projects which the developing countries could not afford to pay for on regular commercial terms. This is international sharing in the aid effort at its best. For to the extent we furnish funds to IDA, and they are augmented by the contributions of others, the needs of developing countries are met,

[20] Public Law 88-205, approved December 16, 1963; excerpts in *Documents, 1963*, pp. 49-53.

[21] Public Law 88-310, approved May 26, 1964.

thus reducing the amounts required for our own bilateral aid programs.

Under the program before you the United States would be authorized to contribute $312 million over a 3-year period. Against this other countries have pledged $438 million which will be lost in the absence of the U.S. contribution. Action is needed now so that the Association may continue to undertake new projects even though the first appropriation will not be required until fiscal year 1966.

I urge the Congress to authorize U.S. participation in this continued IDA subscription.

Fifth: Let us insist on steadily increasing efficiency in assistance operations.

After careful study, I have decided to continue the basic organization of aid operations, established after intensive review in 1961. Economic assistance operations will continue to be centered in the Agency for International Development, military assistance operations in the Department of Defense. Both will be subject to firm foreign policy guidance from the Secretary of State.

STEPS TO INCREASE EFFICIENCY OF AID

One officer, Assistant Secretary of State [*Thomas C.*] Mann, has been assigned firm policy control over all aspects of our activities in Latin America.

Full support will be given to the newly created Inter-American Alliance for Progress Committee which is designed to strengthen the aspect of partnership in the Alliance.

The AID Administrator has instructions to embark on a major program to improve the quality of his staff—and to reduce the total number of AID employees by 1,200 by the end of fiscal year 1965.

The AID Administrator has been directed to continue to consolidate AID missions with U.S. Embassies and, wherever possible, to eliminate altogether separate AID field missions.

The Secretary of Defense has been directed to continue to make substantial reductions in the number of personnel assigned to military assistance groups and missions.

In this connection, I recommend two specific legislative steps:

One, legislation to provide the AID Administrator with authority to terminate a limited number of supervisory and policy-making employees notwithstanding other provisions of law, and to extend the existing Foreign Service "selection out" authority to other personnel.

This is essential if the Administrator is to carry out my desire—and that of the Congress—that he improve the quality of the AID staff, and at the same time, reduce its total size.

Two, legislation to permit outstanding U.S. representation on the Inter-American Alliance for Progress Committee under the leadership of Ambassador Teodoro Moscoso.[22]

Finally, I am appointing a general advisory committee, as suggested by Senator [*John Sherman*] Cooper and others, on foreign economic and military assistance problems. It will be composed of distinguished private citizens with varied backgrounds and will serve as a continuing source of counsel to me. In addition to its general responsibility the committee will examine aid programs in individual countries. These reviews will be made by members of the advisory committee, augmented as necessary by additional persons. I would hope that at least four or five country reviews, including two or three in Latin America, will be completed in the present year.

A PROGRAM TO STRENGTHEN THE FAMILY OF THE FREE

I am convinced this program will enable the United States to live in a turbulent world with a greater measure of safety and of honor.

There is in our heart the larger and nobler hope of strengthening the family of the free, quite apart from our duty to disappoint the evil designs of the enemies of freedom.

We wish to build a world in which the weak can walk without fear and in which even the smallest nation can work out its own destiny without the danger of violence and aggression.

This program, based on the principle of mutual help, can make an essential contribution to these purposes and objectives which have guided our Nation across the difficulties of these dangerous years.

I recommend this program to the judgment and the conscience of the Congress in the belief that it will enlarge the strength of the free world—

aid in frustrating the ambitions of Communist imperialism;

reduce the hazards of widespread conflict; and

[22] Mr. Moscoso resigned on May 4, 1964. President Johnson appointed W. W. Rostow as his successor on May 11, 1964.

support the moral commitment of freemen everywhere to work for a just and peaceful world.

(5) *Myths and Realities: Address by Senator J. W. Fulbright to the United States Senate, March 25, 1964.*[23]

(Excerpts)

Mr. President, there is an inevitable divergence, attributable to the imperfections of the human mind, between the world as it is and the world as men perceive it. As long as our perceptions are reasonably close to objective reality, it is possible for us to act upon our problems in a rational and appropriate manner. But when our perceptions fail to keep pace with events, when we refuse to believe something because it displeases or frightens us, or because it is simply startlingly unfamiliar, then the gap between fact and perception becomes a chasm, and action becomes irrelevant and irrational.

There has always—and inevitably—been some divergence between the realities of foreign policy and our ideas about it. This divergence has in certain respects been growing, rather than narrowing; and we are handicapped, accordingly, by policies based on old myths, rather than current realities. This divergence is, in my opinion, dangerous and unnecessary—dangerous, because it can reduce foreign policy to a fraudulent game of imagery and appearances; unnecessary, because it can be overcome by the determination of men in high office to dispel prevailing misconceptions by the candid dissemination of unpleasant, but inescapable, facts.

Before commenting on some of the specific areas where I believe our policies are at least partially based on cherished myths, rather than objective facts, I should like to suggest two possible reasons for the growing divergence between the realities and our perceptions of current world politics. The first is the radical change in relations between and within the Communist and the free world; and the second is the tendency of too many of us to confuse means with ends and, accordingly, to adhere to prevailing practices with a fervor befitting immutable principles.

* * *

It seems reasonable, therefore, to suggest that the character of the cold war has, for the present, at least, been profoundly

[23] *Congressional Record,* March 25, 1964, pp. 6028-6034.

altered: by the drawing back of the Soviet Union from extremely aggressive policies; by the implicit repudiation by both sides of a policy of "total victory"; and by the establishment of an American strategic superiority which the Soviet Union appears to have tacitly accepted because it has been accompanied by assurances that it will be exercised by the United States with responsibility and restraint. These enormously important changes may come to be regarded by historians as the foremost achievements of the Kennedy administration in the field of foreign policy. Their effect has been to commit us to a foreign policy which can accurately—though perhaps not prudently—be defined as one of "peaceful coexistence."

Another of the results of the lowering of tensions between East and West is that each is now free to enjoy the luxury of accelerated strife and squabbling within its own domain. The ideological thunderbolts between Washington and Moscow which until a few years ago seemed a permanent part of our daily lives have become a pale shadow of their former selves. Now instead the United States waits in fascinated apprehension for the Olympian pronouncements that issue from Paris at 6-month intervals while the Russians respond to the crude epithets of Peiping with almost plaintive rejoinders about "those who want to start a war against everybody."

* * *

We are confronted with a complex and fluid world situation and we are not adapting ourselves to it. We are clinging to old myths in the face of new realities and we are seeking to escape the contradictions by narrowing the permissible bounds of public discussion, by relegating an increasing number of ideas and viewpoints to a growing category of "unthinkable thoughts." I believe that this tendency can and should be reversed, that it is within our ability, and unquestionably in our interests, to cut loose from established myths and to start thinking some "unthinkable thoughts"—about the cold war and East-West relations, about the underdeveloped countries and particularly those in Latin America, about the changing nature of the Chinese Communist threat in Asia and about the festering war in Vietnam.

The master myth of the cold war is that the Communist bloc is a monolith composed of governments which are not really governments at all but organized conspiracies, divided among themselves perhaps in certain matters of tactics, but all equally resolute and implacable in their determination to destroy the free world.

I believe that the Communist world is indeed hostile to the free world in its general and long-term intentions but that the existence of this animosity in principle is far less important for our foreign policy than the great variations in its intensity and character both in time and among the individual members of the Communist bloc. Only if we recognize these variations, ranging from China, which poses immediate threats to the free world, to Poland and Yugoslavia, which pose none, can we hope to act effectively upon the bloc and to turn its internal differences to our own advantage and to the advantage of those bloc countries which wish to maximize their independence. It is the responsibility of our national leaders both in the executive branch and in Congress, to acknowledge and act upon these realities, even at the cost of saying things which will not win immediate widespread enthusiasm.

* * *

Important opportunities have been created for Western policy by the development of "polycentrism" in the Communist bloc. The Communist nations, as George Kennan has pointed out,[24] are, like the Western nations, currently caught up in a crisis of indecision about their relations with countries outside their own ideological bloc. The choices open to the satellite states are limited but by no means insignificant. They can adhere slavishly to Soviet preferences or they can strike out on their own, within limits, to enter into mutually advantageous relations with the West.

Whether they do so, and to what extent, is to some extent at least within the power of the West to determine. If we persist in the view that all Communist regimes are equally hostile and equally threatening to the West, and that we can have no policy toward the captive nations except the eventual overthrow of their Communist regimes, then the West may enforce upon the Communist bloc a degree of unity which the Soviet Union has shown itself to be quite incapable of imposing—just as Stalin in the early postwar years frightened the West into a degree of unity that it almost certainly could not have attained by his own unaided efforts. If, on the other hand, we are willing to reexamine the view that all Communist regimes are

[24] See George F. Kennan, *On Dealing with the Communist World* (New York and Evanston: Harper & Row, published for the Council on Foreign Relations, 1964).

alike in the threat which they pose for the West—a view which had a certain validity in Stalin's time—then we may be able to exert an important influence on the course of events within a divided Communist world.

We are to a great extent the victims, and the Soviets the beneficiaries, of our own ideological convictions, and of the curious contradictions which they involve. We consider it a form of subversion of the free world, for example, when the Russians enter trade relations or conclude a consular convention or establish airline connections with a free country in Asia, Africa, or Latin America—and to a certain extent we are right. On the other hand, when it is proposed that we adopt the same strategy in reverse—by extending commercial credits to Poland or Yugoslavia, or by exchanging Ambassadors with a Hungarian regime which has changed considerably in character since the revolution of 1956—then the same patriots who are so alarmed by Soviet activities in the free world charge our policymakers with "giving aid and comfort to the enemy" and with innumerable other categories of idiocy and immorality.

It is time that we resolved this contradiction and separated myth from reality. The myth is that every Communist state is an unmitigated evil and a relentless enemy of the free world; the reality is that some Communist regimes pose a threat to the free world while others pose little or none, and that if we will recognize these distinctions, we ourselves will be able to influence events in the Communist bloc in a way favorable to the security of the free world.

* * *

On the basis of recent experience and present economic needs, there seems little likelihood of a spectacular increase in trade between Communist and Western countries, even if existing restrictions were to be relaxed. Free world trade with Communist countries has been increasing at a steady but unspectacular rate, and it seems unlikely to be greatly accelerated because of the limited ability of the Communist countries to pay for increased imports. A modest increase in East-West trade may nonetheless serve as a modest instrument of East-West detente—provided that we are able to overcome the myth that trade with Communist countries is a compact with the Devil and to recognize that, on the contrary, trade can serve as an effective and honorable means of advancing both peace and human welfare.

* * *

There is little in history to justify the expectation that we can either win the cold war or end it immediately and completely. These are favored myths, respectively, of the American right and of the American left. They are, I believe, equal in their unreality and in their disregard for the feasibilities of history. We must disabuse ourselves of them and come to terms, at last, with the realities of a world in which neither good nor evil is absolute and in which those who move events and make history are those who have understood not how much but how little it is within our power to change.

* * *

Latin America is one of the areas of the world in which American policy is weakened by a growing divergency between old myths and new realities.

The crisis over the Panama Canal [25] has been unnecessarily protracted for reasons of domestic politics and national pride and sensitivity on both sides—for reasons, that is, of only marginal relevance to the merits of the dispute. I think the Panamanians have unquestionably been more emotional about the dispute than has the United States. I also think that there is less reason for emotionalism on the part of the United States than on the part of Panama. It is important for us to remember that the issue over the canal is only one of a great many in which the United States is involved, and by no means the most important. For Panama, on the other hand, a small nation with a weak economy and an unstable government, the canal is the preeminent factor in the nation's economy and in its foreign relations. Surely in a confrontation so unequal, it is not unreasonable to expect the United States to go a little farther than halfway in the search for a fair settlement.

We Americans would do well, for a start, to divest ourselves of the silly notion that the issue with Panama is a test of our courage and resolve. I believe that the Cuban missile crisis of 1962, involving a confrontation with nuclear weapons and intercontinental missiles, was indeed a test of our courage,[26] and we acquitted ourselves extremely well in that instance. I am unable to understand how a controversy with a small and poor country, with virtually no military capacity, can possibly be regarded as a test of our bravery and will to defend our interests. It takes stubbornness but not courage to reject the entreaties of

[25] Documents 71-75.
[26] *Documents, 1962,* pp. 367-410.

the weak. The real test in Panama is not of our valor but of our wisdom and judgment and common sense.

* * *

Under these circumstances, it seems to me entirely proper and necessary for the United States to take the initative in proposing new arrangements that would redress some of Panama's grievances against the treaty as it now stands. I see no reason—certainly no reason of "weakness" or "dishonor"—why the United States cannot put an end to the semantic debate over whether treaty revisions are to be "negotiated" or "discussed" by stating positively and clearly that it is prepared to negotiate revisions in the canal treaty and to submit such changes as are made to the Senate for its advice and consent.

* * *

The problem of Cuba is more difficult than that of Panama, and far more heavily burdened with the deadweight of old myths and prohibitions against "unthinkable thoughts." I think the time is overdue for a candid reevaluation of our Cuban policy even though it may also lead to distasteful conclusions.

There are and have been three options open to the United States with respect to Cuba: first, the removal of the Castro regime by invading and occupying the island; second, an effort to weaken and ultimately bring down the regime by a policy of political and economic boycott; and finally, acceptance of the Communist regime as a disagreeable reality and annoyance but one which is not likely to be removed in the near future because of the unavailability of acceptable means of removing it.

The first option, invasion, has been tried in a halfhearted way and found wanting.

* * *

It has been rejected by our Government and by public opinion and I think that, barring some grave provocation, it can be ruled out as a feasible policy for the United States.

The approach which we have adopted has been the second of those mentioned, an effort to weaken and eventually bring down the Castro regime by a policy of political and economic boycott. This policy has taken the form of extensive restrictions against trade with Cuba by United States citizens, of the exclusion of Cuba from the inter-American system and efforts to secure Latin American support in isolating Cuba politically and economically, and of diplomatic efforts, backed by certain trade and aid sanctions, to persuade other free world countries to maintain economic boycotts against Cuba.

This policy, it now seems clear, has been a failure, and there is no reason to believe that it will succeed in the future. Our efforts to persuade our allies to terminate their trade with Cuba have been generally rebuffed.

* * *

The boycott policy has not failed because of any "weakness" or "timidity" on the part of our Government. This charge, so frequently heard, is one of the most pernicious myths to have been inflicted on the American people. The boycott policy has failed because the United States is not omnipotent and cannot be. The basic reality to be faced is that it is simply not within our power to compel our allies to cut off their trade with Cuba, unless we are prepared to take drastic sanctions against them, . . .

* * *

Having ruled out military invasion and blockade, and recognizing the failure of the boycott policy, we are compelled to consider the third of the three options open to us with respect to Cuba: the acceptance of the continued existence of the Castro regime as a distasteful nuisance but not an intolerable danger so long as the nations of the hemisphere are prepared to meet their obligations of collective defense under the Rio Treaty.[27]

In recent years we have become transfixed with Cuba, making it far more important in both our foreign relations and in our domestic life than its size and influence warrant.

* * *

But it is important to bear in mind that, despite their best efforts, the Cuban Communists have not succeeded in subverting the hemisphere and that in Venezuela, for example, where communism has made a major effort to gain power through terrorism, it has been repudiated by a people who in a free election have committed themselves to the course of liberal democracy. It is necessary to weigh the desirability of an objective against the feasibility of its attainment, and when we do this with respect to Cuba, I think we are bound to conclude that Castro is a nuisance but not a grave threat to the United States and that he cannot be gotten rid of except by means that are wholly disproportionate to the objective. Cuban communism does pose a

[27] Same, *1947*, pp. 534-540.

grave threat to other Latin American countries, but this threat can be dealt with by prompt and vigorous use of the established procedures of the inter-American system against any act of aggression.

I think that we must abandon the myth that Cuban communism is a transitory menace that is going to collapse or disappear in the immediate future and face up to two basic realities about Cuba: first, that the Castro regime is not on the verge of collapse and is not likely to be overthrown by any policies which we are now pursuing or can reasonably undertake; and second, that the continued existence of the Castro regime, though inimical to our interests and policies, is not an insuperable obstacle to the attainment of our objectives, unless we make it so by permitting it to poison our politics at home and to divert us from more important tasks in the hemisphere.

The policy of the United States with respect to Latin America as a whole is predicated on the assumption that social revolution can be accomplished without violent upheaval. This is the guiding principle of the Alliance for Progress and it may in time be vindicated. We are entitled to hope so and it is wise and necessary for us to do all that we can to advance the prospects of peaceful and orderly reform.

At the same time, we must be under no illusions as to the extreme difficulty of uprooting long-established ruling oligarchies without disruptions involving lesser or greater degrees of violence. The historical odds are probably against the prospects of peaceful social revolution. There are places, of course, where it has occurred and others where it seems likely to occur. In Latin America, the chances for such basic change by peaceful means seem bright in Colombia and Venezuela and certain other countries; in Mexico, many basic changes have been made by peaceful means, but these came in the wake of a violent revolution. In other Latin American countries, the power of ruling oligarchies is so solidly established and their ignorance so great that there seems little prospect of accomplishing economic growth or social reform by means short of the forcible overthrow of established authorities.

I am not predicting violent revolutions in Latin America or elsewhere. Still less am I advocating them. I wish only to suggest that violent social revolutions are a possibility in countries where feudal oligarchies resist all meaningful change by peaceful means. We must not, in our preference for the democratic procedures envisioned by the Charter of Punta del Este,[28] close

[28] Same, *1961*, pp. 416-435.

our minds to the possibility that democratic procedures may fail in certain countries and that where democracy does fail violent social convulsions may occur.

* * *

The Far East is another area of the world in which American policy is handicapped by the divergence of old myths and new realities. Particularly with respect to China, an elaborate vocabulary of make believe has become compulsory in both official and public discussion. We are committed, with respect to China and other areas in Asia, to inflexible policies of long standing from which we hesitate to depart because of the attribution to these policies of an aura of mystical sanctity. It may be that a thorough reevaluation of our Far Eastern policies would lead us to the conclusion that they are sound and wise, or at least that they represent the best available options. It may be, on the other hand, that a reevaluation would point up the need for greater or lesser changes in our policies. The point is that, whatever the outcome of a rethinking of policy might be, we have been unwilling to undertake it because of the fear of many Government officials, undoubtedly well founded, that even the suggestion of new policies toward China or Vietnam would provoke a vehement public outcry.

I do not think the United States can, or should, recognize Communist China, or acquiesce in its admission to the United Nations under present circumstances. It would be unwise to do so, because there is nothing to be gained by it so long as the Peiping regime maintains its attitude of implacable hostility toward the United States. I do not believe, however, that this state of affairs is necessarily permanent. As we have seen in our relations with Germany and Japan, hostility can give way in an astonishingly short time to close friendship; and, as we have seen in our relations with China, the reverse can occur with equal speed. It is not impossible that in time our relations with China will change again—if not to friendship, then perhaps to "competitive coexistence." It would therefore be extremely useful if we could introduce an element of flexibility, or, more precisely, of the capacity to be flexible, into our relations with Communist China.

* * *

The situation in Vietnam poses a far more pressing need for a reevaluation of American policy. Other than withdrawal, which

I do not think can be realistically considered under present circumstances, three options are open to us in Vietnam: First, continuation of the antiguerrilla war within South Vietnam, along with renewed American efforts to increase the military effectiveness of the South Vietnamese Army and the political effectiveness of the South Vietnamese Government; second, an attempt to end the war, through negotiations for the neutralization of South Vietnam, or of both North and South Vietnam; and, finally, the expansion of the scale of the war, either by the direct commitment of large numbers of American troops or by equipping the South Vietnamese Army to attack North Vietnamese territory, possibly by means of commando-type operations from the sea or the air.

It is difficult to see how a negotiation, under present military circumstances, could lead to termination of the war under conditions that would preserve the freedom of South Vietnam.

* * *

It seems clear that only two realistic options are open to us in Vietnam in the immediate future: the expansion of the conflict in one way or another, or a renewed effort to bolster the capacity of the South Vietnamese to prosecute the war successfully on its present scale. The matter calls for thorough examination by responsible officials in the executive branch; and until they have had an opportunity to evaluate the contingencies and feasibilities of the options open to us, it seems to me that we have no choice but to support the South Vietnamese Government and Army by the most effective means available. Whatever specific policy decisions are made, it should be clear to all concerned that the United States will continue to meet its obligations and fulfill its commitments with respect to Vietnam.

These, I believe, are some, although by no means all, of the issues of foreign policy in which it is essential to reevaluate longstanding ideas and commitments in the light of new and changing realities. In all the issues which I have discussed, American policy has to one degree or another been less effective than it might have been because of our national tendency to equate means with ends and therefore to attach a mythological sanctity to policies and practices which in themselves have no moral content or value except insofar as they contribute to the achievement of some valid national objective. I believe that we must try to overcome this excessive moralism, which binds us to old myths and blinds us to new realities and, worse still, leads us to regard new and unfamiliar ideas with fear and mistrust.

* * *

We must dare to think about "unthinkable things," because when things become "unthinkable," thinking stops and action becomes mindless. If we are to disabuse ourselves of old myths and to act wisely and creatively upon the new realities of our time, we must think and talk about our problems with perfect freedom, remembering, as Woodrow Wilson said, that "The greatest freedom of speech is the greatest safety because, if a man is a fool, the best thing to do is to encourage him to advertise the fact by speaking."

(6) *America as a Great Power: Address by President Johnson to the Associated Press, New York, April 20, 1964.*[29]

The world has changed many times since General Washington counseled his new and weak country to "observe good faith and justice toward all nations." Great empires have risen and dissolved. Great heroes have made their entrances and have left the stage. And America has slowly, often reluctantly, grown to be a great power and a leading member of world society.

So we seek today, as we did in Washington's time, to protect the life of our nation, to preserve the liberty of our citizens, and to pursue the happiness of our people. This is the touchstone of our world policy.

Thus we seek to add no territory to our dominion, no satellites to our orbit, no slavish followers to our policies. The most impressive witness to this restraint is that for a century our own frontiers have stood quiet and stood unarmed. But we have also learned in this century, and we have learned it at painful and bloody cost, that our own freedom depends on the freedom of others, that our own protection requires that we help protect others, that we draw increased strength from the strength of others.

Thus, to allies we are the most dependable and enduring of friends, for our own safety depends upon the strength of that friendship. To enemies we are the most steadfast and determined of foes, for we know that surrender anywhere threatens defeat everywhere. For a generation, without regard to party or region

[29] White House Press Release, April 20, 1964; text from *Department of State Bulletin,* May 11, 1964, pp. 726-732.

or class, our country has been united in a basic foreign policy that grows from this inescapable teaching.

Tested Principles of Foreign Policy

The principles of this foreign policy have been shaped in battle, have been tested in danger, have been sustained in achievement. They have endured under four Presidents of the United States, because they reflect the realities of our world and they reflect the aims of our country.

Particular actions must change as events change conditions. We must be alert to shifting realities, to emerging opportunities, and always alert to any fresh dangers. But we must not mistake day-to-day changes for fundamental movements in the course of history. It often requires greater courage and resolution to maintain a policy which time has tested than to change it in the face of the moment's pressures. Our foreign policy rests on very tested principles.

First, since Korea, we have labored to build a military strength of unmatched might. We have succeeded. If the threat of war has lessened, it is largely because our opponents realize attack would bring destruction. This effort has been costly. But the costs of weakness are far greater than the costs of strength, and the payment far more painful. That is why, in the last 3 years, your Government has strengthened the whole range of America's defenses.

We have increased defense spending in these 3 years by approximately $6 billion over the last year of the Eisenhower administration, and this year we are spending approximately $8 billion more on defense than we were during that last year.

Second, we have strongly resisted Communist efforts to extend their dominion and expand their power. We have taken the risks and we have used the power which this principle demanded. We have avoided purposeless provocation and needless adventure. The Berlin airlift, the Korean war, the defense of Formosa, the Cuba crisis, the struggle in Viet-Nam, prove our determination to resist aggression and prove our ability to adapt particular response to particular challenge.

Third, we have worked for the revival of strength among our allies, initially, to oppose Communist encroachment on war-weakened nations; in the long run, because our own future rests on the vitality and the unity of the Western society to which we belong.

Fourth, we have encouraged the independence and the progress of developing countries. We are safer and we are more comfortable in a world where all people can govern themselves in their own way, and where all nations have the inner strength to resist external domination.

Fifth, we have pursued every hope of a lasting peace. From the [*Bernard*] Baruch Plan,[30] named after that noble resident of this city, to the test ban treaty,[31] we have sought and welcomed agreements which decrease danger without decreasing security. In that pursuit, for 20 years we have been the leading power in the support of the United Nations. In that pursuit, this year as in every year, we will work to reach agreement on measures to reduce armament and lessen the chance of war.

Today we apply these same principles in a world that is much changed since 1945. Europe seeks a new role for strength rather than contenting itself with protection for weakness. The unity of communism is being eroded by the insistent forces of nationalism and diverging interest. A whole new group of societies is painfully struggling toward the modern world.

Our basic principles are adequate to this shifting world.

But foreign policy is more than just a set of general principles. It is the changing application of those principles to specific dangers and to specific opportunities. It involves knowledge of strengths and awareness of limitations in each new situation.

The presence of offensive missiles in Cuba was a fact. The presence of fallout in the atmosphere has been a fact. The presence of guerrillas in Viet-Nam, at this hour, is a fact.

Such facts cannot be dealt with simply by historical judgments or general precepts. They require concrete acts of courage, and wisdom, and often restraint. These qualities of endurance and innovation, these qualities of continuity and change are at work in at least six major areas of continuing concern to you.

Relations with the Soviet Union

First is our relationship with the Soviet Union, the center of our concern for peace. Communists, using force and intrigue, seek to bring about a Communist-dominated world. Our convictions, our interests, our life as a nation, demand that we resolutely oppose, with all of our might, that effort to dominate the world. This activity, and this alone, is the cause of the cold war between us.

[30] *Documents, 1945-1946,* pp. 557-559.
[31] Same as note 5 to Document 1.

For the United States has nothing to fear from peaceful competition. We welcome it, and we will win it. It is our system which flourishes and grows stronger in a world free from the threat of war. And in such a competition all people, everywhere, will be the gainers. Today there are new pressures, new realities, which make it permissible to hope that the pursuit of peace is in the interests of the Soviet Union as it is in ours.

And our own restraint may be convincing the Soviet leaders of the reality that we, in America, seek neither war nor the destruction of the Soviet Union. Thus I am very hopeful that we can take important steps toward the day when in the words of the Old Testament, "nation shall not lift up sword against nation, neither shall they learn war any more."

We must remember that peace will not come suddenly. It will not emerge dramatically from a single agreement or a single meeting. It will be advanced by concrete and limited accommodations, by the gradual growth of common interests, by the increased awareness of shifting dangers and alinements, and by the development of trust in a good faith based on a reasoned view of the world.

Our own position is clear. We will discuss any problem, we will listen to any proposal, we will pursue any agreement, we will take any action which might lessen the chance of war without sacrificing the interests of our allies or our own ability to defend the alliance against attack. In other words, our guard is up but our hand is out.

I am taking two actions today which reflect both our desire to reduce tensions and our unwillingness to risk weakness. I have ordered a further substantial reduction in our production of enriched uranium, to be carried out over a 4-year period. When added to previous reductions, this will mean an overall decrease in the production of plutonium by 20 percent, and of enriched uranium by 40 percent. By bringing production in line with need—and the chart shows now that our production is here [*gesturing*], and our need is here, and our reduction today will bring it here—we think we will reduce tension while we maintain all the necessary power.

We must not operate a WPA nuclear project, just to provide employment, when our needs have been met. And in reaching these decisions, I have been in close consultation with Prime Minister [*Sir Alec*] Douglas-Home [*of the United Kingdom*]. Simultaneously with my announcement now, Chairman [*Nikita S.*] Khrushchev is releasing a statement in Moscow, at 2 o'clock our time, in which he makes definite commitments to steps toward a more peaceful world.[32] He agrees to discontinue the construction of two big new atomic reactors for the production of plutonium over the next several years, to reduce substantially the production of U-235 for nuclear weapons, and to allocate more fissionable material for peaceful uses.

This is not disarmament. This is not a declaration of peace. But it is a hopeful sign, and it is a step forward which we welcome and which we can take in hope that the world may yet, one day, live without the fear of war. At the same time, I have reaffirmed all the safeguards against weakening our nuclear strength which we adopted at the time of the test ban treaty.

The Atlantic Partnership

The second area of continuing effort is the development of Atlantic partnership with a stronger and more unified Europe. Having begun this policy when peril was great, we will not now abandon it as success moves closer. We worked for a stronger and more prosperous Europe, and Europe is strong and prosperous today because of our work and beyond our expectation.

We have supported a close partnership with a more unified Europe, and in the past 15 years more peaceful steps have been taken in this direction than have been taken at any time in our history. The pursuit of this goal, like the pursuit of any large and worthy cause, will not be easy or untroubled. But the realities of the modern world teach that increased greatness and prosperity demand increased unity and partnership. The underlying forces of European life are eroding old barriers, and they are dissolving old suspicions. Common institutions are expanding common interest.

National boundaries continue to fade under the impact of travel and commerce and communication. A new generation is coming of age, unscarred by old hostilities or old ambitions, thinking of themselves as Europeans, their values shaped by a common Western culture. These forces, and the steadfast effort of all who share common goals, will shape the future. And unity based on hope will ultimately prove stronger than unity based on fear.

We realize that sharing the burden of leadership requires us

[32] Chairman Khrushchev's statement of April 20 and Prime Minister Douglas Home's statement of April 21 in *Further Documents Relating to the Conference of the Eighteen-Nation Committee on Disarmament (Session January 21-April 28, 1964)* (Miscellaneous No. 20 [1964]; Cmnd. 2486; London: H.M.S.O., 1963), pp. 22-23 and 25 respectively.

to share the responsibilities of power. As a step in this direction we support the establishment of a multilateral nuclear force composed of those nations which desire to participate. We also welcome agreed new mechanisms for political consultation on mutual interests throughout the world with whatever changes in organization are necessary to make such consultation rapid and effective.

The experience of two world wars has taught us that the fundamental security interests of the United States and of Europe are the same. What we learned in time of war, we must not now forget in time of peace. For more than a decade we have sought to enlarge the independence and ease the rigors of the people of Eastern Europe. We have used the tools of peaceful exchange in goods, in persons, and in ideas, to open up communication with these restless nations that Mr. Khrushchev refers to sometimes as "children who are grown up too big to spank." We have used limited direct assistance where the needs of our security have allowed us to follow the demands of our compassion.

In that spirit within the last month I have exercised the power granted the President by the Congress and I have reaffirmed the right of open trade with Poland and Yugoslavia.[33]

Latin America

In the third area of continuing concern, Latin America, we have renewed our commitment to the Alliance for Progress, we have sought peaceful settlement of disputes among the American nations, and we have supported the OAS effort [34] to isolate Communist-controlled Cuba. The Alliance for Progress is the central task today of this hemisphere. That task is going ahead successfully.

But that alliance means more than economic assistance or investment. It requires us to encourage and to support those democratic political forces which seek essential change within the framework of constitutional government. It means preference for rapid evolution as the only real alternative to violent revolution. To struggle to stand still in Latin America is just to "throw the sand against the wind."

We must, of course, always be on guard against Communist subversion. But anticommunism alone will never suffice to insure our liberty or fulfill our dreams. That is going to take leadership, leadership that is dedicated to economic progress without

[33] *Department of State Bulletin*, April 20, 1964, pp. 626-628.
[34] Document 70.

uneconomic privilege, to social change which enhances social justice, to political reform which widens human freedom.

The resumption of relations with Panama [35] proves once again the unmatched ability of our inter-American system to resolve these disputes among our good neighbors. At the outset of that dispute with Panama, the first morning I stated to the President [*Roberto F. Chiari*] of Panama by telephone our willingness to seek a solution to all problems without conditions of any kind. And I told him that our negotiators would meet theirs anywhere, anytime, to discuss anything, and we would do what was fair, just, and right. We never departed from that willingness. And on that basis, the dispute was settled.

We now move toward solution with the generosity of friends who realize, as Woodrow Wilson once said, "You cannot be friends on any other terms than upon the terms of equality."

The use of Cuba as a base for subversion and terror is an obstacle to our hopes for the Western Hemisphere. Our first task must be, as it has been, to isolate Cuba from the inter-American system, to frustrate its efforts to destroy free governments, and to expose the weakness of communism so that all can see. That policy is in effect, and that policy is working. The problems of this hemisphere would be far more serious if [*Premier Fidel*] Castro today sat at the councils of the Organization of American States disrupting debates and blocking decision, if Castro had open channels of trade and communication along which subversion and terror could flow, if his economy had been a successful model rather than a dismal warning to all of his neighbors.

The effectiveness of our policy is more than a matter of trade statistics. It has increased awareness of difference and danger, it has revealed the brutal nature of the Cuban regime, it has lessened opportunities for subversion, it has reduced the number of Castro's followers, and it has drained the resources of our adversaries, who are spending more than $1 million a day. We will continue this policy with every peaceful means at our command.

The Far East

A fourth area of continuity and change is the battle for freedom in the Far East. In the last 20 years, in two wars, millions of Americans have fought to prevent the armed conquest of free Asia. Having invested so heavily in the past, we will not weaken

[35] Document 74.

in the present. The first American diplomatic mission to the Far East was instructed to inform all countries that "we will never make conquests, or ask any nation to let us establish ourselves in their countries."

That was our policy in 1832. That is our policy in 1964. Our conquering forces left Asia after World War II with less territory under our flag than ever before. But if we have desired no conquest for ourselves, we have also steadfastly opposed it for others. The independence of Asian nations is a link in our own freedom.

In Korea we proved the futility of direct aggression. In Viet-Nam the Communists today try the more insidious, but equally dangerous, methods of subversion, terror, and guerrilla warfare. They conduct a campaign organized, directed, supplied, and supported from Hanoi. This, too, we will prove futile. Armed Communist attack on Viet-Nam is a reality. The fighting spirit of South Viet-Nam is a reality, as Secretary [*of State Dean*] Rusk told us from there yesterday.[36] The request of a friend for our help in this terrible moment is a reality.

The statement of the SEATO [*Southeast Asia Treaty Organization*] allies that Communist defeat is "essential" is a reality.[37] To fail to respond to these realities would reflect on our honor as a nation, would undermine worldwide confidence in our courage, would convince every nation in South Asia that it must now bow to Communist terms to survive.

The situation in Viet-Nam is difficult. But there is an old American saying that "when the going gets tough, the tough get going." So let no one doubt that we are in this battle as long as South Viet-Nam wants our support and needs our assistance to protect its freedom.

I have already ordered measures to step up the fighting capacity of the South Vietnamese forces, to help improve the welfare and the morale of their civilian population, to keep our forces at whatever level continued independence and freedom require. No negotiated settlement in Viet-Nam is possible, as long as the Communists hope to achieve victory by force.

Once war seems hopeless, then peace may be possible. The door is always open to any settlement which assures the independence of South Viet-Nam and its freedom to seek help for its protection.

[36] The reference is to Secretary Rusk's visit of April 17-20 to South Vietnam at the conclusion of the SEATO meeting in Manila. For background see *The United States in World Affairs, 1964,* pp. 142-143.
[37] Document 46.

In Laos we continue to support the Geneva agreements[38] which offer what we think is the best hope of peace and independence for that strife-torn land. At my instruction yesterday Assistant Secretary of State William [*P.*] Bundy went to Laos, and he has already arrived there for a firsthand examination of the developments, developments that have come in the last 48 hours. At the moment we are encouraged by reports of progress toward the reestablishment of orderly, legal government.

As for China itself, so long as the Communist Chinese pursue conflict and preach violence, there can be and will be no easing of relationships. There are some who prophesy that these policies will change. But America must base its acts on present realities and not on future hopes. It is not we who must reexamine our view of China. It is the Chinese Communists who must reexamine their view of the world.

Nor can anyone doubt our unalterable commitment to the defense and liberty of free China. Meanwhile, we will say to our historic friends, the talented and courageous Chinese people on the mainland, that just as we opposed aggression against them, we must oppose aggression by their rulers and for the same reasons.

The New Nations of Africa and Asia

Fifth is our concern with the new nations of Africa and Asia. We welcome their emergence, for their goals flow from hopes like our own. We began the revolt from colonial rule which is now reshaping continents and which is now creating new nations. Our mastery of technology has helped men to learn that poverty is not inevitable, that disease and hunger are not laws of nature. Having helped create hopes, we must now help satisfy them, or we will witness a rising discontent which may ultimately menace our own welfare.

What we desire for the developing nations is what we desire for ourselves—economic progress which will permit them to shape their own institutions, and the independence which will allow them to take a dignified place in the world community.

Let there be no mistake about our intention to win the war against poverty at home, and let there be no mistake about our intention to fight that war around the world. This battle will not be easy and it will not be swift. It takes time to educate young minds and shape the structure of a modern economy. But the

[38] *Documents, 1962,* pp. 284-294.

world must not be divided into rich nations and poor nations, or white nations and colored nations. In such division, I know you must realize, are the seeds of terrible discord and danger in decades to come. For the wall between rich and poor is a wall of glass through which all can see.

We recognize the need for more stable prices for raw materials, for broader opportunity for trade among nations. We are ready to help meet these claims, as we have already done, for example, with the negotiation of the international coffee agreement,[39] and as we will do in the weeks ahead in the Kennedy Round.[40] We will continue with the direct economic assistance which has been a vital part of our policy for 20 years.

Foreign Aid

Last year the Congress reduced foreign aid from $4.9 billion—later modified by General [*Lucius D.*] Clay's committee [41] to $4.5 billion—and Congress reduced that to a total of $3.4 billion that they appropriated to me to deal with the problems of 120 nations. This year I ordered that our request be cut to the absolute minimum consistent with our commitments and our security,[42] allowing for no cushions or no padding, and that was done.

Every dollar cut from that request for $3.4 billion will directly diminish the security of the United States. And if, in spite of this clear need and this clear warning, substantial cuts are made again this year in either military or economic funds, I want to sound a warning that it will be my solemn duty as President to submit supplemental requests for additional amounts until the necessary funds of $3.4 billion are appropriated.

In these areas, and in other areas of concern, we remain faithful to tested principle and deep conviction while shaping our actions to shifting dangers and to fresh opportunity. This year is an election year in the United States. And in this year let neither friend nor enemy abroad mistake growing discussion for growing dissension, conflict over programs for conflict over principles, or political division for political paralysis. This mistake in judgment has been made twice in our lifetime, to the sorrow of our adversaries.

[39] The International Coffee Agreement, signed on September 28, 1962, entered into force December 27, 1963.
[40] Document 28.
[41] The report of General Clay's committee in *Documents, 1963*, pp. 25-34.
[42] Document 4.

Now let those at home, who share in the great democratic struggle, remember that the world is their audience and that attack and opposition to old policies must not be just for opposition's sake, that it requires responsible presentation of new choices, that in the protection of our security—the protection of American security—partisan politics must always yield to national need.

I recognize that those who seek to discuss great public issues in this election year must be informed on those issues. Therefore I have today instructed the Departments of State and Defense and the Central Intelligence Agency to be prepared and to provide all major candidates for the office of President with all possible information helpful to their discussion of American policy. I hope candidates will accept this offer in the spirit in which it is made, the encouragement of the responsible discussion which is the touchstone of the democratic process.

In the past 20 years we have gradually become aware that America is forever bound up in the affairs of the whole world. Our own future is linked to the future of all. In great capitals and in tiny villages, in the councils of great powers and in the rooms of unknown planners, events are being set in motion which will continually call upon our attention and our resources.

Prophecy is always unsure. But if anything is certain, it is that this nation can never again retreat from world responsibility. You must know, and we must realize, that we will be involved in the world for the rest of our history. We must accustom ourselves to working for liberty in the community of nations as we have pursued it in our community of States.

The struggle is not merely long. The struggle is unending. For it is part of man's ancient effort to master the passions of his mind, the demands of his spirit, the cruelties of nature. Yes, we have entered a new arena. The door has closed behind us, and the old stage has passed into history.

Dangers will replace dangers, challenges will take the place of challenges, new hopes will come as old hopes fade. There is no turning from a course which will require wisdom and much endurance so long as the name of America still sounds in this land and around the world.

B. The Presidential Campaign.[43]

(7) *Speech by Senator Barry M. Goldwater Accepting the Republican Nomination, San Francisco, July 16, 1964.*[44]

(Excerpts)

* * *

Now, we Americans understand freedom, we have earned it; we have lived for it, and we have died for it. This nation and its people are freedom's models in a searching world. We can be freedom's missionaries in a doubting world.

But, ladies and gentlemen, first we must renew freedom's mission in our own hearts and in our own homes.

During four futile years the Administration which we shall replace has distorted and lost that faith. It has talked and talked and talked and talked the words of freedom but it has failed and failed and failed in the works of freedom.

Now failure cements the wall of shame in Berlin; failures blot the sands of shame at the Bay of Pigs; failures marked the slow death of freedom in Laos; failures infest the jungles of Vietnam; and failures haunt the houses of our once great alliances and undermine the greatest bulwark ever erected by free nations, the NATO [*North Atlantic Treaty Organization*] community.

Failures proclaim lost leadership, obscure purpose, weakening wills and the risk of inciting our sworn enemies to new aggressions and to new excesses.

And because of this Administration we are tonight a world divided. We are a nation becalmed. We have lost the brisk pace of diversity and the genius of individual creativity. We are plodding along at a pace set by centralized planning, red tape, rules without responsibility and regimentation without recourse.

* * *

And I needn't remind you that it was the strength and the believable will of the Eisenhower years that kept the peace by using our strength, by using it in the Formosa [*Taiwan*] Strait,[45] and in Lebanon,[46] and by showing it courageously at all times.

[43] For discussion see *The United States in World Affairs, 1964,* pp. 13-17.
[44] *New York Times,* July 17, 1964.
[45] The reference is to the Formosa crisis of 1955. For relevant documentation see *Documents, 1955,* pp. 294-305.
[46] The reference is to the dispatch of U.S. troops to Lebanon in July 1958. Cf. *Documents, 1958,* pp. 302-311.

It was during those Republican years that the thrust of Communist imperialism was blunted. It was during those years of Republican leadership that this world moved closer not to war but closer to peace than at any other time in the last three decades.

And I needn't remind you, but I will, that it's been during Democratic years that our strength to deter war has been stilled and even gone into a planned decline. It has been during Democratic years that we have weakly stumbled into conflicts, timidly refusing to draw our own lines against aggression, deceitfully refusing to tell even our own people of our full participation and tragically letting our finest men die on battlefields unmarked by purpose, unmarked by pride or the prospect of victory.

Yesterday it was Korea; tonight it is Vietnam. Make no bones of this. Don't try to sweep this under the rug. We are at war in Vietnam. And yet the President, who is the Commander in Chief of our forces, refuses to say, refuses to say mind you, whether or not the objective over there is victory, and his Secretary of Defense [*Robert S. McNamara*] continues to mislead and misinform the American people, and enough of it has gone by.

And I needn't remind you, but I will, it has been during Democratic years that a billion persons were cast into Communist captivity and their fate cynically sealed.

Today—today in our beloved country we have an Administration which seems eager to deal with Communism in every coin known—from gold to wheat; from consulates [47] to confidence, and even human freedom itself.

Now the Republican cause demands that we brand Communism as the principal disturber of peace in the world today. Indeed, we should brand it as the only significant disturber of the peace. And we must make clear that until its goals of conquest are absolutely renounced, and its relations with all nations tempered, Communism and the governments it now controls are enemies of every man on earth who is or wants to be free.

Now, we here in America can keep the peace only if we remain vigilant, and only if we remain strong. Only if we keep our eyes open and keep our guard up can we prevent war.

And I want to make this abundantly clear—I don't intend to let peace or freedom be torn from our grasp because of lack of strength, or lack of will—and that I promise you Americans.

I believe that we must look beyond the defense of freedom today to its extension tomorrow. I believe that the Communism

[47] Document 30.

which boasts it will bury us will instead give way to the forces of freedom.

* * *

I can see, and I suggest that all thoughtful men must contemplate, the flowering of an Atlantic civilization, the whole world of Europe reunified and free, trading openly across its borders, communicating openly across the world.

This is a goal far, far more meaningful than a moon shot.

* * *

I can see a day when all the Americas—North and South—will be linked in a mighty system—a system in which the errors and misunderstandings of the past will be submerged one by one in a rising tide of prosperity and interdependence.

We know that the misunderstandings of centuries are not to be wiped away in a day or wiped away in an hour. But we pledge, we pledge, that human sympathy—what our neighbors to the South call an attitude of sympatico—no less than enlightened self-interest will be our guide.

And I can see this Atlantic civilization galvanizing and guiding emergent nations everywhere.

* * *

And I pledge that the America I envision in the years ahead will extend its hand in help in teaching and in cultivation so that all new nations will be at least encouraged to go our way; so that they will not wander down the dark alleys of tyranny or to the dead-end streets of collectivism.

* * *

Anyone who joins us in all sincerity we welcome. Those, those who do not care for our cause, we don't expect to enter our ranks in any case. And let our Republicanism so focused and so dedicated not be made fuzzy and futile by unthinking and stupid labels.

I would remind you that extremism in the defense of liberty is no vice.

And let me remind you also that moderation in the pursuit of justice is no virtue!

* * *

Our Republican cause is not to level out the world or make its people conform in computer-regimented sameness. Our Republican cause is to free our people and light the way for liberty throughout the world.

* * *

(8) *Speech by President Johnson Accepting the Democratic Nomination, Atlantic City, August 28, 1964.*[48]

(Excerpts)

Chairman [*John W.*] McCormack. My fellow Americans.

I accept your nomination.

I accept the duty of leading this party to victory this year.

* * *

And let none of us stop to rest until we have written into the law of the land all the suggestions that made up the John Fitzgerald Kennedy program and then let us continue to supplement that program with the kind of laws that he would have us write.

* * *

America's cause is still the cause of all mankind. Over the last four years, the world has begun to respond to a simple American belief—the belief that strength and courage and responsibility are the keys to peace.

Since 1961, under the leadership of that great President, John F. Kennedy, we have carried out the greatest peacetime build-up of national strength of any nation, at any time in the history of the world.

And I report tonight that we have spent $30 billions more on preparing this nation in the four years of the Kennedy Administration than would have been spent if we had followed the appropriations of the last year of the previous Administration.

I report tonight as President of the United States and as Commander in Chief of the Armed Forces on the strength of your country and I tell you that it is greater than any adversary's.

I assure you that it is greater than the combined might of all the nations in all the wars in all the history of this planet.

And I report our superiority is growing.

Weapons do not make peace; men make peace. And peace comes not through strength alone, but through wisdom and patience and restraint.

[48] *New York Times,* August 28, 1964.

And these qualities under the leadership of President Kennedy brought a treaty banning nuclear tests in the atmosphere [49] and a hundred other nations in the world joined us.

Other agreements were reached and other steps were taken. And their single guide was to lessen the danger to men without increasing the danger of freedom.

Their single purpose was peace in the world. And as a result of these policies, the world tonight knows where we stand and our allies know where we stand, too.

And our adversaries have learned again that we will never waver in the defense of freedom.

The true courage of this nuclear age lies in the quest for peace. There is no place in today's world for weakness, but there is also no place in today's world for recklessness.

We cannot act rashly with the nuclear weapons that could destroy us all. The only course is to press with all our minds and all our will to make sure, doubly sure, that these weapons are never really used at all.

This is a dangerous and a difficult world in which we live tonight. I promise no easy answers. But I do promise this: I pledge the firmness to defend freedom; the strength to support that firmness; and a constant, patient effort to move the world toward peace instead of war.

* * *

Tonight we of the Democratic party confidently go before the people offering answers, not retreats; offering unity, not division; offering hope, not fear or smear.

We do offer the people a choice. A choice of continuing on the courageous and the compassionate course that has made this nation the strongest and the freest and the most prosperous and the most peaceful nation in the history of mankind.

To those who have sought to divide us, they have only helped to unite us.

To those who would provoke us, we have turned the other cheek.

So as we conclude our labors, let us tomorrow turn to our new task. Let us be on our way.

[49] Same as note 5 to Document 1.

(9) *The Defense Question.*

(a) ***Address by Senator Goldwater to the American Legion, Dallas, September 23, 1964.***[50]

(Excerpts)

* * *

I want to talk today about peace. No man anywhere wants peace more than I do, and no man anywhere wants to avoid war more than I do. I know war, and I have sons and daughters and grandchildren whom I do not want touched by war. I think one war in a man's life is par for the course.

And we can begin, I know, with the assumption that all Americans share the desire for peace, and they share also the responsibility for answering the terrible question of how we are to have and hold peace in a deeply troubled and a deeply divided world.

* * *

I believe that in the first place, we must recognize that it's not possible or at least not honest, to talk about peace without talking about and understanding Communism.

Now, the great, harsh fact of today's troubled world is that Communism is at war, and it's at war against us, at war against all non-Communist nations.

The great, harsh fact is that Communism is the only major threat to the peace of the world anywhere in this world today, and the sooner we realize this the better.

The great, harsh fact is that Communism wants the whole world. In Cuba, in the Congo, at the Berlin wall, in Indonesia, in Vietnam—wherever the flames of conflict are being fanned, Communism is the cause.

Now, the methods it uses in its unrelenting drive to conquer the world are based solely upon expediency. What Communism will do, how far it will go, at any given moment, depends upon their hardheaded, cold-blooded assessment of the risks that they must face.

If they can bury us, as they've promised to do—if they can win the world, as they've said they will—if they can do this without nuclear war, then they will try to avoid nuclear war.

But remember this: It is not compassion or decency which prevents their attacking us. It's not concern for our children. It's

[50] *New York Times*, September 24, 1964.

just plain fear. They respect our power and they fear provoking its use against them.

Now, this is the reason that we must maintain peace through preparedness.

But, you might ask, can we, in good heart and conscience, look forward to a cold war which will last forever unless it ends suddenly in nuclear destruction or take-over by a Communist dictator?

We can't, and I say we need not, look forward to such a bleak future. There is a rational solution to the problem which confronts us. The present policy that guides us, however, is based upon false answers. American foreign policy based on those false answers has made it altogether too easy for Communists to seize complete control of 18 nations and enslave one-third of the world's population.

Now, the worst of the false answers is that the Communists will stop being hostile if we just accommodate them, if we can convince them that we really want to be friends. Now, according to this theory, then they will become friends. This naive assumption is based on a complete misunderstanding of Communism as we know it today. It puts us in the position of a lamb trying to convince a lion that he's not really hungry.

I might remind you that 30 years of tragic experience have proven this theory utterly false.

* * *

This thesis directed the settlement of the Cuba crisis, the nuclear test ban treaty, and the sale of wheat to Russia—just to mention a few.

Now, it should be clear, I believe, to everyone that the "let's be friends" theory has not worked. Communism has not moderated its goals. It's [*sic*] continued to gain ground.

Now, the Communists have been stymied in Europe by the mighty shield of NATO which, incidentally, is cracking up under this present Administration, and they've been thrown back to the 38th parallel in Korea—but these reversals have been brought about by the use, or the threatened use, of military force. Almost everywhere else, the Communists have gained ground.

Now, if we want to halt their gains, if we want to save America's future and freedom, we must be stronger than the enemy—not just by a little bit, but by far. We certainly can't make the Reds reasonable, but we can make Communism count the odds.

But merely possessing the weapons of strength is not the same as being strong. We need the will to be strong. All the weapons in the world can't save us if our will is weak.

Now, we must realize that the responsible use of power—to deter those with hostile intent—is not nearly so likely to provoke all-out war as it is to prevent war by keeping the aggressor within bounds.

* * *

If we follow in this country the notion that a "let's be friends" approach, coupled with a defense establishment we are reluctant to use, can save us from Communism, we will run a very, very grave risk of war.

Now, the balance of power can't remain static forever. The threat of a technological breakthrough by the Soviets must be considered. And if the Communists believe the odds favor them, they will not hesitate to hit us with their most fearsome weapons.

Therefore, the first and central duty of the Federal Government is to provide for the common defense, and in the present state of the world, military spending is and must be high. But it alone amounts to less than one-half of the total Federal expenditures. In the 12 months ending June 30, 1964, the Federal Government spent the astounding total of $120 billion, or nearly $650 for every man, woman and child in the United States. Of this amount, $55 billion was spent on our military forces. Nondefense expenses, however, amounted to $65 billion.

And more importantly, the sharp rise in Federal spending in the present Administration has been mainly for purposes other than our common defense. In 1960, the final full year of the Eisenhower Administration, the Federal Government spent $94 billion, of which $46 billion was for defense.

And in the four years since, total expenditures have risen by nearly $30 billion, or by about one-third, and this is what this Administration calls economy. Federal expenses, for example, on our military forces have risen by $10 billion, so two-thirds of the rise in expenditures was for other purposes. Nondefense expenditures alone rose by 40 per cent in the last four years.

Currently, the Administration proposes actually to cut our military spending in order to provide funds for sticking the Government's fingers in still a larger mess of pies—for handouts here, subsidies there, and all, no doubt, said to be for the good purposes but, like past efforts in these directions, likely to end up having effects quite the opposite of those intended, yet draining the public purse.

That way lies national suicide. There is no surer way to condemn this nation to the status of a second-rate power, incapable of exerting influence in the world at large, than to fritter away taxable capacity in do-gooder schemes that waste our substance. Let me remind you that the experience of Britain is a striking example of how this can happen. We must not let it happen here.

The defenses of our nation need to be strengthened, not weakened. We must be ready to spend more on them when it's needed, not less. And we mustn't try to save money by putting all our trust in untried missiles, while scrapping tried and true weapons.

And we can't afford to reduce our defense establishment in the hope that a friendly Russian regime will accommodate us by doing the same thing.

We mustn't let our guard drop because of a temporarily friendly mask.

* * *

On the count of freedom, the present Secretary of Defense must be charged with mistake after mistake in evaluating the intentions of Communism and in understanding the dynamics of Communism.

His efforts to turn the Defense Department into a Disarmament Department, his participation in the massive misevaluation of Soviet intentions which led to the Cuban missile crisis, are parts of the indictment on this score.

His ceaseless attempts to downgrade professional military men and his persistent attempts to turn basic decisions—basic defense decisions—to political purposes must also be included in the indictment.

On the count of economy, the present Secretary of Defense must be charged with mistake after mistake in seeking to save pennies and dollars at the expense of the weapons, equipment and plans upon which the lives of our citizens and our citizen soldiers may depend. And a careful accounting, I am willing to predict, will show that even the high claims for saving will have to be lowered or denied.

* * *

And I am speaking for peace when I say we must build our strength and show the will to halt the Reds' aggression. I am speaking for peace when I say we must quit helping the Reds—

by sending them wheat,[51] for example—to keep their oppressive and unsound system alive.

Their system has so many intrinsic faults it would collapse if it wasn't braced from the outside as we've been bracing it.

These are old words to you. But appease an aggressor and try to make friends with him and eventually you'll have to go to war with him—unless you're willing to hand over your freedom without a fight. And I don't think Americans are.

Three times in the lives of most of us in this chamber, the way of weakness has led us to war under similar administrations. Don't let it happen again. The next war—and God forbid that it will ever come—would be more devastating than all the others put together.

* * *

(b) *Address by President Johnson, Seattle, September 16, 1964.*[52]

(Excerpts)

* * *

Tonight I want to talk to you about one of the most solemn responsibilities of the President of the United States, and that is the duty to direct and control the nuclear power of the United States.

Nineteen years ago President Truman announced "The force from which the sun draws its power has been loosed." In a single, fiery flash the world as we had known it was forever changed. Into our hands had come much of the responsibility for the life of freedom, for the life of our civilization, and for the life of man on this planet, and the realities of atomic power placed much of that burden in the hands of the President of the United States.

Let no one think atomic weapons are simply bigger and more destructive than other weapons; just another development like the airplane or the tank. The total number of Americans killed in battle from the Revolution until tonight is a little over 526,000 people. Today a single nuclear weapon can kill more than 526,000.

Our experts tell us as of today that a full-scale nuclear exchange between the East and the West would kill almost 300 mil-

[51] For President Kennedy's statement authorizing the wheat sale see *Documents, 1963*, pp. 160-162.
[52] White House Press Release, September 16, 1964.

lion people around the world, and in the midst of that terror and tragedy we could expect that weapon after weapon would soon engulf a portion of mankind. A cloud of deadly radiation would drift and destroy, menacing every living thing on God's earth, and in those unimaginable hours unborn generations would forever be lamed.

Now, in the face of these facts, every American President has drawn the same conclusion:

President Harry Truman said: "Such a war is not a possible policy for rational man."

President Eisenhower said: "In a nuclear war, there can be no victory—only losers."

President Kennedy said: "Total war makes no sense . . ."

And I say that we must learn to live with each other or we will destroy each other.

Many forces have converged to make the modern world. Atomic power is very high among those forces, but what has the atomic age meant for us who have come here to this dinner tonight?

It means, I think, that we have a unique responsibility, unique in history, for the defense of freedom. Our nuclear power alone has deterred Soviet aggression. Under the shadow of our strength, our friends have kept their freedom and have built their nations.

It means that we can no longer wait for the tides of conflict to touch our shores.

It means that great powers can never again delude themselves into thinking that war will be painless or that victory will be easy. Thus, atomic power creates urgent pressure for peaceful settlements, and for the strengthening of the United Nations.

It means a change must come in the life of nations. Man has fought since time began, and now it has become clear that the consequences of conflict are greater than any gain, and man just simply must change if man is to survive.

For Americans, it means that control over nuclear weapons must be centralized in the hands of the highest and the most responsible officer of government—the President of the United States. He, alone, has been chosen by all the people to lead all the Nation. He, alone, is the constitutional Commander-in-Chief of the Nation. On his prudence and wisdom alone can rest the decision which can alter or destory the Nation. The responsibility for the control of U.S. nuclear weapons rests solely with the President, who exercises the control of their use in all foreseeable circumstances. This has been the case since 1945, under four President[*s*]. It will continue to be the case as long as I am President of the United States.

In this atomic age we have always been required to show restraint as well as strength. At moments of decisive tests, our nuclear power has been essential. But we have never rattled our rockets or come carelessly to the edge of war. Each of the great conflicts of this century have begun when nations wrongly thought others would shrink before their might. As I and my predecessors have said, we may have to use nuclear weapons to defend American freedom, but I will never let slip the engines of destruction because of a reckless and rash miscalculation about our adversaries.

We have worked consistently to bring nuclear weapons under careful control, and to lessen the danger of nuclear conflict, and this policy has been the policy of the United States of America for 19 years now, under both Democratic and Republican Administrations, and this will continue to be the policy of the United States of America.

First, we have worked to avoid war by accident or miscalculation. I believe the American people should know the steps that we have taken to eliminate the danger of accidental attack by our strategic forces, and I am going to talk about that tonight. The release of nuclear weapons would come by Presidential decision alone. Complex codes and electronic devices prevent any unauthorized action. Every further step along the way from decision to destruction is governed by the two-man rule. Two or more men must act independently and must decide the order has been given. They must independently take action. An elaborate system of checks and counter-checks, procedural and mechanical, guard against any unauthorized nuclear bursts. In addition, since 1961 we have placed Permissive Action Links on several of our weapons. These are electromechanical locks which must be opened by secret combination before action at all is possible, and we are extending this system. The American people and all the world can rest assured that we have taken every step man can devise to insure that neither a madman nor a malfunction could ever trigger nuclear war.

We have also worked to avoid war by miscalculation. There may be little time for decision between our first warning and our need to reply. If our weapons could be easily destroyed, we would have to make the final decision in a matter of minutes. By protecting our power against surprise attack, we give ourselves more time to confirm that war has actually begun. Thus, we have placed missiles in protected, underground sites.

We have placed missiles beneath the seas. And we have provided constant and secure communication between strategic forces and the Commander-in-Chief, the President of the United States.

I do not want to fight a war that no one meant to begin. We have worked to limit the spread of nuclear weapons. The dignity and the interest of our allies demands that they share nuclear responsibility, and we have proposed such measures. The secrets of the atom are known to many people. No single nation can forever prevent their use. If effective arms control is not achieved, we may see the day when these frightful, fearful weapons are in the hands of many nations. Their concern and capacity for control may be more limited than our own.

So our work against nuclear spread must go on.

Third, we have developed ways to meet force with appropriate force by expanding and modernizing our conventional forces. We have increased our ground forces. We have increased our tactical air force. We have increased our airlift. We have increased our stock of the most modern weapons.

Thus, we do not need to use nuclear power to solve every problem. We will not let our might make us muscle-bound.

Fourth, we have worked to damp down disputes and to contain conflict. In an atomic world, any spark might ignite the bonfire. Thus, our responses are firm, but measured. We saw an example of that in the Tonkin Gulf just the other day.[53] Thus, we pursue peaceful settlement in many remote corners of the globe.

Fifth, we constantly work toward arms control. A test ban agreement has ended atmospheric explosions which were poisoning the atmosphere.[54] We have established a hot line for instant communication between the United States and Moscow in case of crisis.[55]

As President, I ordered a cutback of unnecessary nuclear production,[56] and this year we submitted several major new proposals to the Disarmament Conference in Geneva.[57] I will pursue with vigor all of those proposals.

These are only first steps. But they point the way toward the ultimate elimination of ultimate destruction. So long as I am your President, I intend to follow that course with all the patience at my command. In these ways, for 19 dangerous years,

[53] Document 49.
[54] Same as note 5 to Document 1.
[55] *Documents, 1963,* pp. 115-116.
[56] Document 1.
[57] Document 36.

my three predecessors have acted to insure the survival of the Nation, to insure survival of our freedom, and to insure survival of our race. That will always be my policy and this is the wish of the people of the United States.

* * *

Conflict among nations will trouble this planet and will test our patience for a long time to come. And as long as weapons are necessary, wisdom in their control is going to be needed. The man who guides them holds in his hands the hopes of survival for the entire world.

* * *

CHAPTER TWO

THE ATLANTIC ALLIANCE IN THE MID-SIXTIES

A. The United States and NATO.[1]

(10) *A Growing Partnership: Remarks by President Johnson on the Fifteenth Anniversary of the Signing of the North Atlantic Treaty, Washington, April 3, 1964.*[2]

Fifteen years ago tomorrow, here in Washington, the North Atlantic Treaty was signed.[3] Less than 5 months later, after due constitutional process in all the signing countries, the treaty entered into force. From that time to this, the treaty has served the peace of the world.

This short treaty commits its parties to meet an armed attack on any of them in Europe or North America as "an attack against them all." For 15 years it has prevented any such attack. Created in response to Stalin's Iron Curtain and the loss of Czechoslovakian freedom, this treaty has lived through war in Korea, the threat of war over Berlin, and a crisis without precedent in Cuba. Each great event has tested NATO, and from each test we have gained increased strength.

We began as 12 countries; today we are 15. Those we have gained are among our most determined partners: Greece, Turkey, and the Federal Republic of Germany.

What began as a treaty soon became a command and then a great international organization. The number of ready divisions, including 6 from the United States, has multiplied by 5. The number of modern aircraft has multiplied by 10—all more effective by far than any were in 1949. So the alliance is real. Its forces operate. Its strength is known. Its weapons cover the full range of power, from small arms to nuclear missiles of the most modern design.

[1] For discussion see *The United States in World Affairs, 1964*, pp. 20-25.
[2] White House Press Release, April 3, 1964; text from *Department of State Bulletin*, April 20, 1964, pp. 606-608.
[3] *Documents, 1949*, pp. 612-615.

From the beginning, this treaty has aimed not simply at defense but has aimed at the cooperative progress of all its members. On the day of its signing back there 15 years ago, President Truman described it as a "bulwark which will permit us to get on with the real business of government and society, the business of achieving a fuller and happier life for our citizens." [4] This treaty, in fact, came 2 years after we and other friends had begun our historic enterprise of economic recovery under the Marshall Plan. Our "real business" was already pretty well advanced.

The 15 years since 1949 have seen the longest upward surge of economic growth that our Atlantic world has ever known. Our production and trade have more than doubled; our population has grown by more than a hundred million; the income of the average man has grown by more than 50 percent. Our inward peace and our outward confidence have grown steadily more secure. The internal threat of communism has shriveled in repeated failure. A new generation, strong and free and healthy, walks our streets and rides in our cars. Yes, we have done well.

Danger has receded, but it has not disappeared. The task of building our defenses is never really done. The temptation to relax must always be resisted. Our own Atlantic agenda has changed, but it is not short.

Our first common task, therefore, is to move onward to that closer partnership which is so plainly in our common interest. The United States, for one, has learned much from 15 years of danger and achievement. In 1949 the solemn commitment of this treaty was for us an historic departure from isolation, and we have many great men, some among us and some away today, to thank for their leadership.

Now it is a tested and recognized foundation stone of America's foreign policy. What Robert Schuman said for France in 1949 I repeat for my country today:

> Nations are more and more convinced that their fates are closely bound together; their salvation and their welfare can no longer be based upon an egotistical and aggressive nationalism, but must rest upon the progressive application of human solidarity.

The ways of our growing partnership are not easy. Though the union of Europe is her manifest destiny, the building of that unity is a long, hard job. But we, for our part, will never turn back to separated insecurity. We welcome the new strength

[4] Same, p. 611.

of our transatlantic allies. We find no contradiction between national self-respect and interdependent mutual reliance. We are eager to share with the new Europe at every level of power and responsibility. We aim to share the lead in the search for new and stronger patterns of cooperation.

We believe in the alliance because in our own interest we must, because in the common interest it works, and because in the world's interest it is right.

We have other duties and opportunities. Our trade with one another and the world is not yet free and not yet broad enough to serve both us and others as it should. Our monetary systems have grown stronger, but they still too often limit us, when they should be, instead, a source of energy and growth.

In ever-growing measure we have set ourselves and others free from the burden of colonialism. We have also set new precedents of generous concern for those that are less prosperous than we. But our connection to the less developed nations is not yet what it should be and must be. This is not a one-way street, but we must work to do our full part to make it straight and make it broad.

We remain vigilant in defending our liberties, but we must be alert to any hope of stable settlement with those who have made vigilance necessary and essential. In particular, we must be alive to the new spirit of diversity that is now abroad in Eastern Europe. We did not make the Iron Curtain. We did not build the [*Berlin*] wall. Gaps in the Curtain are welcome, and so are holes in the wall, whenever they are not hedged by traps. We continue to believe that the peace of all Europe requires the reunification of the German people in freedom. We will be firm, but we will always be fair. Our guard is up, but our hand is out.

We must build on our tradition of determined support for the United Nations. We are pledged to this purpose by the very articles of our treaty, and we have kept our pledge. The members of NATO provide most of the resources of the United Nations and most of its ability to help in keeping peace. When we began, we promised that our treaty was consistent with the charter. Today we know that the charter and the treaty are indispensable to one another. Neither can keep the peace alone. We need them both, in full effectiveness, for as many years ahead as any of us can see.

The Atlantic peoples have a magnificent history, but they have known too much war. It is the splendor of this great alliance that, in keeping peace with its opponents, it has kept the road clear for a worldwide upward march toward the good life for free people. Proven in danger, strengthened in freedom, and resolute in purpose, we will go on, with God's help, to serve not only our own people but to serve the bright future of all mankind.

(11) *The Atlantic Alliance: Address by Secretary of State Dean Rusk to the Overseas Press Club, New York, April 7, 1964.*[5]

(Excerpts)

* * *

Tonight I should like to discuss some of the specific tasks to which we think the North Atlantic nations should address their efforts.

Security in a Changing Environment

The first of these tasks is to maintain security in a changing environment. Dangerous issues between the Communist and free worlds remain unresolved. Although the Central European front remains quiet, massive Soviet ground and nuclear forces are still arrayed against Europe. In the absence of assured arrangements for the mutual reduction of arms, it would be foolhardy to dismantle the military strength of NATO. The task is rather to adapt that strength to a changing political and military environment. This means two things:

First: While maintaining our efforts to deter or defeat deliberate attack with every needed weapon, we should continue also to increase NATO's capability to cope with lesser forms of conflict —effectively and without automatic escalation to the type of conflict no one can rationally seek.

Second: There is a need to respond, in ways consistent with nonproliferation, to European desires for a responsible role in strategic nuclear deterrence.

Several hundred Soviet medium- and intermediate-range ballistic missiles [*MRBM*] are aimed at free Europe—many more missiles than are aimed at the United States. To cover some of these targets which threaten Europe, two successive NATO Supreme Commanders have proposed that MRBM's be deployed to the European area.

[5] Department of State Press Release 148, April 7, 1964; text from *Department of State Bulletin,* April 27, 1964, pp. 650-655. For discussion concerning the M.L.F. see *The United States in World Affairs, 1964,* pp. 25-31, and pp. 42-51.

We believe that it makes more sense to put MRBM's thus deployed to the European area at sea, instead of in heavily populated European areas. One way of deploying sea-based MRBM's would be under procedures involving national Allied manning and ownership of the missile and bilateral United States–Allied control over the warhead's use. New nationally owned and manned strategic missile forces could, however, be divisive within the alliance and unsettling in terms of East–West relations.

If Allied forces are to participate in MRBM deployment, but not under national manning and ownership, the only remaining possibility is mixed manning and ownership.

These conclusions suggested the need for an imaginative breakthrough to a new pattern of ownership and control of medium-range nuclear weapons—a new pattern involving a greater degree of Allied integration than anything yet attempted.

This is the origin of the so-called multilateral missile fleet—or MLF [multilateral force]. Eight nations are now discussing this concept in a working group at Paris, where substantial and encouraging progress has been made.

The MLF will effectively discharge the task to which it is addressed. General [Lyman L.] Lemnitzer has said that its 200 well-protected MRBM's would be effective in covering some of the airfields and missiles threatening Europe. Indeed, its capabilities will be taken into full account in the development of future American forces, because we consider it a reliable component of overall NATO defense.

The MLF plan also would permit nations interested in this specific problem to move ahead, without requiring the participation of nations which do not wish to take part.

Furthermore, the plan follows the classic pattern of Atlantic partnership: The United States will be in the venture from the start, but the concept and structure of the force is such that Europe's role and influence can grow as more European countries join and as Europe moves toward unity.

The MLF is, of course, not the end of the process of bringing our allies closer together in the field of nuclear defense. From this first step, much could flow.

First, this truly integrated force will provide practical experience suggesting perhaps further applications—and even new ventures in Atlantic partnership.

Second, this venture is bound to give the participants a deeper insight into the responsibility and the problems that go with strategic nuclear weapons. In so doing, it should make possible improved interallied consultation about the use of strategic forces, toward which a good start was made in the arrangements agreed to at Ottawa last year.[6] And it should contribute to a common approach to the problems of disarmament.

Third, military integration may have important nonmilitary implications. Countries which join in owning, manning, and managing a major nuclear force are likely to find themselves drawn into increasingly intimate relations in a wide variety of ways.

Finally, let me emphasize this: We do not see security for anybody in a world of proliferating national weapons systems. The detailed arrangements for the MLF will include mutually agreed strong and enduring safeguards against any one nation's securing control of any of the MLF weapons. We believe that when the Soviet Government understands this, it will recognize that the MLF does not constitute a proliferation of national nuclear systems but, on the contrary, is an alternative to it.

These are important reasons why support for the MLF is the firm policy of President Johnson's administration, as it was of two previous U.S. administrations. They are [*the*] reasons why we expect to move ahead vigorously with other interested countries in its execution. As President Johnson said at Brussels last November: [7]

> The movement to Atlantic partnership makes this possible. The movement to European unity makes this desirable—as a first step toward a greater European voice in nuclear matters.

Political Consultation Within NATO

We have never, however, considered the North Atlantic partnership as purely military—or as temporary or static.

The great goal of our foreign policy is a world in which both peace and freedom are secure. We regard the nations of free Europe as senior partners in this vast effort.

For various tasks, new patterns of collective action will be needed.

In the political field we have increasingly recognized the need for consultation about policies both toward the Communist nations and in other areas.

We continuously review together the changes that are occurring within the Communist world—the dispute between Peiping and Moscow, the trends toward more autonomy in Eastern Europe, the economic troubles of the Communist countries, the

[6] Cf. *Documents, 1963*, pp. 199-201.
[7] *Department of State Bulletin,* December 2, 1963, p. 852.

modest signs here and there of yearnings for more individual freedom. We must remain alert to opportunities for constructive action growing out of these changes.

We should not forget that the division of Germany is a continuing obstacle to permanent peace in Central Europe. A major task of our diplomacy should be to mitigate and eventually to eliminate this danger by moving toward German self-determination and unification. We believe that this can be done under terms which meet the legitimate security concerns of the Soviet Union and the smaller states of Eastern Europe.

We must try unceasingly to abate the perils of the arms race. We hope that the Soviet Union will agree to various safeguards against war from miscalculation or accident. We should like to see real progress in reducing armaments. We hope that the Soviets will make that possible by modifying their opposition to effective verification and inspection.

The North Atlantic nations should also deal cooperatively and effectively with Communist aggression and subversive threats—in Asia, Latin America, and Africa. I have in mind especially such countries as Laos and South Viet-Nam, which are targets of aggression by Hanoi, with the support of the Chinese Communists; and Cuba, which is engaged in the export of arms, subversive agents, and guerrilla leaders to other Latin American nations. We believe that the North Atlantic nations should recognize a common interest in seeing that these aggressions are brought to an end. They should also contribute, where they can, to the settlement of disputes within the non-Communist world.

I do not intend to lay out here a precise blueprint for improved political consultation within NATO. A great deal has been accomplished in that direction in the last 3 years. But more can be done to the mutual benefit of all concerned. I would suggest a few broad guidelines, which we are trying increasingly to follow.

Consultation should focus on specific problems and should include the countries most interested in joint action on these problems, while insuring that all the Atlantic allies are kept closely informed about concerted actions.

Officials who bear responsibility for these problems in their own governments should be intimately involved. This expedites agreement and makes it possible for those who do agree to move ahead in concert.

The means of fulfilling these principles will vary. Continuing discussions of Cuba in the North Atlantic Council, the latest involving Under Secretary [*of State George W.*] Ball,[8] have improved understanding of the purpose and effectiveness of restrictions on trade with Cuba. Consultation about Berlin and Germany in the Washington quadripartite group [France, Federal Republic of Germany, U.K., U.S.] has resulted in agreed Western positions. It is not generally realized that the NATO permanent representatives continually carry on consultations regarding a broad range of political subjects. These include not only problems within the NATO treaty area but outside as well. In the past year the United States has initiated consultation or exchange of information in NATO on approximately 30 issues of significance.

In addition to the regular consideration of current political problems, geographic experts from the NATO countries meet in Paris twice a year to exchange views and prepare reports on the various areas of the world—such as Africa, the Middle East, and Far East. These reports are considered by the NATO ministers at their spring and winter meetings. The NATO Council also benefits from the periodic meetings of the Atlantic Political Advisory Group (APAG), NATO's long-range planning arm, whose members seek to anticipate problems or crises around the world.

There is particularly close consultation within NATO on disarmament issues and questions of European security. Approximately every 2 weeks, for example, a senior representative of one of the four Western Powers at the Geneva Disarmament Conference visits Paris to brief the NATO Permanent Council on developments in the disarmament talks. And before any major United States initiative in the disarmament field is put forward at Geneva, it is subjected to close consultation with our allies to insure that it does not adversely affect their interests.

Our political consultations are, of course, not confined to NATO. We have other allies and friends. We consult intimately with many other countries in all parts of the world about problems of common interest, including some of those which are discussed in NATO. And our NATO allies do the same.

We intend to go forward pragmatically and flexibly in political consultation within NATO, adapting the procedure in each case to the end in view. And we shall bear in mind, as we do, the possible need for evolution in these procedures as Europe moves toward unity.

* * *

But this is a matter in which we must wait for our European friends to come to a common view.

[8] The reference is to Mr. Ball's attendance at a meeting of the NATO Council held on March 27, 1964 in Paris.

We support European unity, but the future of Europe is for the free peoples of Europe to determine. We have been consistently unwilling to try to settle Europe's future in bilateral dealings with individual European governments. For that reason, we have not been prepared to provide additional help to the development of national nuclear capabilities or to accept proposals for a directorate of a self-chosen few to manage the affairs of the West. These are not issues in bilateral relations with individual European countries. They are issues which affect the interests of, and must be settled by, the Atlantic allies together. But let no one mistake the free discussion of these issues which goes on within the alliance for disunity on the prime question of mutual defense; the Cuban crisis of October 1962 demonstrated again how quickly NATO closes ranks in the face of an external threat.

Concerted Action Needed in Economic Field

New tasks also confront us in the economic field. There are three main areas in which concerted action is needed.

First, there is trade. The achievement of a truly integrated European Economic Community has created large opportunities here.

We cannot afford to lose sight of the basic goal of trade liberalization that motivates the Common Market and that led our Congress to enact the Trade Expansion Act.[9] Liberalization must apply to both industrial and agricultural trade. The inherent difficulties in easing restrictions on trade can be overcome, and the Kennedy Round can succeed, only if the negotiations are approached on both sides of the Atlantic with statesmanship and mutual understanding.[10] It is essential that we keep in mind that the reductions in tariffs resulting from these negotiations will be to the mutual advantage of all the participants and will serve to strengthen the foundation of the free world.

At present in Geneva the United Nations Conference on Trade and Development is highlighting the vast needs of the developing countries for expanded export markets.[11] These countries depend in part for their growth on enlarging trade with Europe and the United States. The Kennedy Round negotiations, which will follow immediately upon this conference, should and will offer concrete and tangible progress toward this end.

Joint economic action is also needed in the field of monetary

[9] Official summary in *Documents, 1962,* pp. 496-508.
[10] Document 28.
[11] Document 97.

and financial policy. For a considerable period after the war, when the United States and the United Kingdom disposed of almost all the West's international reserve assets, full and multilateral consultation was not as essential as it is now. The large accumulation of gold and foreign exchange assets on the Continent in the last several years has necessitated a more general pattern of Atlantic cooperation.

Such cooperation is well advanced in insuring orderly conditions in foreign exchange markets. Further steps are needed to ease the international flow of capital and to make sure that liquidity can expand as the volume of trade expands. We must seek arrangements through which the Atlantic nations can work out their temporary balance-of-payments problems in an orderly fashion, without hampering the larger ends of Atlantic policy. The countries of the European Economic Community have special responsibilities, under the Treaty of Rome,[12] for helping each other to this end. We are confident that progress toward both European and Atlantic cooperation will continue in the Organization for Economic Cooperation and Development.

Finally, joint action is needed in aid to developing countries. The time when it was fitting for the United States to provide the lion's share is past. It is essential that all the economically advanced countries act together to help the developing countries expand their economies and improve their welfare.

The members of the Development Assistance Committee of the OECD, which include Japan, have increased materially the flow of resources to the developing countries. From 1958 to 1962 the total flow of governmental aid from the DAC countries to the developing countries increased from $4,300,000,000 to $6,000,000,000. Aid from DAC countries other than the United States rose from $1,900,000,000 to $2,400,000,000. Members of this Committee have also been seeking to improve consultation on important aid problems and to achieve better coordination of their individual aid programs. We must expect needs in this respect to grow, rather than to diminish.

In each of these economic fields, therefore, closer concert is necessary—and is being sought with increasing effect.

[12] Text of the Rome treaty of March 25, 1957 in *American Foreign Policy: Current Documents 1957*, Department of State Publication 7101 (Washington: G.P.O., February 1961), pp. 426-518.

"The Time Is Now Ripe for Wider Tasks"

My theme, as you have seen, is simply this:

NATO is an alliance of free men determined to remain free, in full knowledge that peace and security are indivisible.

It has performed the central task for which it was created. It remains essential for the protection of its members and the security of the free world. The time is now ripe for wider tasks—in sharing responsibility for nuclear power; in concerting policies toward Communist nations and the settlement of disputes within the free world; and in cooperating more closely on worldwide problems of aid, trade, and monetary policy.

These new tasks can be fulfilled only by developing new forms of common action.

We are moving ahead to do just this—joining with those nations which wish to cooperate, leaving the door open for others and for a larger European role as Europe moves toward unity.

So let us proceed with quiet determination, avoiding both the drag of inertia and outmoded concepts and the seduction of sloganeering and apparent shortcuts, seizing the opportunities for more cohesive action with vigorous and open minds. In so doing we will demonstrate anew the vitality of the North Atlantic alliance in meeting the needs of the time.

As far ahead as any of us can perceive, the preservation of the values and ideals of the West requires that the parties to this partnership work with increasing intimacy.

As Carl Schurz reminds us: "Ideals are like stars; you will not succeed in touching them with your hands. But like the seafaring man on the desert of waters, you choose them as your guides, and following them you will reach your destiny."

(12) *NATO and World Responsibilities: Address by Under-Secretary of State George W. Ball, Georgetown University, Washington, May 7, 1964.*[13]

(Excerpts)

* * *

NATO was born in a time of crisis. It developed its present shape and form during a sustained period of tension. Today the

[13] Department of State Press Release 215, May 7, 1964; text from *Department of State Bulletin,* May 25, 1964, pp. 823-825.

fact—or at least the appearance—of relaxation between East and West is subjecting it to a new strain and test.

In today's relaxed environment there is danger that NATO may gradually lose some of its vitality through apathy and a kind of international wishful thinking. The present generally good state of economic health on both sides of the ocean has produced a pervasive sense of well-being, almost of euphoria. The Atlantic world feels increasingly strong and confident of the future. There is danger that, if this happy state persists for long, some may be tempted to regard the obligations of a massive enterprise such as NATO as unnecessarily heavy, and some of our European friends, out of a sense of newfound confidence, may be led to consider NATO as too much an American show—there is already an apparent trend that way.

Character and Meaning of NATO

No human institution is ever perfect, and over time we should continue to improve further the present NATO alliance. But at the same time we must be extremely wary of any suggestion that the alliance is, of course, a good thing but that the NATO structure is a bad idea. Such a suggestion, if seriously regarded, could do great harm. For it might reduce NATO to the status of a classical alliance—an alliance inactive in peace and impotent in war.

* * *

Like any living organism, NATO must grow and change in order to survive. Several of the papers submitted to this conference emphasize two major pieces of unfinished business: *First,* we must develop ways and means for managing the nuclear deterrent power of the West in a manner that will take account of the aspirations for participation by member states not now possessing atomic weapons. At the same time we must avoid the manifest dangers of proliferation.

Second, we must continue to perfect NATO as an instrument by which the member nations can concert policies with respect to problems that arise not merely within the NATO area but elsewhere in the world.

Each of these pieces of unfinished business is, in my view, complicated by the same central difficulty—that most of the nation-states which form the membership of NATO are not large enough by themselves to play roles commensurate with the requirements of the present age.

Management and Control of a Nuclear Deterrent

Clearly this is true with regard to atomic weapons. The defense of the West requires not merely that an individual nation have the ability to mobilize vast resources of men, money, material, industrial plant, and technology but also that there be unity of control of the life-or-death decision of nuclear destruction.

I am sure that no one here favors nuclear proliferation as an objective of policy. Its dangers are manifest. For first one country, then another, to develop a national nuclear system could not help but heighten feelings of distrust within the Western alliance, while at the same time increasing tensions between the free world and the [*Communist*] bloc. The multiplication of national deterrents would increase the danger that a nuclear holocaust might be triggered through accident or miscalculation. At the same time it would multiply the chance that—at some point—nuclear weapons might fall under the control of an irresponsible individual or government. And finally, it would render progressively more difficult the achievement of an ultimate agreement to control or limit nuclear armament. But the road toward proliferation has no logical ending, and as we start down that road there are no logical stopping points other than the limits which nations impose on themselves or the limits imposed by the availability of resources or technology.

The renunciation of proliferation as a general principle is clearly not good enough. Such a solemn pronouncement is unlikely to influence the decisions of individual governments. Unless we can produce workable alternatives, proliferation will almost certainly occur whether we like it or not.

Here is where the political organization of Europe becomes relevant. If Europe were sufficiently far advanced toward political unity that it could by itself manage and control an atomic deterrent, we could hopefully look forward to an effective and integrated Atlantic defense founded on a true nuclear partnership. But this is not the case today, nor is it likely to be for some time. Effective nuclear control means the delegation to a central executive of the power of life or death involved in the use of atomic weapons. Obviously this presupposes a very high degree of political unity—a degree that far transcends anything immediately in contemplation.

Meanwhile, time will not stand still. Whatever the situation today—and the evidence on the point is confusing—we would delude ourselves if we assumed that the gifted and vigorous people in several of the countries of Western Europe would not sooner or later insist on playing an effective role in their own nuclear defense. If we provide no opportunity for even partial fulfillment of this quite natural desire, the consequences are easily foreseeable. Political pressures for the multiplication of national nuclear deterrents will accumulate, and governments will yield to them. The process, moreover, will feed on itself; the decision of one country to build a nuclear deterrent will almost certainly increase pressures for similar decisions in others.

The dilemma we face cannot, therefore, be safely brushed aside. If we regard the proliferation of national deterrent systems as undesirable and if we consider that the present exclusion of a large part of the members of the Western alliance from nuclear management is not likely to last, what other options do we have?

It is our attempt to answer this question that led us in 1960 to propose the creation of a multilateral nuclear force.[14] I recognize that this force has become a subject of some controversy not merely among you *cognoscenti* in this conference but in similar discussions elsewhere. Yet, as I see it, those who challenge the wisdom or effectiveness of such a force are yet to suggest an adequate alternative.

The Multilateral Nuclear Force

The multilateral force we are proposing would be organized within the framework of the Western alliance. To constitute a truly international force, we have felt that it should meet four conditions:

First, it should be assigned to NATO by all countries participating in the force. To meet this condition, we propose that it be collectively owned by the participants and that all participating nations share in the costs of creating, maintaining, and operating it.

Second, it should not be predominantly based on the soil of any one nation. To meet this condition, we are proposing a sea-based force consisting of Polaris-type missiles mounted on surface warships. This force, deployed on the high seas, would operate outside the national limits of any state.

Third, it should be managed and operated by nationals of

[14] Cf. *The United States in World Affairs, 1960,* pp. 148-149.

all participating countries under such conditions that it could not be withdrawn from the alliance to serve the national uses of any participating government. To meet this requirement, we propose that the ships themselves be manned by mixed crews of nationals of the participating nations.

The United States Joint Chiefs of Staff and the Secretary of Defense [*Robert S. McNamara*] have concluded that an efficient first-class force can be created in this fashion. SACEUR [Supreme Allied Commander Europe] has stated he would welcome the force as a significant addition to NATO's deterrent forces.

Fourth, the decision to fire the Polaris weapons should be a collective decision of the participating nations. One proposal is that political control be exercised through an executive body representing the participating nations. Obviously this control question is the heart of the matter. We are confident it can be solved.

In an ideal world we could no doubt devise less elaborate means for managing nuclear weapons. But we must work within the limitations of existing political arrangements. Those limitations arise from the fact that Western political institutions have not evolved in pace with the march of our technology. Until the West has achieved a far greater political unity than it possesses today, we believe that the development of a multilateral force is the best available course to pursue.

Not only does it offer the most effective means of dealing with the nuclear problem in the present political framework; it can also make possible a gradual and constructive evolution within that framework. The multilateral force would provide a new opportunity for working toward a greater unity in Europe and a closer partnership between the two sides of the Atlantic.

For the striking progress that has been achieved toward these goals in the past decade and a half has, to a considerable extent, come about from necessity—from the fact that governments have been compelled to cope with specific and immediate problems in Europe and the Atlantic area. And, as we seek to cope with the problem of nuclear management, I have no doubt that we shall—of necessity—make further strides toward a greater political unity in the years ahead.

Over the long pull, it will not be abstract principle but importunate necessity—the urgent need to get hard things done in order that we may survive and flourish—that will move us toward the attainment of the ultimate objective of unity and partnership.

Unequal Allocation of Responsibility

If the lack of political unity in Europe complicates the management of nuclear weapons systems within the NATO alliance, it also limits the development of NATO as an instrument for effective political consultation.

This question of consultation has been a favorite subject for discussions in conferences such as you have been having here today. A strong case can be made—and is frequently made—for greater consultation among NATO members, particularly with regard to world problems that lie outside the scope of the alliance.

The logic of this is clear enough. The member nations of NATO represent 90 percent of the industrial strength of the free world. They are, in Dean Acheson's words, "the central power which will support—if it is to be supported at all—a non-Communist world system."

I do not mean to suggest that, in the modern decentralized world, it would make sense to reserve the management of world affairs to an exclusive board of directors drawn solely from the NATO nations. Such a proposal would be an affront to friendly nations the world over that are playing responsible roles in their own areas. The United States, for example, has military alliances with 28 countries in addition to its NATO partners. At the same time it is clear that unity of policy among the members of NATO is an essential component of free-world power. To quote Mr. Acheson again: "If the center is not solid, relations with the periphery will not provide strength."

Unity of policy should presumably be hammered out through consultation. But consultation—essential though it be—can be fruitful only if all powers concerned are determined to make it so. It can produce little, for example, in the face of rigid philosophical differences such as those we have encountered in attempting to develop a common economic policy toward Cuba. It will also produce little when the consulting parties hold widely differing concepts of responsibility for world problems.

* * *

We Americans have few national interests—in the narrow sense—outside own own territory, but we have assumed vast world responsibility.

The result is an unequal allocation among the Atlantic nations both of responsibility and of the burden of decision that goes with it. This imbalance derives from the imperatives of history—not from deliberate American choice. We are aware that policy and responsibility must not be divorced. We recognize that no nation can be expected to share one without the other.

The United States today is quite prepared to share both with its NATO partners. So far, however, such sharing has been severely limited by differences of attitude within the NATO alliance. The willingness to accept world responsibility—as distinct from the preservation of national interests—is, in our observation and experience, not universal among the NATO membership.

Hopefully this is a passing phenomenon. For the past decade and a half most European nations have been preoccupied with pressing postwar business—the liquidation of colonial arrangements and the building of strong domestic economies. Now this business is largely finished.

Yet this alone will not solve the problem. The problem will never be fully solved until Europe gets on further with the achievement of its own unity, until it organizes itself on a scale commensurate with the requirements of the age.

There are quite obvious reasons for this. The undertaking of world responsibility requires a world view. The discharge of such responsibility under postcolonial conditions must be based on the command of vast resources for defense and foreign aid—and on the will to use them. Western Europe collectively has more than enough resources, but a fragmented Europe cannot efficiently mobilize them in support of a common effort and a common view.

The existing structure of Europe, therefore, sets limits to the effective sharing both of responsibility and decision. But this does not mean that—within the limits thus imposed—we should not continue to improve the present imperfect allocation. In fact, the United States is quite ready to go forward in sharing its responsibilities around the world wherever there is a will on the part of its European partners to share—and this includes a willingness to provide resources to make that sharing effective.

It was this thought which underlay President Johnson's comment in his recent speech to the Associated Press in New York when he said, in speaking of our Atlantic relations: [15]

> We also welcome agreed new mechanisms for political consultation on mutual interests throughout the world with whatever changes in organization are necessary to make such consultation rapid and effective.

[15] Document 6.

The Ultimate Goal of NATO

I approach the end of my observations tonight with three general conclusions:

The *first* is that NATO as it exists today—an Atlantic alliance with a unified force in being under a unified command—is an extraordinary peacetime achievement, a platform of accomplishment on which we should continue to build. And we should be wary, indeed, of any actions that might reduce its full effectiveness.

The *second* is that we cannot safely ignore the problem of widening participation in the management of our atomic defense, complicated as it may be by the fragmented structure of Western Europe. And unless you gentlemen are able, out of the collected wisdom represented here, to come up with a better solution than the multilateral force, I strongly urge your support for that proposal.

Finally, if NATO is to fulfill its purpose as the central arrangement for the defense of the free world, it must gradually extend its concern to the larger questions of free-world policy. Here again the limitations that obtain are not hard to isolate. They do not derive from any fault in the institutional structure of NATO but rather from the limited sense of world responsibility—as distinct from national interests—felt by many of our NATO partners.

These, then, are some of the problems for which we must find solutions over the coming months and years. Effective solutions will not be achieved merely by tinkering with the NATO structure but rather by progress in achieving a greater cohesion in relations among the member nations. This, it seems to me, is already in process. It has already produced substantial results, but there is much more to be done.

NATO, therefore, should not be regarded as an end in itself. It should be thought of as one of the pillars in a more comprehensive Atlantic relationship—an Atlantic relationship we must achieve in due course if we are to gain that ultimate goal of which Woodrow Wilson spoke with such prophetic passion—the "universal dominion of right by such a concert of free peoples as shall bring peace and safety to all nations and make the world itself at last free."

(13) *The Atlantic Community: Address by President Johnson, Washington, December 3, 1964.*[16]

(Excerpt)

* * *

Solving Our Problems by Common Consent

The United States has no policy *for* the people of Europe, but we do have a policy *toward* the people of Europe. And we do have common hopes and common objectives shared with most of the people of Europe. Answers to our common problems must emerge from the consent of free countries, and that consent, in turn, will be based on discussion and debate and respect for the ideas and the proposals of all. But there must be progress. A Chinese proverb says there are many paths up the mountain but the view from the top is always the same. We are always ready to look for a better or easier path, but we intend to climb to the summit.

First, we must all seek to assist in increasing the unity of Europe as a key to Western strength and a barrier to resurgent and erosive nationalism.

Second, we must all work to multiply in number and intimacy the ties between North America and Europe. For we shape an Atlantic civilization with an Atlantic destiny.

Third, we must all make sure that the Federal Republic of Germany is always treated as an honorable partner in the affairs of the West. Germany has labored to build a stable and a free society in complete loyalty to European unity and to Atlantic partnership. And the people and the leaders of Germany have bound themselves to peace and reconciliation with their European neighbors, and especially with France. They have rejected all separate adventures, especially, and I think most wisely, in the field of nuclear weapons. In particular, our friends and comrades throughout Germany deserve assurance from their allies that there shall be no acceptance of the lasting threat to peace which is the forced division of Germany. No one seeks to end this grim and dangerous injustice by force. But there can be no stable peace in Europe while one part of Germany is denied the basic right to choose freely its

[16] White House Press Release, December 3, 1964; text from *Department of State Bulletin,* December 21, 1964, pp. 866-876. For discussion see *The United States in World Affairs, 1964,* pp. 47-48.

own destiny and to choose, without threat to anyone, reunion with the Germans in the Federal Republic.

Fourth, those of us who are ready to proceed in common ventures must decide to go forward together, always with due deliberation, with due respect for the interests of others, and with an open door for those who may join later. We shall always seek agreement. We shall never insist on unanimity. This is the course which has brought fruitful results and almost every major advance in the 20 years since World War II.

An Agenda for Future Progress

The Atlantic alliance is not in the midst of crisis, as some alarm mongers would have you believe. But it is in the midst of change. Every important period of progress has been marked by the same kind of discussion and debate that is now in progress. The Coal and Steel Community, the integration of Germany into NATO, the Common Market [*European Economic Community*] itself, raise some blood pressures among excitable people, arouse question and concern and warning. And we were told that such steps might be against the interests of America. We were told that it might become harder to deal with the Soviet Union. We were told that we might encourage German militarism. We were told that we might divide Europe or arouse hostilities. To change patterns of thought or the shape of institutions is never very easy. Today's discussion and debate, the flow of ideas and proposals, is proof of coming change and a spur to continuing action.

The agenda for future progress does not consist of an isolated or a single dramatic step. It is made up of action—action across the whole range of common interest, which is the bedrock of our alliance. We have a common interest in the defense of the West. For 20 years the atomic might of the United States has been the decisive guard of freedom. Ours remains the largest strength and ours a most awesome obligation. But we recognize the reasonable interest and concerns of other allies, those who have nuclear weapons of their own and those who do not. We seek ways to bind the alliance even more strongly together by sharing the tasks of defense through collective action and meeting the honorable concerns of all.

This is the meaning of the proposals that we have made. This is the meaning of the discussions that we expect, and that we welcome, with all interested allies. We come to reason, not to dominate. We do not seek to have our way but to find a common way. And any new plans for the handling of weapons so powerful we think deserve most careful discussion and deliberation. No solution will be perfect in the eyes of everyone. But we all know that the problem is there. It must be solved. And we will continue to work for its solution.

We have a common interest in a rising standard of living for humanity. This will require a continuing effort to lower industrial tariffs in the Kennedy Round [17] and a joint study of the political and human problems of agriculture. We have a common interest in assisting the freedom and the growth of the developing world, and none of us will be finally secure in a world that is divided into hostile camps of rich and poor, or black and white.

We must also seek progress toward stable prices and nondiscriminatory trade for our basic commodities. We have a common interest in building bridges of trade and ideas, of understanding and humanitarian aid to the countries of Eastern Europe. These countries are increasingly asserting their own independence, and we will work together to demonstrate that their prospects for progress lie in greater ties with the West.

We have a common interest in increasing political consultation among the nations of the alliance. This may well require more frequent meetings among all the ministers or deputy ministers of the NATO alliance. It clearly demands that all of us be ready for those patient and determined efforts to meet each other halfway, without which no real agreement is ever possible among strong and honorable states.

Most of all, the Atlantic nations have a common interest in the peace of the world. In the past 4 years we have taken several steps toward lessening the danger of war. The United States is prepared in full consultation with its allies to discuss any proposal with the Soviet Union which might increase the chances of a lasting peace.

These are some of the areas in which we must work together. At every turning point for 20 years we have risen above national concerns to the more spacious vision of European unity and Atlantic partnership. This, too, must be such a time.

* * *

[17] Same as note 10 to Document 11.

B. The North Atlantic Treaty Organization.

(14) *Communiqué of the North Atlantic Council, The Hague, May 14, 1964.*[18]

The North Atlantic Council held its Spring Ministerial Meeting at The Hague from 12th to 14th May, 1964.

The Ministers reviewed the international situation. They discussed the annual political appraisal of the state of the Alliance presented by the Secretary-General. They emphasized the role of the Atlantic Alliance as the indispensable guardian of security and peace, and thus as the prerequisite for social and economic progress.

The Ministers reaffirmed their determination to achieve a genuine relaxation of tension in international relations. Although in recent months no serious crises have arisen in Europe, the Union of Soviet Socialist Republics has nevertheless continued to try to exert different forms of pressure. The Communist countries continue their various efforts to extend their system to the whole world. The fundamental causes of tension in the world therefore persist.

In particular, no solution has yet been found for the problems of Germany and Berlin. The Council reaffirmed that a just and peaceful solution to the problem of Germany can be reached only on the basis of the right of self-determination, and agreed that every suitable opportunity should be taken to bring nearer to realization the wish of the German people for reunification in freedom, and thereby ensure an enduring peace in Central Europe. This problem will continue to be examined. The Council also reaffirmed that the Government of the Federal Republic of Germany is the only German Government freely and legitimately constituted and therefore entitled to speak for Germany as the Representative of the German people in international affairs. With regard to Berlin, the Alliance stands by the terms of its Declaration of 16th December, 1958.[19]

The Ministers noted with satisfaction that limited steps had recently been taken towards arresting the arms race. They reiterated their desire to bring about a settlement of the basic problems of disarmament, but noted that such a prospect would remain remote as long as the Soviet Union refused to accept effective measures of control and inspection.

[18] Department of State Press Release 237, May 15, 1964; text from *Department of State Bulletin,* June 1, 1964, p. 852.
[19] *Documents, 1958,* pp. 233-234.

In present circumstances, the members of the Alliance are in duty bound to improve their overall defensive capability. They will strengthen their unity by extending and deepening their political consultation. They will intensify their economic effort in order to raise living standards, whether of their own peoples or in developing countries.

The Ministers, referring to the previous resolution concerning the study of the military and economic problems of the defense of the Southeastern region of NATO,[20] expressed the wish that the conclusions of this study be submitted at the next Ministerial Meeting.

The Ministers expressed their concern at the situation in this region arising from the continuing disorders in Cyprus. They reaffirmed the full support of their governments for the action decided on by the United Nations Organization with a view to restoring law and order, and for the efforts of the mediator appointed by the United Nations to seek an agreed solution of the problem.[21]

The Ministers expressed their deep regret at the impending departure of Mr. Dirk U. Stikker, who had announced his intention of retiring from the Secretary-Generalship of the Organization. In their tributes to Mr. Stikker, who was one of those who signed the North Atlantic Treaty in 1949,[22] the Ministers expressed their profound appreciation of his outstanding services to the Alliance.

The Council invited Signor Manlio Brosio, former Deputy Prime Minister and Defense Minister in the Italian Government and at present Italian Ambassador in Paris, to become Secretary-General of the Organization in succession to Mr. Stikker as from 1 August, 1964. Signor Brosio has informed the Council of his acceptance of this invitation.

The next Ministerial Meeting will be held in Paris in December 1964.[23]

(15) *Communiqué of the North Atlantic Council, Paris, December 17, 1964.*[24]

1. The North Atlantic Council met in Ministerial Session in Paris on December 15, 16 and 17, 1964.

[20] Same, *1963*, pp. 243-245.
[21] Documents 23 and 25.
[22] Same as note 3 to Document 10.
[23] Document 15.
[24] Department of State Press Release 523, December 18, 1964; text from *De-*

2. The Ministers surveyed the whole field of East-West relations. The basic causes of tension still persist, and will persist as long as it remains the aim of the Communist countries to extend their system to the whole world. The Ministers noted that recent developments in China and the Soviet Union have increased the uncertainties with which the world is faced. They reiterated their conviction that it remained essential for the Alliance to maintain and strengthen its unity.

3. The Ministers also reviewed the situation in various areas in Asia, Africa and Latin America. They reaffirmed their interest in the stability of these areas and in the economic and social welfare of the peoples concerned.

4. In their discussions on the state and future progress of the Alliance, the Ministers emphasized the importance of strengthening and deepening their political consultation. Recognizing the challenges that may face the organization in the years ahead, they directed the Council in permanent session to study the state of the Alliance and the purposes and objectives commonly accepted by all members, and to keep the Ministers informed.

5. The Ministers reaffirmed their determination to continue their efforts to find a peaceful solution to the questions at issue between East and West. In particular, they continue to attach great importance to making progress towards meeting the legitimate aspirations of the German people to reunification on the basis of their right to self-determination. In regard to Berlin, the Ministers confirmed the terms of their declaration of 16th December 1958.[25]

6. The Ministers expressed their conviction that the unity and military preparedness of the Alliance had safeguarded peace and preserved the freedom of the West in the past. So long as general and complete disarmament under effective international control has not been achieved, any weakening of the Allied defensive posture would expose the Alliance to increased pressures. The Ministers therefore stressed the importance of maintaining the cohesion of the member states in the strategic as well as the political field. Only a military structure demonstrably capable of swift and vigorous reaction to any aggression can meet the threat. To maintain such a structure, involving as it does a continuous adaptation to changing requirements, necessitates a persistent effort to improve the readiness, state of training, and equipment of the forces of the Alliance. It further requires a sound economic

partment of State Bulletin, January 4, 1965, pp. 2-4. For discussion see *The United States in World Affairs, 1964,* pp. 49-51.

[25] Same as note 19 to Document 14.

basis for the defense effort and the most rational use of available resources.

7. The Ministers also confirmed their determination to continue their efforts to arrive at agreements in the field of disarmament. In this connection, they stressed the importance of avoiding the dissemination of nuclear weapons.

8. The Ministers examined the problems confronting the Alliance in the field of conventional and nuclear weapons. A thorough exchange of views on these problems took place and will be continued.

9. The Ministers took note of developments in the studies of the inter-related questions of strategy, force requirements and resources, initiated in pursuance of the decisions taken at their meeting in Ottawa in May 1963.[26] They reaffirmed the significance they attached to these studies and instructed the Council in permanent session to continue them with the assistance of the NATO military authorities.

10. The Ministers also considered the special military and economic problems of Greece and Turkey. They reaffirmed the need for accelerating the economic development of these two Allied countries, and for an effort to strengthen the defense of the Southeastern region of NATO. They instructed the Council in permanent session to continue to examine these questions urgently.

11. In the spirit of previous resolutions on defense aid to Greece in 1963 and 1964, the Ministers established a procedure aimed at contributing to the solution of the special defense problems of Greece and Turkey in 1965.

12. With regard to Greek-Turkish relations, the Ministers heard a report by the Secretary General on the "watching brief" conferred on his predecessor [*Dirk U. Stikker*] at The Hague in May 1964.[27] In an effort to improve these relations and in the interests of the solidarity of the Alliance, they agreed that this "watching brief" should continue. They reaffirmed their determination to lose no opportunity of contributing to a reduction in tension and a peaceful, agreed and equitable solution of the problem of Cyprus, confirming also their support for the efforts of the United Nations and the mediator.[28]

13. The Ministers considered a report on civil emergency planning. They reaffirmed the importance of such planning within

[26] Same as note 6 to Document 11.
[27] Document 14.
[28] Same as note 21 to Document 14.

the context of overall defense, noting the progress which had been achieved and the work which remained to be done.

14. The next meeting of the North Atlantic Council at the Ministerial level will be held on the invitation of the United Kingdom Government in London in May 1965.

C. Exchange of Atomic Information.

(16) *Agreement for Cooperation Regarding the Exchange of Atomic Information, Submitted by President Johnson to the Congress, June 30, 1964.*[29]

PREAMBLE

The Parties to the North Atlantic Treaty, signed at Washington on 4th April, 1949,[30]

Recognising that their mutual security and defence requires that they be prepared to meet the contingencies of atomic warfare, and

Recognising that their common interest will be advanced by making available to the North Atlantic Treaty Organization and its member states information pertinent thereto, and

Taking into consideration the United States Atomic Energy Act of 1954, as amended,[31] which was prepared with these purposes in mind,

Acting on their own behalf and on behalf of the North Atlantic Treaty Organization,

Agree as follows:

ARTICLE I

In accordance with and subject to the requirements of the United States Atomic Energy Act of 1954, as amended, the Government of the United States of America will, while the North Atlantic Treaty Organization continues to make substantial and material contributions to the mutual defence and security, co-operate by communicating, from time to time, to the North Atlantic Treaty Organization and its member states, while they continue to make such contributions, atomic information in accordance with the provisions of this Agreement, provided that the Government of the United States of America determines that such co-operation will promote and will not constitute an unreasonable risk to its defence and security.

[29] *Department of State Bulletin,* July 20, 1964, pp. 96-98.
[30] Same as note 3 to Document 10.
[31] Public Law 85-479, approved July 2, 1958.

ARTICLE II

Paralleling the undertaking of the Government of the United States of America under this Agreement, the other member states of the North Atlantic Treaty Organization will, to the extent they deem necessary, communicate to the North Atlantic Treaty Organization, including its military and civilian elements, and to member states atomic information of their own origin of the same types provided for in this Agreement. The terms and conditions governing these communications by other member states will be the subject of subsequent agreements, but will be the same or similar to the terms and conditions specified in this Agreement.

ARTICLE III

The Government of the United States of America will communicate to the North Atlantic Treaty Organization, including its military and civilian elements, and to member states of the North Atlantic Treaty Organization requiring the atomic information in connection with their functions related to NATO missions, such atomic information as is determined by the Government of the United States of America to be necessary to:

(a) the development of defence plans;

(b) the training of personnel in the employment of and defence against atomic weapons and other military applications of atomic energy;

(c) the evaluation of the capabilities of potential enemies in the employment of atomic weapons and other military applications of atomic energy; and

(d) the development of delivery systems compatible with the atomic weapons which they carry.

ARTICLE IV

1. Co-operation under this Agreement will be carried out by the Government of the United States of America in accordance with its applicable laws.

2. Under this Agreement there will be no transfer by the Government of the United States of America of atomic weapons, non-nuclear parts of atomic weapons, or non-nuclear parts of atomic weapons systems involving Restricted Data.

3. The atomic information communicated by the Government of the United States of America pursuant to this Agreement shall be used exclusively for the preparation or implementation of NATO defence plans and activities and the development of de-

livery systems in the common interests of the North Atlantic Treaty Organization.

ARTICLE V

1. Atomic information communicated pursuant to this Agreement shall be accorded full security protection under applicable NATO regulations and procedures, agreed security arrangements, and national legislation and regulations. In no case will the North Atlantic Treaty Organization or its member states maintain security standards for the safeguarding of atomic information less restrictive than those set forth in the pertinent NATO security regulations and other agreed security arrangements in effect on the date this Agreement comes into force.

2. The establishment and co-ordination of the security programme in all NATO military and civilian elements will be effected under the authority of the North Atlantic Council in conformity with procedures set forth in agreed security arrangements.

3. Atomic information communicated by the Government of the United States of America pursuant to this Agreement will be made available through channels for communicating atomic information now existing or as may be hereafter agreed.

4. Atomic information communicated or exchanged pursuant to this Agreement shall not be communicated or exchanged by the North Atlantic Treaty Organization or persons under its jurisdiction to any unauthorized persons or, except as provided in paragraph 5 of this article, beyond the jurisdiction of that Organization.

5. Unless otherwise specified by the Government of the United States of America, United States atomic information provided to the North Atlantic Treaty Organization may be communicated by the North Atlantic Treaty Organization to its member states as necessary to carry out functions related to NATO missions, provided that dissemination of such atomic information within such member states is limited to those specific individuals concerned with the NATO missions for which the information is required. Member states agree that atomic information so received from the North Atlantic Treaty Organization or otherwise pursuant to this Agreement will not be transferred to unauthorised persons or beyond the jurisdiction of the recipient member state; however, such information may be communicated to the North Atlantic Treaty Organization or, when authorised by the Government of the United States of America, to other member states re-

quiring the information for functions related to NATO missions.

ARTICLE VI

Other provisions of this Agreement notwithstanding, the Government of the United States of America may stipulate the degree to which any of the atomic information made available by it to the North Atlantic Treaty Organization or member states may be disseminated, may specify the categories of persons who may have access to such information, and may impose such other restrictions on the dissemination of information as it deems necessary.

ARTICLE VII

1. A Party receiving atomic information under this Agreement shall use it for the purposes specified herein only. Any inventions or discoveries resulting from possession of such information on the part of a recipient Party or persons under its jurisdiction shall be made available to the Government of the United States of America for defence purposes without charge in accordance with such arrangements as may be agreed and shall be safeguarded in accordance with the provisions of Article V of this Agreement.

2. The application or use of any information communicated under this Agreement shall be the responsibility of the Party receiving it; the Party communicating the information does not provide any indemnity or warranty with respect to its application or use.

ARTICLE VIII

Nothing in this Agreement shall be considered to supersede or otherwise affect bilateral agreements between Parties to this Agreement providing for co-operation in the exchange of atomic information.

ARTICLE IX

For the purposes of this Agreement:

(a) "Atomic weapon" means any device utilising atomic energy, exclusive of the means for transporting or propelling the device (where such means is a separable and divisible part of the device), the principal purpose of which is for use as, or for development of, a weapon, a weapon prototype, or a weapon test device.

(b) "Atomic information" to be provided by the Government of the United States of America under this Agreement means information which is designated "Restricted Data" or "Formerly

Restricted Data" by the Government of the United States of America.

ARTICLE X

1. This Agreement shall enter into force upon receipt by the Government of the United States of America of notification from all Parties to the North Atlantic Treaty that they are willing to be bound by the terms of the Agreement.

2. The Government of the United States of America will inform all parties to the North Atlantic Treaty, and will also inform the North Atlantic Treaty Organization, of each notification and of the entry into force of this Agreement.

3. This Agreement shall remain in force until terminated by unanimous agreement or superseded by another agreement, it being understood, however, that termination of this Agreement as a whole shall not release any Party from the requirements of this Agreement to safeguard information made available pursuant to it.

ARTICLE XI

Notwithstanding the provisions of Article VI (4) of the Agreement between the Parties to the North Atlantic Treaty for Cooperation regarding Atomic Information, signed in Paris on 22nd June, 1955,[32] the present Agreement shall upon its entry into force supersede the above-mentioned Agreement, it being understood, however, that information communicated under that Agreement shall be considered for all purposes to have been communicated under the provisions of this Agreement.

ARTICLE XII

This Agreement shall bear the date on which it is opened for signature and shall remain open for signature until it has been signed by all the States Parties to the North Altantic Treaty.

In witness whereof the undersigned Representatives have signed the present Agreement on behalf of their respective States, members of the North Atlantic Treaty Organization, and on behalf of the North Atlantic Treaty Organization.

Done at Paris this 18th day of June 1964, in the English and French languages, both texts being equally authoritative, in a single original which shall be deposited in the archives of the Government of the United States of America. The Government of the United States of America shall transmit certified copies thereof to all the signatory and acceding States.

[32] *Documents, 1955*, p. 89.

D. France, the United States, and the European Community.[33]

(17) *Press Conference Statement of President Charles de Gaulle, Paris, July 23, 1964.*[34]

(Excerpts)

* * *

Europe and the French-German Agreement

Question: Mr. President, what meaning do you attach to the pursuit of the political unification of Europe after your recent talks with Chancellor [*Ludwig*] Erhard in Bonn?

Question: Mr. President, what results has the French-German treaty produced in political, economic and military matters? Do you deem these results satisfactory, disappointing or simply insufficient?

* * *

Undoubtedly it [*Europe*] should maintain an alliance with America in which, in the North Atlantic, both are interested so long as the Soviet threat remains. But the reasons which, for Europe, made this alliance a form of subordination are fading away day by day. Europe must assume its share of the responsibilities. Everything indicates, moreover, that this event would be in accordance with the interest of the United States, whatever may be its merit, its power and its good intentions. For the multiplicity and complexity of the tasks henceforth go beyond, and perhaps dangerously, its means and its capacity. That is why the United States declares that it wishes to see the old continent unite and organize itself while many among the Gallic, Germanic and Latin people cry out "Let us build Europe!"

But which Europe? That is the question. Indeed, the established conveniences, the accepted renunciations, the deep-rooted reservations do not fade away easily. According to we French, it is a question of Europe's being made in order for it to be European. A European Europe means that it exists by itself for itself, in other words in the midst of the world it has its own policy. But that is precisely what is rejected consciously or unconsciously by some who claim, however, to want it to be established. In reality, the fact that Europe, not having a policy, would be subject to the policy that came to it from the other side

[33] For discussion see *The United States in World Affairs, 1964,* pp. 34-35.

[34] Ambassade de France, Service de Presse et d'Information (New York), *Speeches and Press Conferences,* No. 208, July 23, 1964.

of the Atlantic appears to them, even today, normal and satisfactory.

We have seen many people—quite often, what is more, worthy and sincere—advocate for Europe not an independent policy, which in reality they do not visualize, but an organization unsuited to have one, linked in this field, as in that of defense and the economy, to an Atlantic system, in other words American, and consequently subordinate to what the United States calls its leadership. This organization, entitled federal, would have had as its bases on the one hand a council of experts withdrawn from the affiliation to the States, and which would have been dubbed "executive"; and on the other hand a Parliament without national qualifications and which would have been called "legislative." Doubtless each of these two elements would have supplied that for which it would have been fitted, that is to say, studies for the council and debates for the Parliament. But, without a doubt, neither of the two would have made what indeed no one wanted them to make, that is a policy, for if the policy must take the debates and studies into account, it is another thing entirely than studies and debates.

A policy is an action, that is to say a body of decisions taken, of things done, of risks assumed, all this with the support of a people. The governments of nations alone can be capable of and responsible for making policy. It is of course not forbidden to imagine that a day will come when all the peoples of our continent will become one and that then there could be a Government of Europe, but it would be ridiculous to act as if that day had come.

That is why France—refusing to let Europe get bogged down, becoming bogged down herself in a guileful undertaking that would have stripped States, misled peoples and prevented the independence of our continent—took the initiative of proposing to her five partners of the Rome Treaty [35] a beginning for the organization of their cooperation. Thus we would begin to live in common, pending the time when habit and evolution would gradually draw the ties closer together. We know that the German Government adhered in principle to this project. We know that a meeting of the six States in Paris, then another one in Bonn, seemed at first on the road to success, but that Rome refused to call the decisive meeting, its objections, joined with those of The Hague and Brussels, being powerful enough to halt everything. Finally, we know that the opponents invoked two ar-

[35] Same as note 12 to Document 11.

guments, moreover contradictory. The first argument: the French plan, which maintains the sovereignty of the States, does not conform to our conception of a Europe having as its Executive a commission of experts, and as its Legislative a Parliament cut off from national realities. The second argument: although Britain does not agree to lose its sovereignty, we will not enter into any European political organization to which it would not belong.

The French plan for European organization not being adopted by Italy and by the Benelux countries; moreover, integration not being able to lead to anything other than an American protectorate; finally, Great Britain having shown throughout the interminable Brussels negotiations that it was not in a position to accept the common economic rules and, by the Nassau agreement,[36] that its defense force, particularly in the nuclear domain, would not be European for lack of being autonomous in relation to the United States—it seemed to the Government of the Federal Republic of Germany and to the Government of the French Republic that their bilateral cooperation could have some value. It was then that, on the proposal of the German Government, the French-German Treaty of January 22, 1963 was concluded, which I had the honor of signing right here with Chancellor [*Konrad*] Adenauer.

However, it must be noted that, if the French-German Treaty made possible limited results in some areas, also if it led the two Governments and their services to establish contacts which, for our part, and altogether, we judge can be useful and which are, in any case, very pleasant, up to now a common line of conduct has not emerged. Assuredly there is not, and there could not be any opposition, strictly speaking, between Bonn and Paris. But, whether it is a matter of the effective solidarity of France and Germany concerning their defense, or even of the stand to take and the action to pursue toward the East, above all the Moscow satellites, or correlatively of the question of boundaries and nationalities in Central and Eastern Europe, or of the recognition of China and of the diplomatic and economic mission which can be opened to Europe in relation to that great people, or of peace in Asia and particularly Indochina and Indonesia, or of the aid to give to the developing countries in Africa, Asia and Latin America, or of the organization of the agricultural common market and consequently the future of the Community of the Six—one could not say that Germany and France have yet agreed to make together a policy and one could not dispute that

[36] *Documents, 1962,* pp. 244-245.

this results from the fact that Bonn has not believed, up to now, that this policy should be European and independent. If this state of affairs were to last, there would be the risk, in the long run, of doubts among the French people, of misgivings among the German people and, among their four partners of the Rome Treaty, an increased tendency to leave things as they are, while waiting, perhaps, to be split up.

But, throughout the world, the force of things is doing its work. In wanting and in proposing the organization of a Europe having its own policy, France is sure of serving the balance, the peace and progress of the world. Moreover, she is now strong enough and sure enough of herself to be able to be patient, except for major external changes which would jeopardize everything and therefore lead her to change her direction. Besides, at the last meeting just held between the Governments in Bonn and Paris, Chancellor Erhard gave an indication of a forthcoming German initiative. In waiting for the sky to clear, France is pursuing, by her own means, that which a European and independent policy can and should be. It is a fact that people everywhere are pleased with it and that for herself it is not an unsatisfactory situation.

* * *

E. Germany, the U.S.S.R., and the West.[37]

(18) *Soviet-East German Treaty of Friendship, Mutual Assistance and Cooperation, Signed in Moscow, June 12, 1964.*[38]

Treaty of Friendship, Mutual Assistance and Co-operation between the Union of Soviet Socialist Republics and the German Democratic Republic.

The Union of Soviet Socialist Republics and the German Democratic Republic,

Guided by the desire to continue to develop and strengthen the fraternal friendship between the Union of Soviet Socialist Republics and the German Democratic Republic, which is in line with the basic interests of the peoples of both countries and of the socialist commonwealth as a whole,

On the basis of the fraternal all-round co-operation which is the cornerstone of the policy determining relations between both states and which has assumed a still closer and cordial nature since the conclusion of the treaty on relations between the Union

[37] For discussion see *The United States in World Affairs, 1964,* pp. 35-41.
[38] *Soviet News* (London), June 15, 1964.

of Soviet Socialist Republics and the German Democratic Republic of September 20, 1955,[39]

Expressing their firm intention to contribute to the cause of consolidating peace in Europe and throughout the world and unswervingly to follow a policy of peaceful co-existence between states with different social systems, fully determined to unite their efforts, on the basis of the Warsaw Treaty of Friendship, Co-operation and Mutual Assistance of May 14, 1955,[40] in order to counter effectively the threat to international security and peace created by the revenge-seeking and militarist forces which are striving for a revision of the results of the Second World War, and to defend the territorial integrity and sovereignty of both states from any attack,

Being of the unanimous opinion that the German Democratic Republic, the first state of workers and peasants in the history of Germany, which has put into effect the principles of the Potsdam Agreement[41] and which follows the path of peace, is an important factor for ensuring security in Europe and averting the threat of war,

Striving to facilitate the conclusion of a German peace treaty and to contribute to the realisation of the unity of Germany on peaceful and democratic principles,

Guided by the aims and principles of the United Nations Charter,

Have agreed on the following:

Article One

The high contracting parties, on the basis of full equality, mutual respect for their state sovereignty, non-interference in their internal affairs and the noble principles of socialist internationalism, implementing the principles of mutual benefit and reciprocal fraternal assistance, will continue to develop and consolidate their relations of friendship and close co-operation in all spheres.

Article Two

In the interests of peace and the peaceful future of the peoples, including the German people, the high contracting parties will unswervingly work for the elimination of the vestiges of the Second World War, for the conclusion of a German peace

[39] *Documents, 1955,* pp. 108-111.
[40] *American Foreign Policy 1950-1955: Basic Documents,* Department of State Publication 6446 (Washington: G.P.O., 1957).
[41] *Documents, 1945-1946,* pp. 925-938.

treaty and for the normalisation of the situation in West Berlin on this basis.

The parties proceed from the premise that, pending the conclusion of a German peace treaty, the United States of America, Great Britain and France continue to bear their responsibility for the realisation on the territory of the Federal Republic of Germany of the demands and commitments jointly assumed by the governments of the four powers under the Potsdam and other international agreements and directed towards the eradication of German militarism and Nazism and towards the prevention of German aggression.

Article Three

The high contracting parties unite their efforts in the direction of ensuring peace and security in Europe and throughout the world in accordance with the aims and principles of the United Nations Charter.

They will take all measures in their power to contribute to the settlement, on the basis of the principles of peaceful coexistence, of the major international problems such as general and complete disarmament, including partial measures contributing to the ending of the arms race and the relaxation of international tension, the abolition of colonialism, the settlement of territorial and frontier disputes between states by peaceful means, and other problems.

Article Four

In face of the existing danger of an aggressive war on the part of the militarist and revenge-seeking forces, the high contracting parties solemnly declare that the integrity of the state frontiers of the German Democratic Republic is one of the basic factors for European security. They confirm their firm determination to guarantee the inviolability of these frontiers in accordance with the Warsaw Treaty of Friendship, Co-operation and Mutual Assistance.

The high contracting parties will also undertake all the necessary measures in order to prevent aggression on the part of the militarist and revenge-seeking forces which are striving for a revision of the results of the Second World War.

Article Five

In the case of one of the high contracting parties becoming the object of an armed attack in Europe by some state or a group of states, the other high contracting party will render it immediate assistance in accordance with the provisions of the Warsaw Treaty of Friendship, Co-operation and Mutual Assistance.

The Security Council will be informed of the measures taken, in accordance with the provisions of the United Nations Charter. These measures will be discontinued as soon as the Security Council takes the necessary measures to restore and maintain international peace and security.

Article Six

The high contracting parties will regard West Berlin as an independent political unit.

Article Seven

The high contracting parties confirm their judgment that in view of the existence of two sovereign German states—the German Democratic Republic and the Federal Republic of Germany—the creation of a peace-loving united democratic German state can be achieved only through negotiations on an equal footing and on the basis of agreement between both sovereign German states.

Article Eight

On the basis of mutual benefit and unselfish fraternal co-operation and in accordance with the principles of the Council of Economic Mutual Assistance, the high contracting parties will develop and consolidate economic, scientific and technical relations between both states in every way and in accordance with the principles of international socialist division of labour, will carry out the co-ordination of national economic plans, specialisation and co-operation in production and ensure the highest productivity through the *rapprochement* and co-ordination of the national economies of both states.

The parties will continue to develop relations between them in the cultural, public and sports fields, and also in the sphere of tourism.

Article Nine

The present treaty does not affect the rights and commitments of the parties under the bilateral and other international agreements which are in force, including the Potsdam agreement.

Article Ten

This treaty will be valid for 20 years from the day on which it enters into force. The treaty will remain in force for a further

10 years if neither of the high contracting parties repudiates it 12 months before the expiration of the term of the treaty.

In case of the establishment of a united democratic and peace-loving German state or the conclusion of a German peace treaty, the present treaty can be revised at the request of either of the high contracting parties before the expiration of its 20 year term.

Article Eleven

The present treaty is subject to ratification and will enter into force at the moment of the exchange of the ratification instruments which will take place in Berlin in the very near future.

Done in Moscow on June 12, 1964, in two copies each in the Russian and German languages, both texts being equally valid.

(19) *The United States Position on the Soviet-East German Treaty: Department of State Statement, June 12, 1964.*[42]

The conclusion or implementation of this agreement[43] by the Soviet Union cannot in any case affect Soviet obligations or responsibilities under agreements and arrangements between the Three Powers and the Soviet Union on the subject of Germany, including Berlin.

The Soviet Union remains bound by the engagements which it assumed vis-à-vis the Three Powers, and continues to be responsible for the fulfillment of its obligations to them.

The United States Government considers that the Government of the Federal Republic of Germany is the only German government freely and legitimately constituted, and therefore entitled to speak for the German people in international affairs.

The United States Government does not recognize the East German regime nor the existence of a state in Eastern Germany. The objective of the United States remains the reunification of Germany in peace and freedom on the basis of self-determination.

[42] *Department of State Bulletin,* June 29, 1964, p. 993.
[43] Document 18.

(20) *Joint Communiqué of President Johnson and Chancellor Ludwig Erhard of the Federal Republic of Germany, Washington, June 12, 1964.*[44]

President Johnson and Chancellor Erhard met on June 12 in Washington. They were accompanied by Secretary Rusk, Foreign Minister [Gerhard] Schroeder and other advisers.

The President expressed his pleasure that the Chancellor had come to Washington following his official visit to Canada and receipt of an honorary degree at Harvard, thus providing an opportunity to review the international situation and to discuss areas of mutual interest and concern to the United States and the Federal Republic of Germany.

The Chancellor and the President discussed the need for finding a just and peaceful solution to the problem of Germany and Berlin and agreed that efforts to find such a solution must continue. They agreed that a solution must be based upon the right of self-determination and take into consideration the security of Europe as a whole. Every suitable opportunity should be used to bring nearer the reunification of Germany through self-determination. So long as Germany remains divided, Europe will not achieve stability.

The President and the Chancellor noted the Soviet Government's announcement that it signed today [June 12] a Treaty of Friendship, Mutual Assistance and Cooperation with the so-called German Democratic Republic.[45] They agreed that no unilateral move by the Soviet Union could in any way affect the rights of the Three Western Powers or modify the obligations and responsibilities of the Soviet Union with respect to Germany and Berlin. They stressed that the Soviet Government would be solely responsible for the consequences of any attempt at interference with Allied rights that might result from implementation of the new treaty. They also reaffirmed that until Germany is unified, only the freely elected and legitimately constituted government of the Federal Republic of Germany and no one else can speak for the German people.

The President restated the determination of the United States to carry out fully its commitments with respect to Berlin, including the maintenance of the right of free access to West Berlin and the continued freedom and viability of the city.

[44] White House Press Release, June 12, 1964; text from *Department of State Bulletin,* June 29, 1964, pp. 992-994. For discussion see *The United States in World Affairs, 1964,* pp. 39-40.
[45] Document 18.

The President and Chancellor stressed the importance of improving relations with the nations of Eastern Europe. The President said that the United States fully supports the actions of the Federal Republic directed toward this goal. They also expressed the conviction that measures designed to reduce the threat of war and to bring about arms control serve to promote the goal of German reunification.

The President and the Chancellor expressed satisfaction at the progress achieved by the nations of the Atlantic Community in developing political stability as well as economic and military strength. They reaffirmed the continuing importance of NATO to the defense and cohesion of the West. They were agreed that the proposed multilateral force would make a significant addition to this military and political strength and that efforts should be continued to ready an agreement for signature by the end of the year. The Chancellor stressed his interest in the promotion of greater political cooperation between the nations of Western Europe.

In their review of the international scene, the President described the serious situation faced by the United states and the free world in Southeast Asia. He and the Chancellor agreed that the Communist regime in Hanoi must cease its aggression in South Viet-Nam and Laos. The two governments also agreed that the Government of the Republic of Viet-Nam must be fully supported in its resistance against the Viet Cong. The Chancellor stated that his government would increase assistance to South Viet-Nam in the political and economic fields.

They reviewed the Kennedy Round negotiations underway at Geneva [45a] and were agreed that expanded trade in all commodities and substantial tariff reductions would be in the interest of all the nations of the free world.

They were agreed on the vital importance of sustaining the flow of economic aid to the developing countries in order to support the efforts of these countries to maintain their independence and to modernize and expand their economies to the point where further growth could be sustained without extraordinary foreign assistance. They were of the view that strengthening the private sector of the developing economies can play a key role in the process and they recognize the need for official aid as well as for foreign private investment to promote this objective. The President stressed his intention to sustain the level of United States aid commitments and expenditures. The Chancellor in turn noted the substantial increase in total

[45a] Document 28.

aid commitments of the Federal Republic of Germany in 1963 and stated that every effort will be made to increase the level of these commitments this year and next.

The President and the Chancellor reviewed also the constructive steps taken so far by Germany to help reduce its large balance of payments surplus. The President told the Chancellor of his appreciation of German support in helping the United States meet its balance of payments problems.

The President and the Chancellor were both happy to have had this opportunity to consult on common problems, as part of the continuing process of full consultation so indispensable to the maintenance of close relations between the two countries. They were gratified to reaffirm that their governments have established a solid basis of cooperation and mutual understanding in their common quest for peace.

(21) *Tripartite Declaration of the United States, the United Kingdom, and France, June 26, 1964.*[46]

The Governments of France, the United Kingdom and the United States, after consulting with the Government of the Federal Republic of Germany, wish to state the following with regard to the agreement signed by the Soviet Union and the so-called "German Democratic Republic" on June 12, 1964.[47] This agreement, among other things, deals with questions related to Germany as a whole and to Berlin in particular.

1. As the Soviet Government was reminded before the signing of this agreement, it is clear that any agreement which the Soviet Union may make with the so-called "German Democratic Republic" cannot affect Soviet obligations or responsibilities under agreements and arrangements with the Three Powers on the subject of Germany including Berlin and access thereto. The Three Governments consider that the Soviet Union remains bound by these engagements, and they will continue to hold the Soviet Government responsible for the fulfillment of its obligations.

2. West Berlin is not an "independent political unit." Within the framework of their responsibilities regarding Germany as a whole, the Four Powers have put the German capital, the city of "Greater Berlin," under their joint administration. Unilateral

[46] Department of State Press Release 300, June 26, 1964; text from *Department of State Bulletin,* July 13, 1964, pp. 44-45. The Declaration was released simultaneously in London, Paris, and Washington.
[47] Same as note 43 to Document 19.

initiatives taken by the Soviet Government in order to block the quadripartite administration of the city cannot in any way modify this legal situation nor abrogate the rights and responsibilities of the Four Powers in regard to Berlin. While reserving their rights relating to Berlin, the Three Western Powers, taking account of the necessities for the development of the city, have authorized, in accordance with the agreements of October 23, 1954,[48] the establishment of close ties between Berlin and the Federal Republic of Germany, including permission to the Federal Republic to ensure representation of Berlin and of the Berlin population outside Berlin. These ties, the existence of which is essential to the viability of Berlin, are in no way inconsistent with the quadripartite status of the city and will be maintained in the future.

3. The Three Governments consider that the Government of the Federal Republic of Germany is the only German government freely and legitimately constituted and therefore entitled to speak for the German people in international affairs. The Three Governments do not recognize the East German regime nor the existence of a state in eastern Germany. As for the provisions related to the "frontiers" of this so-called state, the Three Governments reiterate that within Germany and Berlin there are no frontiers but rather a "demarcation line" and the "sector borders" and that, according to the very agreements to which the agreement of June 12 refers, the final determination of the frontiers of Germany must await a peace settlement for the whole of Germany.

4. The charges of "revanchism" and "militarism" contained in the agreement of June 12 are without basis. The Government of the Federal Republic of Germany in its statement of October 3, 1954,[49] has renounced the use of force to achieve the reunification of Germany or the modification of the present boundaries of the Federal Republic of Germany. This remains its policy.

5. The Three Governments agree that the safeguarding of peace and security is today more than ever a vital problem for all nations and that a just and peaceful settlement of outstanding problems in Europe is essential to the establishment of lasting peace and security. Such a settlement requires the application in the whole of Germany of the principle of self-determination. This principle is reaffirmed in the United Nations Charter, which the agreement of June 12 itself invokes. By ignoring this principle, the agreement of June 12 seeks to perpetuate the arbi-

[48] *Documents, 1954,* pp. 241-245.
[49] Same, p. 115.

trary division of Germany, which is a continuing source of international tension and an obstacle to a peaceful settlement of European problems. The exercise of self-determination, which should lead to the reunification of Germany in peace and freedom, remains a fundamental objective of the Three Governments.

6. The Three Governments are convinced that such a settlement should be sought as soon as possible. This settlement should include progressive solutions which would bring about German reunification and security in Europe. On such a basis, the Three Governments are always ready to take advantage of any opportunity which would peacefully reestablish German unity in freedom.

F. United States-United Kingdom Relations.[50]

(22) *Joint Communiqué of President Johnson and Prime Minister Harold Wilson, Washington, December 8, 1964.*[51]

The President of the United States and the Prime Minister of the United Kingdom met in Washington 7th December to 9th December. They were assisted by Secretary of State Rusk, Secretary of Defense McNamara and Under Secretary of State Ball and by the Foreign Secretary, Mr.[Patrick] Gordon Walker and the Secretary of State for Defense, Mr. [Denis] Healey.

In the course of a wide ranging exchange of views, the President and the Prime Minister reviewed the current international situation in light of the responsibilities which their countries carry for maintaining, together with their allies and friends, peace and stability throughout the world. They reaffirmed their determination to support the peace-keeping operations of the United Nations and to do all in their power to strengthen the systems of regional alliance in Europe, the Middle East and the Far East to which they both contribute.

They recognized the importance of strengthening the unity of the Atlantic Alliance in its strategic nuclear defense. They discussed existing proposals for this purpose and an outline of some new proposals presented by the British Government. They agreed that the objective in this field is to cooperate in finding the arrangements which best meet the legitimate interests of all

[50] For discussion see *The United States in World Affairs, 1964*, pp. 42-45, and p. 48.

[51] White House Press Release, December 8, 1964; text from *Department of State Bulletin*, December 28, 1964, pp. 903-904.

members of the Alliance, while maintaining existing safeguards on the use of nuclear weapons, and preventing their further proliferation. A number of elements of this problem were considered during this initial exchange of views as a preliminary to further discussions among interested members of the Alliance.

They also agreed on the urgency of a world-wide effort to promote the non-dissemination and non-acquisition of nuclear weapons, and of continuing Western initiatives towards arms control and disarmament. They recognized the increasing need for initiatives of this kind in light of the recent detonation of a Chinese nuclear device.[52]

The President and the Prime Minister reaffirmed their determination to continue to contribute to the maintenance of peace and stability in the Middle East and the Far East. In this connection they recognized the particular importance of the military effort which both their countries are making in support of legitimate Governments in South East Asia, particularly in Malaysia and South Vietnam, which seek to maintain their independence and to resist subversion.

They recognized also that a nation's defense policy must be based on a sound economy. The President and the Prime Minister, while determined that their countries should continue to play their full parts in the world-wide peace-keeping effort, affirmed their conviction that the burden of defense should be shared more equitably among the countries of the free world.

They agreed also on the need for improvement in the balance of payments and in the productivity and competitive position of both their economies in order to ensure the underlying economic strength which is essential for fulfilling their heavy international responsibilities. In this connection they arranged to explore in detail the possibilities of closer cooperation between their two countries in defense research and development and in weapons production.

The President and the Prime Minister reaffirmed their belief in the importance of close allied cooperation in international affairs. They agreed that this meeting was only the first stage in their consultation in which the matters that they had discussed would need to be examined in greater detail. They looked forward, too, to continuing discussions at all levels both within the Alliance and in wider international negotiations in pursuit of nuclear and conventional disarmament and all measures to reduce world tension.

[52] Document 41.

CHAPTER THREE

PROBLEMS WITHIN THE WESTERN COMMUNITY

A. The Cyprus Crisis.[1]

(23) *The Establishment of a Peace-Keeping Force.*

(a) *Statement by United States Representative Adlai E. Stevenson to the United Nations Security Council, February 19, 1964.*[2]

During the 1950's, the political problems of Cyprus were the subject of bitter dispute in the General Assembly of the United Nations year after year. Finally, however, a carefully balanced settlement was reached with the agreement of all of the parties—Greece, Turkey, the two communities inside Cyprus, and the United Kingdom. I think we all breathed a sigh of relief at that time and allowed ourselves to hope that, with the conclusion of the Zurich agreements [3] and the establishment of the Republic of Cyprus, the peace which was so longed for and so needed by the people of that historic island had finally been achieved. We were, therefore, deeply distressed when new fighting broke out last December and resulted in hundreds of deaths and has now threatened to rupture the whole fabric of peace in the eastern Mediterranean.

All members of the Council are familiar with the melancholy events of the past several weeks to which Sir Patrick Dean has just referred. Tension between the two communities reached a flashpoint on December 21, and violence and bloodshed erupted on a serious scale. When it became clear that additional help was needed, President Makarios on behalf of the Greek community and Vice President [Fazil] Kutchuk on behalf of the Turkish community invited the United Kingdom, in cooperation with the Governments of Greece and Turkey, to undertake

[1] For discussion see *The United States in World Affairs, 1964,* pp. 53-67.
[2] U.S. Delegation Press Release 4364; text from *Department of State Bulletin,* March 9, 1964, pp. 374-376.
[3] *Documents, 1959,* pp. 381-392.

to restore stability and preserve the peace. Since December 26, a British force has sought to keep the peace on the island. Today the United Kingdom has dispatched further troops to troubled Cyprus. I believe all of us here, Mr. President, and most particularly the representatives of Cyprus owe a debt of gratitude to the United Kingdom for undertaking this unenviable task.

Political efforts to resolve the problems were also promptly started. A conference of the parties was convened, as we know, in London in an effort to work out a solution of the political issues which divided the two communities on the island. But that conference, alas, was unable to produce an agreement.

Despite the determined efforts of the British forces on Cyprus, violent incidents multiplied and bloodshed continued. With the Government of Cyprus and the leaders of the Cypriot communities apparently unable or unwilling to control the passions which had been unleashed, it became clear that the restoration of public order so imperative before the long-range political problems could be attacked anew would require a considerably larger number of troops. The United Kingdom told the Government of Cyprus that she could not continue to shoulder alone the responsibility for peace in the island. The conclusion was obvious that a larger and a more broadly based peacekeeping force was required to augment the British forces if order were to be reestablished and maintained throughout the island. The Government of the United Kingdom then proceeded to consult with the Governments of Greece and Turkey, who are also parties to the international agreements which led to the establishment of the Republic of Cyprus in [*August 16,*] 1960. It also consulted with my Government.

A plan for the establishment of such a force, including provision for an impartial mediator to help settle the dispute, was agreed to by Greece and Turkey and the Cypriot Vice President, Dr. Kutchuk. Archbishop Makarios, however, raised a number of objections.

The other parties made a new effort to meet these objections and a revised plan within the framework of the United Nations and agreed to by Greece, Turkey, and the United Kingdom and my Government, was put before him on February 12. On the following day President Makarios informed representatives of the United Kingdom and of my Government that this revised proposal was also unacceptable, although he agreed in principle to the need for an international peacekeeping force.

We are frank to say that we deeply regret that the President of Cyprus was not able to agree to that latter proposal, a proposal which represented a solid recommendation of the Governments of all of the guarantor powers—the United Kingdom, Greece, and Turkey—and also of the United States.

Tragic loss of life and property occurs daily in Cyprus. International complications increase, and a solution daily becomes more difficult. The recommendations of the guarantors would, we believe, have helped to avoid all of this.

Mr. President, I think we all know that the Treaty of Guarantee forms an integral part of the organic arrangements that created the Republic of Cyprus. In fact, it is a so-called basic article of the Constitution of Cyprus. That treaty assures the independence, territorial integrity, and security of the Republic, as well as respect for its Constitution. It assigns to the guarantor powers certain responsibilities regarding the maintenance of the Constitution and of the treaty itself, including the carefully negotiated balance and protection of the two Cypriot communities. It was signed after literally years of soul-searching negotiation and approved by all of the parties.

This treaty, or any international treaty, cannot be abrogated, cannot be nullified, cannot be modified either in fact or in effect by the Security Council of the United Nations. The treaty can be abrogated or altered only by agreement of all of the signatories themselves, or in accordance with its terms.

No one, Mr. President, is threatening to take the territory of Cyprus; no one is threatening its independence—Turkey or Greece or anyone else. What is possible—and I quote the language of the treaty—[*is*] "action" expressly authorized by Article 4 of the treaty "with the sole aim of reestablishing the state of affairs created by the treaty." [4]

Gentlemen, time is wasting. While we talk people are dying, and any moment violence and bloodshed may erupt again on a large scale with predictable and grave consequences. The important, the imperative, the urgent thing to do is to restore order and communal tranquillity—and do it quickly before new violence breaks out, before the atmosphere is further poisoned, before the positions of the parties on the political issues that divide them become more inflexible, and, indeed, before peace in the eastern Mediterranan is endangered.

I repeat—that the urgent business before the Council and the responsibility of the Government of Cyprus is to restore communal peace and order and to stop the bloodshed. The sooner that we and the Security Council turn our attention to this, the better it will be for all.

[4] *Cyprus,* Cmnd. 1093 (London: H.M.S.O., July 1960), pp. 86-87.

I respectfully urge that the Security Council not be deflected from this purpose. Once we have met this problem and communal peace is restored, no question of any action under the Treaty of Guarantee would arise.

The United States has no position as to the form or the shape of a final settlement of the Cyprus problem. The leaders of the two communities must work out their differences together. But in the present climate this is patently impossible. The two communities are holding each other at gunpoint. To serve any helpful purpose in this inflammable case, the Security Council must make an effective contribution to the reestablishment of conditions in which a long-term political solution can be sought with due regard to the interests, the rights, and the responsibilities of all parties concerned.

We have made it clear at all times that the United States is prepared to participate in a peacekeeping force, but only on the request of all of the parties. We have made this unequivocally clear to Archbishop Makarios, and I can assure the representative of the Soviet Union that the United States, while prepared to help, will be delighted if it does not have to be involved in keeping the peace between Greeks and Turks in Cyprus. And it must be equally clear, Mr. President, that neither the United States nor any of the Western Powers are seeking to impose their will on the Government of Cyprus.

I shall not dwell at this time upon the assertions of the distinguished representative of the Soviet Union that the anxiety most of us feel that peace be restored to Cyprus is some sort of a NATO plot. No one is even proposing that the international force be comprised just of NATO military units. The parties will have to agree upon the participants in any such force.

Now, sir, I have outlined why the United States supported the proposals developed for a peacekeeping force in Cyprus. I have said that the United States is deeply concerned with this grave situation and the imperative need to keep the peace in the Mediterranean area. Peace on that island today is as precarious as it is precious, and we don't know what new violence tomorrow may bring. The need for such a peacekeeping force is, I repeat, critically urgent. Clandestine arms shipments have recently increased the dangers. The world cannot stand by as an idle and a silent witness to the fire that is consuming Cyprus and could spread so rapidly.

Mr. President, we must ask ourselves what the Council can and should do in these circumstances. That is clear. We should go straight to the point at which we can really be most helpful.

I suggest that we must bring about a prompt agreement on an international peacekeeping force for Cyprus, the need for which has been recognized by all, including President Makarios. This may require that we introduce into these consultations an expert in the peacekeeping field of recognized impartiality and stature. No one better fills such a requirement than the Secretary-General [*U Thant*] of the United Nations. We, therefore, recommend that the Council appeal to the parties concerned, in consultation with the Secretary-General, to move ahead quickly in working out such arrangements. Other states can make a contribution toward the establishment of a peacekeeping force. Those that can do so should cooperate freely and generously in this endeavor.

Strenuous efforts will also be required to bring about an agreement between the two parties on a political settlement which will permit them to live in peace with each other. Therefore we would also strongly urge that the Government of Cyprus and the guarantor powers, in consultation with the Secretary-General, be asked to designate an impartial mediator to assist in achieving a settlement. Let us address ourselves to these two priorities, and let us, I beg leave to say, do so quickly.

Mr. President, in conclusion let me say how much the United States values the spirit of cooperation which Greece and Turkey have shown in these dangerous weeks. They have demonstrated great restraint at a difficult moment in history. Both Governments, I believe, are to be commended for approaching Cyprus' problem, which has such sensitive implications for both of them, with a sense of responsibility not only to the respective communities in Cyprus but, even more importantly, to the entire world community. We should be grateful to both of them.

(b) *Resolution of the United Nations Security Council, Adopted March 4, 1964.*[5]

The Security Council,

Noting that the present situation with regard to Cyprus is likely to threaten international peace and security and may further deteriorate unless additional measures are promptly taken to maintain peace and to seek out a durable solution,

Considering the positions taken by the parties in relation to the Treaties signed at Nicosia on 16 August 1960,

Having in mind the relevant provisions of the Charter of the United Nations and its Article 2, paragraph 4, which reads: "All Members shall refrain in their international relations from

[5] U.N. Document S/5575, March 4, 1964; adopted unanimously.

the threat or use of force against the territorial integrity or political independence of any State, or in any other manner inconsistent with the Purposes of the United Nations".

1. *Calls upon* all Member States, in conformity with their obligations under the Charter of the United Nations, to refrain from any action or threat of action likely to worsen the situation in the sovereign Republic of Cyprus, or to endanger international peace;

2. *Asks* the Government of Cyprus, which has the responsibility for the maintenance and restoration of law and order, to take all additional measures necessary to stop violence and bloodshed in Cyprus;

3. *Calls upon* the communities in Cyprus and their leaders to act with the utmost restraint;

4. *Recommends* the creation, with the consent of the Government of Cyprus, of a United Nations peace-keeping force in Cyprus. The composition and size of the force shall be established by the Secretary-General, in consultation with the Governments of Cyprus, Greece, Turkey and the United Kingdom. The commander of the force shall be appointed by the Secretary-General and report to him. The Secretary-General, who shall keep the Governments providing the force fully informed, shall report periodically to the Security Council on its operation;

5. *Recommends* that the function of the force should be, in the interest of preserving international peace and security, to use its best efforts to prevent a recurrence of fighting and, as necessary, to contribute to the maintenance and restoration of law and order and a return to normal conditions;

6. *Recommends* that the stationing of the force shall be for a period of three months, all costs pertaining to it being met, in a manner to be agreed upon by them, by the Governments providing the contingents and by the Government of Cyprus. The Secretary-General may also accept voluntary contributions for that purpose;

7. *Recommends further* that the Secretary-General designate, in agreement with the Government of Cyprus and the Governments of Greece, Turkey and the United Kingdom, a mediator,[6] who shall use his best endeavours with the representatives of the communities and also with the aforesaid four Governments, for the purpose of promoting a peaceful solution and an agreed settlement of the problem confronting Cyprus, in accordance

[6] On March 25 Secretary-General Thant appointed Sakari S. Tuomioja of Finland as mediator. Mr. Tuomioja died on September 9, 1964; he was succeeded on September 17, 1964, by Galo Plaza Lasso of Ecuador.

with the Charter of the United Nations, having in mind the well-being of the people of Cyprus as a whole and the preservation of international peace and security. The mediator shall report periodically to the Secretary-General on his efforts;

8. *Requests* the Secretary-General to provide, from funds of the United Nations, as appropriate, for the remuneration and expenses of the mediator and his staff.

(24) *President Johnson Confers with Turkey and Greece.*

(a) *Joint Communiqué of the President and Prime Minister Ismet Inönü of Turkey, Washington, June 23, 1964.*[7]

Prime Minister Inonu of Turkey and President Johnson have discussed all aspects of the problem of Cyprus. Both leaders welcomed the opportunity presented by the Prime Minister's visit at the President's invitation for a full exchange of views.

The discussion, proceeding from the present binding effects of existing treaties, covered ways in which present difficulties might be adjusted by negotiation and agreement. The urgent necessity for such agreement upon lasting solutions was underlined.

The Prime Minister and the President also considered ways in which their countries could strengthen the efforts of the United Nations [8] with respect to the safety and security of the communities on Cyprus.

The cordial and candid conversations of the two leaders strengthened the broad understanding already existing between Turkey and the United States.

The President and the Prime Minister expressed their conviction that their peoples are devoted to common democratic principles, to individual freedom, to human dignity and to peace in justice.

(b) *Joint Communiqué of the President and Prime Minister George Papandreou of Greece, Washington, June 25, 1964.*[9]

During the visit to Washington of the Prime Minister of Greece conversations were held between Mr. George A. Papan-

[7] White House Press Release, June 22, 1964; text from *Department of State Bulletin,* July 13, 1964, p. 49.

[8] The Security Council met from June 18 to June 20 and unanimously adopted a resolution (U.N. Document S/5778, July 20, 1964) extending the peace-keeping force in Cyprus until September 26, 1964. Details and text of resolution in *UN Monthly Chronicle,* July 1964, pp. 3-16.

[9] White House Press Release, June 25, 1964; text from *Department of State Bulletin,* July 13, 1964, p. 50.

dreou and the President of the United States, the Secretary of State, and other officials of the United States Government.

The conversations, which were conducted in an atmosphere of friendship and warm cordiality, have contributed to the strengthening of the close ties between Greece and the United States.

The visit provided the opportunity to the Greek Prime Minister and the President of the United States to review various aspects of the international situation and to discuss subjects of mutual interest.

The President of the United States and the Greek Prime Minister had a sincere and useful exchange of views on the Cyprus situation. Both expressed full support of the efforts undertaken by the Security Council and the Secretary-General of the United Nations for the establishment of peace in the island and for rapidly finding a permanent solution. The Greek Prime Minister explained in detail the Greek position on the problem. He emphasized that a permanent solution should be based upon the principles of democracy and justice. The two leaders reiterated their determination to make every effort to increase the understanding among allies.

The Greek Prime Minister expressed the deep appreciation for the generous support of the United States Government and people in the hard struggle of the Greek people for their freedom and welfare.

(25) *Call for a Cease-Fire.*

(a) *Statement by Ambassador Stevenson to the United Nations Security Council, August 9, 1964.*[10]

All of us who have been present at the discussions of this question have had ample evidence of the depth of feeling that exists between the two communities in Cyprus and the homicidal consequences of their mistrust and bitterness. And we have had repeated and bloody reminders that the danger is not just to the inhabitants of Cyprus. The danger is even greater: The danger is international war.

The responsibility of the Council is to stop hostilities—and until *all* are stopped, *none* will stop. Archbishop Makarios says that unless Turkey stops its air attacks by 12:00 noon he will launch a full-scale attack on the Turkish community and forces. The Government of Turkey says that until the Greeks in Cyprus stop attacking the Turks the air attacks will continue.

[10] U.S. Delegation Press Release 4430, August 9, 1964; text from *Department of State Bulletin,* August 31, 1964, p. 318.

I repeat that in these circumstances until *all* hostilities stop, *none* will stop, and, perhaps in a matter of hours, we will be over the brink and in the abyss. And none can see the bottom. Most of us, perhaps all of us, wanted an immediate cease-fire last night. We didn't get it.

Today the situation is even more urgent. The situation demands swift action. Our first responsibility is to stop the fighting before it is too late.

To ascertain and debate the facts, to try to apportion the blame for this deplorable situation, may be an appropriate task for the Security Council when time and circumstance permit. But unless the present flames are quenched, and quenched quickly, they will spread, fanned by these hot fires of fear. If that happens, our deliberations will not be an inquiry; they will be an autopsy.

An appeal for a cease-fire is the swiftest action the Council can take. The President [of the Security Council] has issued such an appeal. Accordingly, I propose the adoption—unanimously and quickly, I would hope—of the following resolution to formally endorse and affirm the President's appeal. The resolution is introduced by the United States and the United Kingdom and reads as follows: [11]

The Security Council,

Concerned by the serious deterioration of the situation in Cyprus,

Reaffirming the appeal the President of the Security Council has just addressed to the Governments of Turkey and Cyprus:

1. *Calls* for an immediate cease-fire by all concerned;
2. *Calls* upon all concerned to cooperate fully with the U.N. Commander in the restoration of peace and security; and
3. *Calls* on all states to refrain from any action that might exacerbate the situation or contribute to the broadening of hostilities.

After the adoption of such a resolution we can resume our discussion of the situation and consider what further steps are desirable to preserve the peace while the mediator continues his efforts to find a peaceful solution.

(b) *Resolution of the United Nations Security Council, Adopted August 9, 1964.*[12]

The Security Council,

Concerned at the serious deterioration of the situation in Cyprus,

[11] U.N. Document S/5866, August 9, 1964.

[12] U.N. Document S/5868, August 9, 1964, adopted by a vote of 9-0-2 (Czechoslovakia and the U.S.S.R.).

Reaffirming the resolutions of the Security Council on this issue dated 4 March (S/5575),[13] 13 March (S/5603) and 20 June 1964 (S/5778),

Anticipating the submission of the Secretary-General's report on the situation,

1. *Reaffirms* the appeal of the President of the Council just addressed to the Governments of Turkey and Cyprus, as follows: "The Security Council has authorized me to make an urgent appeal to the Government of Turkey to cease instantly the bombardment and the use of military force of any kind against Cyprus, and to the Government of Cyprus to order the armed forces under its control to cease firing immediately".

2. *Calls* for an immediate cease-fire by all concerned;

3. *Calls* upon all concerned to co-operate fully with the United Nations Commander in the restoration of peace and security; and

4. *Calls* on all States to refrain from any action that might exacerbate the situation or contribute to the broadening of hostilities.

B. United States-Canadian Relations.[14]

(26) *Columbia River Development.*

(a) *Joint Statement of President Johnson and Prime Minister Lester B. Pearson of Canada, Washington, January 22, 1964.*[15]

President Johnson and Prime Minister Pearson presided today at the White House at the signing of further important agreements between the two governments regarding the cooperative development of the water resources of the Columbia River Basin.[16] Mr. Rusk, Secretary of State, signed for the United States, and Mr. [*Paul*] Martin, Secretary of State for External Affairs, signed for Canada.

The arrangements which are now being made will be of great benefit to both countries, particularly to the province of British Columbia in Canada and to the States of Washington, Idaho, Montana, and Oregon in the United States. Today's signing took place in the presence of representatives of the area on both sides of the border.

[13] Document 23b.
[14] For discussion see *The United States in World Affairs, 1964*, pp. 67-72.
[15] White House Press Release, January 22, 1964; text from *Department of State Bulletin*, February 10, 1964, pp. 199-201.
[16] Text of agreements in same, pp. 201-206.

The treaty of January 17, 1961 [17] provided for effective regulation of the flow from the Canadian portion of the Columbia River for flood control and increased power production in the United States as well as for benefits in Canada. The downstream power benefits resulting from increased generation in the United States are to be shared by the two countries, and the United States is to compensate Canada for the flood protection which it receives. Effective storage amounting to 15,500,000 acre-feet will be provided in Canada from two dams on the main stem of the Columbia at Mica Creek and Arrow Lakes, and from one dam near Duncan Lake, all in British Columbia. The additional storage approximately doubles that presently available for regulation of the flows of the Columbia River.

Under the terms of the treaty, the United States has the option to commence construction of the Libby project on the Kootenai River in northern Montana with 5,000,000 acre-feet of usable storage. Canada and the United States each will retain all of the benefits from the Libby project which accrue in their respective countries.

At the Hyannis Port meeting in May 1963 President Kennedy and Prime Minister Pearson [18]

> . . . noted especially the desirability of early progress on the cooperative development of the Columbia River. The Prime Minister indicated that if certain clarifications and adjustments in arrangements proposed earlier could be agreed on, to be included in a protocol to the treaty, the Canadian Government would consult at once with the provincial Government of British Columbia, the province in which the Canadian portion of the river is located, with a view to proceeding promptly with the further detailed negotiations required with the United States and with the necessary action for approval within Canada. The President agreed that both Governments should immediately undertake discussions on this subject looking to an early agreement.

These things have now been done. The way has been cleared for the completion of the necessary financial and related arrangements in the United States and the ratification of the treaty by Canada.

The primary purpose of the first set of documents signed today was to agree now on the clarifications and adjustments that would eliminate possible sources of controversy between the two countries in later years. These documents contain important, if rather technical, provisions regarding such varied matters as con-

[17] Text in *Department of State Bulletin,* February 13, 1961, pp. 234-243.
[18] *Documents, 1963,* p. 234.

ditions governing flood control; the intention to complete arrangements for the initial sale of Canada's share of the downstream power benefits at the time when ratifications of the treaty are exchanged; [19] the avoidance by Canada of stand-by transmission charges in the event of sales of downstream benefits in the United States; provision for cooperation in connection with the operation of the Libby Dam in the light of the Canadian benefits from it; clarification regarding water diversions; the procedures relating to hydroelectric operating plans; the adoption of a longer stream flow period as a basis for calculating downstream power benefits; various matters relating to power load calculations; adjustments to be considered in the event of the provision of flood control by Canada ahead of schedule; the avoidance of any precedent regarding waters other than those of the Columbia River Basin; and clarification regarding the position of the boundary waters treaty of 1909.

The other set of documents relates to the arrangement to be made for the sale of the Canadian entitlement to downstream power benefits for a period limited to 30 years. The arrangements which the two governments have agreed upon will be beneficial to the United States in facilitating the coming into force of the treaty and thereby removing uncertainty about the availability of power and flood control protection for the northwestern part of the United States for a considerable period of time. Equally, they will benefit Canada by removing uncertainty about the return to be received by Canada from the Columbia River development during the first 30 years after the completion of each dam.

The treaty, together with the arrangements now being made, represents an important step in achieving optimum development of the water resources of the Columbia River Basin as a whole, from which the United States and Canada will each receive benefits materially larger than either could obtain independently.

The arrangements fully respect the sovereignty and the interests of the two countries. As was said in the Hyannis Port Communique, "Close cooperation across the border can enhance rather than diminish the sovereignty of each country by making it stronger and more prosperous than before." [20]

[19] Document 26b.
[20] See note 18. The Hyannis Port communiqué used the word "wise" instead of "close."

(b) *Proclamation by the President, September 16, 1964.*[21]

A PROCLAMATION

WHEREAS the treaty between the United States of America and Canada relating to cooperative development of the water resources of the Columbia River basin was signed at Washington on January 17, 1961 [22] by their respective Plenipotentiaries, the original of which treaty is word for word as follows:

WHEREAS the Senate of the United States of America by their resolution of March 16, 1961, two-thirds of the Senators present concurring therein, did advise and consent to the ratification of the aforesaid treaty:

WHEREAS the aforesaid treaty was duly ratified by the President of the United States of America on March 23, 1961, in pursuance of the aforesaid advice and consent of the Senate, and was duly ratified on the part of Canada;

WHEREAS it is provided in Article XIX of the aforesaid treaty that the treaty shall come into force on the ratification date and in Article XX of the aforesaid treaty that the instruments of ratification shall be exchanged at Ottawa;

AND WHEREAS the respective instruments of ratification of the aforesaid treaty were duly exchanged at Ottawa on September 16, 1964 by the respective Plenipotentiaries of the United States of America and Canada;

NOW, THEREFORE, be it known that I, Lyndon B. Johnson, President of the United States of America, do hereby proclaim and make public the aforesaid treaty to the end that the said treaty and each and every article and clause thereof may be observed and fulfilled, on and after September 16, 1964, with good faith by the United States of America and by the citizens of the United States of America and all other persons subject to the jurisdiction thereof.

IN TESTIMONY WHEREOF, I have hereunto set my hand and caused the Seal of the United States of America to be affixed.

DONE at the International Peace Arch, Blaine, Washington, this sixteenth day of September in the year of our Lord [SEAL] one thousand nine hundred sixty-four and of the Independence of the United States of America the one hundred eighty-ninth.

(signed) Lyndon B. Johnson

By the President:
DEAN RUSK,
Secretary of State

21 *Department of State Bulletin,* October 12, 1964, p. 507.
22 Same as note 17 to Document 26a.

(27) *Communiqué of the Ninth Meeting of the Joint United States-Canadian Committee on Trade and Economic Affairs, Ottawa, April 30, 1964.*[23]

The Ninth Meeting of the Joint United States–Canadian Committee on Trade and Economic Affairs was held in Ottawa April 29-30, 1964. The Committee noted with satisfaction the progress which had been made in matters of interest to both countries and the general improvement in relations between them.

The Committee received from Mr. Arnold Heeney, on behalf of himself and Mr. Livingston T. Merchant, their interim report of progress on their joint study of United States–Canadian relations. They were appointed by President Johnson and Prime Minister [Lester B.] Pearson to examine the desirability and practicability of developing acceptable principles which would facilitate cooperation in economic and other policies.[24] Their report noted agreement on method of procedure and states that preliminary investigations have been initiated.

The Committee noted that economic activity in Canada and the United States had continued to expand and that another favorable year was anticipated for 1964. They agreed that the two countries should continue to follow policies designed to stimulate economic growth and employment in the context of economic stability. They noted that trade between the United States and Canada was running at record levels. The Committee discussed policies which each country was following to improve its balance of payments. The United States members expressed agreement with Canada's desire to improve its current account through an expansion of exports, and stressed the importance of adhering to the principles of non-discrimination in achieving this objective. The Committee also noted the recent improvement in the United States balance of payments position and expressed the expectation that this improvement would continue.

The members of the Committee looked forward to the opening of the GATT tariff and trade negotiations in Geneva,[25] in which both countries would be participating actively, for the reduction of trade barriers and the expansion of trade in both industrial and agricultural products between the two countries and with the rest of the world. They took note also of the

[23] *Department of State Bulletin,* May 18, 1964, pp. 774-776.
[24] For background see *Department of State Bulletin,* March 23, 1964, p. 448.
[25] Document 28.

progress at the current United Nations Conference on Trade and Development [26] and agreed on the importance of continuing international cooperative efforts to assist the less developed countries to expand their trading opportunities and facilitate their economic development.

The Committee discussed the trade in automobiles and automobile parts between Canada and the United States. United States members stressed their concern over the possible adverse effects of the Canadian automotive programme on certain United States parts producers. Canadian members emphasized that the programme is designed to promote increased specialization and lower production costs in the Canadian automotive industry.

The Committee examined problems affecting trade between the two countries. Canadian Ministers expressed concern about increases in levels of certain United States tariffs arising from the recent reclassification of the U.S. tariff, including rates on parts and components. They urged that the U.S. Government take action to correct this situation. They requested that action should be taken to remove long standing U.S. restrictions on imports from Canada of lead and zinc, and cheese. The United States members expressed their concern over possible Canadian measures which might adversely affect certain U.S. publications. A number of other matters were discussed including Great Lakes water levels, tourist customs privileges, and the trade in softwood lumber and coal.

The Committee discussed the energy resources and energy problems of both countries and their relationship to economic efficiency. There was general agreement that U.S.-Canadian cooperation should be encouraged in areas where such cooperation serves the long-term mutual advantage of both nations. They established a joint working group to prepare a programme of studies relating to trade in all kinds of energy between the United States and Canada.

The meeting concluded with a general review of the international situation by Mr. Rusk and Mr. Martin.

The Canadian Delegation included Mr. Paul Martin, Secretary of State for External Affairs; Mr. Walter Gordon, Minister of Finance; Mr. Mitchell Sharp, Minister of Trade and Commerce; Mr. Harry Hays, Minister of Agriculture; Mr. C. M. Drury, Minister of Industry; the Governor of the Bank of Canada, Mr. L. Rasminsky; Mr. Norman Robertson, the Chief Canadian Trade Negotiator; the Canadian Ambassador to the United States, Mr. C. S. A. Ritchie; and other advisers.

[26] Document 97.

The United States Delegation included Mr. Dean Rusk, Secretary of State; Mr. Douglas Dillon, Secretary of the Treasury; Mr. Stuart Udall, Secretary of the Interior; Mr. Luther H. Hodges, Secretary of Commerce; Mr. Orville L. Freeman, Secretary of Agriculture; Mr. George W. Ball, Under Secretary of State; Mr. Walter W. Heller, Chairman of the President's Council of Economic Advisers; Mr. William M. Roth, Deputy Special Trade Representative; the United States Ambassador to Canada, Mr. W. W. Butterworth; and other advisers.

C. The Kennedy Round.[27]

(28) *Meeting of the Trade Negotiations Committee of the General Agreement on Tariffs and Trade (GATT), Geneva, May 4-6, 1964.*

(a) *Remarks by Christian A. Herter, Special Representative for Trade Negotiations, May 4, 1964.*[28]

Before beginning my own remarks, Mr. Chairman, may I read a message from the President of the United States.

Upon the opening of this meeting of GATT, an important and effective instrument for the expansion of world trade, I should like to send you best wishes for success from the people of the United States. Your meetings, universally known as the Kennedy Round, exemplify the hope and commitment of our late President to bring together the nations of the world in peaceful pursuits. I believe, as he did, in the necessity of success in your work.

We in the United States look upon these negotiations as an important opening to a better world. If we act together with dedication and purpose, all can gain and none need lose. Not only the major commercial nations, but all the countries of this shrinking world—poor and rich alike—have the right to expect success from our endeavors.

For the United States, I can assure you that we shall spare no effort in seeking to help bring this meeting, and the meetings which will follow, to a happy and fruitful conclusion.

Mr. Chairman, in 17 years of practical experience the GATT has proven itself to be the world's most successful vehicle for reducing the obstacles to the flow of international trade and promoting its expansion. This sixth round of GATT negotiations, which we are formally opening today, can be the most comprehensive and productive in its history. Building upon its

[27] For discussion see *The United States in World Affairs, 1964*, pp. 72-79.
[28] *Department of State Bulletin*, June 1, 1964, pp. 878-879.

solid record of success—and taking into account the changes in the world and particularly the importance of the developing nations' playing a greater role in international trade—GATT can move forward into new and wider areas of service. It was just a year ago that we met to lay the groundwork for these negotiations. The resolution that we adopted set out the principles by which our work should be guided: [29]

—that we should achieve a significant liberalization of world trade.
—that the negotiations shall include all classes of products and shall deal not only with tariffs but also with nontariff barriers. In the case of agricultural products, the negotiations should provide for acceptable conditions of access to world markets.
—that the negotiations should proceed on the basis of substantial linear tariff reductions with a bare minimum of exceptions and special rules of general and automatic application to govern cases where there are significant disparities in tariff levels.
—and that every effort should be made to reduce trade barriers to exports of the less developed countries, though the latter cannot be expected to provide reciprocity.

Mr. Chairman, these are ambitious objectives, but in the months of negotiations that lie ahead we—and the GATT—will be measured by them. In living up to them, as we must, it will be necessary for all countries to reach a balanced agreement at a maximum rather than a minimum level. After all, we should never lose sight of the fact that trade liberalization is good for all. It is good:

—because our peoples as consumers will gain readier access, at reasonable prices, to a wider variety of goods.
—because our businessmen and industrialists will have a clear picture of the new challenges and new opportunities in international trade and will be stimulated to respond to them.
—because producers and consumers alike will benefit from an increased international flow of an abundant supply of reasonably priced food.
—because the developing countries will gain wider opportunities to earn through exports the funds needed for their development programs. These negotiations—and GATT itself —can promote the expansion of their trade on a practical and workable basis.

[29] Resolution of May 21, 1963 in *Documents, 1963*, pp. 196-199.

In addition to adopting a set of principles at the meeting last year, we established procedures for putting them into effect.[30] The Trade Negotiations Committee was formed in order to work out a negotiating plan to be adopted before the start of the conference. It is now time to take stock of what has been accomplished.

We are agreed, as we were a year ago, that there should be a bare minimum of exceptions and that they should be subject to confrontation and justification. We are now also agreed that the negotiations should be based on offers of linear tariff reductions of 50 percent.

We are conditionally agreed on some elements of the "special rules of general and automatic application" on disparities, but all elements of this formula have still not fallen into place. We have, unfortunately, made little progress on agriculture. We have not yet come to grips with the problem of nontariff barriers. While considerable achievements have been made on rules and procedures relating to less developed countries, we have a good deal more ground to cover.

It is now our joint responsibility to move ahead, more rapidly and successfully than in the past, to fill the remaining gaps. The longer the rules are left open, the longer we procrastinate in setting the formulas by which these negotiations will proceed, the more we risk the success of the entire trade negotiations. Let us use this meeting to dedicate ourselves and our governments to prompt, effective efforts to settle these issues quickly.

Gentlemen, I have been brief—because time is pressing. We have in GATT an unequaled instrument for trade expansion. We are breaking new ground in the worldwide attack on trade barriers through negotiations of unparalleled complexity. In this difficult but essential task we have the invaluable assistance of GATT's Executive Secretary [Eric Wyndham White], to whose skilled and selfless services all of us owe so much. What we can and must contribute is the determination to get on with the job.

(b) *Declaration of the Trade Negotiations Committee, Adopted May 6, 1964.*[31]

A. *Tariffs*

1. The Trade Negotiations Committee in opening the trade negotiations, notes that:

[30] Same, 198-199.
[31] Text from *Department of State Bulletin,* June 1, 1964, pp. 879-880; adopted unanimously.

(i) The rate of 50 per cent has been agreed as a working hypothesis for the determination of the general rate of linear reduction provided for in paragraph 4 of the Resolution of 21 May 1963; [32]

(ii) the ultimate agreement on tariff reductions in accordance with the application of this hypothesis is linked with the solution of other problems arising in the negotiations, for example, tariff disparities, agricultural problems, exceptions and non-tariff problems, and, in general, with the achievement of reciprocity;

(iii) it is the intention of the participants to cooperate to solve these problems.

2. The Trade Negotiations Committee decides that exceptions lists will be tabled on the basis of the hypothesis of a 50 per cent linear reduction.

It is recognized that nothing in the negotiating rules would preclude any participant from making a larger reduction in, or completely eliminating, duties on particular products.

3. The Trade Negotiations Committee notes the progress made towards solving the problems relating to the question of disparities.

4. The Trade Negotiations Committee recalls that it was agreed, on 21 May 1963, that there should be a bare minimum of exceptions which should be subject to confrontation and justification.

It decides that the method to be followed for such confrontation and justification shall be elaborated as rapidly as possible and that the study of that method shall be undertaken immediately. The method shall take account of the need to safeguard the confidential nature of the negotiations.

It decides also that exceptions lists shall be tabled on 10 September 1964,[33] such exceptions to be necessitated only by reasons of overriding national interest.[34]

B. *Agriculture*

The Committee, while reaffirming that the trade negotiations shall provide for acceptable conditions of access to world mar-

[32] *Documents, 1963*, p. 197.

[33] The deadline for submission of the exceptions lists was extended to November 16, 1964.

[34] These exceptions are distinct from any modification of its offers which, as agreed by the Ministers at their meeting in May 1963, it shall be open to each country to make in the course of the negotiations, where this is necessary to obtain an over-all balance of advantages between it and the other participants. [Footnote in original.]

kets for agricultural products in furtherance of a significant development and expansion of world trade in such products, notes that it has not yet been possible to formulate agreed rules to govern, and methods to be employed in, the negotiations. In view of the importance of this subject to the success of the negotiations, the necessary rules and procedures shall be established at an early date.

The Committee notes that negotiations have been initiated with a view to the formulation of general arrangements on certain products. The negotiations have so far related to cereals and meat, and preparations have been made for the early initiation of such negotiations on dairy products.

C. *Non-tariff barriers*

The Committee recalls that the trade negotiations must relate not only to tariffs but also to non-tariff barriers.

It notes that many participants have already indicated the measures on which they wish to negotiate, and that others will shortly do so. In view of the importance for the full success of the negotiations of solving these problems, the Trade Negotiations Committee shall, at an early date, draw up the necessary procedures.

D. *Participation of less-developed countries*

The Committee reaffirms that in the trade negotiations every effort shall be made to reduce barriers to exports of less-developed countries and agrees that this consideration should be borne particularly in mind in the approach to the question of exceptions.

The Committee notes with satisfaction that all participants are prepared to consider the possibility of taking such steps as are open to them to make cuts deeper than 50 per cent in, or to eliminate completely, duties on products of special interest to less-developed countries.

The Committee also notes with satisfaction the intention to entrust to a special body the task of examining and calling attention to any problems arising in the negotiations which are of special interest to the less-developed countries and of action as a focal point for bringing together all issues of interest to these countries.

The Committee agreed that it would pursue further the question of trade in tropical products with a view to working out arrangements and procedures for their treatment in the negotiations.

The Committee recalls the decision of the Ministers that developed countries cannot expect to receive reciprocity from the less-developed countries. It agrees that the contribution of the less-developed countries to the overall objective of trade liberalization should be considered in the light of the development and trade needs of these countries.[35]

E. *The problem of countries with a very low average level of tariffs or a special economic or trade structure such that equal linear tariff reductions may not provide an adequate balance of advantages*

(a) *Countries with a very low average level of tariffs*

The Committee notes that the countries concerned reserve the right to submit proposals in this connection at a later date.

(b) *Countries with a special economic or trade structure*

1. The Committee agrees that Canada falls in the category of countries with a special economic or trade structure such that equal linear tariff reductions may not provide an adequate balance of advantages.

2. The Committee further agrees that Australia, New Zealand and South Africa are countries which have a very large dependence on exports of agricultural and other primary products and therefore, by virtue of the understanding reached at the Ministerial Meeting in May 1963, also fall in the category of countries referred to in 1 above.

3. The Committee reaffirms that the objective in the case of all these countries should be the negotiation of a balance of advantages based on trade concessions by them of equivalent value.

4. The Committee notes that appropriate procedures in pursuance of this objective have been agreed.

5. The Committee notes with satisfaction that Greece and Portugal have indicated their intention to participate actively in the negotiations and will be submitting proposals at a later date on the basis for their participation.

F. *Participation of Poland in the trade negotiations*

The Committee notes that there has been under consideration for some time the question of ways and means of Poland's parti-

[35] Argentina and Brazil accepted this paragraph on the understanding that the phrase "development and trade needs" covers the requirements of the current financial situation. [Footnote in original.]

cipation in the Kennedy Round. This consideration has taken place on the basis of the Polish proposals listed and explained in TN.64/NTB/15. The interest of Poland in participating actively in the trade negotiations is warmly welcomed and there is general agreement that it should be feasible to work out a practical arrangement. The Committee recommends that these discussions should be actively pursued to an early conclusion.

CHAPTER FOUR

EAST-WEST RELATIONS AND EASTERN EUROPE

A. The United States and the Soviet Union.[1]

(29) *U.S.S.R. Interference with Ships.*

(a) *United States Note to the U.S.S.R., April 22, 1964.*[2]

The Department of State requests that the Embassy of the Union of Soviet Socialist Republics call to the attention of its Government the following recent serious violation by the Soviet merchant ship POLOTSK of the International Regulations for Preventing Collisions at Sea, approved by the International Conference on Safety of Life at Sea, London 1948 and adhered to by the U.S.S.R.

During daylight hours, shortly after 2:00 p.m., on April 9, 1964, while proceeding on the high seas in the waters of the southern end of the Red Sea, the United States Navy Seaplane Tender DUXBURY BAY was harassed and placed in serious jeopardy of imminent collision by the negligent and unlawful maneuvers of the Soviet merchant ship POLOTSK.

At about 2:20 p.m., local time (11:20 G.M.T.), on April 9, 1964, in the approximate position of 13°38′ N, 42°59′ E, and while proceeding on the high seas in the waters of the Red Sea on course 159° true at a speed of 13 knots, DUXBURY BAY was overtaken by the Soviet merchant vessel POLOTSK. POLOTSK maneuvered from a position of about 500 yards on the port quarter of DUXBURY BAY to within 230 yards off her port beam and then cut sharply across the bow of the United States Navy ship, clearing by a mere 10 yards. POLOTSK, thereafter, continued drawing ahead to a position of about 2,000 yards on the starboard bow of DUXBURY BAY.

These radical maneuvers of POLOTSK were in clear and flagrant violation of Rule 24 of the International Rules for Pre-

[1] For discussion see *The United States in World Affairs, 1964,* pp. 83-90.
[2] *Department of State Bulletin,* October 5, 1964, p. 482.

venting Collisions at Sea in that POLOTSK, as the overtaking ship, did fail to keep clear of the DUXBURY BAY which was the privileged overtaken ship. On the contrary, POLOTSK created serious imminent risk of collision, jeopardizing the safety of the ship and the lives of the crew on board DUXBURY BAY. The navigational situation, moreover, was aggravated by the presence of the West German Tug and Tow (SURABAYA–1) in the vicinity which restricted and hampered maneuvering room of DUXBURY BAY.

Despite the dangerous and unlawful actions of the Soviet ship POLOTSK against DUXBURY BAY, the United States naval ship at all times complied with the International Regulations for Preventing Collisions at Sea, 1948, and successfully avoided collision.

The Government of the United States, protesting the illegal actions of the Soviet merchant vessel POLOTSK which hazarded the safe navigation of DUXBURY BAY, requests that the Government of the Union of Soviet Socialist Republics undertake all necessary and appropriate measures to ensure compliance in the future by Soviet vessels with the International Regulations for Preventing Collisions at Sea.

(b) *United States Note to the U.S.S.R., September 15, 1964.*[3]

The Embassy of the United States of America acknowledges the receipt of the note of the Soviet Ministry of Foreign Affairs dated August 3, 1964.[4]

The Embassy has been instructed by the United States Government to inform the Soviet Ministry of Foreign Affairs that the investigation mentioned in the Embassy's interim note of August 18, 1964[5] of alleged dangerously-low overflights of Soviet vessels by United States aircraft and of charges of dangerous maneuvers by United States vessels in the Ministry's note No. 45 of August 3, 1964 and the Soviet Embassy note No. 24 delivered in Washington August 5, 1964[6] has been completed. The investigations reveal that the Soviet charges are without foundation.

Detailed investigation of each of the Soviet charges found that in no case did American aircraft harass, endanger, or provoke any Soviet ships. The distances maintained by United States aircraft were at all times appropriate and in no instance constituted "dangerously-low overflights." In the one specific

[3] Department of State Press Release 403, September 15, 1964; text from *Department of State Bulletin*, October 5, 1964, pp. 483-484.
[4] Same, pp. 484-485.
[5] Same, p. 483.
[6] Same, pp. 482-483.

charge in the Soviet note of August 3 that two American military aircraft overflew the Soviet vessel "Frunze" at a height of 50 meters on June 27, investigation establishes that the Soviet charge is in error. The two United States aircraft at no time approached closer than an altitude of 500 feet and a lateral range of 3,000 feet. The aircraft did not overfly the "Frunze" nor make any harassing or provocative maneuvers. In the incident in the Soviet note of August 3 involving the Soviet steamer "Dubna" on July 8, it has been established that no United States aircraft were in the area of the alleged incident and furthermore that the aircraft number cited in the Soviet note of August 3 is not a United States Government aircraft number.

Detailed investigation of the shipping incidents protested in the Soviet notes of August 3 and August 5 revealed the following: In the case of the Soviet vessel "Gruziya" on July 21, the American vessel at no time approached closer than 300 yards to the starboard of the vessel nor in any way created a threat of collision. In one incident of April 25 involving the Soviet merchant vessel "Leonid Leonidev" there was no United States Navy or United States Coast Guard ship in the area at the time and place specified. In both of the other cases in the Soviet note of August 5, United States vessels were in the vicinity of Soviet vessels, but did not engage in any dangerous maneuvers. The Soviet note charging that a Coast Guard vessel on June 1 approached within 50 meters of the Soviet vessel "Dalni Vostok," is in error. The Coast Guard vessel confirms, however, that it witnessed another ship, which was *not* of United States registry, run parallel to the Soviet vessel and cut across the bow of the Soviet ship.

United States commanders are under strictest instructions not to approach foreign vessels closer than is necessary for common practice of establishing identification in international waters. The United States adheres to the rights of all ships and aircraft to engage in peaceful operations in and over international waters without harassment and United States vessels and aircraft are instructed to perform accordingly.

On the other hand, on a number of occasions in recent months, United States vessels have encountered harassment by Soviet ships.

In the last three months alone the following incidents occurred: On June 30 at a position of 40°35′ north and 65°43′ west, the Soviet trawler "Rauda" P5054 with stern designation "2516–Port Dayoda," maneuvered dangerously within 150 yards of the U.S.S. "D.A. Joy" causing the United States vessel to sound the danger signal and use emergency speeds to avoid collision. On August 18, 1964 the Soviet vessel "Dubna," in passage between Cuba and Haiti, maneuvered irresponsibly near the U.S.S. "Dash" and created a dangerous situation.

In bringing these incidents to the attention of the Soviet Government, the Government of the United States assumes that the Soviet Government will take the necessary measures to assure that Soviet pilots and masters do not violate international practices.

(30) *United States-Soviet Consular Convention.*[7]

(a) *Statement by President Johnson, May 27, 1964.*[8]

We have just concluded negotiations with the Soviet Union on a consular convention. The agreement will be signed in Moscow on June 1. I have authorized Ambassador [Foy D.] Kohler to sign for the United States. I understand Soviet Foreign Minister [Andrei A.] Gromyko will be signing for the Soviet Union.

This treaty, which I will submit to the Senate for its advice and consent, is a significant step in our continuing efforts to increase contacts and understanding between the American people and the peoples of the Soviet Union. It will make possible improved consular services in both countries. American citizens visiting the Soviet Union, either as tourists or for business reasons, will have available to them a greater degree of consular protection than ever before. For example, Americans detained in the Soviet Union for any reasons will be assured of access without delay to American consular officials. American businessmen and shipping companies will be able to call on U.S. consular services to assist in representing their interests. And the mechanics for dealing with a whole range of legal problems from complicated questions of inheritance to simply notary services will be considerably eased.

It is my hope that this treaty—the first bilateral treaty between the United States and the Soviet Union—will be a step forward in developing understanding between our two countries, which is so important in the continuing struggle for peace.

[7] For discussion see *The United States in World Affairs, 1964*, pp. 87-88.
[8] White House Press Release, May 27, 1964; text in *Department of State Bulletin*, June 22, 1964, p. 979.

(b) *Convention and Protocol, Signed in Moscow, June 1, 1964.*[9]

CONSULAR CONVENTION

BETWEEN THE GOVERNMENT OF THE UNITED STATES OF AMERICA AND THE GOVERNMENT OF THE UNION OF SOVIET SOCIALIST REPUBLICS

The Government of the United States of America and the Government of the Union of Soviet Socialist Republics,

Desiring to cooperate in strengthening friendly relations and to regulate consular relations between both states,

Have decided to conclude a consular convention and for this purpose have agreed on the following:

DEFINITIONS

ARTICLE 1

For the purpose of the present Convention, the terms introduced hereunder have the following meaning:

1) "Consular establishment"—means any consulate general, consulate, vice consulate or consular agency;

2) "Consular district"—means the area assigned to a consular establishment for the exercise of consular functions;

3) "Head of consular establishment"—means a consul general, consul, vice consul, or consular agent directing the consular establishment;

4) "Consular officer"—means any person, including the head of the consular establishment, entrusted with the exercise of consular functions. Also included in the definition of "consular officer" are persons assigned to the consular establishment for training in the consular service;

5) "Employee of the consular establishment"—means any person performing administrative, technical, or service functions in a consular establishment.

OPENING OF CONSULAR ESTABLISHMENTS, APPOINTMENT OF CONSULAR OFFICERS AND EMPLOYEES

ARTICLE 2

1. A consular establishment may be opened in the territory of the receiving state only with that state's consent.

[9] Department of State Press Release 262, June 1, 1964, as corrected; text from *Department of State Bulletin,* June 22, 1964, pp. 979-985.

2. The location of a consular establishment and the limits of its consular district will be determined by agreement between the sending and receiving states.

3. Prior to the appointment of a head of a consular establish ment, the sending state shall obtain the approval of the receiving state to such an appointment through diplomatic channels.

4. The diplomatic mission of the sending state shall transmit to the foreign affairs ministry of the receiving state a consular commission which shall contain the full name of the head of the consular establishment, his citizenship, his class, the consular district assigned to him, and the seat of the consular establishment.

5. A head of a consular establishment may enter upon the exercise of his duties only after having been recognized in this capacity by the receiving state. Such recognition after the presentation of the commission shall be in the form of an exequatur or in another form and shall be free of charge.

6. The full name, function and class of all consular officers other than the head of a consular establishment, and the full name and function of employees of the consular establishment shall be notified in advance by the sending state to the receiving state.

The receiving state shall issue to each consular officer an appropriate document confirming his right to carry out consular functions in the territory of the receiving state.

7. The receiving state may at any time, and without having to explain its decision, notify the sending state through diplomatic channels that any consular officer is persona non grata or that any employee of the consular establishment is unacceptable. In such a case the sending state shall accordingly recall such officer or employee of the consular establishment. If the sending state refuses or fails within a reasonable time to carry out its obligations under the present paragraph, the receiving state may refuse to recognize the officer or employee concerned as a member of the consular establishment.

8. With the exception of members of the staff of the diplomatic mission of the sending state, as defined in paragraph c of Article 1 of the Vienna Convention on Diplomatic Relations, no national of the sending state already present in the receiving state or in transit thereto may be appointed as a consular officer or employee of the consular establishment.

ARTICLE 3

Consular officers may be nationals only of the sending state.

ARTICLE 4

The receiving state shall take the necessary measures in order that a consular officer may carry out his duties and enjoy the rights, privileges, and immunities provided for in the present Convention and by the laws of the receiving state.

ARTICLE 5

1. The receiving state shall either facilitate the acquisition on its territory, in accordance with its laws and regulations, by the sending state of premises necessary for its consular establishment or assist the latter in obtaining accommodation in some other way.

2. It shall also, where necessary, assist the sending state in obtaining suitable accommodation for the personnel of its consular establishment.

ARTICLE 6

1. If the head of the consular establishment cannot carry out his functions or if the position of head of a consular establishment is vacant, the sending state may empower a consular officer of the same or another consular establishment, or one of the members of the diplomatic staff of its diplomatic mission in the receiving state, to act temporarily as head of the consular establishment. The full name of this person must be transmitted in advance to the foreign affairs ministry of the receiving state.

2. A person empowered to act as temporary head of the consular establishment shall enjoy the rights, privileges and immunities of the head of the consular establishment.

3. When, in accordance with the provisions of paragraph 1 of the present Article, a member of the diplomatic staff of the diplomatic mission of the sending state in the receiving state is designated by the sending state as an acting head of the consular establishment, he shall continue to enjoy diplomatic privileges and immunities.

CONSULAR FUNCTIONS

ARTICLE 7

A consular officer shall be entitled within his consular district to perform the following functions, and for this purpose may apply orally or in writing to the competent authorities of the consular district:

1) To protect the rights and interests of the sending state and its nationals, both individuals and bodies corporate;

2) To further the development of commercial, economic, cultural and scientific relations between the sending state and the receiving state and otherwise promote the development of friendly relations between them;

3) To register nationals of the sending state, to issue or amend passports and other certificates of identity, and also to issue entry, exit, and transit visas;

4) To draw up and record certificates of birth and death of citizens of the sending state taking place in the receiving state, to record marriages and divorces, if both persons entering into marriage or divorce are citizens of the sending state, and also to receive such declarations pertaining to family relationships of a national of the sending state as may be required under the law of the sending state, unless prohibited by the laws of the receiving state;

5) To draw up, certify, attest, authenticate, legalize and take other actions which might be necessary to validate any act or document of a legal character, as well as copies thereof, including commercial documents, declarations, registrations, testamentary dispositions, and contracts, upon the application of a national of the sending state, when such document is intended for use outside the territory of the receiving state, and also for any person, when such document is intended for use in the territory of the sending state;

6) To translate any acts and documents into the English and Russian languages and to certify to the accuracy of the translations;

7) To perform other official consular functions entrusted to him by the sending state if they are not contrary to the laws of the receiving state.

ARTICLE 8

1. The acts and documents specified in paragraph 5 of Article 7 of the present Convention which are drawn up or certified by the consular officer with his official seal affixed, as well as copies, extracts, and translations of such acts and documents certified by him with his official seal affixed, shall be receivable in evidence in the receiving state as official or officially certified acts, documents, copies, translations, or extracts, and shall have the same force and effect as though they were drawn up or certified by the competent authorities or officials of the receiving state; provided that such documents shall have been drawn and executed in conformity with the laws and regulations of the country where they are designed to take effect.

2. The acts, documents, copies, translations, or extracts, enu-

merated in paragraph 1 of the present Article shall be authenticated if required by the laws of the receiving state when they are presented to the authorities of the receiving state.

ARTICLE 9

If the relevant information is available to the competent authorities of the receiving state, such authorities shall inform the consular establishment of the death of a national of the sending state.

ARTICLE 10

1. In the case of the death of a national of the sending state in the territory of the receiving state, without leaving in the territory of his decease any known heir or testamentary executor, the appropriate local authorities of the receiving state shall as promptly as possible inform a consular officer of the sending state.

2. A consular officer of the sending state may, within the discretion of the appropriate judicial authorities and if permissible under then existing applicable local law in the receiving state:

a) take provisional custody of the personal property left by a deceased national of the sending state, provided that the decedent shall have left in the receiving state no heir or testamentary executor appointed by the decedent to take care of his personal estate; provided that such provisional custody shall be relinquished to a duly appointed administrator;

b) administer the estate of a deceased national of the sending state who is not a resident of the receiving state at the time of his death, who leaves no testamentary executor, and who leaves in the receiving state no heir, provided that if authorized to administer the estate, the consular officer shall relinquish such administration upon the appointment of another administrator;

c) represent the interests of a national of the sending state in an estate in the receiving state, provided that such national is not a resident of the receiving state, unless or until such national is otherwise represented: provided, however, that nothing herein shall authorize a consular officer to act as an attorney at law.

3. Unless prohibited by law, a consular officer may, within the discretion of the court, agency, or person making distribution, receive for transmission to a national of the sending state who is not a resident of the receiving state any money or prop-

erty to which such national is entitled as a consequence of the death of another person, including shares in an estate, payments made pursuant to workmen's compensation laws, pension and social benefits systems in general, and proceeds of insurance policies.

The court, agency, or person making distribution may require that a consular officer comply with conditions laid down with regard to: (a) presenting a power of attorney or other authorization from such non-resident national, (b) furnishing reasonable evidence of the receipt of such money or property by such national, and (c) returning the money or property in the event he is unable to furnish such evidence.

4. Whenever a consular officer shall perform the functions referred to in paragraphs 2 and 3 of this Article, he shall be subject, with respect to the exercise of such functions, to the laws of the receiving state and to the civil jurisdiction of the judicial and administrative authorities of the receiving state in the same manner and to the same extent as a national of the receiving state.

ARTICLE 11

A consular officer may recommend to the courts or to other competent authorities of the receiving state appropriate persons to act in the capacity of guardians or trustees for citizens of the sending state or for the property of such citizens when this property is left without supervision.

In the event that the court or competent authorities consider that the recommended candidate is for some reason unacceptable, the consular officer may propose a new candidate.

ARTICLE 12

1. A consular officer shall have the right within his district to meet with, communicate with, assist, and advise any national of the sending state and, where necessary, arrange for legal assistance for him. The receiving state shall in no way restrict the access of nationals of the sending state to its consular establishments.

2. The appropriate authorities of the receiving state shall immediately inform a consular officer of the sending state about the arrest or detention in other form of a national of the sending state.

3. A consular officer of the sending state shall have the right without delay to visit and communicate with a national of the sending state who is under arrest or otherwise detained in

custody or is serving a sentence of imprisonment. The rights referred to in this paragraph shall be exercised in conformity with the laws and regulations of the receiving state, subject to the proviso, however, that the said laws and regulations must not nullify these rights.

ARTICLE 13

1. A consular officer may provide aid and assistance to vessels sailing under the flag of the sending state which have entered a port in his consular district.

2. Without prejudice to the powers of the receiving state, a consular officer may conduct investigations into any incidents which occurred during the voyage on vessels sailing under the flag of the sending state, and may settle disputes of any kind between the master, the officers and the seamen insofar as this may be authorized by the laws of the sending state. A consular officer may request the assistance of the competent authorities of the receiving state in the performance of such duties.

3. In the event that the courts or other competent authorities of the receiving state intend to take any coercive action on vessels sailing under the flag of the sending state while they are located in the waters of the receiving state, the competent authorities of the receiving state shall, unless it is impractical to do so in view of the urgency of the matter, inform a consular officer of the sending state prior to initiating such action so that the consular officer may be present when the action is taken. Whenever it is impractical to notify a consular officer in advance, the competent authorities of the receiving state shall inform him as soon as possible thereafter of the action taken.

4. Paragraph 3 of this Article shall not apply to customs, passport, and sanitary inspections, or to action taken at the request or with the approval of the master of the vessel.

5. The term "vessel," as used in the present Convention, does not include warships.

ARTICLE 14

If a vessel sailing under the flag of the sending state suffers shipwreck, runs aground, is swept ashore, or suffers any other accident whatever within the territorial limits of the receiving state, the competent authorities of the receiving state shall immediately inform a consular officer and advise him of the measures which they have taken to rescue persons, vessel, and cargo.

The consular officer may provide all kinds of assistance to

such a vessel, the members of its crew, and its passengers, as well as take measures in connection with the preservation of the cargo and repair of the ship, or he may request the authorities of the receiving state to take such measures.

The competent authorities of the receiving state shall render the necessary assistance to the consular officer in measures taken by him in connection with the accident to the vessel.

No customs duties shall be levied against a wrecked vessel, its cargo or stores, in the territory of the receiving state, unless they are delivered for use in that state.

If the owner or anyone authorized to act for him is unable to make necessary arrangements in connection with the vessel or its cargo, the consular officer may make such arrangements. The consular officer may under similar circumstances make arrangements in connection with cargo owned by the sending state or any of its nationals and found or brought into port from a wrecked vessel sailing under the flag of any state except a vessel of the receiving state.

ARTICLE 15

Articles 13 and 14, respectively, shall also apply to aircraft.

RIGHTS, PRIVILEGES AND IMMUNITIES

ARTICLE 16

The national flag of the sending state and the consular flag may be flown at the consular establishment, at the residence of the head of the consular establishment, and on his means of transport used by him in the performance of his official duties. The shield with the national coat-of-arms of the sending state and the name of the establishment may also be affixed on the building in which the consular establishment is located.

ARTICLE 17

The consular archives shall be inviolable at all times and wherever they may be. Unofficial papers shall not be kept in the consular archives.

The buildings or parts of buildings and the land ancillary thereto, used for the purposes of the consular establishment and the residence of the head of the consular establishment, shall be inviolable.

The police and other authorities of the receiving state may not enter the building or that part of the building which is used for the purposes of the consular establishment or the residence of the head of the consular establishment without the consent of the head thereof, persons appointed by him, or the head of the diplomatic mission of the sending state.

Article 18

1. The consular establishment shall have the right to communicate with its Government, with the diplomatic mission and the consular establishments of the sending state in the receiving state, or with other diplomatic missions and consular establishments of the sending state, making use of all ordinary means of communication. In such communications, the consular establishment shall have the right to use code, diplomatic couriers, and the diplomatic pouch. The same fees shall apply to consular establishments in the use of ordinary means of communication as apply to the diplomatic mission of the sending state.

2. The official correspondence of a consular establishment, regardless of what means of communication are used, and the sealed diplomatic pouch bearing visible external marks of its official character, shall be inviolable and not subject to examination or detention by the authorities of the receiving state.

Article 19

1. Consular officers shall not be subject to the jurisdiction of the receiving state in matters relating to their official activity. The same applies to employees of the consular establishment, if they are nationals of the sending state.

2. Consular officers and employees of the consular establishment who are nationals of the sending state shall enjoy immunity from the criminal jurisdiction of the receiving state.

3. This immunity from the criminal jurisdiction of the receiving state of consular officers and employees of the consular establishment of the sending state may be waived by the sending state. Waiver must always be express.

Article 20

1. Consular officers and employees of the consular establishment, on the invitation of a court of the receiving state, shall appear in court for witness testimony. Taking measures to compel a consular officer or an employee of the consular establishment who is a national of the sending state to appear in court as a witness and to give witness testimony is not permissible.

2. If a consular officer or an employee of the consular establishment who is a national of the sending state for official reasons

or for reasons considered valid according to the laws of the receiving state cannot appear in court, he shall inform the court thereof and give witness testimony on the premises of the consular establishment or in his own abode.

3. Whenever under the laws of the receiving state an oath is required to be taken in court by consular officers and employees of the consular establishment, an affirmation shall be accepted in lieu thereof.

4. Consular officers and employees of the consular establishment may refuse to give witness testimony on facts relating to their official activity.

5. The provisions of paragraphs 1, 2, 3, and 4 shall also apply to proceedings conducted by administrative authorities.

ARTICLE 21

1. Immovable property, situated in the territory of the receiving state, of which the sending state or one or more persons acting in its behalf is the owner or lessee and which is used for diplomatic or consular purposes, including residences for personnel attached to the diplomatic and consular establishments, shall be exempt from taxation of any kind imposed by the receiving state or any of its states or local governments other than such as represent payments for specific services rendered.

2. The exemption from taxation referred to in paragraph 1 of this Article shall not apply to such charges, duties, and taxes if, under the law of the receiving state, they are payable by the person who contracted with the sending state or with the person acting on its behalf.

ARTICLE 22

A consular officer or employee of a consular establishment, who is not a national of the receiving state and who does not have the status in the receiving state of an alien lawfully admitted for permanent residence, shall be exempt from the payment of all taxes or similar charges of any kind imposed by the receiving state or any of its states or local governments on official emoluments, salaries, wages, or allowances received by such officer or employee from the sending state in connection with the discharge of his official functions.

ARTICLE 23

1. A consular officer or employee of a consular establishment who is not a national of the receiving state and who does not have the status in the receiving state of an alien lawfully ad-

mitted for permanent residence, shall, except as provided in paragraph 2 of this Article, be exempt from the payment of all taxes or similar charges of any kind imposed by the receiving state or any of its states or local governments, for the payment of which the officer or employee of the consular establishment would otherwise be legally liable.

2. The exemption from taxes or charges provided in paragraph 1 of this Article does not apply in respect to taxes or charges upon:

a) The acquisition or possession of private immovable property located in the receiving state if the persons referred to in paragraph 1 of this Article do not own or lease this property on the behalf of the sending state for the purposes of the consular establishment;

b) Income received from sources in the receiving state other than as described in Article 22 of the present Convention;

c) The transfer by gift of property in the receiving state;

d) The transfer at death, including by inheritance, of property in the receiving state.

3. However, the exemption from taxes or similar charges provided in paragraph 1 of this Article, applies in respect to movable inherited property left after the death of a consular officer or employee of the consular establishment or a member of his family residing with him if they are not nationals of the receiving state or aliens lawfully admitted for permanent residence, and if the property was located in the receiving state exclusively in connection with the sojourn in this state of the deceased as a consular officer or employee of the consular establishment or member of his family residing with him.

Article 24

A consular officer or employee of a consular establishment and members of his family residing with him who are not nationals of the receiving state and who do not have the status in the receiving state of aliens lawfully admitted for permanent residence, shall be exempt in the receiving state from service in the armed forces and from all other types of compulsory service.

Article 25

A consular officer or employee of a consular establishment and members of his family residing with him who do not have the status in the receiving state of aliens lawfully admitted for permanent residence, shall be exempt from all obligations under the laws and regulations of the receiving state with regard to the registration of aliens, and obtaining permission to reside, and from compliance with other similar requirements applicable to aliens.

ARTICLE 26

1. The same full exemption from customs duties and internal revenue or other taxes imposed upon or by reason of importation shall apply in the receiving state to all articles, including motor vehicles, imported exclusively for the official use of a consular establishment, as applies to articles imported for the official use of the diplomatic mission of the sending state.

2. Consular officers, and employees of the consular establishment, and members of their families residing with them, who are not nationals of the receiving state, and who do not have the status in the receiving state of aliens lawfully admitted for permanent residence, shall be granted, on the basis of reciprocity, the same exemptions from customs duties and internal revenue or other taxes imposed upon or by reason of importation, as are granted to corresponding personnel of the diplomatic mission of the sending state.

3. For the purpose of paragraph 2 of this Article the term "corresponding personnel of the diplomatic mission" refers to members of the diplomatic staff in the case of consular officers, and to members of the administrative and technical staff in the case of employees of a consular establishment.

ARTICLE 27

Subject to the laws and regulations of the receiving state concerning zones entry into which is prohibited or regulated for reasons of national security, a consular officer shall be permitted to travel freely within the limits of his consular district to carry out his official duties.

ARTICLE 28

Without prejudice to their privileges and immunities, it is the duty of all persons enjoying such privileges and immunities to respect the laws and regulations of the receiving state, including traffic regulations.

ARTICLE 29

1. The rights and obligations of consular officers provided for in the present Convention also apply to members of the

diplomatic staff of the diplomatic mission of the Contracting Parties charged with the performance of consular functions in the diplomatic mission and who have been notified in a consular capacity to the foreign affairs ministry of the receiving state by the diplomatic mission.

2. Except as provided in paragraph 4 of Article 10 of the present Convention, the performance of consular functions by the persons referred to in paragraph 1 of this Article shall not affect the diplomatic privileges and immunities granted to them as members of the diplomatic mission.

FINAL PROVISIONS

Article 30

1. The present Convention shall be subject to ratification and shall enter into force on the thirtieth day following the exchange of instruments of ratification, which shall take place in Washington as soon as possible.

2. The Convention shall remain in force until six months from the date on which one of the Contracting Parties informs the other Contracting Party of its desire to terminate its validity.

In witness whereof the Plenipotentiaries of the two Contracting Parties have signed the present Convention and affixed their seals thereto.

Done in Moscow on June 1, 1964 in two copies, each in the English and the Russian language, both texts being equally authentic.

For the Government of the United States of America	For the Government of the the Union of Soviet Socialist Republics
Foy D. Kohler Ambassador of the United States of America to the USSR	A. Gromyko Minister for Foreign Affairs of the Union of Soviet Socialist Republics

PROTOCOL

To the Consular Convention Between the Government of the United States of America and the Government of the Union of Soviet Socialist Republics

1. It is agreed between the Contracting Parties that the notification of a consular officer of the arrest or detention in other

form of a national of the sending state specified in paragraph 2 of Article 12 of the Consular Convention between the Government of the United States of America and the Government of the Union of Soviet Socialist Republics of June 1, 1964, shall take place within one to three days from the time of arrest or detention depending on conditions of communication.

2. It is agreed between the Contracting Parties that the rights specified in paragraph 3 of Article 12 of the Consular Convention of a consular officer to visit and communicate with a national of the sending state who is under arrest or otherwise detained in custody shall be accorded within two to four days of the arrest or detention of such national depending upon his location.

3. It is agreed between the Contracting Parties that the rights specified in paragraph 3 of Article 12 of the Consular Convention of a consular officer to visit and communicate with a national of the sending state who is under arrest or otherwise detained in custody or is serving a sentence of imprisonment shall be accorded on a continuing basis.

The present Protocol constitutes an integral part of the Consular Convention between the Government of the United States of America and the Government of the Union of Soviet Socialist Republics of June 1, 1964.

Done at Moscow on June 1, 1964 in two copies, each in the English and the Russian language, both texts being equally authentic.

For the Government of the United States of America	For the Government of the Union of Soviet Socialist Republics
FOY D. KOHLER	A. GROMYKO
Ambassador of the United States of America to the USSR	Minister for Foreign Affairs of the Union of Soviet Socialist Republics

(31) *United States-Soviet Cooperation in Desalination Research: Agreement Signed at Moscow, November 18, 1964.*[10]

AGREEMENT ON COOPERATION BETWEEN THE UNITED STATES OF AMERICA AND THE UNION OF SOVIET SOCIALIST REPUBLICS IN THE FIELD OF DESALINATION, INCLUDING THE USE OF ATOMIC ENERGY

The Government of the United States of America and the Government of the Union of Soviet Socialist Republics, hereinafter referred to as the "Parties,"

Taking into account that the problem of desalination has great significance for the USA and the USSR and also for many other countries experiencing a shortage of fresh water;

Taking into account that contemporary scientific and technical achievements, including the use of atomic energy, permit the practical solution of the problem of desalination;

Have agreed on the following:

I. The Parties will engage in wide scientific and technical cooperation in the field of desalination, including the use of atomic energy, in accordance with the provisions of this Agreement.

II. The Parties will conduct scientific research and development work in the field of desalination, including the use of atomic energy, in accordance with their own programs and at their own expense.

III. The Parties will exchange, on a reciprocal basis, scientific accounts, reports, and other documents, including the results obtained from work at pilot and demonstration plants of the Parties.

IV. The Parties will periodically organize, on a reciprocal basis, symposia and scientific meetings for discussion of scientific and technical problems and projects in accordance with previously agreed programs.

V. The Parties will periodically organize visits, on a reciprocal basis, by technical experts to appropriate installations and laboratories.

VI. In order that the International Atomic Energy Agency (IAEA) and its members receive benefits in full measure from this cooperation, the Parties will give the IAEA copies of accounts, reports, and other documents which they exchange and also in appropriate cases invite IAEA observers to symposia and

[10] *Department of State Bulletin,* December 7, 1964, p. 829.

scientific meetings held by the Parties. The Parties will jointly inform the IAEA Director-General of this agreement.

VII. The implementation of this Agreement shall be subject to the provisions of Sections I and XIII of the US–USSR Agreement on Exchanges in the Scientific, Technical, Educational, Cultural and Other Fields signed at Moscow February 22, 1964.[11]

VIII. This Agreement shall enter into force upon signature. It shall continue in force for two years, and shall be subject to renewal by the Parties.

In witness whereof, the undersigned, duly authorized, have signed the present agreement.

Done, in duplicate, in the English and Russian languages, both equally authentic, at Moscow this Eighteenth day of November, One Thousand Nine Hundred Sixty-Four.

By authority of the Government of the United States of America

FOY D. KOHLER
DONALD F. HORNIG

By authority of the Government of the Union of Soviet Socialist Republics

A. GROMYKO
A. PETROSYANTS

B. Change in Soviet Leadership.[12]

(32) *The Removal of Chairman Nikita S. Khrushchev.*

(a) *Official Announcement by the Central Committee of the C.P.S.U., October 15, 1964.*[13]

A plenary meeting of the central committee of the C.P.S.U. [*Communist Party of the Soviet Union*] was held on October 14.

The plenary meeting of the C.P.S.U. central committee granted N. S. Khrushchov's request that he be relieved of his duties as first secretary of the C.P.S.U. central committee, member of the presidium of the C.P.S.U. central committee and Chairman of the U.S.S.R. Council of Ministers in view of his advanced age and the deterioration of his health.

The plenary meeting of the C.P.S.U. central committee elected L. I. Brezhnev first secretary of the C.P.S.U. central committee.

[11] Department of State, *Treaties and Other International Acts Series 5582.*
[12] For discussion see *The United States in World Affairs, 1964,* pp. 88-90.
[13] *Soviet News* (London), October 16, 1964.

(b) *Official Announcement by the Presidium of the U.S.S.R., October 15, 1964.*[14]

The Presidium of the U.S.S.R. Supreme Soviet met on October 15, with Comrade A. I. Mikoyan, President of the Presidium of the U.S.S.R. Supreme Soviet, in the chair.

The Presidium of the U.S.S.R. Supreme Soviet discussed the question of the Chairman of the U.S.S.R. Council of Ministers.

The Presidium of the U.S.S.R. Supreme Soviet granted Nikita Sergeyevich Khrushchov's request that he be relieved of the duties of Chairman of the U.S.S.R. Council of Ministers in view of his advanced age and the deterioration of his health.

The Presidium of the U.S.S.R. Supreme Soviet appointed Comrade Alexei Nikolayevich Kosygin as Chairman of the Council of Ministers of the U.S.S.R., releasing him from his duties as First Vice-Chairman of the U.S.S.R. Council of Ministers.

The decrees of the Presidium of the U.S.S.R. Supreme Soviet on the release of Comrade N. S. Khrushchov from his duties as Chairman of the U.S.S.R. Council of Ministers and on the appointment of Comrade A. N. Kosygin as Chairman of the U.S.S.R. Council of Ministers were adopted unanimously by the members of the Presidium of the U.S.S.R. Supreme Soviet.

The members of the Presidium of the U.S.S.R. Supreme Soviet warmly congratulated Comrade Kosygin on his appointment to the post of Chairman of the U.S.S.R. Council of Ministers.

Comrade Kosygin heartily thanked the central committee of the Communist Party of the Soviet Union and the Presidium of the Supreme Soviet of the U.S.S.R. for the confidence shown in him and gave an assurance that he would do his utmost to discharge his duties.

(c) *Broadcast Statement by President Johnson, October 18, 1964.*[15]

(Excerpts)

My fellow Americans: On Thursday of last week [October 15], from the Kremlin in Moscow, the Soviet Government announced a change in its leadership.[16]

* * *

[14] Same.
[15] White House Press Release, October 18, 1964; text from *Department of State Bulletin,* November 2, 1964, pp. 610-611.
[16] Document 32a and 32b.

Events in Moscow

* * *

We do not know exactly what happened to Nikita Khrushchev last Thursday. We do know that he has been forced out of power by his former friends and colleagues. Five days ago he had only praise in Moscow. Today we learn only of his faults. Yet the men at the top today are the same men that he picked for leadership. These men carried on the administration of the Soviet Government when he was absent from the Soviet capital, and that was nearly half of the time that he was in power.

Mr. Khrushchev was clearly the dominant figure in making Soviet policy. After [*V. I.*] Lenin and [*Joseph V.*] Stalin, he is only the third man in history to have made himself the undisputed master of Communist Russia. There were times when he was guilty of dangerous adventure. It required great American firmness and good sense—first in Berlin and later in the Cuban missile crisis—to turn back his threats and actions without war. Yet he learned from his mistakes, and he was not blind to realities. In the last 2 years, his Government had shown itself aware of the need for sanity in the nuclear age.

He joined in the nuclear test ban treaty.[17] He joined in the "hot line," which can help prevent a war by accident.[18] He agreed that space should be kept free of nuclear weapons. In these actions, he demonstrated good sense and sober judgment. We do not think it was these actions that led to his removal.

We cannot know for sure just what did lead to this secret decision. Our intelligence estimate is that Khrushchev learned of the decision only when for him it was too late.

There has been discontent and strain and failure, both within the Soviet Union and within the Communist bloc as a whole. All of this has been evident for all to see. These troubles are not the creation of one man. They will not end with his removal.

When Lenin died in 1924, Stalin took 4 years to consolidate his power. When Stalin died in 1953, it was not Mr. Khrushchev who first emerged. But two men now share top responsibility in the Soviet Union, and their exact relation to each other and their colleagues is not yet very clear. They are experienced, but younger, men and perhaps less rooted in the past. They are said

[17] *Documents, 1963,* pp. 130-132.
[18] Same, pp. 115-116.

to be realistic. We can hope that they will share with us our great objective—the prevention of nuclear war.

But what does all this mean for us in America? It means at least four things:

First: We must never forget that the men in the Kremlin remain dedicated, dangerous Communists. A time of trouble among Communists requires steady vigilance among free men—and most of all among Americans, for it is the strength of the United States that holds the balance firm against danger.

Second: There will be turmoil in the Communist world. It is likely that the men in the Kremlin will be concerned primarily with problems of communism. This would not be all good, because there are problems and issues that need attention between our world and theirs. But it is not all bad, because men who are busy with internal problems may not be tempted to reckless external acts.

Third: This great change will not stop the forces in Eastern Europe that are working for greater independence. Those forces will continue to have our sympathy. We will not give up our hope of building new bridges to these peoples.

Fourth: Our own course must continue to prove that we, on our side, are ready to get on with the work of peace.

The new Soviet Government has officially informed me, through Ambassador [Anatoliy F.] Dobrynin, day before yesterday, that it plans no change in basic foreign policy. I spoke frankly, as always, to the Soviet Ambassador. I told him that the quest for peace in America had never been more determined than it is now. I told him that we intend to bury no one and we do not intend to be buried. I reminded the Ambassador of the danger that we all faced 2 years ago in Cuba. I told him that any Soviet Government which is ready to work for peace will find us ready in America. I said to the Ambassador that I would be ready to talk to anyone when it would help the cause of peace. I believe that this was a good beginning on both sides.

* * *

C. The Loosening of the Soviet Bloc.[19]

(33) *United States Policy and Eastern Europe: Address by Secretary of State Rusk, Washington, February 25, 1964.*[20]

(Excerpts)

* * *

I should like to discuss with you today a central question—one which rightfully looms large in the concern of the American people about foreign affairs. What is the policy of this Government toward international communism?

At the present time, as throughout the postwar period, there are some who, for political or other reasons, deliberately sow confusion about our real intentions. Also, both at home and abroad, puzzlement may arise on more legitimate grounds.

We are asked how we can object to other free countries selling goods to Cuba when we are willing to sell wheat to the Soviet Union. We are asked why we refuse to recognize the Peiping regime when we recognize the Soviet Union. We are asked why we have treated Yugoslavia and Poland somewhat differently from other Communist states in Eastern Europe. We are asked why we enter into cultural exchange agreements, or a test ban treaty, with a government whose leader has continued to boast that he will "bury" us.

If the Communists, as a group, have as their aim the destruction of our way of life, how is it that we can treat one Communist country differently from another? And why do we enter into an agreement or understanding with a Communist government over one matter, while accepting the hard necessity of continued hostility and conflict over other matters?

No Illusions as to Communist Designs

Before answering those questions, let me make one point clear. We, in this administration, and in this country, are under no illusions as to the designs of the Communists against us and the entire free world. No one needs to tell us that the Communist menace is deadly serious, that the Communists seek their goals through varied means, that deception is a standard element in

[19] For discussion see *The United States in World Affairs, 1964,* pp. 96-103.
[20] Department of State Press Release 83, February 25, 1964; text from *Department of State Bulletin,* March 16, 1964, pp. 390-396.

their tactics, that they move easily from the direct attack to the indirect, or to combinations of the two.

To know what the Communists are up to, and to understand their varied techniques, is a major order of business with us in the State Department and other branches of the Government. It is an order of business we do not neglect.

We are fully aware that Moscow, as well as Peiping, remains committed to the Communist world revolution. Chairman Khrushchev tells us bluntly that coexistence cannot extend to the ideological sphere, that between him and us there will be continued competition and conflict. We hope this will not always be so. But as long as Mr. Khrushchev says it is and acts accordingly, we must believe him and act accordingly ourselves.

Combating Communist Imperialism

The first objective of our policy toward the Communist states must be, and is, to play our part in checking Communist imperialism. This administration will vigorously oppose the expansion of the Communist domain—whoever the Communists in question may be—by force or the threat of force, whether directly or indirectly applied.

* * *

The free world must prevent the Communists from extending their sway through force, whether through frontal assault, piecemeal territorial grabs, or infiltration of men and arms across frontiers. We will continue to do our part to make aggression not only unprofitable to the Communists but increasingly costly and dangerous to them.

* * *

Seeking Steps Toward a More Reliable Peace

But our policy does not end there. In the longer run we want the Communists to come to see that their aggressive hostility toward the free world is not only costly and dangerous but futile. Meanwhile, we want to reduce as much as we can the chance that the hostility they have created between them and us may lead to a great war. Thus we search patiently for agreements and understandings to settle or blunt dangerous disputes between them and us and to bring armaments under control.

The Soviets appear to recognize that there is a common interest in preventing a mutually destructive thermonuclear exchange. We have managed to reach a few limited agreements with them. These do not yet constitute a *détente.* We hope for further agreements or understandings. But in the field of disarmament there are severe limits to the progress that can be made without reliable inspection and verification of arms retained. And on many vital political issues Moscow's views and the West's remain far apart. Nevertheless, we shall pursue unceasingly our earnest quest for mutually acceptable steps toward a more reliable peace.

Communist World Not a "Single Flock of Sheep"

But it is not enough to "contain" communism and to try to negotiate specific agreements to reduce the danger of a great war. The conflict between the Communists and the free world is as fundamental as any conflict can be. Their proclaimed objectives and our conception of a decent world order just do not and cannot fit together.

We view communism as a system incapable of satisfying basic human needs, as a system which will ultimately be totally discredited in the minds of men everywhere. We believe that the peoples who have been brought under Communist rule aspire to a better life—of peace, economic opportunity, and a chance to pursue happiness. This, indeed, has always been so. But in recent years an important new trend has been perceptible: Some of the Communist governments have become responsive, in varying degrees, if not directly to the aspirations of their subjects, at least to kindred aspirations of their own. The Communist world is no longer a single flock of sheep following blindly behind one leader.

The Soviet Union and Communist China are engaged in a deep and comprehensive quarrel involving ideology—how best to promote the Communist world revolution—a struggle for influence in other countries and other Communist parties, conflicting national interests, and personal rivalries. The dispute between Moscow and Peiping has spread through the world Communist movement and, in many countries, has divided the local parties.

The Chinese Communists have demanded that the Russians risk their national interests, and even their national survival, to promote the world revolution, as that cause is defined by Peiping. The rulers of the Soviet Union have rejected this doctrine. They appear to have begun to realize that there is an irresolvable contradiction between the demands to promote world communism by force and the needs and interests of the Soviet state and people.

The smaller Communist countries of Eastern Europe have increasingly, although in varying degree, asserted their own policies. We have always considered it unnatural for the diverse peoples of Eastern Europe, with their own talents and proud traditions, to be submerged in a monolithic bloc. We have wanted these peoples, while living in friendship with their Russian and other neighbors, to develop in accordance with their own national aspirations and genius. And they seem to feel a strong nostalgia for their traditional ties with the West. Most of them are increasing their trade and other contacts with Western Europe and, to some extent, with us.

Within the Soviet bloc the Stalinist terror has been radically changed. And within the Soviet Union, as well as most of the smaller European Communist nations, there are signs—small but varied and persistent signs—of yearnings for more individual freedom. And there are practical reasons why men must be allowed freedom if they are to achieve their best.

* * *

Our capacity to influence events and trends within the Communist world is very limited. But it is our policy to do what we can to encourage evolution in the Communist world toward national independence and open societies. We favor more contacts between the peoples behind the Iron Curtain and our own peoples. We should like to see more Soviet citizens visit the United States. We would be glad to join in cooperative enterprises to further mankind's progress against disease, poverty, and ignorance. We applaud the interest of the Soviet leadership in improving the lot of the Soviet people.

Thus our policy toward international communism has three objectives:

(1) To prevent the Communists from extending their domain and to make it increasingly costly, dangerous, and futile for them to try to do so;

(2) To achieve agreements or understandings which reduce the danger of a devastating war;

(3) To encourage evolution within the Communist world toward national independence, peaceful cooperation, and open societies.

U.S. Policy Toward Various Communist States

We believe that we can best promote these objectives by adjusting our policies to the differing behavior of different Communist states—or to the changing behavior of the same state.

When Yugoslavia challenged Stalin's centralized control of Communist affairs in 1948, we gave that country military and economic assistance. Yugoslavia not only defied Stalin but stopped supporting the guerrilla aggression against Greece, reached an agreement with Italy on Trieste, and increased its economic, political, and cultural ties with the West. It is not a member of the Warsaw Pact. As a nonalined state, it has gained influence among the uncommitted nations of the world. Sometimes it agrees with the Soviet Union on particular points of foreign policy, sometimes not. In brief, Yugoslavia is an independent state. Its success in defending its independence made other peoples in Eastern Europe wonder why they could not do likewise. And not least important from our viewpoint, Yugoslavia is not shipping arms to be used against a democratic government in Venezuela and is not trying to destroy non-Communist governments in South Viet-Nam and Laos.

For some years we have treated Poland somewhat differently from other Soviet bloc states. A good deal of the national autonomy and domestic liberalization which the Poles won in 1956 persists. Most of Polish agriculture remains in private hands; religion is strong; Poland has developed a broad range of relations and exchanges with the West. Poland has historic ties with the West. And its people are the close blood relatives of many citizens of the United States. We apologize to none for our efforts to help the brave people of Poland to preserve their national identity and their own aspirations.

At one time we felt compelled to break diplomatic relations with Bulgaria. Since the ruthless suppression of the Hungarian national revolution in 1956, we have been represented in Budapest not by a regular envoy but by a Chargé.

We have never had diplomatic relations with Communist Albania, the most blatantly Stalinist state in Europe.

Thus, for good reasons, we have treated various Soviet bloc states differently and the same state differently at different times. And we shall continue to differentiate our policy according to the conduct of the various Communist states.

Recently Rumania has asserted a more independent attitude and has expanded its trade and other contacts with the West. It has taken steps to improve its relations with the United States.[21] We are responding accordingly.

Hungary has turned to a more permissive policy of national conciliation. We of course welcome any tendencies promising to ease the lot of the Hungarian people. We will do what we can to encourage them.

In Czechoslovakia and Bulgaria there are some signs of movement away from earlier and harsher policies. We are watching these developments with close attention.

* * *

(34) *United States-Rumanian Relations: Joint Communiqué, Washington, June 1, 1964.*[22]

Representatives of the Governments of the United States of America and of the Rumanian People's Republic met in Washington from May 18 to June 1, 1964 to discuss matters of common interest, particularly economic and trade matters. The Rumanian delegation was headed by Gheorghe Gaston-Marin, Vice-Chairman of the Council of Ministers and Chairman of the State Planning Committee. The United States delegation was headed by W. Averell Harriman, Under Secretary of State for Political Affairs.

In the course of the negotiations, the two delegations noted the improvement in the relations between the two countries following the agreement of March 30, 1960 which provided for the reciprocal settlement of claims and other financial questions.[23] They noted in particular the mutually beneficial results of the increased cultural, educational, scientific, and other exchanges between the two countries in the past several years.

The representatives of the two Governments agreed that further steps should be taken to carry forward the improvement in mutual relations. To this end they reached the following understandings:

1. The United States Government agreed to establish a General License procedure under which most commodities may be exported to Rumania without the necessity for individual export license. In addition the United States Government agreed to grant licenses for a number of particular industrial facilities in which the Rumanian delegation expressed special interest.

21 Cf. Document 34.
22 Department of State Press Release 263, June 1, 1964; text from *Department of State Bulletin,* June 15, 1964, pp. 924-926.
23 Text in *Department of State Bulletin,* April 25, 1960, pp. 671-673.

The Government of the Rumanian People's Republic agreed to authorize enterprises and institutes in Rumania to sell or license Rumanian technology to United States firms.

The two Governments agreed that products, designs, and technology exported to Rumania from the United States would not be transshipped or re-exported without the prior consent of the United States Government. They agreed further that contracts between United States firms and Rumanian state enterprises for imports from Rumania could provide for limitations on re-export or transshipments without prior consent of the Rumanian supplier. The two Governments will mutually facilitate the exchange of information on the use and disposition of products, designs and technology exported from one country to the other.

2. The two Governments also agreed on arrangements for the mutual protection of industrial property rights and processes. It was agreed that commercial contracts between United States firms and Rumanian state enterprises could provide for the settlement of commercial differences and disputes by arbitration in third countries or by appropriate international tribunals, as agreed by the parties to the contracts.

3. The two Governments further agreed to consult, at the request of either party, about any other problems that might arise as the trade between the two countries grows.

4. In order to promote trade between Rumania and the United States, the representatives of the Rumanian Government expressed their desire to expand the activity of the New York Trade Office of the Rumanian Mission in the United States. The United States delegation discussed plans for setting up in Bucharest a trade promotion office of the United States Mission in Rumania. It was also understood that tourist promotion offices could be established in the two countries.

5. Both Governments agreed to facilitate the entry, travel and work of the representatives of firms and enterprises, and of trade missions. They also agreed to facilitate the exchange of trade exhibits and the publication of trade promotion materials.

6. Both delegations recognized that the development of significant and durable trade relations between the two countries requires the promotion of trade in both directions.

The Rumanian delegation emphasized that Rumanian products cannot compete on an equal basis in the United States market under the tariff treatment accorded such products. It stated that this factor could limit the expansion of trade between the two countries. The United States delegation took note of this concern, and explained the applicable provisions of United States law. The two delegations agreed to give continuing consideration to means of increasing trade between the United States and Rumania.

7. The two delegations noted the forward steps that had been taken in consular matters, and on behalf of their Governments agreed that further measures would be taken to facilitate the mutual settlement of consular problems. In the interest of further improvement of consular relations, they agreed that representatives of the two Governments would meet in Washington in September 1964 to negotiate a new consular convention between the two countries.

8. The delegations stated the intention of the two Governments to expand the existing program of cultural, educational, scientific, and other exchanges between the United States and Rumania.

9. The Governments of the United States of America and of the Rumanian People's Republic today raised the level of their diplomatic missions in Washington and Bucharest from Legations to Embassies. Ambassadors will be exchanged at an early date.

At the conclusion of the meetings, Under Secretary Harriman and Vice-Chairman Gaston-Marin expressed the hope on behalf of their Governments that progress in carrying out the understandings reached would furnish the basis for a further broadening and improvement in the relations between the United States and Rumania.

D. Disarmament and Related Developments.[24]

(35) *Proposal for the Renunciation of the Use of Force in Settling Territorial and Frontier Disputes.*

(a) *Message of Soviet Chairman Khrushchev to the Heads of State or Government of All Countries, Released January 2, 1964.*[25]

(Excerpts)

I am sending you this message in order to draw your attention to one of the problems which in my opinion is of particularly great significance for strengthening peace—the question of ter-

[24] For discussion see *The United States in World Affairs, 1964,* pp. 103-109.

[25] Text of Soviet message dated December 31, 1963 from *Department of State Bulletin,* February 3, 1964, pp. 158-163. For discussion see *The United States in World Affairs, 1964,* pp. 83-85.

ritorial disputes between countries and the ways of settling them. I should like to explain first of all the reason why the Soviet Government is raising this question precisely at this moment and why it regards it as one of great urgency and significance.

I hope you will agree that life itself has now implacably placed the problem of maintaining and strengthening peace in the center of attention of all people, regardless of their nationality and race, of their political and religious convictions.

By the combined efforts of many states it has been possible of late to achieve a certain success in reducing international tension. By common opinion, the signing of the treaty banning nuclear weapons tests in the atmosphere, in outer space, and under water,[26] which has been warmly acclaimed by the peoples, is a major forward step toward a peaceful settlement of urgent international problems. The agreement between the U.S.S.R. and the United States, sealed by the unanimous resolution of the United Nations [27] to keep vehicles with nuclear weapons and other weapons of mass destruction out of orbit, has also been positively acclaimed by all those who want to strengthen peace. These steps have made a good beginning and now must be pursued further.

In recent months, it will be recalled, opinions have been exchanged between the governments of several states concerning the possibility of carrying out a number of further measures toward the relaxation of international tension and the strengthening of peace. Agreement on such measures would naturally have a positive effect on the international situation. The Soviet Government proceeds from the assumption that the search for agreements on ripe international questions will be continued.

Making due appraisal of what it is customary to call the realities of the atomic age, one would have to acknowledge that it is the common duty of statesmen bearing a high responsibility for the destinies of the world and the future of the peoples to agree to even more radical steps capable of eliminating the danger of another war.

* * *

Analyzing the present situation, the Soviet Government came to the conclusion that it would be advisable, while tirelessly working to settle the problem of general and complete disarmament, to step up our efforts for removing friction in the

[26] Same as note 17 to Document 32c.

[27] Resolution 1884 (XVIII), adopted October 17, 1963 in *Documents, 1963* p. 155.

relations between states and the breeding grounds of tension.

I think that you will agree with me that if we try to pick out the questions which most often give rise to dangerous friction between states in different parts of the world, these undoubtedly will be territorial disputes, the problems of frontiers between states, mutual or unilateral claims of states to each other's territory.

* * *

The question of boundaries or, to be more specific, of territorial claims and disputes is not new, of course.

* * *

But while it is true that territorial claims in many cases have led to wars and armed conflicts, it is also equally true that wars as means of settling territorial disputes have always been very costly to the peoples. No sooner had one state seized by armed force the disputed territory from another state, than the latter began to prepare a new war to regain the lost territory. After that the cycle repeated itself.

* * *

Of course territorial claims and disputes between states are different in character. There are some that are associated with the completion of the liberation of this or that people from colonial oppression or foreign occupation.

It is well known that not all young national states by any means managed to liberate from the power of the colonialists all the territories that are theirs by right immediately after they became independent.

Taiwan is a case in point. This island has since time immemorial been an integral part of the Chinese state. Taiwan's unlawful occupation by American troops should be terminated. The island is an inalienable part of the Chinese People's Republic and would have long since been reunited with it but for outside interference by another state.

If other examples were needed, they are there for all to see. Take, for instance, such a recent case as West Irian's reunification with Indonesia. The demands of the liberated states for the return of territories that are still under the colonial yoke or under foreign occupation are unquestionably just.

Of course all this also applies to the territories of the peoples who have not yet achieved national independence and whose status is still colonial. One cannot recognize the casuistry of the colonialists who still hold colonies and contend that these colonial territories are component parts of the metropolis. There should be no ambiguity about that: the right of all colonial peoples to liberation, to freedom and independence, proclaimed in the U.N. declaration [28] to give independence to colonial countries and peoples, cannot be questioned by anyone.

* * *

The peoples still under colonialist domination are striving to achieve their freedom and independence by peaceful means. But these means do not always prove adequate, because those who are interested in preserving and perpetuating the remnants of the colonial system frequently reply by force of arms to the legitimate demands of these peoples for the abolition of colonial regimes. In this event the oppressed peoples have no other choice but to take up arms themselves. And this is their sacred right.

War bases established on foreign territories alienated from other states should be liquidated in the same way. And no one should be misled by the arguments that the land on which such bases are built and foreign troops stationed was leased under some treaty or agreement some time in the past.

* * *

There is one more problem, that of unification of Germany, Korea, and Viet-Nam, which is associated to a certain degree with the territorial question. In the postwar period each of these countries was divided into two states with different social systems. The desire of the peoples of these countries for unification should be treated, of course, with understanding and respect.

It goes without saying, however, that the matter of reunification should be settled by the peoples of these countries and their governments themselves, without any interference or pressure from the outside and certainly without foreign military intervention—occupation, as is actually the case, for instance, in South Korea and South Viet-Nam.

No force should be used in settling this matter, and the peoples of these countries should be given an opportunity to solve the problems of unification by peaceful means. All other states should contribute to this.

But this is not the question we are examining here. The

[28] Text of Declaration, embodied in Resolution 1514 (XV), December 14, 1960, in same, *1960*, pp. 575-577.

question before us is how to deal with territorial disputes and claims which arise over the presently existing well-established frontiers of states. Let us have a look, first of all, into the nature of these disputes and claims.

A special class among such claims are the demands of the revenge-seeking circles of certain states which were the aggressors in the Second World War. These circles craving revenge for the lost war are harboring plans for a revision of the just postwar territorial settlement. In the first place they want to get hold of those territories which went to other states by way of eliminating the consequences of the aggression and providing guarantees of security for the future. Such territorial "claims" must be resolutely rejected as incompatible with the interests of peace, because nothing but a new world war may grow out of these claims.

There exist, however, other territorial claims and border disputes, and they are perhaps the most numerous. These disputes have nothing to do with the postwar settlement. To justify their claims the parties to these disputes advance arguments and considerations relating to history, ethnography, blood affinity, religion and so forth.

It often happens that one state justifies by such arguments its territorial claim to another state, and the latter in turn finds other arguments of the same kind but of an absolutely opposed nature, and itself advances a territorial counterclaim. The result is the kindling of passions and deepening of mutual strife.

How can one tell which side is right, whose position is just and whose unjust? In some cases this is very difficult because the existing borders came into being as a result of the influence of many factors.

* * *

Occasionally it is difficult to get one's bearings among numerous "arguments" based on national, ethnographic, or blood affinity grounds. The development of mankind was such that some peoples are now living on the territories of several states. On the other hand there exist states of the multinational type inhabited sometimes by dozens of peoples belonging even to different races.

Unfortunately, disputes about borders take place not only between historians and ethnographers but also between states each of which possesses armed forces and quite big ones sometimes. Life shows that the majority of territorial disputes are fraught with the danger of complication of relations between the parties, with the possibility of a serious armed conflict, and consequently constitute a potential threat to universal peace. This means that one has to display due understanding of boundaries as they have been formed in the course of history.

* * *

I believe you would agree with me that especially dangerous to all humanity would be an armed conflict over borders in the area of the world where both World Wars started in the past and where at the present time are concentrated great masses of troops and armaments of states belonging to the two principal antagonistic military groupings. Europe is such an area—this is undeniable.

Undoubtedly if a world thermonuclear war breaks out over a local clash of states striving to settle their territorial disputes by armed forces, it will spare no one. No one would be able to shun it. No one except madmen or political figures blinded by hatred can resign themselves to such a prospect.

* * *

It is our deep conviction that the use of force for the solution of territorial disputes is not in the interest of any people or any country. It is not in the interest of the European peoples inhabiting countries where almost every inch of soil is drenched with blood shed in past wars. It is not to plunge headlong into fateful military adventures for the sake of seizing a strip of land from their neighbors that these peoples by their labor created their economy, built factories and mills, plowed land.

And is it not dangerous for the peoples of Asia to use force for the purposes of revising the state borders existing in this part of the world? Of course they don't need that. Is it not a fact that the border conflicts existing between some states of Asia even now have a most adverse effect on their life?

* * *

The question of frontiers between African states is a very complicated and knotty question they inherited from colonialism. But despite the complexity of territorial problems the summit conference of African states, in its charter of the Organization of African Unity adopted in May 1963,[29] unanimously stressed the impermissibility of settling territorial differences and disputes

[29] English text of charter and resolutions in *Current Notes on International Affairs,* August 1963, pp. 12-26.

between African states by force and the necessity of resolving such questions exclusively by peaceful means.

* * *

And what about Latin America? To this day some of the Latin American countries are unable to recover from the consequences of military clashes caused by territorial disputes which occurred in the past. Suffice it to recall the war between Paraguay and neighboring countries at the end of the 19th century, in which so much blood was spilled that the population of Paraguay is still smaller than before this war. Is it worth it for the Latin American countries to sharpen knives against each other in our days, when there is so much they yet have to do at home?

* * *

One may ask—and I reckon this question has already come to your mind—is it that the Soviet Union proposes to cross out with one stroke all territorial issues between states, to abandon all attempts to settle them, as if these issues do not exist at all? No, this is not the point. We realize that some countries have weighty reasons for their claims. In all current frontier disputes between states the sides must of course study the matter thoroughly in order to settle these issues. We are wholly for this. The only thing we are against are the military methods of solving territorial disputes. This is what we should agree upon, precisely upon this.

As for peaceful means of settling territorial disputes, experience proves them to be feasible. Even the existence of different social systems and forms of state power in the modern world need not be an obstacle to peaceful solution of territorial problems, provided of course it is sincerely desired by both sides. Life shows that whenever states firmly abide by the principles of peaceful coexistence and display good will, restraint, and due regard for each other's interests, they are quite capable of extricating themselves from the maze of historical, national, geographical, and other factors and finding a satisfactory solution.

* * *

A peaceful settlement of territorial disputes is also favored by the fact that in the practice of international relations there already exists a store of improved methods of peaceful settlement of outstanding issues—direct negotiations between the states concerned, use of good offices, request of assistance from international organizations, etc. Although in my opinion the United Nations in its present form is far from being an ideal instrument of peaceful cooperation of states, even this organization, granted an impartial approach, can make a positive contribution to the cause of peaceful settlement of territorial and border issues.

Considering this, the Soviet Government, guided by the interests of strengthening peace and preventing war, is submitting the following proposal to the consideration of the governments of all states: to conclude an international agreement—or treaty—on the renunciation by states of the use of force for the solution of territorial disputes or questions of frontiers. In our opinion such an agreement should include the following principal propositions:

First, a solemn undertaking by the states that are parties to the agreement not to resort to force to alter existing state frontiers,

Second, recognition that the territory of states should not even temporarily be the object of any invasion, attack, military occupation, or any other forcible measure directly or indirectly undertaken by other states for whatever political, economic, strategic, frontier, or any other considerations,

Third, a firm declaration that neither differences in social or political systems, nor denial of recognition or the absence of diplomatic relations, nor any other pretexts can serve as a justification for the violation by one state of the territorial integrity of another,

Four, an undertaking to settle all territorial disputes exclusively by peaceful means, such as negotiations, mediation, conciliatory procedures, and also other peaceful means at the option of the parties concerned in accordance with the U.N. Charter.

Needless to say, such an international agreement should cover all territorial disputes concerning the existing borders between states. The proposed agreement would be a confirmation, specification, and development of the principles of the U.N. Charter concerning the relations between states on territorial matters, an expression of good will and the determination of states firmly to abide by these principles.

The Soviet Government is deeply convinced that the undertaking by states to settle territorial disputes by peaceful means only would go a long way toward putting international relations in order. Conclusion of an international agreement by states renouncing the use of force for the solution of territorial disputes would dispel like a fresh wind many of the things in international life that are artificially exaggerated and create obstacles to the relaxation of tension in the world and to the consolidation of peace. It would bring about a considerable new improvement of the international climate and create a good basis for greater confidence among states.

* * *

(b) *Reply of President Johnson, January 18, 1964.*[30]

DEAR MR. CHAIRMAN: I welcome the stated objective of your December 31 letter and agree with much of its contents. It is my hope that we can build on these areas of agreement instead of merely emphasizing our well-known disagreements. This Nation is committed to the peaceful unification of Germany in accordance with the will of the people. This Nation, which has fundamental commitments to the Republic of China, has for many years sought the renunciation of force in the Taiwan Strait. This Nation's forces and bases abroad are for collective defense, and in accordance with treaties and agreements with the countries concerned.

Let us emphasize, instead, our agreement on the importance your letter places on preserving and strengthening peace—and on the need to accompany efforts for disarmament with new efforts to remove the causes of friction and to improve the world's machinery for peacefully settling disputes. In this spirit, let us both present new proposals to the Geneva Disarmament Conference[31]—in pursuit of the objectives we have previously identified:

—to prevent the spread of nuclear weapons;
—to end the production of fissionable material for weapons;
—to transfer large amounts of fissionable materials to peaceful purposes;
—to ban all nuclear weapons tests;
—to place limitations on nuclear weapons systems;
—to reduce the risk of war by accident or design;
—to move toward general disarmament.

I am sure you will agree that our task is to work hard and persistently on these and other specific problems and proposals—as you and President Kennedy did on the Test Ban Treaty—instead of confining ourselves to vague declarations of principle that oppose some wars but not all.

Your letter singles out the problem of territorial disputes

[30] White House Press Release, January 20, 1964; text from *Department of State Bulletin,* February 3, 1964, pp. 157-158.
[31] Cf. Documents 36 and 37.

and concludes that "the use of force for the solution of territorial disputes is not in the interest of any people or any country." I agree; moreover, the United States proposes guidlines to implement this principle which are even broader and stronger than your own.

First, all governments or regimes shall abstain from the direct or indirect threat or use of force to change

—international boundaries;
—other territorial or administrative demarcation or dividing lines established or confirmed by international agreement or practice;
—the dispositions of truce or military armistice agreements; or
—arrangements or procedures concerning access to, passage across or the administration of those areas where international agreement or practice has established or confirmed such arrangements or procedures.

Nor shall any government or regime use or threaten force to enlarge the territory under its control or administration by overthrowing or displacing established authorities.

Second, these limitations shall apply regardless of the direct or indirect form which such threat or use of force might take, whether in the form of aggression, subversion, or clandestine supply of arms; regardless of what justification or purpose is advanced; and regardless of any question of recognition, diplomatic relations, or differences of political systems.

Third, the parties to any serious dispute, in adhering to these principles, shall seek a solution by peaceful means—resorting to negotiation, mediation, conciliation, arbitration, judicial settlement, action by a regional or appropriate United Nations agency or other peaceful means of their own choice.

Fourth, these obligations, if they are to continue, would have to be quite generally observed. Any departure would require reappraisal; and the inherent right of self-defense which is recognized in Article 51 of the United Nations Charter would, in any event, remain fully operative.

You will note the basic similarities in our position. Agreement should not be impossible on this or other propositions—and I share your hope that such agreement will stimulate disarmament and peaceful relations.

The prevention of wars over territorial and other disputes requires not only general principles but also the "growth and improvement" to which you refer regarding the machinery and methods for peaceful settlement. The United States believes that the peace-keeping processes of the United Nations—and specifically its Security Council—should be more fully used and strengthened and that the special responsibilities and contributions of the larger countries—particularly the permanent members of the Security Council—deserve greater attention in solving its financial problems.

In consultation with our allies, we shall offer specific proposals along these lines in the weeks ahead. Both the Geneva Disarmament Conference and the United Nations are appropriate places for such discussions.

Mr. Chairman, let me assure you that practical progress toward peace is my most fervent desire. This requires, not only agreements in principle but also concrete actions in accord with those principles. I believe this exchange of letters offers real hope for that kind of progress—and that hope is shared by all peace-loving men in every land.

(36) *Message of President Johnson to the Conference of the Eighteen-Nation Committee on Disarmament, January 21, 1964.*[32]

There is only one item on the agenda of this Conference—it is the leading item on the agenda of mankind—and that one item is peace.

Already this Conference has led to more concrete and effective results than any disarmament Conference in modern history. Your efforts and deliberations laid the groundwork for the nuclear test ban treaty[33]—for the communications link between Washington and Moscow[34]—and for the UN General Assembly action against nuclear weapons in space.[35]

Today your search begins anew in a climate of hope. Last year's genuine gains have given us new momentum. Recent Soviet and American announcements of reduction in military

[32] White House Press Release, January 21, 1964; text from *Department of State Bulletin,* February 10, 1964, pp. 224-225. For discussion see *The United States in World Affairs, 1964,* pp. 103-109. As Conference Document ENDC/120, President Johnson's message is also included, together with many additional documents, in *Report of the Conference of the Eighteen-Nation Committee on Disarmament,* A/5731 (DC/209), September 22, 1964. The Eighteen-Nation Disarmament Committee's two sessions in 1964 were held from January 21 to April 8 and June 9 to September 17.
[33] Same as note 17 to Document 32c.
[34] Same as note 18 to Document 32c.
[35] Same as note 27 to Document 35.

spending, even though modest, have brightened the atmosphere further. Let us pray that the tide has turned—that further and more far-reaching agreements lie ahead—and that future generations will mark 1964 as the year the world turned for all time away from the horrors of war and constructed new bulwarks of peace.

Specifically, this nation now proposes five major types of potential agreement:

1) *First,* as Chairman Khrushchev and I have observed, the use of force for the solution of territorial disputes is not in the interest of any people or country.[36] In consultation with our allies, we will be prepared to discuss means of prohibiting the threat or use of force, directly or indirectly—whether by aggression, subversion, or the clandestine supply of arms—to change boundaries or demarcation lines; to interfere with access to territory; or to extend control or administration over territory by displacing established authorities.

2) *Second,* while we continue our efforts to achieve general and complete disarmament under effective international control, we must first endeavor to halt further increases in strategic armaments now. The United States, the Soviet Union and their respective allies should agree to explore a verified freeze of the number and characteristics of strategic nuclear offensive and defensive vehicles. For our part, we are convinced that the security of all nations can be safeguarded within the scope of such an agreement and that this initial measure preventing the further expansion of the deadly and costly arms race will open the path to reductions in all types of forces from present levels.

3) *Third,* in this same spirit of early action, the United States believes that a verified agreement to halt all production of fissionable materials for weapons use would be a major contribution to world peace. Moreover, while we seek agreement on this measure, the US is willing to achieve prompt reductions through both sides closing comparable production facilities on a plant by plant basis, with mutual inspection. We have started in this direction—we hope the Soviet Union will do the same—and we are prepared to accept appropriate international verification of the reactor shut-down already scheduled in our country.

4) *Fourth,* we must further reduce the danger of war by accident, miscalculation or surprise attack. In consultation with

[36] Document 35.

our allies, we will be prepared to discuss proposals for creating a system of observation posts as a move in this direction.

5) *Fifth,* and finally, to stop the spread of nuclear weapons to nations not now controlling them, let us agree:

(a) that nuclear weapons not be transferred into the national control of states which do not now control them, and that all transfers of nuclear materials for peaceful purposes take place under effective international safeguards;

(b) that the major nuclear powers accept in an increasing number of their peaceful nuclear activities the same inspection they recommend for other states; and

(c) on the banning of all nuclear weapons tests under effective verification and control.

Each of these proposed steps is important to peace. No one of them is impossible of agreement. The best way to begin disarming is to begin—and the United States is ready to conclude firm agreements in these areas and to consider any other reasonable proposal. We shall at all times pursue a just and lasting peace—and with God's help, we shall achieve it.

(37) *Memorandum on Measures for Slowing Down the Arms Race and Relaxing International Tension, Submitted to the Conference of the Eighteen-Nation Committee on Disarmament by the U.S.S.R., January 28, 1964.*[37]

As a result of the joint efforts of all men of good will, it has been possible to achieve a certain relaxation of international tension; this has been reflected in the conclusion of a treaty on the prohibition of nuclear weapon tests in the atmosphere, in outer space and under water [38] and in an agreement not to place in orbit objects carrying nuclear weapons.[39]

The Soviet Government considers that more favourable conditions have now been created for agreeing upon and carrying out other measures aimed at a further relaxation of international tension. If the efforts of all governments and peoples are united in the cause of peace, 1964 may become a turning point towards an improvement in the whole international situation.

The Soviet Government, which considers that the main task of governments is to achieve the speediest possible agreement on general and complete disarmament, at the same time proposes

[37] Conference Document ENDC/123, January 28, 1964 (annex to U.N. Document A/5731 (DC/209), September 22, 1964).
[38] Same as note 17 to Document 32c.
[39] Same as note 27 to Document 35.

that agreement be reached on the implementation of measures aimed at slowing down the armaments race and further lessening international tension.

1. *Withdrawal of foreign troops from the territories of other countries*

The question of the withdrawal of foreign troops stationed in the territories of other countries to within the boundaries to their national territories is now acquiring particular importance and urgency.

The presence of foreign troops in the territories of other countries is one of the principal sources of international tension and gives rise to conflicts fraught with danger to the cause of the peace and the security of the peoples. As recent events in various parts of the world have shown, the withdrawal of foreign troops from the territories of other countries is becoming increasingly imperative and urgent. Of particularly important significance would be the withdrawal of foreign troops from the territories of European States, where the troops and armaments of the NATO countries, on the one hand, and of the Warsaw Treaty countries, on the other, are concentrated in large numbers.

Agreement on the withdrawal of foreign troops would not cause detriment to either side, since this would not disrupt the general balance of forces between the States belonging to the two groups, namely NATO and the Warsaw Treaty. After all, the military leaders of the NATO countries themselves, to judge by their statements, take as their starting point the assumption that the total number of NATO forces is not less, but is even greater than the number of troops of the Warsaw Treaty countries.

The Soviet Union proposes the most radical way of solving this question, namely, that all foreign troops should be withdrawn from all foreign territories and that not a single foreign soldier should be left anywhere, in any part of the world. On its part, the Soviet Union is prepared to withdraw all its troops from the territories of foreign States where they are now stationed, if the Western Powers will do likewise. If, however, the Western Powers are not as yet prepared for such a radical solution of this important question, the Soviet Government proposes that agreement be reached immediately that the number of armed forces in foreign territories should first be reduced on a basis of reciprocity, and afterwards it will be possible to lead up gradually, step by step, to their complete withdrawal to within the boundaries of their national territories. The Soviet Union is prepared to set about such a reduction of its troops in the territory of the German Democratic Republic and other European States, if the Western Powers begin to reduce the number of their troops in the Federal Republic of Germany and other countries.

The implementation of these measures would undoubtedly lead to the normalization of the situation in Europe and would thereby contribute to the strengthening of universal peace.

2. *Reduction of the total numbers of the armed forces of States*

The Soviet Government has always declared itself in favour of the reduction of the armed forces of States, and the Soviet Union has on a number of occasions undertaken a considerable reduction of its army even unilaterally. At the present time, more favourable possibilities have come about for settling this important question on a reciprocal basis, without waiting for the implementation of the programme of general and complete disarmament to begin.

As Mr. N. S. Khrushchev, the Chairman of the Council of Ministers of the USSR, has stated, the Soviet Union has now set about further reducing the number of its armed forces. The Soviet Government is prepared to go in the direction of reducing the numbers of its armed forces still further, if the governments of the Western Powers show willingness to take similar measures.

3. *Reduction of military budgets*

Being anxious to put an end to the unbridled growth of military expenditure which is a heavy burden on the shoulders of the peoples, the Soviet Government has on a number of occasions made proposals for the reduction of military budgets. As is well known, the Soviet Union has recently shown initiative in solving this question by unilaterally reducing its military budget for 1964 by 600 million roubles. It is also known that the United States Government in its turn is taking measures for a certain reduction of its military expenditure. Thus there now exist favourable pre-conditions for agreement on a further reciprocal reduction of military budgets. The Soviet Government proposes that agreement be reached to reduce the military budgets of States by 10 to 15 per cent.

4. *Conclusion of a non-aggression pact between the NATO and the Warsaw Treaty countries*

The Soviet Government considers it essential to agree to conclude a non-aggression pact between the States parties to the Warsaw Treaty and the States members of NATO.[40] The conclusion of such a pact would in no way disrupt the existing balance of forces between the two groups and, at the same time, would introduce into international relations the element of stability and calm which is so much needed.

In the years which have elapsed since the Soviet Government first put forward a proposal for the conclusion of such a pact, this idea has met with the support of statesmen and public figures in many countries. The time has come to discuss this proposal in a businesslike way and to arrive at a mutually acceptable agreement. Moreover, this is called for by the commitments laid down in the joint communiqué of the USSR, the United States and the United Kingdom of 25 July 1963.[41] The Soviet Government reaffirms its willingness to conclude a non-aggression pact with the States members of NATO.

With regard to the form that the non-aggression pact should take, the Soviet Government considers that this question can be solved without any particular difficulty.

5. *Establishment of denuclearized zones*

The Soviet Government attaches great importance to the establishment of denuclearized zones in various parts of the world. This idea has met with universal response and approval during recent years. Proposals have been put forward for the establishment of denuclearized zones in Central and Northern Europe, in the Mediterranean, in the Balkans, in Africa and Latin America, as well as in other regions of the world.

In supporting the plans for the establishment of denuclearized zones in various regions of the world, the Soviet Government attaches special importance to the formation of such zones in those regions where the danger of nuclear conflict is greatest, and first and foremost in Central Europe.

The Soviet Government, on its part, will be prepared to give an undertaking to respect the status of denuclearized zones wherever and whenever they are established.

[40] Cf. *Documents, 1963,* pp. 95-97.
[41] Same, pp. 129-130.

6. *Prevention of the further spread of nuclear weapons*

As the stocks of nuclear weapons increase, and the methods of manufacturing them are improved, and as ever new types of such weapons are being devised, the question of preventing their further dissemination becomes increasingly important. A widening of the circle of States possessing nuclear weapons would increase many times over the danger of the outbreak of a thermonuclear war. At the same time a widening of the circle of nuclear States would also make it much more difficult to solve the problem of disarmament.

The Soviet Government notes that at present there is an increasing awareness throughout the world of the danger threatening mankind in connexion with the further spread of nuclear weapons. It is the duty of all governments to make every effort to avert this danger before it is too late. It is particularly important from the point of view of the interests of peace to close all the channels, whether direct or indirect, through which nuclear weapons could come into the hands of those who twice during this century have caused the conflagration of a world war and who are now actively striving to obtain nuclear weapons.

In order to shut off all possibilities for the spread of nuclear weapons, the Soviet Government proposes that an agreement on this question should contain, besides the prohibition to transfer such weapons or to give information on their manufacture to any particular government, also provisions to guarantee that such a transfer of nuclear weapons or access to them shall not take place indirectly, through military blocs, for example, through the so-called multilateral nuclear force of NATO.

7. *Measures to prevent surprise attack*

The Soviet Government has declared itself and continues to declare itself in favour of taking active and effective measures to prevent surprise attack. As is well known, for this purpose the Soviet Union put forward a proposal for the establishment of a network of observation posts in the territories of the countries belonging to the two opposing groups of States in conjunction with certain measures for lessening international tension such as a reduction in the numbers of foreign troops in the territories of European countries and an undertaking not to station nuclear weapons in the German Democratic Republic and the Federal Republic of Germany.

The Soviet Government considers that, if unaccompanied by these concrete measures for the lessening of international tension and the limitation of armaments, the establishment of observation posts could not lead to the achievement of the desired aim, namely, the growth of confidence between States, and thereby a lessening of the danger of war. On the contrary, it might even lead to an increase of mutual suspicions and to the aggravation of international relations.

The establishment of a system of observation posts may prove to be useful only in conjunction with concrete measures for reducing the threat of war. Practical steps for a real lessening of the possibility of an outbreak of military conflict in Europe and observation posts would in that case be two complementary aspects of a single process—the lessening of tension in the danger zones where the armed forces of the two opposing groups face each other.

8. *Elimination of bomber aircraft*

Bomber aircraft, though obsolete, still remain one of the powerful means of carrying on a war of aggression, used to deliver nuclear weapons many thousands of kilometres from their bases in order to inflict massive blows in the territories of other States. The elimination of this type of armament would diminish the risk of war and help to strengthen the security of all peoples. The Soviet Government is prepared to examine this question.

9. *Prohibition of underground nuclear tests*

The Soviet Government declares its readiness, as before, to reach agreement on extending the treaty banning nuclear weapons tests in the atmosphere, in outer space and under water, to underground testing.

Actual experience has fully confirmed that no special international control need be organized to detect underground tests any more than it is needed to detect tests in the atmosphere, outer space, and under water.

The Soviet Government assumes, of course, that in concluding agreements providing for measures of actual disarmament, agreement must be achieved on appropriate, mutually acceptable forms of control over the implementation of these measures.

In the opinion of the Soviet Government, the implementation

of the measures enumerated in this Memorandum would lead to a further considerable lessening of international tension and would constitute an important step forward towards solving the main problem—general and complete disarmament.

(38) *Memorandum of the Polish People's Republic on the Freezing of Nuclear and Thermonuclear Armaments in Central Europe, Made Public in Warsaw, March 5, 1964.*[42]

The Government of the Polish People's Republic has already on numerous occasions manifested its consistent desire in the search for solutions aimed at bringing about international détente and disarmament and lent its support to all constructive proposals designed to achieve this end. The reduction of international tension and creation of conditions of security in Central Europe have always been and continue to be matters of particular concern to the Polish Government. This objective can and should be achieved above all by way of arresting the armaments race in this part of the world.

With this in mind the Government of the Polish People's Republic presented some time ago a plan for the creation of a nuclear-free zone in Europe [43] which as is known aroused the interest of numerous states and of world public opinion. In the view of the Polish Government that plan continues to be fully topical.

The Polish Government believes that there are at the present time suitable conditions for undertaking immediate measures the implementation of which could facilitate further steps leading to a détente, to a strengthening of security and to progress in the field of disarmament.

Basing itself on these premises the Government of the Polish People's Republic is submitting a proposal to freeze nuclear and thermonuclear armaments in Central Europe. The implementation of such a proposal would be of particular significance to the security both of Poland and of all countries of this region as well as of the whole of Europe, since, while in no way affecting the existing relation of forces, it would contribute to the arrest of the nuclear armaments race.

I. The Polish Government proposes that the freezing of nuclear and thermonuclear armaments include in principle the territories of the Polish People's Republic, the Czechoslovak So-

[42] Press Release of the Embassy of the Polish People's Republic, March 6, 1964.

[43] Cf. *Documents, 1958,* pp. 195-199.

cialist Republic, the German Democratic Republic and the Federal Republic of Germany, with the respective territorial waters and air space.

The Government of the Polish People's Republic sees the possibility of extending that area through the accession of other European states.

II. The freeze would apply to all kinds of nuclear and thermonuclear charges, irrespective of the means of their employment and delivery.

III. Parties maintaining armed forces in the area of the proposed freeze of armaments would undertake obligations not to produce, not to introduce or import, not to transfer to other parties in the area or to accept from other parties in the area the aforementioned nuclear and thermonuclear weapons.

IV. To ensure the implementation of those obligations an appropriate system of supervision and safeguards should be established.

The supervision over the implementation of the obligation not to produce nuclear and thermonuclear weapons covered by the freeze would be exercised in plants which are or could be used for such production.

To ensure the implementation of other obligations control would be established to be exercised in accordance with an agreed procedure in proper frontier railway, road, waterway junctions, sea and airports.

The supervision and control could be exercised by mixed commissions composed of representatives of the Warsaw Pact and of the North Atlantic Treaty on a parity basis. Those commissions could be enlarged to include also representatives of other states. The composition, structure and procedure of the control organs will be subject of detailed arrangements.

Parties whose armed forces are stationed in the area of the armaments freeze and which have at their disposal nuclear and thermonuclear weapons would exchange at periodical meetings of their representatives all information and reports indispensable for the implementation of the obligations with regard to the freezing of nuclear and thermonuclear armaments.

V. Provisions relating to the implementation of the proposal submitted above should be embodied in appropriate documents.

The Government of the Polish People's Republic is ready to enter into discussions and negotiations with the interested parties to reach an agreement on the implementation of these objectives.

The Polish Government will give due attention to all constructive suggestions, which would be in accordance with the objectives of the present proposal and would aim at the freezing of armaments in Central Europe.

The Government of the Polish People's Republic expects a favourable attitude to the proposal submitted hereby.

(39) *Statement by William C. Foster, Director, U.S. Arms Control and Disarmament Agency to the Conference of the Eighteen-Nation Committee on Disarmament, September 17, 1964.*[44]

(Excerpt)

* * *

Message from President Johnson

At our first meeting this year I read a message from President Johnson.[45] It began: "There is only one item on the agenda of this Conference—it is the leading item on the agenda of mankind—and that one item is peace." Today I should like to read another message from President Johnson, as follows: [46]

Peace is still the one item on your agenda and the leading item on the agenda of mankind.

Our Conference was formed because nations have learned that peace cannot be assured by military preparedness alone. They have learned that they must work together if our world is to be moved toward lasting peace instead of war.

War is senseless in the world of today when a single nuclear weapon can contain more explosive force than all the bombs dropped in World War II.

War is senseless when nations can inflict devastating damage and incalculable suffering on each other and the rest of the world in the space of an hour.

I pledge the best efforts of which my country is capable to prevent such a war. To this end—to deter aggression—my country is maintaining the most powerful defense force in its peace-time history. But in the world of today, the quest for peace demands much more than military preparedness. It demands the elimination of the causes of war and the building of a firm foundation for peace.

In the quest for peace, this Conference has already played a significant role.

[44] *Department of State Bulletin,* October 12, 1964, pp. 524-527.
[45] Document 36.
[46] Also released as White House Press Release, September 16, 1964.

Already the world is somewhat safer because of the efforts of the nations represented here. The air we breathe is no longer being contaminated by nuclear tests. Nuclear weapons are being kept out of space. Announcements have been made that planned production of fissionable material for nuclear weapons is being limited. Better means of emergency communications exist to help prevent an unintended nuclear exchange. For the first time, friends and adversaries alike have taken steps together to bring the nuclear arms race under control.

Limited as they are, these achievements are cause for some satisfaction. They followed sixteen years of post-war disarmament talks which produced neither agreement nor the basis for agreement.

The year 1961 saw the first steps to build the basis for later agreement. The McCloy-Zorin negotiations produced a Joint Statement of Agreed Principles to guide disarmament deliberations.[47] This was followed by agreement on the framework for this Conference.[48] In my country, a new Arms Control and Disarmament Agency was created to give new impetus toward the goal which we all share.[49] This is a goal which the United States Congress described as "a world which is free from the scourge of war and the dangers and burdens of armaments; in which the use of force has been subordinated to the rule of law; and in which international adjustments to a changing world are achieved peacefully."

This Conference began in [*March 14*] 1962. In that year, your deliberations included three proposals which formed the foundation for the three forward steps taken in 1963—the nuclear test ban treaty,[50] the communications link between Washington and Moscow,[51] and the United Nations resolution against nuclear weapons in space.[52]

The year 1964 has witnessed announcements by my country, the Soviet Union and the United Kingdom that the planned production of fissionable material for nuclear weapons would be limited.[53]

This year also brought more concrete proposals for safeguarded and realistic agreements than any other year since before World War II. These proposals have included urgently needed steps to prevent the spread of nuclear weapons. They have included measures to cease the production of fissionable materials for nuclear weapons and to freeze the numbers and characteristics of strategic delivery systems. They have included plans to decrease the danger of war by accident, miscalculation or surprise attack.

This year has not witnessed agreement on any of these proposals.

[47] *Documents,* 1961, pp. 200-205.
[48] Cf. *Documents, 1962,* pp. 68-69.
[49] Public Law 87-297, approved September 26, 1961.
[50] Same as note 17 to Document 32c.
[51] Same as note 18 to Document 32c.
[52] Same as note 27 to Document 35.
[53] *Further Documents Relating to the Conference of the Eighteen-Nation Committee on Disarmament,* cited, pp. 22-25; see also Document 6.

We hope that, like 1961 and 1962, it has witnessed the groundwork being laid for the agreements of the future.

The road to peace is not an easy one. The concrete gains so far achieved required long and diligent effort. So will the accomplishments of tomorrow.

As you recess temporarily your deliberations in Geneva, let each nation represented here resolve to continue at home its consideration of the proposals made at this Conference. Let each nation use this time for reflection. Let each nation return to the reconvened conference prepared to take additional steps toward peace.

Let us all contribute to building a safer tomorrow.

I ask that that message from President Johnson be circulated for the information of the Conference.

Conference's Role in Quest for Peace

Now let me call the attention of members of the Committee to President Johnson's remark that this Conference has already played a significant role in the quest for peace. My Government has long believed that this Conference is an extremely useful forum for the exchange of views and the conduct of negotiations. As I have probably said to many of you, if it did not exist we should have to create something like it.

During the first 2 years of our Conference differences over the manner of achieving disarmament became increasingly apparent. Those differences arose over the need to provide balance, verification, and peacekeeping machinery. All three points featured in our consideration of nuclear delivery vehicles this year, and, in spite of this year's passage, we do not seem closer to our goal. Yet the exchange of views has at least clarified the differences.

The radical reduction in strategic armaments which the Soviet Union has proposed for the first stage of disarmament would be decidedly in its favor. It would upset the present balance and create more danger than it eliminated. No nation can be expected to risk war in order to achieve disarmament. There is no safe short-cut to the millennium.

We must recognize the facts of the present, establish goals for the future, and move toward those goals in a step-by-step, evolutionary process. That is the approach of the United States plan for disarmament. That is also our approach to collateral measures.

The sharp disagreements over methods of achieving disarmament led the Conference this year to focusing greater attention on collateral measures. The United States presented proposals to the Conference which were intended to reduce the area of disagreement on all three main points of disagreement—balance, verification, and peacekeeping. We designed those proposals so that they would not disrupt the present rough balance between the two sides. We designed them so that effective verification could be provided without as much inspection as that required for general disarmament. We designed them so that their adoption would not produce an immediate requirement for a significant strengthening of present institutions for keeping the peace.

By planning our proposals to reduce the areas of difference on each of the three points of disagreement, we hoped to make them more acceptable to all concerned. Moreover, by focusing on methods to halt the nuclear arms race and turn it around, we hoped to find the easiest way to lay a foundation for disarmament.

We proposed a freeze on strategic delivery vehicles for nuclear weapons.[54] To begin the actual disarmament process, we suggested the mutual destruction of substantial numbers of B–47 and TU–16 bombers.[55]

We proposed a cutoff in the production of material for use in nuclear weapons.[56] To reduce the stocks of those explosives available for weapons, we suggested the transfer of large quantities of such material to peaceful purposes.

To halt the spread of nuclear weapons to nations not now controlling them, we called for agreement on four additional steps: [57]

(1) that nuclear weapons should not be transferred into the national control of nations which do not now possess them;

(2) that all transfers of nuclear materials for peaceful purposes should take place under IAEA [International Atomic Energy Agency] or similar safeguards;

(3) that major nuclear powers should accept in an increasing number of their peaceful activities the same safeguards as those they recommend for nonnuclear powers; and

(4) that an effectively verified ban should be placed on all nuclear tests—those underground as well as those above ground.

Finally, we suggested measures which would help to reduce

[54] *Department of State Bulletin,* March 2, 1964, pp. 350-352; same, May 11, 1964, pp. 756-759; same, September 21, 1964, pp. 413-417.

[55] Statement of March 19, 1964 in *Department of State Bulletin,* April 20, 1964, pp. 643-645.

[56] Conference Document ENDC/134, submitted June 25, 1964 (annex to U.N. Document A/5731 (DC/209), September 22, 1964).

[57] *Department of State Bulletin,* March 9, 1964, pp. 376-379; same. April 20, 1964, pp. 641-643.

the risk of war, increase the peaceful settlement of international disputes, and improve the ability of the United Nations to mobilize peace forces for coping with limited conflicts.

Comprehensive Test Ban

Having summarized the proposals made by my country this year, I should like to comment briefly on the joint memorandum which relates to one of them—the eight-nation memorandum on a treaty banning all nuclear weapon tests.[58]

We have long urged a comprehensive test ban to help prevent the spread of nuclear weapons to countries that do not now possess them. Our support for such a ban was reaffirmed by President Johnson in his message to the Conference of 21 January 1964. It was reiterated by my delegation as recently as 8 September, at our 214th meeting.

We read the joint memorandum as proposing an agreement to ban all nuclear tests—an agreement which would provide verification satisfactory to both sides. The United States is, of course, not willing to accept a prohibition on all its tests unless it can have adequate assurance that the other side is actually adhering to the same restraint.

The joint memorandum proposes an exchange of scientific and other information between nuclear powers. My delegation has repeatedly suggested that if the Soviet Union has information on how to detect and identify all underground events by using distant instrumentation it should supply that information to other governments. As far as my Government is concerned, it will gladly cooperate in an exchange which will give each side information available to the other on techniques for detection and identification of underground tests.

The joint memorandum also suggests improvement of detection and identification techniques, if necessary. Because my Government has long believed that such improvement is necessary, we are continuing to carry out an extensive research program for this purpose.

The joint memorandum reflects the sincere desire of the eight nations to hasten the achievement of a comprehensive test ban. That desire is shared by my nation and, I believe, by most of the nations of the world. We believe the memorandum to be a most useful contribution to this Conference, another among the significant contributions made by the eight nations.

[58] Conference Document ENDC/145, September 14, 1964 (annex to U.N. Document A/5731 (DC/209), September 22, 1964).

The main reason for the adoption of a comprehensive test ban is to erect a further obstacle to the spread of nuclear weapons to countries that do not now possess them. That is an interest which we all share. One of our foremost concerns here is the danger of nuclear war. Think for a moment how that danger would be increased if 5, 10, or even 20 nations had nuclear weapons. Every increase in the number of nations having nuclear weapon capabilities multiplies the chances of an accidental or unintentional nuclear exchange—an exchange the effects of which would, as we all know, not be limited to the nuclear powers.

That is why, out of all the proposals referred to by President Johnson in the message I have just read, he placed in the "urgently needed" category steps to prevent the spread of nuclear weapons. That is why, in a speech which he made yesterday in Seattle, Washington,[59] he said that our work against nuclear spread must go on. That is why my delegation has laid so much stress on nonproliferation this year; and that is why I hope we shall make early progress on nonproliferation when we meet again.

* * *

[59] Document 9b.

CHAPTER FIVE

COMMUNIST CHINA AND THE FAR EAST

A. The Sino-Soviet Conflict and the West.[1]

(40) *Problems in East Asia: Address by Assistant Secretary of State for Far Eastern Affairs William P. Bundy, Tokyo, September 29, 1964.*[2]

(Excerpts)

* * *

Communist China's foreign policy is fashioned by men whose whole life has been one of struggle, who are thoroughly wedded to a fundamentalist concept of communism, who have grown rigid and intransigent even in the face of overwhelming proof that the 19th-century doctrines of Karl Marx are hopelessly inadequate to meet the 20th-century problems of China. Monumentally convinced of the correctness of their position, they view all who disagree with them, including even the Russians, as old and bad and decadent. Neutralists are tolerated only to the extent that they are moving in the direction desired by Peiping.

I do not claim to know what their precise goals are. Are these goals to be defined in territorial terms, and, if so, what territories? Or could their goals be better described in terms of their quest for power and status and of gaining control and influence over other nations? Or are their goals directed more at exploiting the divisions and the difficulties of the countries of the free world, especially those in bordering areas? I suspect that all these and other elements are involved. But in any event the record of Communist China's behavior in recent years—against the offshore islands [*Quemoy and Matsu*], Tibet, and India—should leave us in no doubt of her militant and expansionist outlook.

[1] For discussion see *The United States in World Affairs, 1964,* pp. 110-113.

[2] Department of State Press Release 422, September 29, 1964; text from *Department of State Bulletin,* October 19, 1964, pp. 534-540.

More recently we have evidence in the continuing statements of Chinese Communist leaders, expressed most forcefully in the course of their ideological dispute with the Soviet Union. They say (as in their June 14, 1964 [*sic*], letter to the Soviet Communist Party) that "two-thirds of the world's population need to make revolution." [3] They add that the revolution must be violent: "Violent revolution is a universal law of proletarian revolution. To realize the transition to socialism the proletariat must wage armed struggle, smash the old state machine, and establish the dictatorship of the proletariat."

Now it may be argued that the leaders of Communist China do not really mean all that they say, but I think it is a good rule of thumb to believe most of what dictators say about their intentions.

Finally, we should note that the severest indictments of Chinese Communist bellicosity come from the Soviet Union itself, and, because of the close relationship that until recently marked Moscow-Peiping affairs, the Soviet Union may be in a good position to judge what Communist China is up to.

To say that Communist China is fundamentally militant is not inconsistent with the view that she may be tactically cautious when confronted with major force. Unquestionably our United States strategic and conventional capabilities, supplementing the efforts of free Asian nations, have made Communist China reluctant to embark on the older forms of naked aggression. Instead they prefer what Premier Khrushchev has called "wars of national liberation"—support to guerrillas, training of saboteurs, and the creation of Communist-dominated "national fronts." Fortunately Japan and other countries with internal stability and strength are not susceptible to this type of aggression.

I do not say that this will always be the picture of the policy of the Asian Communist nations. They confront tremendous internal problems. Like Communist countries everywhere they have not yet found the answer to the basic problem of agricultural production, much less of carrying out a true industrial or scientific revolution along the lines on which you in Japan have led the way. If their leaders were reasonable, or even pragmatic, the Communist nations of Asia should recognize that they cannot afford to embark on outside adventures that draw upon resources so urgently needed at home.

Thus we do not rule out the possibility that the passage of time will bring about desirable changes in the outlook of Com-

[3] *Peking Review,* June 21, 1963, p. 6.

munist China, North Korea, and North Viet-Nam. But clearly this cannot come about unless Communist expansionism is deterred and completely frustrated and unless, too, the conduct of all our relationships with Communist China gives her no encouragement that a continued militant course can be accepted.

So long as Peiping, as well as Hanoi and Pyongyang, continue on their present course, I see no basic change in United States policy toward mainland China. It is inconceivable to me that, at a time when Communist China is stridently proclaiming a militant revolutionary thesis and bearing out its threats with actions that undermine the security of nations both in Asia and Africa and even in the Americas, we should relax our guard. It remains the first requirement of our policy to help maintain adequate free-world military strength in order to deter aggression or, where aggression or threats to the peace occur, to be able to cope with such threats effectively. Without such capability to keep the peace, there can be no peace. Nor can there be any real progress in improving the well-being and satisfying the aspirations of the people in Asia. From this general policy there follow a number of specific applications that bear on the relations between Japan and the United States:

1. We believe that the Treaty of Mutual Cooperation and Security [4] concluded between us in 1960 still remains fundamental to our common security. The very fact that we have never needed to invoke the treaty in defense against an attack is proof of its worth. There are those who, for one reason or another, would like to see our defensive arrangements altered or terminated. Admittedly it would be to our advantage if Japan's security could be assured without the enormous drain of money and manpower which the maintenance of our bases here involves. But so long as Japan's Communist neighbors openly proclaim their desire to impose their own economic and political system upon the rest of Asia, our mutual security arrangements would seem essential and the United States will continue to cooperate with the Japanese people in the defense of Japan.

We believe that the presence of our men here gives credibility to our pledge to defend Japan in a way that no mere commitment on paper could achieve. We do not, in short, see any need to alter the fundamental concept of our existing security arrangements until there is real evidence that the threat of aggression has disappeared from the Far East.

2. The importance of Okinawa to the security of East Asia remains unchanged. In his statement of March 1962 President

[4] *Documents, 1960,* pp. 425-431.

Kennedy set forth United States policies for the Ryukyus,[5] which remain unchanged under President Johnson. In that statement, you will recall, President Kennedy reaffirmed the importance the United States attaches to our military bases in the Ryukyus. He went on to say that he recognized the Ryukyus to be a part of the Japanese homeland and looked forward to the day when the security interests of the free world will permit their restoration to full Japanese sovereignty. He then outlined several courses of action to increase the autonomy granted to the Ryukyuan people, to improve their well-being, and to enhance the cooperation of Japan and America in programs of assistance to the islands. Two new joint committees have recently been set up to implement this latter purpose, and it has been made clear that these committees are only a beginning step, not a limiting boundary.[6] I feel confident that the cooperation between Japan and the United States in the Ryukyu Islands will permit the continuance of the essential role of the islands in free-world defense and at the same time will contribute to the welfare of the people and to the solidarity of relations between our two countries.

As you know, our new High Commissioner in the Ryukyus, General [Albert] Watson, was able to visit Japan on his way to take up his post in Okinawa and had highly profitable discussions with the leaders of your Government. We expect to stay in close touch with the Government of Japan on this matter and to continue to work toward the objectives laid down by President Kennedy.

3. We continue to believe that the security of South Korea is essential to the security of Japan. We will continue to support the required level of the Armed Forces of the Republic of Korea, and these, supplemented by our own forces, will be maintained at a level adequate to prevent repetition from any quarter of the attack of 1950. Concurrently, we continue to attach fundamental importance to the economic development and welfare of the Republic of Korea as an integral part of its security and of that of Japan and the United States as well.

4. With regard to your own defense effort here in Japan, our grant military assistance is now naturally drawing to a close and is now represented by our cooperative efforts particularly in the field of air defense and technical equipment for your naval self-defense forces. It is natural and inevitable that Japan should assume the burden of her own defense to an increasing degree,

[5] White House Press Release, March 19, 1962.
[6] *Department of State Bulletin,* May 11, 1964, p. 755.

but at the same time we welcome the continuing consultation made possible by our close and cooperative relationships under the treaty.

5. We recognize the profound implications of the Sino-Soviet rift and the possibility that it may lead to greater tension between the U.S.S.R. and Communist China in the northern regions. But we doubt that the U.S.S.R. has yet abandoned her Communist expansionist aims, and certainly not to the point where in the foreseeable future she could be relied upon to play a constructive role in assisting other nations to defend themselves against Communist China. There may be a long-term hope in this direction, but let us recognize always that the differences between the U.S.S.R. and Communist China are still concerned primarily not with their basic objectives but rather with the degree of violence to be employed to achieve those objectives. And let us recognize too that, to the extent that Soviet policy has changed or may change in the future, this will be in large part due to the fact that we, in partnership with other free-world nations, have maintained a military posture adequate to deter and to defeat any aggressive action.

* * *

Need for Economic and Social Progress

But I do not want to leave the impression that we regard communism as the only major problem facing Asia. Security is fundamental. But economic and social progress remains an equally important need for the welfare of nations and of the individuals who must always be our primary concern.

The headlines in the newspapers today sometimes create the impression that the whole of East Asia is in turmoil. It is true that we face serious problems in Southeast Asia today, but we faced at least equally serious ones 10 years ago after Dien Bien Phu, when the Huks were still active in the Philippines, and the jungle insurgents were in Malaya. Problems and dangers are always with us. They are a fact of life in our rapidly changing world.

Meanwhile, over the past several decades there has been progress in the Far East of a slow, steady, unsensational kind which will, I firmly believe, have far more long-range significance than the problems with which we are so deeply concerned today. In most of the countries of free Asia there has been a notable degree of improvement in what the economists call "human resources" but what I still like to call "people." People are, by and large, healthier. They are better educated. They live longer. Students have far more opportunities for advanced and specialized studies at home and abroad.

Within the last 15 years there have been some remarkable success stories—Japan, the Republic of China, and, despite some remaining weaknesses, the Republic of Korea, the Philippines, Thailand, and even South Viet-Nam in the 1954-59 period.

Undoubtedly, however, Japan has provided the outstanding example of progress during the past 10 years. This progress extends well beyond the material things of life, beyond the economic growth which has surpassed that of any other nation in the postwar era. Japan's progress has also been in the arts, in health, education, and broadening intellectual horizons in all directions.

The United States has ties of friendship, confidence, and mutual interest with many Far Eastern countries but none of which we are prouder and which we cherish more than those with Japan. Our friendship began long before the war, survived the war, and is now almost unique between two great nations of different historical and cultural background.

Inevitably, in view of the breadth of our relations, we have problems. Sometimes United States actions run counter to what Japan considers its best interests. But neither of us, because of this reality of international life, loses sight of the larger picture of our common devotion to a world of freedom under law, of our vast and steadily growing trade, of our vital mutual security ties, and of our proven friendship. I have not the slightest doubt, as I hope that you do not, that the negotiation process, with each side taking account of the other's views, is simply an outward expression of this status.

The Tokyo Olympics, for which you have prepared so well, have focused world attention on Japanese endeavors in still another field. The people of America look forward eagerly to watching telecasts of the Olympics via Syncom III, a triumph of U.S.-Japanese cooperation.

* * *

(41) *Communist China Joins the Nuclear Club.*[7]

(a) *Statement by Secretary of State Rusk, September 29, 1964.*[8]

For some time it has been known that the Chinese Communists were approaching the point where they might be able to detonate a first nuclear device. Such an explosion might occur in the near future. If it does occur, we shall know about it and will make the information public.

It has been known since the 1950's that the Chinese Communists have been working to develop a nuclear device. They not only failed to sign but strongly opposed the nuclear test ban treaty [9] which has been signed by over 100 countries. The detonation of a first device does not mean a stockpile of nuclear weapons and the presence of modern delivery systems. The United States has fully anticipated the possibility of Peiping's entry into the nuclear weapons field and has taken it into full account in determining our military posture and our own nuclear weapons program. We would deplore atmospheric testing in the face of serious efforts made by almost all other nations to protect the atmosphere from further contamination and to begin to put limitations upon a spiraling arms race.

(b) *Statement by the Government of the People's Republic of China, October 16, 1964.*[10]

China exploded an atom bomb at 15:00 hours on October 16, 1964, and thereby conducted successfully its first nuclear test. This is a major achievement of the Chinese people in their struggle to increase their national defence capability and oppose the U.S. imperialist policy of nuclear blackmail and nuclear threats.

To defend oneself is the inalienable right of every sovereign state. And to safeguard world peace is the common task of all peace-loving countries. China cannot remain idle and do nothing in the face of the ever increasing nuclear threat posed by the United States. China is forced to conduct nuclear tests and develop nuclear weapons.

The Chinese Government has consistently advocated the complete prohibition and thorough destruction of nuclear weapons.

[7] For discussion see *The United States in World Affairs, 1964,* pp. 118-121.
[8] Department of State Press Release 423, September 29, 1964; text from *Department of State Bulletin,* October 19, 1964, pp. 542-543.
[9] *Documents, 1963,* pp. 130-132.
[10] *Peking Review,* October 16, 1964, Supplement.

Should this have been realized, China need not develop the nuclear weapon. But this position of ours has met the stubborn resistance of the U.S. imperialists. The Chinese Government pointed out long ago that the treaty on the partial halting of nuclear tests signed by the United States, Britain and the Soviet Union in Moscow in July 1963 was a big fraud to fool the people of the world, that it tried to consolidate the nuclear monopoly held by the three nuclear powers and tie up the hands and feet of all peace-loving countries, and that it not only did not decrease but had increased the nuclear threat of U.S. imperialism against the people of China and of the whole world. The U.S. Government declared undisguisedly even then that the conclusion of such a treaty does not at all mean that the United States would not conduct underground tests, or would not use, manufacture, stockpile, export or proliferate nuclear weapons. The facts of the past year and more fully prove this point.

During the past year and more, the United States has not stopped manufacturing various nuclear weapons on the basis of the nuclear tests which it had already conducted. Furthermore, seeking for ever greater perfection, the United States has during this same period conducted several dozen underground nuclear tests, thereby further perfecting the nuclear weapons it manufactures. In stationing nuclear submarines in Japan, the United States is posing a direct threat to the Japanese people, the Chinese people and the peoples of all other Asian countries. The United States is now putting nuclear weapons into the hands of the West German revanchists through the so-called multilateral nuclear force and thereby threatening the security of the German Democratic Republic and the other East European socialist countries. U.S. submarines carrying Polaris missiles with nuclear warheads are prowling the Taiwan Straits, the Tonkin Gulf, the Mediterranean Sea, the Pacific Ocean, the Indian Ocean and the Atlantic Ocean, threatening everywhere peace-loving countries and all peoples who are fighting against imperialism, colonialism and neo-colonialism. Under such circumstances, how can it be considered that the U.S. nuclear blackmail and nuclear threat against the people of the world no longer exist just because of the false impression created by the temporary halting of atmospheric tests by the United States?

The atom bomb is a paper tiger. This famous saying by Chairman Mao Tse-tung is known to all. This was our view in the past and this is still our view at present. China is developing nuclear weapons not because we believe in the omnipotence of nuclear weapons and that China plans to use nuclear weapons.

The truth is exactly to the contrary. In developing nuclear weapons, China's aim is to break the nuclear monopoly of the nuclear powers and to eliminate nuclear weapons.

The Chinese Government is loyal to Marxism-Leninism and proletarian internationalism. We believe in the people. It is the people who decide the outcome of a war, and not any weapon. The destiny of China is decided by the Chinese people and the destiny of the world by the peoples of the world, and not by the nuclear weapon. The development of nuclear weapons by China is for defence and for protecting the Chinese people from the danger of the United States launching a nuclear war.

The Chinese Government hereby solemnly declares that China will never at any time and under any circumstances be the first to use nuclear weapons.

The Chinese people firmly support the struggles for liberation waged by all oppressed nations and people of the world. We are convinced that, by relying on their own struggles and also through mutual aid, the peoples of the world will certainly win victory. The mastering of the nuclear weapon by China is a great encouragement to the revolutionary peoples of the world in their struggles and a great contribution to the cause of defending world peace. On the question of nuclear weapons, China will neither commit the error of adventurism nor the error of capitulationism. The Chinese people can be trusted.

The Chinese Government fully understands the good wishes of peace-loving countries and people for the halting of all nuclear tests. But more and more countries are coming to realize that the more the U.S. imperialists and their partners hold on to their nuclear monopoly, the more is there danger of a nuclear war breaking out. They have it and you don't, and so they are very haughty. But once those who oppose them also have it, they would no longer be so haughty, their policy of nuclear blackmail and nuclear threat would no longer be so effective, and the possibility for a complete prohibition and thorough destruction of nuclear weapons would increase. We sincerely hope that a nuclear war would never occur. We are convinced that, so long as all peace-loving countries and people of the world make common efforts and persist in the struggle, a nuclear war can be prevented.

The Chinese Government hereby formally proposes to the governments of the world that a summit conference of all the countries of the world be convened to discuss the question of the complete prohibition and thorough destruction of nuclear weapons, and that as a first step, the summit conference should reach an agreement to the effect that the nuclear powers and those countries which may soon become nuclear powers undertake not to use nuclear weapons, neither to use them against non-nuclear countries and nuclear-free zones, nor against each other.

If those countries in possession of huge quantities of nuclear weapons are not even willing to undertake not to use them, how can those countries not yet in possession of them be expected to believe in their sincerity for peace and not to adopt possible and necessary defensive measures?

The Chinese Government will, as always, exert every effort to promote the realization of the noble aim of the complete prohibition and thorough destruction of nuclear weapons through international consultations. Before the advent of such a day, the Chinese Government and people will firmly and unswervingly march along their own road of strengthening their national defences, defending their motherland and safeguarding world peace.

We are convinced that nuclear weapons which are after all created by man, certainly will be eliminated by man.

(c) ***Statement by President Johnson, October 16, 1964.***[11]

The Chinese Communists have announced that they conducted their first nuclear test today. By our own detection system we have confirmed that a low-yield test actually took place in western China at about 3 a.m., e.d.t.

As Secretary Rusk noted on September 29,[12] we have known for some time that the Chinese Communists had a nuclear development program which was approaching the point of a first detonation of a test device.

This explosion comes as no surprise to the United States Government. It has been fully taken into account in planning our own defense program and nuclear capability. Its military significance should not be overestimated. Many years and great efforts separate testing of a first nuclear device from having a stockpile of reliable weapons with effective delivery systems.

Still more basic is the fact that, if and when the Chinese Communists develop nuclear weapons systems, free-world nuclear strength will continue to be enormously greater.

The United States reaffirms its defense commitments in Asia. Even if Communist China should eventually develop an effective nuclear capability, that capability would have no effect upon the readiness of the United States to respond to requests from

[11] White House Press Release, October 16, 1964; text from *Department of State Bulletin,* November 2, 1964, p. 612.
[12] Document 41a.

Asian nations for help in dealing with Communist Chinese aggression. The United States will also not be diverted from its efforts to help the nations of Asia to defend themselves and to advance the welfare of their people.

The Chinese Communist nuclear weapons program is a tragedy for the Chinese people, who have suffered so much under the Communist regime. Scarce economic resources which could have been used to improve the well-being of the Chinese people have been used to produce a crude nuclear device which can only increase the sense of insecurity of the Chinese people. Other Asian nations have wisely chosen instead to work for the well-being of their people through economic development and peaceful use of the atom. In this way they have made a great contribution to the peace and security of the world.

The Chinese Communist nuclear detonation is a reflection of policies which do not serve the cause of peace. But there is no reason to fear that it will lead to immediate dangers of war. The nations of the free world will recognize its limited significance and will persevere in their determination to preserve their independence.

We join all humanity in regretting the contamination of the atmosphere caused by the Chinese Communist test. We will continue in our own efforts to keep the atmosphere clean. We will pursue with dedication and determination our purpose of achieving concrete practical steps on the road that leads away from nuclear armaments and war and toward a world of co-operation, development, and peace.

B. The Republic of China.[13]

(42) *The United States Reaffirms Its Commitments to Taiwan: Statement by Secretary of State Rusk, Taipei, April 16, 1964.*[14]

I greatly welcome this opportunity to visit Taiwan. I bring you warmest greetings from the President of the United States, Lyndon B. Johnson, and the American people.

The United States Government and the American people are associated with you in a Treaty of Mutual Defense.[15] I wish to reaffirm our dedication to the commitments in this treaty, our support of the Republic of China as the Government of China,

[13] For discussion see *The United States in World Affairs, 1964,* pp. 123-127.
[14] *Department of State Bulletin,* May 4, 1964, p. 694.
[15] *Documents, 1954,* pp. 360-364.

and our opposition to any proposal to deprive the Republic of China of its rightful place in the United Nations and to seat the Chinese Communists in its place.

The Communist regime on the mainland of China calls itself revolutionary and boasts of progress, despite the fact that its policies have inflicted terrible setbacks on the people of the mainland. It is the Government and people of the Republic of China who have been carrying out successfully progressive programs which reflect the true revolutionary inheritance of the Three People's Principles of Dr. Sun Yat-sen. These forward-looking programs continue to improve the well-being of the people of the Republic of China.

I salute the resolute will and positive achievement of the Republic of China under the leadership of President Chiang Kai-shek. The American people have always regarded the Chinese people with admiration. We value you as stalwart comrades in the struggle to secure a more prosperous, just, and satisfying life for all free men everywhere, and a peace safe from the threats of aggression. I look forward to discussions with your leaders on the major problems facing free men today. May the friendship and close understanding between our two peoples, as your own phrase puts it, live 10,000 years!

(43) *Redefinition of United States Aid Policies: Department of State Announcement, May 28, 1964.*[16]

Because of the healthy economic growth of the Republic of China on Taiwan, the Agency for International Development is planning to terminate its programs there at the end of the next fiscal year, that is June 1965.

The United States Government notes the interest and willingness of industrial and financial institutions, private money markets, and foreign private investments to provide an increasing flow of development capital to Taiwan.

The United States will continue to encourage this trend. While the AID program in Taiwan will be ended, the United States will continue its military assistance program and the sale of surplus agricultural commodities under P.L. 480, that is the Food for Peace program.[17]

At the same time, the effect of funds committed in prior years to development programs on Taiwan will be felt for several years to come as the development loans are drawn down.

[16] *Department of State Bulletin,* June 15, 1964, p. 934.
[17] Public Law 480, 83rd Cong., approved July 10, 1954.

The United States has shared with the Government of China its gratification over the country's exceptional growth, which has been due to successful accomplishments of an industrious and capable people, making good use of large-scale U.S. assistance.

Since 1953 the country's gross national product has increased at a rate of more than 6 percent per year. Agricultural production has increased 4 percent annually, and industrial production between 10 and 12 percent annually.

Reflecting this outstanding growth, Taiwan's export earnings rose 11 percent in 1962 and 50 percent in 1963. Since 1949 the United States has provided Taiwan with $3.6 billion in military and economic aid. This breaks down to $2.2 billion in military aid, $205 million in Public Law 480 agricultural commodities, and $1.2 billion from AID and predecessor agencies.

For the final year of its program in Taiwan, the AID appropriation request to Congress includes about $500,000 for advisory services in industrial development.

C. The Republic of Korea.[18]

(44) *Joint Communiqué of Secretary of State Rusk and President Park Chung Hee, Seoul, January 29, 1964.*[19]

At the invitation of the Government of the Republic of Korea, Secretary of State Dean Rusk of the United States of America made a visit to the Republic of Korea on January 29, 1964. President Park Chung Hee and Secretary Rusk held cordial discussions on matters of mutual interest including recent international developments and the situation in Korea.

Secretary Rusk expressed appreciation for President Park's act of friendship and sympathy for the American people in their sorrow when he came to Washington to attend the funeral of the late President John Fitzgerald Kennedy. He brought to President Park the personal greetings of President Lyndon Johnson.

President Park and Secretary Rusk discussed the implications of the recognition of Communist China by France for the security of free-world countries in the Pacific area.[20]

President Park explained the current status of the negotiations with the Government of Japan. The two agreed that early completion of these negotiations would be of significant benefit to

[18] For discussion see *The United States in World Affairs, 1964,* pp. 128-131.
[19] Department of State Press Release 41, February 4, 1964; text from *Department of State Bulletin,* February 17, 1964, pp. 238-239.
[20] For State Department statement on the French decision to recognize Communist China see same, p. 260.

Korea, to Japan and to general free-world interests. The Secretary assured the President that the basic policy of United States military and economic assistance to the Republic of Korea would not be affected by normalization of relations between Korea and Japan.

Arrangements to ensure the continued defense of the Republic of Korea against Communist aggression were also discussed. It was agreed that powerful Korean and U.S. forces adequate to the defense of the Republic of Korea would be maintained in order to meet the continuing Communist menace in the Far East.

It was agreed that the Republic of Korea was making good progress toward economic independence but would continue to require economic aid for the further development of the Korean economy. It was also agreed that it is important to stabilize the national economy and to make the best possible uses of all the resources available.

They also noted that the status-of-forces negotiations have made good progress, and were confident that progress would continue to achieve earliest possible agreement.

President Park and Secretary Rusk reaffirmed the friendship between the two countries and pledged themselves to continued cooperation in the economic, monetary, and political fields.

At the same time other high United States and Korean officials met together in several separate meetings to discuss activities of common interest: Secretary of Commerce Luther H. Hodges with Minister of Commerce and Industry Lee Pyong-ho and Minister of Transportation Kim Yun-ki; Secretary of Labor W. Willard Wirtz with Minister of Health and Social Affairs Park Chu-pyong; Chairman of the Council of Economic Advisers Walter W. Heller with Deputy Prime Minister Kim Yu-taek, Finance Minister Park Dong-kyu and the Governor of the Bank of Korea Kim Se-yon; and Under Secretary of the Interior James K. Carr and Under Secretary of Agriculture Charles S. Murphy with Minister of Agriculture and Forestry Won Yong-sok. These meetings were of great benefit in developing a closer understanding between the two Governments.

D. Japan.[21]

(45) *Communiqué of the Third Meeting of the Joint United States-Japan Committee on Trade and Economic Affairs, Tokyo, January 28, 1964.*[22]

I

The Third Meeting of the Joint United States—Japan Committee on Trade and Economic Affairs was held at Tokyo on January 27 and 28, 1964 under the chairmanship of the Minister of Foreign Affairs, Masayoshi Ohira.

At the outset of its deliberations, the committee recalled the tragic death of President John F. Kennedy which necessitated the delay in convening the present meeting. Secretary of State Rusk, after expressing the United States Delegation's deep appreciation for the sympathy and support of the Japanese Government and people, stated that President Lyndon B. Johnson's administration would continue to promote the increasingly close partnership which had developed between the two countries under the leadership of Prime Minister [*Hayato*] Ikeda and the late President Kennedy.

The meeting was characterized throughout by a recognition on the part of the committee members that developments in world affairs now demand that the interests and concerns of both countries in trade and economic matters be considered from a global perspective.

II

After a general review of the world situation in the light of its bearing on trade and economic relations between Japan and the United States, the two delegations had a lively exchange of views on a wide range of subjects. A high degree of mutual understanding was reached on the points which follow:

1. On the basis of the satisfactory economic momentum achieved in both countries in 1963 and the policies in prospect for 1964, the committee looked forward to 1964 as a record year for U.S.–Japan economic exchanges. In view of the fact that any major change in the economic policy or level of business activity of one country may affect the economy of the other, the com-

[21] For discussion see *The United States in World Affairs, 1964,* pp. 131-135.
[22] Department of State Press Release 29, January 29, 1964; text from *Department of State Bulletin,* February 17, 1964, pp. 235-238.

mittee reaffirmed its agreement that the Japanese and U.S. Governments should exchange information as early and in as much detail as possible on their economic prospects and programs.

2. In both countries, the balance of payments is a matter of basic economic concern. The United States Delegation pointed to the marked reduction in the U.S. payments deficit after the first half of 1963 and expressed again the determination of the United States Government to restore equilibrium in its external accounts, and to do so in a manner consistent with its international obligations. The Japanese Delegation, for its part, expressed serious concern over the effects of the proposed interest equalization tax [23] on Japan's balance of payments and reiterated the position of the Japanese Government that Japan should be exempted from the application of the proposed tax. After full discussion, it was reaffirmed that, in the words of the August 2 communique,[24] "if contrary to U.S. expectations, serious economic difficulties were to arise in Japan, the United States would consider appropriate measures that might then be taken to meet the problem, including some form of exemption from the proposed interest equalization tax for new issues of securities."

3. The volume of commodity trade between Japan and the United States which reached a record level of more than $3 billion in 1963, is important to employment and to living standards in both countries

In this context, the two delegations pointed out that from time to time there are moves for restrictive measures against trade both in the United States and in Japan and expressed the hope that the governments would deal judiciously with them.

The committee noted that as trade in large volume continues to flourish between the two countries, difficulties are likely to arise. It was agreed that it is the task of both governments to keep in perspective such problems as may arise so that in seeking to meet particular difficulties, care will be exercised to preserve harmonious relations between Japan and the United States which are fundamental to a continued healthy growth of trade. It was emphasized that solutions satisfactory to both countries on many of these problems can be expedited through greater mutual understanding of the respective situations in the two countries.

[23] Public Law 88-563, approved September 2, 1964.
[24] Not reproduced here.

4. The committee exchanged views on matters pertaining to transportation and tourism between the two countries.

5. The importance of close cooperation between Japan and the United States in international economic affairs was emphasized.

A. The two delegations stressed the vital importance of the forthcoming sixth or Kennedy round [25] of tariff negotiations at Geneva for the reduction of tariffs and other impediments which now restrict world trade. It was agreed that the two countries would maintain close contact in Geneva and in their respective capitals to study the possibilities of achieving the maximum practicable reduction of both tariff and non-tariff barriers on both industrial and agricultural products on a fully non-discriminatory basis.

B. With regard to the United Nations Conference on Trade and Development which will convene in Geneva in March,[26] it was agreed that the United States and Japanese delegations would cooperate in promoting practicable ways to increase the export earnings of the developing countries. Concerning the institutional questions likely to [*a*]rise at the conference, the committee reaffirmed the conviction of both countries that the General Agreement on Tariffs and Trade (GATT) is an indispensable means for the further expansion of world commerce. It was also anticipated that existing institutions of the United Nations could assist in this vital work.

C. With regard to the Organization for Economic Cooperation and Development, the committee looked forward to Japan's early accession and to the prospects for close cooperation between the United States and Japan in all the activities of that body.[27]

D. In view of the continued and increasing need for assistance to the developing countries, the committee noted United States and Japanese aid efforts and reaffirmed the desirability of closer bilateral and multilateral coordination of aid. The United States Delegation noted the high level of aid which it would be extending and stated that its ability to sustain or increase this effort would be influenced by the degree to which other donor countries contributed to the common effort. It also pointed to the necessity of donors achieving greater comparability and liberalization of lending terms. The Japanese Delegation explained its aid efforts and policies and stated Japan's intention

25 Document 28a.
26 Documents 96 and 97.
27 Japan acceded to the O.E.C.D. on April 28, 1964.

to further strengthen its aid efforts in accordance with its capabilities.

The contribution and importance of private investment and technical assistance to the development process also was noted.

III

The committee exchanged frank views on trade with the Communist nations. The Japanese Delegation explained that it was Japan's policy to carry out its trade with Communist countries on a commercial basis, in accordance with the principle of separating the political and economic aspects of Japanese relations with countries of the Communist bloc and acting in consonance with the practices of free world countries. The U.S. Delegation explained why the United States has no economic relations with Communist China. The recent U.S. sale of wheat to the Soviet Union [28] was discussed. The United States also set forth the strategic reasons for its own economic embargo of Cuba, expressing its hope for cooperation from its friends in this respect.

IV

The committee agreed that both countries could benefit from new government-to-government exchanges of technical personnel and research findings in the area of human and natural resources. Officials from Japan and the United States will meet at an early date to discuss procedures through which this agreement can be carried forward. It was foreseen that cooperation in such a program would usefully complement the work of the U.S.–Japan Committee on Scientific Cooperation which is concerned primarily with pure rather than applied science.

V

The committee noted progress made in dealing with international fisheries problems of concern to both Japan and the United States. Both countries undertook to make further efforts to seek solutions satisfactory to all the countries concerned.

VI

The committee expressed the unanimous view that annual meetings of the U.S.–Japan Committee on Trade and Economic Affairs had proved to have great value. Both delegations looked forward to an exchange of views and consultation on policies at its next meeting.

[28] Cf. *Documents, 1963*, pp. 160-162.

VII

Japan was represented by Masayoshi Ohira, Minister for Foreign Affairs; Kakuei Tanaka, Minister of Finance; Munenori Akagi, Minister of Agriculture and Forestry; Hajime Fukuda, Minister of International Trade and Industry; Takeo Ohashi, Minister of Labor; Kentaro Ayabe, Minister of Transportation; Kiichi Miyazawa, Director of the Economic Planning Agency; and Yasumi Kurogane, Chief Cabinet Secretary. Ryuji Takeuchi, Japanese Ambassador to the United States as well as Takio Oda, Deputy Vice Minister for Foreign Affairs, and other advisers from the various Ministries concerned, also were present. The United States was represented by Dean Rusk, Secretary of State; Luther H. Hodges, Secretary of Commerce; W. Willard Wirtz, Secretary of Labor; Walter W. Heller, Chairman of the President's Council of Economic Advisers; James K. Carr, Under Secretary of the Interior; Charles S. Murphy, Under Secretary of Agriculture; and John C. Bullitt, Assistant Secretary of the Treasury. Edwin O. Reischauer, United States Ambassador to Japan, Robert Manning, Assistant Secretary of State for Public Affairs, and advisers from the several Departments concerned were also present.

CHAPTER SIX

THE UNITED STATES AND SOUTHEAST ASIA

A. The Southeast Asia Treaty Organization (SEATO).

(46) *Communiqué of the Ninth Meeting of the SEATO Council, Manila, April 15, 1964.*[1]

1. The Council of the South-East Asia Treaty Organization held its ninth meeting in Manila from April 13 to 15, 1964, under the chairmanship of the Honourable Salvador P. Lopez, Secretary of Foreign Affairs of the Republic of the Philippines. The inaugural address was delivered by the Honourable Diosdado Macapagal, President of the Republic of the Philippines.

General Observations

2. The Council discussed the international situation with particular attention to the conditions existing in the treaty area at the close of SEATO's first decade. It was agreed that SEATO has had, and continues to have, a most important stabilizing influence in South-East Asia.

3. The Council noted that, while the member nations of the alliance have continued over the past year to enjoy peaceful progress and national security, the Communist threat remains. The Council studied the various manifestations of this threat in the treaty area and the means required to combat them. Despite the sharpening of the Sino-Soviet dispute, world domination remains the aim of communism and thus vigilance must not be relaxed. In addition to measures to deter overt aggression and active insurgency, there should continue to be emphasis on the development of economic and social conditions which strengthen national resistance to subversion.

4. Re-affirming that the determination of national policy rests

[1] Department of State Press Release 166, April 15, 1964; text from *Department of State Bulletin,* May 4, 1964, pp. 692-693. For discussion see *The United States in World Affairs, 1964,* pp. 142-143.

with individual governments, the Council declared that material support and encouragement should be given to those nations which, in defending themselves, need and request such support.

Republic of Vietnam

5. The Council (see paragraph 10 regarding the position of France) surveyed with special attention the situation in Vietnam. It noted the efforts made there to check increasing subversive and aggressive activities and expressed its continuing deep interest and sympathy for the Government and people of Vietnam in their struggle.

6. The Council expressed grave concern about the continuing Communist aggression against the Republic of Vietnam, a protocol state under the terms of the Manila Pact.[2] Documentary and material evidence continues to show that this organized campaign is directed, supplied and supported by the Communist regime in North Vietnam, in flagrant violation of the Geneva accords of 1954 and 1962.[3]

7. The Government and people of the Republic of Vietnam have given eloquent testimony to their determination to fight for their country. The Council affirmed its confidence that the program of political and administrative reform, military action, pacification, and economic and social development recently instituted by the Government of the Republic of Vietnam, together with the support it is receiving from member nations of SEATO and from other nations in the free world, will greatly enhance the ability of the Vietnamese people to defeat the Communist campaign and will at the same time improve their prospects for a better life.

8. The Council agreed that the members of SEATO should remain prepared, if necessary, to take further concrete steps within their respective capabilities in fulfillment of their obligations under the treaty.

9. The Council agreed that the defeat of the Communist campaign is essential not only to the security of the Republic of Vietnam, but to that of South-East Asia. It will also be convincing proof that Communist expansion by such tactics will not be permitted.

10. The French Council member, while expressing the sympathy and friendship of France for the Vietnamese people, who

[2] *Documents, 1954,* pp. 319-323.
[3] Same, pp. 283-314 and same, *1962,* pp. 284-294.

for such a long time have been undergoing such severe trials and who aspire towards real independence, stated that under the present serious circumstances it was wise to abstain from any declaration.

Laos

11. The Council expressed concern that the achievement of a neutral and independent government of national union in Laos is being jeopardized by repeated violations of the Geneva agreement of 1962, particularly by North Vietnamese military assistance and intervention and by repeated Pathet Lao attacks. It is urged that the International Control Commission be accorded the necessary facilities to fulfill its duty, under the provisions of that agreement, of investigating violations in all parts of the kingdom. It is agreed to keep the situation under close scrutiny.

Counter-Subversion

12. The Council noted that regional members of the alliance continue to be prime targets for Communist subversion, but that effective counter-measures are being taken by the respective governments to prevent the exploitation of vulnerable areas. SEATO has assisted in the co-ordination of material and other aid provided at the request of member countries.

Interests of Member States

13. The Council noted the anxiety expressed by certain member countries for due consideration of their individual problems in the context of the region as a whole, keeping in view the provisions of the Manila Pact. In this connection, the Council noted the observation of the President of the Philippines that the interests of member states should not be placed at a disadvantage in relation to those of non-member states.

14. The Council heard full reports from its various members about problems of interest to members involving their relations with non-member states.

Economic, Medical and Cultural Co-operation

15. The Council reviewed the progress made by existing SEATO civil projects, and agreed that other proposals should

be examined through which SEATO might make similar contributions to the welfare of the region.

16. The SEATO General Medical Research Laboratory in Bangkok, the SEATO Clinical Research Centre in Bangkok, and the SEATO Cholera Research Laboratory in Dacca are investigating and publishing the causes, treatment and control of diseases.

17. The SEATO Regional Community Development Technical Assistance Centre in Ubol, Thailand, is developing techniques and disseminating information on economic self-help and local development.

18. The SEATO Graduate School of Engineering in Bangkok plays an important part in the development of trained personnel needed in the region. The Council directed that a study should be made of the financing of the school so as to ensure its future as a regional institution of higher learning.

19. The skilled labour projects in the Asian member countries are helping to provide skilled manpower for the developing industrial plants of the Asian member nations.

20. The Council also reviewed the program for cultural cooperation and agreed that the established practice of awarding research fellowships, post-graduate and undergraduate scholarships and professorships is contributing to the advancement of knowledge and to international cultural relations.

Military Planning and Exercises

21. The Council recorded its conviction that adequate defences, individual and collective, are essential to the maintenance of security. The experience gained from regular and systematic military planning among the eight member nations and from the conduct of military exercises, of which 25 have been held to date, is one of the most important and valuable assets of the Alliance.

22. The Council commended the conduct of the military defence exercises held during the past year, including the civic action programs which were of direct benefit to the local population.

23. The Council approved the report of the military advisers, and noted with satisfaction that the Military Planning Office had revised and refined defence plans in the light of changing or anticipated situations.

Staff Changes

24. The Council expressed its deep appreciation to His Excellency Mr. Pote Sarasin, who served as Secretary-General from the creation of that position in 1957 until his resignation in December 1963 upon his appointment as a member of the Cabinet of Thailand. The Council took especial recognition of his skill and untiring efforts in improving and strengthening the organization and of the eminent contribution he made to the cause of collective security.

25. The Council conveyed its gratitude to Mr. William Worth, whose tenure of office as Deputy Secretary-General and Chairman of the Permanent Working Group ends shortly after the conclusion of the Council meeting. It commended him for his outstanding and dedicated service during the seven years he has held those positions.

26. The Council welcomed the incumbent Secretary-General, His Excellency Mr. Konthi Suphamongkhon, who was appointed in February of this year. It also welcomed Mr. David A. Wraight, who has been appointed to succeed Mr. Worth.

Secretariat-General

27. The Council expressed its warm appreciation to the staff of the organization for their valuable services.

Next Meeting

28. The Council accepted with pleasure the invitation of Her Majesty's Government in the United Kingdom to hold its next meeting in London in 1965.

Expression of Gratitude

29. The Council expressed its gratitude to the Government of the Republic of the Philippines for its hospitality and the excellent arrangements made for the conference. The meeting voted warm thanks to the Chairman, the Honourable Mr. Salvador P. Lopez.

Leaders of National Delegations

30. The leaders of the national delegations to the Council meeting were:

The Honourable Sir Garfield Barwick, Minister for External Affairs of Australia
His Excellency Mr. Maurice Couve de Murville, Minister of Foreign Affairs of France
The Right Honourable Keith Holyoake, Prime Minister and Minister of External Affairs of New Zealand
His Excellency Dr. A. M. Malik, Ambassador of Pakistan to the Philippines
The Honourable Salvador P. Lopez, Secretary of Foreign Affairs of the Philippines
His Excellency Mr. Thanat Khoman, Minister of Foreign Affairs of Thailand
The Right Honourable Lord Carrington, Minister Without Portfolio, United Kingdom
The Honourable Dean Rusk, Secretary of State of the United States

B. South Vietnam Battleground.[4]

(47) *United States Policy in Vietnam: Address by Secretary of Defense Robert S. McNamara, Washington, March 26, 1964.*[5]

(Excerpts)

In South Viet-Nam, as you well know, the independence of a nation and the freedom of its people are being threatened by Communist aggression and terrorism. In response to requests from the Government of South Viet-Nam the United States since 1954 has been providing assistance to the Vietnamese in their struggle to maintain their independence.

My purpose this evening is threefold. After recalling some facts about Viet-Nam and its history, I want:

—First, to explain our stake and objectives in South Viet-Nam;
—Second, to review for you the current situation there as General [Maxwell D.] Taylor and I found it on our recent trip;
—And finally, to outline in broad terms the plans which have been worked out with General [*Nguyen*] Khanh for achieving our mutual objectives in South Viet-Nam.

[4] For discussion see *The United States in World Affairs, 1964,* pp. 138-146.
[5] *Department of State Bulletin,* April 13, 1964, pp. 562-570.

Description and History

Let me begin by reminding you of some details about South Viet-Nam, that narrow strip of rich coastal mountain and delta lands running 900 miles in the tropics along the South China Sea to the Gulf of Siam. It contains the mouth of the Mekong River, the main artery of Southeast Asia. It has a population of about 14 million—almost that of California—in an area slightly larger than England and Wales. South Viet-Nam does not exist by itself. Mainland Southeast Asia includes Laos, Cambodia, and the two Viet-Nams, together comprising former French Indochina. It also includes Thailand, Burma, and part of Malaysia. The Southeast Asian peninsula is a richly endowed land area of over 800,000 square miles, roughly the size of the United States east of the Mississippi, and containing almost 100 million people. And immediately beyond to the east are the Philippines; not far to the west is India, to the north is Communist China, and to the south is what the Chinese Communists may consider the greatest prize of all—Indonesia's resources, territory, and the world's fifth largest population, whose strategic location straddles and dominates the gateway to the Indian Ocean.

* * *

U.S. Objectives

I turn now to a consideration of United States objectives in South Viet-Nam. The United States has no designs whatever on the resources or territory of the area. Our national interests do not require that South Viet-Nam serve as a Western base or as a member of a Western alliance. Our concern is threefold.

First, and most important, is the simple fact that South Viet-Nam, a member of the free-world family, is striving to preserve its independence from Communist attack. The Vietnamese have asked our help. We have given it. We shall continue to give it.

We do so in their interest; and we do so in our own clear self-interest. For basic to the principles of freedom and self-determination which have sustained our country for almost two centuries is the right of peoples everywhere to live and develop in peace. Our own security is strengthened by the determination of others to remain free, and by our commitment to assist them. We will not let this member of our family down, regardless of its distance from our shores.

The ultimate goal of the United States in Southeast Asia, as in the rest of the world, is to help maintain free and independent nations which can develop politically, economically, and socially and which can be responsible members of the world community. In this region and elsewhere many peoples share our sense of the value of such freedom and independence. They have taken the risks and made the sacrifices linked to the commitment to membership in the family of the free world. They have done this in the belief that we would back up our pledges to help defend them. It is not right or even expedient—nor is it in our nature—to abandon them when the going is difficult.

Second, Southeast Asia has great strategic significance in the forward defense of the United States. Its location across east-west air and sea lanes flanks the Indian subcontinent on one side and Australia, New Zealand, and the Philippines on the other and dominates the gateway between the Pacific and Indian Oceans. In Communist hands this area would pose a most serious threat to the security of the United States and to the family of free-world nations to which we belong. To defend Southeast Asia, we must meet the challenge in South Viet-Nam.

And third, South Viet-Nam is a test case for the new Communist strategy. Let me examine for a moment the nature of this strategy.

Just as the Kennedy administration was coming into office in January 1961, Chairman Khrushchev made one of the most important speeches on Communist strategy of recent decades. In his report on a party conference entitled "For New Victories of the World Communist Movement," Khrushchev stated: [6] "In modern conditions, the following categories of wars should be distinguished: world wars, local wars, liberation wars and popular uprisings." He ruled out what he called "world wars" and "local wars" as being too dangerous for profitable indulgence in a world of nuclear weapons. But with regard to what he called "liberation wars," he referred specifically to Viet-Nam. He said, "It is a sacred war. We recognize such wars. . . ."

I have pointed out on other occasions the enormous strategic nuclear power which the United States has developed to cope with the first of Mr. Khrushchev's types of wars; deterrence of deliberate, calculated nuclear attack seems as assured as it can be. With respect to our general-purpose forces designed especially for local wars, within the past 3 years we have increased the number of our combat-ready Army divisions by about 45 percent, tactical air squadrons by 30 percent, airlift capabilities by 75 percent, with a 100-percent increase in ship construction

[6] Condensed text in *Current Digest of the Soviet Press,* February 15, 1961, pp. 16-17 and same, February 22, 1961, pp. 8-15 and 24.

and conversion. In conjunction with the forces of our allies our global posture for deterrence and defense is still not all that it should be, but it is good.

President Kennedy and President Johnson have recognized, however, that our forces for the first two types of wars might not be applicable or effective against what the Communists call "wars of liberation," or what is properly called covert aggression or insurgency. We have therefore undertaken and continue to press a variety of programs to develop skilled specialists, equipment, and techniques to enable us to help our allies counter the threat of insurgency.

Communist interest in insurgency techniques did not begin with Khrushchev, nor for that matter with Stalin. Lenin's works are full of tactical instructions, which were adapted very successfully by Mao Tse-tung, whose many writings on guerrilla warfare have become classic references. Indeed, Mao claims to be the true heir of Lenin's original prescriptions for the worldwide victory of communism. The North Vietnamese have taken a leaf or two from Mao's book—as well as Moscow's—and added some of their own.

Thus today in Viet-Nam we are not dealing with factional disputes or the remnants of a colonial struggle against the French but rather with a major test case of communism's new strategy. That strategy has so far been pursued in Cuba, may be beginning in Africa, and failed in Malaya and the Philippines only because of a long and arduous struggle by the people of these countries with assistance provided by the British and the United States.

In Southeast Asia the Communists have taken full advantage of geography—the proximity to the Communist base of operations and the rugged, remote, and heavily foliated character of the border regions. They have utilized the diverse ethnic, religious, and tribal groupings and exploited factionalism and legitimate aspirations wherever possible. And, as I said earlier, they have resorted to sabotage, terrorism, and assassination on an unprecedented scale.

Who is the responsible party—the prime aggressor? First and foremost, without doubt, the prime aggressor is North Viet-Nam, whose leadership has explicitly undertaken to destroy the independence of the South. To be sure, Hanoi is encouraged on its aggressive course by Communist China. But Peiping's interest is hardly the same as that of Hanoi.

For Hanoi, the immediate objective is limited: conquest of the South and national unification, perhaps coupled with control of

Laos. For Peiping, however, Hanoi's victory would be only a first step toward eventual Chinese hegemony over the two Viet-Nams and Southeast Asia and toward exploitation of the new strategy in other parts of the world.

Communist China's interests are clear: It has publicly castigated Moscow for betraying the revolutionary cause whenever the Soviets have sounded a cautionary note. It has characterized the United States as a paper tiger and has insisted that the revolutionary struggle for "liberation and unification" of Viet-Nam could be conducted without risks by, in effect, crawling under the nuclear and the conventional defense of the free world. Peiping thus appears to feel that it has a large stake in demonstrating the new strategy, using Viet-Nam as a test case. Success in Viet-Nam would be regarded by Peiping as vindication for China's views in the worldwide ideological struggle.

Taking into account the relationship of Viet-Nam to Indochina—and of both to Southeast Asia, the Far East, and the free world as a whole—five U.S. Presidents have acted to preserve free-world strategic interests in the area. President Roosevelt opposed Japanese penetration in Indochina; President Truman resisted Communist aggression in Korea; President Eisenhower backed [*President Ngo Dinh*] Diem's efforts to save South Viet-Nam and undertook to defend Taiwan; President Kennedy stepped up our counterinsurgency effort in Viet-Nam; and President Johnson, in addition to reaffirming last week that the United States will furnish assistance and support to South Viet-Nam for as long as it is required to bring Communist aggression and terrorism under control,[7] has approved the program that I shall describe in a few minutes.

The U.S. role in South Viet-Nam, then, is: *first,* to answer the call of the South Vietnamese, a member nation of our free-world family, to help them save their country for themselves; *second,* to help prevent the strategic danger which would exist if communism absorbed Southeast Asia's people and resources; and *third,* to prove in the Vietnamese test case that the free world can cope with Communist "wars of liberation" as we have coped successfully with Communist aggression at other levels.

The Current Situation

* * *

. . . the situation in South Viet-Nam has unquestionably worsened, at least since last fall.

[7] *Department of State Bulletin,* April 6, 1964, pp. 522-523.

The picture is admittedly not an easy one to evaluate and, given the kind of terrain and the kind of war, information is not always available or reliable. The areas under Communist control vary from daytime to nighttime, from one week to another, according to seasonal and weather factors. And, of course, in various areas the degree and importance of control differ. Although we estimate that in South Viet-Nam's 14 million population there are only 20,000 to 25,000 "hard core" Viet Cong guerrillas, they have been able to recruit from among the South Vietnamese an irregular force of from 60,000 to 80,000—mainly by coercion and "bandwagon" effect, but also by promising material and political rewards. The loyalties of the hard core have been cemented by years of fighting, first against the Japanese, then against the French, and, since 1954, against the fledgling government of South Viet-Nam. The young men joining them have been attracted by the excitement of the guerrilla life and then held by bonds of loyalty to their new comrades-in-arms, in a nation where loyalty is only beginning to extend beyond the family or the clan. These loyalties are reinforced both by systematic indoctrination and by the example of what happens to informers and deserters.

Clearly, the disciplined leadership, direction, and support from North Viet-Nam is a critical factor in the strengh of the Viet Cong movement. But the large indigenous support that the Viet Cong receives means that solutions must be as [*much*] political and economic as military. Indeed, there can be no such thing as a purely "military" solution to the war in South Viet-Nam.

The people of South Viet-Nam prefer independence and freedom. But they will not exercise their choice for freedom and commit themselves to it in the face of the high personal risk of Communist retaliation—a kidnaped son, a burned home, a ravaged crop—unless they can have confidence in the ultimate outcome. Much therefore depends on the new government under General Khanh, for which we have high hopes.

Today the government of General Khanh is vigorously rebuilding the machinery of administration and reshaping plans to carry the war to the Viet Cong. He is an able and energetic leader. He has demonstrated his grasp of the basic elements—political, economic, and psychological, as well as military—required to defeat the Viet Cong. He is planning a program of economic and social advances for the welfare of his people. He has brought into support of the Government representatives of key groups previously excluded. He and his colleagues have developed plans for systematic liberation of areas now submissive to Viet Cong duress and for mobilization of all available Vietnamese resources in the defense of the homeland.

At the same time, General Khanh has understood the need to improve South Viet-Nam's relations with its neighbors, Cambodia and Laos; he has taken steps toward conciliation, and he has been quick and forthright in expressing his Government's regret over the recent Vietnamese violation of Cambodia's borders. In short, he has demonstrated the energy, comprehension, and decision required by the difficult circumstances that he faces.

A Program to Meet Our Objectives

Before describing the means by which we hope to assist the South Vietnamese to succeed in their undertaking, let me point out the options that President Johnson had before him when he received General Taylor's and my report last week.

Some critics of our present policy have suggested one option—that we simply withdraw. This the United States totally rejects for reasons I have stated.

Other critics have called for a second and similar option—a "neutralization" of Viet-Nam. This, however, is the game of "what's mine is mine, and what's yours is negotiable." No one seriously believes the Communists would agree to neutralization of North Viet-Nam. And, so far as South Viet-Nam is concerned, we have learned from the past that the Communists rarely honor the kind of treaty that runs counter to their compulsion to expand.

Under the shadow of Communist power, neutralization would in reality be an interim device to permit Communist consolidation and eventual takeover. When General Taylor and I were in Hue, at the north end of South Viet-Nam, 2 weeks ago, several Vietnamese students carried posters which showed their recognition of the reality of neutralization. The signs read: "Neutralize today, communize tomorrow."

Neutralization of South Viet-Nam, which is today under unprovoked subversive attack, would not be in any sense an achievement of the objectives I have outlined. As we tried to convey in Laos, we have no objection in principle to neutrality in the sense of nonalinement. But even there we are learning lessons. Communist abuse of the Geneva accords,[8] by treating the Laos corridor as a sanctuary for infiltration, constantly threatens the precarious neutrality. "Neutralization of South

[8] Same as note 3 to Document 46.

Viet-Nam"—an ambiguous phrase at best—was therefore rejected.

The third option before the President was initiation of military actions outside South Viet-Nam, particularly against North Viet-Nam, in order to supplement the counterinsurgency program in South Viet-Nam. This course of action—its implications and ways of carrying it out—has been carefully studied.

Whatever ultimate course of action may be forced upon us by the other side, it is clear that actions under this option would be only a supplement to, not a substitute for, progress within South Viet-Nam's own borders.

The fourth course of action was to concentrate on helping the South Vietnamese win the battle in their own country. This, all agree, is essential no matter what else is done.

The President therefore approved the 12 recommendations that General Taylor and I made relating to this option.

We have reaffirmed U.S. support for South Viet-Nam's Government and pledged economic assistance and military training and logistical support for as long as it takes to bring the insurgency under control.

We will support the Government of South Viet-Nam in carrying out its anti-insurgency plan. Under that plan, Prime Minister Khanh intends to implement a national mobilization program to mobilize all national resources in the struggle. This means improving the quality of the strategic hamlets, building them systematically outward from secure areas, and correcting previous overextension. The security forces of Viet-Nam will be increased by at least 50,000 men. They will be consolidated, and their effectiveness and conditions of service will be improved. They will press the campaign with increased intensity. We will provide required additional materiel. This will include strengthening of the Vietnamese Air Force with better aircraft and improving the mobility of the ground forces.

A broad national program is to be carried out, giving top priority to rural needs. The program includes land reform, loans to tenant farmers, health and welfare measures, economic development, and improved status for ethnic minorities and paramilitary troops.

A Civil Administrative Corps will be established to bring better public services to the people. This will include teachers, health technicians, agricultural workers, and other technicians. The initial goal during 1964 will be at least 7,500 additional persons; ultimately there will be at least 40,000 men for more than 8,000 hamlets, in 2,500 villages and 43 provinces.

Farm productivity will be increased through doubled use of fertilizers to provide immediate and direct benefits to peasants in secure areas and to increase both their earnings and the nation's export earnings.

We have learned that in Viet-Nam political and economic progress are the *sine qua non* of military success and that military security is equally a prerequisite of internal progress. Our future joint efforts with the Vietnamese are going to apply these lessons.

To conclude: Let me reiterate that our goal is peace and stability, both in Viet-Nam and Southeast Asia. But we have learned that "peace at any price" is not practical in the long run and that the cost of defending freedom must be borne if we are to have it at all.

The road ahead in Viet-Nam is going to be long, difficult, and frustrating. It will take work, courage, imagination, and—perhaps more than anything else—patience to bear the burden of what President Kennedy called a "long twilight struggle." In Viet-Nam, it has not been finished in the first hundred days of President Johnson's administration, and it may not be finished in the first 1,000 days; but, in cooperation with General Khanh's government, we have made a beginning. When the day comes that we can safely withdraw, we expect to leave an independent and stable South Viet-Nam, rich with resources and bright with prospects for contributing to the peace and prosperity of Southeast Asia and of the world.

(48) *The President Urges Increased United States Aid: Message to the Congress, May 18, 1964.*[9]

To the Congress of the United States:

Last January, in my budget message to the Congress,[10] I pointed out that this budget made no provision for any major new requirements that might emerge later for our mutual defense and development program. I stated then that if such requirements should arise I would request prompt action by the Congress to provide additional funds.

That need has emerged in Vietnam. I now request that the Congress provide $125 million in addition to the $3.4 billion already proposed for foreign assistance;[11] $70 million is re-

[9] House Document 307, 88th Cong., 2d sess.; text from *Department of State Bulletin*, June 8, 1964, pp. 891-893.
[10] Document 2.
[11] Document 4.

quired for economic and $55 million for military uses in Vietnam.

Since the 1965 budget was prepared, two major changes have occurred in Vietnam:

First, the Viet Cong guerrillas, under orders from their Communist masters in the north, have intensified terrorist actions against the peaceful people of South Vietnam. This increased terrorism requires increased response.

Second, a new government under Prime Minister [Nguyen] Khanh has come to power, bringing new energy and leadership and new hope for effective action. I share with Ambassador [Henry Cabot] Lodge the conviction that this new government can mount a successful campaign against the Communists.

In March, Prime Minister Khanh declared his intention to mobilize his nation. This intention has now been confirmed by his new and enlarged budget for 1964. It provides for:

> Expanding the Vietnamese Army, Civil Guard, Self-Defense Corps, and police forces, and integrating their operations with political, economic, and social measures in a systematic clear-and-hold campaign.
>
> Greatly expanding and upgrading the Vietnamese civil administrative corps to increase the Government's effectiveness and services at the village, district, and Province level. Local government capacity, responsiveness to popular needs, and initiatives are to be strengthened.
>
> Better pay scales for the men and adequate budgets for the organizations engaged in this struggle of many fronts.
>
> Manifold expansion of training programs, to provide teachers, health workers, agricultural, financial, and administrative staffs for the rural areas.

These and other measures, if promptly carried out, will require an increase of about 40 percent in Vietnam's domestic budget expenditures over the 1963 level—a far greater expansion of Vietnamese effort than was assumed in the assistance plans submitted in January. Under present circumstances, Vietnam's domestic revenues cannot be increased proportionately. Severe inflation resulting from a budget deficit would endanger political as well as economic stability, unless offsetting financial actions are taken. We expect the Vietnamese Government to take all possible self-help measures to deal with this problem internally, but substantial increases in economic assistance also will be required. We must share the increased costs of the greatly intensified Vietnamese effort.

Our more direct support of the expanded Vietnamese military and civil operations also must keep pace with the intensified Vietnamese effort. On the civil side—through AID's [Agency for International Development] counterinsurgency program—this means more fertilizer, medical supplies and services, repair parts and replacements for war-damaged railway rolling stock, school supplies and building materials, well-drilling equipment and teams to bring fresh water to the villagers, and enlarged advisory staffs in the Provinces.

On the military and paramilitary side, additional equipment, ammunition, training, and supplies will be needed as the organization and functioning of the armed forces improves. Additional aircraft, pilot training for the Vietnamese, and airfield improvements are required. Increased activity will require additional ammunition. Additional support equipment is required for all forces.

The vigorous decisions taken by the new Government of Vietnam to mobilize the full resources of the country merit our strongest support. Increased Communist terror requires it.

By our words and deeds in a decade of determined effort, we are pledged before all the world to stand with the free people of Vietnam. Sixteen thousand Americans are serving our country and the people of Vietnam. Daily they face danger in the cause of freedom. Duty requires, and the American people demand, that we give them the fullest measure of support.

We have reviewed the entire budget for mutual defense and development programs once again to determine whether we can accommodate within it these added requirements. We cannot. In fact, recent events in Brazil and elsewhere may add to the economic programs originally planned. Military programs have already been cut to the bare minimum. We cannot respond to the new situation in Vietnam within the limits of the original budget proposal without unacceptable danger to our other basic security interests.

I am today forwarding to the Speaker of the House of Representatives [*John W. McCormack*] amendments to my 1965 budget increasing my request for appropriations for supporting assistance from $335 million to $405 million, and for military assistance from $1 billion to $1.055 billion.[12] Both of these increases are covered by the budget's allowance for contingencies, so that they will not affect overall budget totals.

I ask the Congress to enact authorization for supporting

[12] House Document 305, 88th Cong., 2d sess.

assistance and military assistance sufficient to permit appropriations in these amounts.

I strongly urge the Congress to provide this additional $125 million to Vietnam, and to appropriate the full $3,517 million now required for our mutual defense and development programs.

(49) *The Gulf of Tonkin Episodes.*[13]

(a) *Broadcast Address by President Johnson to the Nation, August 4, 1964.*[14]

My fellow Americans: As President and Commander in Chief, it is my duty to the American people to report that renewed hostile actions against United States ships on the high seas in the Gulf of Tonkin have today required me to order the military forces of the United States to take action in reply.

The initial attack on the destroyer *Maddox,* on August 2, was repeated today by a number of hostile vessels attacking two U.S. destroyers with torpedoes. The destroyers and supporting aircraft acted at once on the orders I gave after the initial act of aggression. We believe at least two of the attacking boats were sunk. There were no U.S. losses.

The performance of commanders and crews in this engagement is in the highest tradition of the United States Navy. But repeated acts of violence against the Armed Forces of the United States must be met not only with alert defense but with positive reply. That reply is being given as I speak to you tonight. Air action is now in execution against gunboats and certain supporting facilities in North Viet-Nam which have been used in these hostile operations.

In the larger sense this new act of aggression, aimed directly at our own forces, again brings home to all of us in the United States the importance of the struggle for peace and security in Southeast Asia. Aggression by terror against the peaceful villagers of South Viet-Nam has now been joined by open aggression on the high seas against the United States of America.

The determination of all Americans to carry out our full commitment to the people and to the Government of South Viet-Nam will be redoubled by this outrage. Yet our response, for the present, will be limited and fitting. We Americans know,

[13] For discussion see *The United States in World Affairs, 1964,* pp. 146-152.
[14] White House Press Release, August 4, 1964; text from *Department of State Bulletin,* August 24, 1964, p. 259.

although others appear to forget, the risks of spreading conflict. We still seek no wider war.

I have instructed the Secretary of State to make this position totally clear to friends and to adversaries and, indeed, to all. I have instructed Ambassador [*Adlai E.*] Stevenson to raise this matter immediately and urgently before the Security Council of the United Nations.[15] Finally, I have today met with the leaders of both parties in the Congress of the United States, and I have informed them that I shall immediately request the Congress to pass a resolution making it clear that our Government is united in its determination to take all necessary measures in support of freedom and in defense of peace in Southeast Asia.

I have been given encouraging assurance by these leaders of both parties that such a resolution will be promptly introduced, freely and expeditiously debated, and passed with overwhelming support. And just a few minutes ago I was able to reach Senator Goldwater, and I am glad to say that he has expressed his support of the statement that I am making to you tonight. It is a solemn responsibility to have to order even limited military action by forces whose overall strength is as vast and as awesome as those of the United States of America, but it is my considered conviction, shared throughout your Government, that firmness in the right is indispensable today for peace. That firmness will always be measured. Its mission is peace.

(b) *Message of the President to the Congress, August 5, 1964.*[16]

To the Congress of the United States:

Last night I announced to the American people that the North Vietnamese regime had conducted further deliberate attacks against U.S. naval vessels operating in international waters, and that I had therefore directed air action against gunboats and supporting facilities used in these hostile operations. This air action has now been carried out with substantial damage to the boats and facilities. Two U.S. aircraft were lost in the action.

After consultation with the leaders of both parties in the Congress, I further announced a decision to ask the Congress for a resolution expressing the unity and determination of the

[15] For Ambassador Stevenson's statement of August 5 to the Security Council see same, pp. 272-274.

[16] House Document 333, 88th Cong., 2d sess.; text from *Department of State Bulletin,* August 24, 1964, pp. 261-263.

United States in supporting freedom and in protecting peace in southeast Asia.

These latest actions of the North Vietnamese regime have given a new and grave turn to the already serious situation in southeast Asia. Our commitments in that area are well known to the Congress. They were first made in 1954 by President Eisenhower.[17] They were further defined in the Southeast Asia Collective Defense Treaty [*SEATO*] approved by the Senate in February 1955.[18]

This treaty with its accompanying protocol obligates the United States and other members to act in accordance with their constitutional processes to meet Communist aggression against any of the parties or protocol states.

Our policy in southeast Asia has been consistent and unchanged since 1954. I summarized it on June 2 in four simple propositions: [19]

1. *America keeps her word.* Here as elsewhere, we must and shall honor our commitments.

2. *The issue is the future of southeast Asia as a whole.* A threat to any nation in that region is a threat to all, and a threat to us.

3. *Our purpose is peace.* We have no military, political, or territorial ambitions in the area.

4. *This is not just a jungle war, but a struggle for freedom on every front of human activity.* Our military and economic assistance to South Vietnam and Laos in particular has the purpose of helping these countries to repel aggression and strengthen their independence.

The threat to the free nations of southeast Asia has long been clear. The North Vietnamese regime has constantly sought to take over South Vietnam and Laos. This Communist regime has violated the Geneva accords for Vietnam. It has systematically conducted a campaign of subversion, which includes the direction, training, and supply of personnel and arms for the conduct of guerrilla warfare in South Vietnamese territory. In Laos, the North Vietnamese regime has maintained military forces, used Laotian territory for infiltration into South Vietnam, and most recently carried out combat operations—all in direct violation of the Geneva agreements of 1962.

In recent months, the actions of the North Vietnamese regime have become steadily more threatening. In May, following new

[17] *Documents, 1954,* pp. 366-367.
[18] Same as note 2 to Document 46.
[19] See *Department of State Bulletin,* June 22, 1964, pp. 953-954.

acts of Communist aggression in Laos, the United States undertook reconnaissance flights over Laotian territory, at the request of the Government of Laos.[20] These flights had the essential mission of determining the situation in territory where Communist forces were preventing inspection by the International Control Commission. When the Communists attacked these aircraft, I responded by furnishing escort fighters with instructions to fire when fired upon. Thus, these latest North Vietnamese attacks on our naval vessels are not the first direct attack on armed forces of the United States.

As President of the United States I have concluded that I should now ask the Congress, on its part, to join in affirming the national determination that all such attacks will be met, and that the United States will continue in its basic policy of assisting the free nations of the area to defend their freedom.

As I have repeatedly made clear, the United States intends no rashness, and seeks no wider war. We must make it clear to all that the United States is united in its determination to bring about the end of Communist subversion and aggression in the area. We seek the full and effective restoration of the international agreements signed in Geneva in 1954, with respect to South Vietnam, and again in Geneva in 1962, with respect to Laos.[21]

I recommend a resolution expressing the support of the Congress for all necessary action to protect our Armed Forces and to assist nations covered by the SEATO Treaty. At the same time, I assure the Congress that we shall continue readily to explore any avenues of political solution that will effectively guarantee the removal of Communist subversion and the preservation of the independence of the nations of the area.

The resolution could well be based upon similar resolutions enacted by the Congress in the past—to meet the threat to Formosa in 1955,[22] to meet the threat to the Middle East in 1957,[23] and to meet the threat in Cuba in 1962.[24] It could state in the simplest terms the resolve and support of the Congress for action to deal appropriately with attacks against our Armed Forces and to defend freedom and preserve peace in southeast Asia in accordance with the obligations of the United States under the Southeast Asia Treaty. I urge the Congress

[20] Document 51.
[21] Same as note 3 to Document 46.
[22] *Documents, 1955,* pp. 298-305.
[23] Same, *1957,* pp. 206-207.
[24] Same, *1962,* pp. 372-373.

to enact such a resolution promptly and thus to give convincing evidence to the aggressive Communist nations, and to the world as a whole, that our policy in southeast Asia will be carried forward—and that the peace and security of the area will be preserved.

The events of this week would in any event have made the passage of a congressional resolution essential. But there is an additional reason for doing so at a time when we are entering on 3 months of political campaigning. Hostile nations must understand that in such a period the United States will continue to protect its national interests, and that in these matters there is no division among us.

(c) *Joint Resolution of the Congress: Public Law 88-408, Approved August 10, 1964.*[25]

To promote the maintenance of international peace and security in southeast Asia.

Whereas naval units of the Communist regime in Vietnam, in violation of the principles of the Charter of the United Nations and of international law, have deliberately and repeatedly attacked United States naval vessels lawfully present in international waters, and have thereby created a serious threat to international peace; and

Whereas these attacks are part of a deliberate and systematic campaign of aggression that the Communist regime in North Vietnam has been waging against its neighbors and the nations joined with them in the collective defense of their freedom; and

Whereas the United States is assisting the peoples of southeast Asia to protect their freedom and has no territorial, military or political ambitions in that area, but desires only that these peoples should be left in peace to work out their own destinies in their own way: Now, therefore, be it

Resolved by the Senate and House of Representatives of the United States of America in Congress assembled, That the Congress approves and supports the determination of the President, as Commander in Chief, to take all necessary measures to repel any armed attack against the forces of the United States and to prevent further aggression.

SEC. 2. The United States regards as vital to its national

[25] H. J. Res. 1145, adopted on August 7 unanimously by the House of Representatives and by the Senate by a vote of 88-2; text from *Department of State Bulletin,* August 24, 1964, p. 268.

interest and to world peace the maintenance of international peace and security in southeast Asia. Consonant with the Constitution of the United States and the Charter of the United Nations and in accordance with its obligations under the Southeast Asia Collective Defense Treaty, the United States is, therefore, prepared, as the President determines, to take all necessary steps, including the use of armed force, to assist any member or protocol state of the Southeast Asia Collective Defense Treaty requesting assistance in defense of its freedom.

SEC. 3. This resolution shall expire when the President shall determine that the peace and security of the area is reasonably assured by international conditions created by action of the United Nations or otherwise, except that it may be terminated earlier by concurrent resolution of the Congress.

(50) *The President Reaffirms United States Policy in Vietnam: White House Statement, December 1, 1964.*[26]

The President today reviewed the situation in South Viet-Nam with Ambassador [Maxwell D.] Taylor, and with the Secretaries of State [Dean Rusk] and Defense [Robert S. McNamara], the Director of Central Intelligence [John A. McCone], and the Chairman of the Joint Chiefs of Staff [Gen. Earle G. Wheeler].

Ambassador Taylor reported that the political situation in Saigon was still difficult but that the new government under Prime Minister [Tran Van] Huong was making a determined effort to strengthen national unity, to maintain law and order, and to press forward with the security program, involving a combination of political, economic, and military actions to defeat the Viet Cong insurgency. The Ambassador also reported that, although the security problems have increased over the past few months in the northern provinces of South Viet-Nam, with uneven progress elsewhere, the strength of the armed forces of the government was being increased by improved recruiting and conscription and by the nearly 100-percent increase in the combat strength of the Vietnamese Air Force. Also, the government forces continue to inflict heavy losses on the Viet Cong.

On the economic front, Ambassador Taylor noted that agricultural output was continuing to increase, with U.S. assistance in fertilizers and pesticides playing an important role. He also noted that the prices of goods and the value of the piaster have

[26] White House Press Release, December 1, 1964; text from *Department of State Bulletin*, December 21, 1964, pp. 869-870.

remained remarkably stable. On the other hand, the Ambassador reported that increased interdiction of the communication routes by the Viet Cong is interfering to some extent with commerce within the country, and the recent typhoons and floods in central Viet-Nam have destroyed a large percentage of the crops and livestock in that region. The Vietnamese Government, with U.S. assistance, has moved promptly to organize a program which is bringing relief and rehabilitation to the stricken areas.

The meeting reviewed the accumulating evidence of continuing and increased North Vietnamese support of the Viet Cong and of North Vietnamese forces in, and passing through, the territory of Laos in violation of the Geneva accords of 1962.[27]

The President instructed Ambassador Taylor to consult urgently with the South Vietnamese Government as to measures that should be taken to improve the situation in all its aspects.

The President reaffirmed the basic U.S. policy of providing all possible and useful assistance to the South Vietnamese people and government in their struggle to defeat the externally supported insurgency and aggression being conducted against them. It was noted that this policy accords with the terms of the congressional joint resolution of August 10, 1964,[28] which remains in full force and effect.

C. Laos.[29]

(51) *United States Reconnaissance Flights Over Laos.*

(a) *Department of State Statement, June 6, 1964.*[30]

A U.S. reconnaissance aircraft has been shot down by ground fire in the area of the Plaine des Jarres over Laos. The pilot was observed to have ejected and landed safely. Efforts to locate and rescue him were underway during the day of June 6.

The U.S. Government had announced these flights on May 21.[31] Such reconnaissance flights are undertaken to disclose informa-

[27] *Documents, 1962,* pp. 284-294.
[28] Document 49c.
[29] For discussion see *The United States in World Affairs, 1964,* pp. 162-167.
[30] *Department of State Bulletin,* June 29, 1964, p. 994.
[31] On May 21 a Department of State spokesman made the following statement: "We are working with the Royal Lao Government in response to its request to assist in every way possible in supplementing its information on intentions and dispositions of attacking forces. For this purpose certain U.S. reconnaissance flights have been authorized in view of the current inability of the International Control Commission to obtain adequate information. Information obtained will be turned over as rapidly as possible to the International Control Commission."

tion about Pathet Lao and Viet Minh military activity which is in direct violation of the Geneva accords on Laos of 1962.[32] They were initiated in accordance with the appeal of the Prime Minister of the Government of National Union in Laos, Prince Souvanna Phouma, in order, in the Prince's words, "to observe the activities and movements of the forces which are invading, attacking and fighting in Laos."

Information from these flights is being transmitted to the Government of Laos and to the International Control Commission.

With the agreement of the Royal Laotian Government these flights by U.S. aircraft over Laos will continue. The U.S. Government has consulted with the Government of Laos with respect to measures required for the protection of these flights.

(b) *Department of State Statement, June 7, 1964.*[33]

An FA–8 aircraft from the carrier *Kitty Hawk* has been shot down by ground fire in the area of the Plaines des Jarres over Laos while participating in a reconnaissance mission. The pilot was observed to have ejected and parachuted to the ground. Efforts to locate and rescue him are underway.

As we have stated previously, the U.S. Government has been undertaking such flights since May 21 to disclose information about Pathet Lao and Viet Minh activity which is in direct violation with the Geneva accords on Laos of 1962.

The flights were initiated in accordance with the appeal of the Prime Minister of the Government of National Union in Laos in order "to observe the activities and movements of the forces which are invading, attacking and fighting in Laos."

Information from these flights is and will continue to be transmitted to the Government of Laos and the International Control Commission.

(c) *Department of State Statement, June 11, 1964.*[34]

There has been no change in the matter of photo reconnaissance flights. They will be undertaken as necessary and in close consultation with the Royal Government of Laos.

As I have said before, we have been in full consultation with Prime Minister Souvanna Phouma on this problem. Yesterday's meeting between Prime Minister Souvanna Phouma and Ambassador [Leonard] Unger was part of the continuing con-

[32] Same as note 27 to Document 50.
[33] *Department of State Bulletin,* June 29, 1964, p. 994.
[34] Same, p. 995.

sultation process. We share the conviction of the Lao Government that the refusal of the Communists to allow any effective functioning by the ICC [*International Control Commission*] combined with Pathet Lao–Viet Minh recent actions of aggression has created an urgent and continuing need for reliable information on eastern Laos. It is for that reason that we agreed to undertake reconnaissance flights.

These flights have taken place and will take place at the intervals necessary for the purpose of obtaining information. We have a clear understanding on this matter with the Laos Government, and we are in agreement with that Government also that it is not in the interest of the Government of Laos or of those who undertake these hazardous missions that any operational part of their work should be discussed.

(52) *Why Laos Is Critically Important: Address by Secretary of State Rusk, Williams College, June 14, 1964.*[35]

(Excerpt)

* * *

Why are we concerned about Laos? First, because of its location. On the north and northeast it has nearly 1,100 miles of border with Communist China and Communist North Viet-Nam. It also shares 1,750 miles of border with four non-Communist countries, including Thailand, the heartland of Southeast Asia, and South Viet-Nam, which is resisting an aggression directed and supplied by Communist North Viet-Nam with the support of Communist China.

In 1949 the French granted Laos independence within the French Union. But the North Vietnamese Communists managed to attract a few Lao dissidents by pledges of military help and technical advice. In September 1950 the North Viet-Nam radio announced formation of the "resistance government of the Pathet Lao." Later broadcasts claimed that this government had a "national assembly," had picked a "prime minister," and had formed a "people's liberation army." All this occurred not in Laos but in North Viet-Nam.

In 1953 North Vietnamese forces invaded Laos, taking with them their puppet Pathet Lao government and troops. When the Indochinese war was brought to an end by the Geneva agree-

[35] Department of State Press Release 282, June 13, 1964; text from *Department of State Bulletin,* July 6, 1964, pp. 3-5.

ments of 1954,[36] the Communists controlled two provinces of Laos. But under those agreements Laos was to be one country, the Pathet Lao forces were to be integrated into the Royal Lao Army, and all foreign military forces were to be withdrawn, excepting limited forces and two bases reserved for France. Those pledges were signed by the Communist regimes of North Viet-Nam and mainland China as well as by the Soviet Union and Poland.

But, because of Pathet Lao intransigence, those agreements did not bring peace and unity to Laos. And, in 1960, fighting among non-Communist elements gave the Communists new opportunities. When President Kennedy took office, the Soviet Union was airlifting arms and ammunition from Hanoi to Communist and neutralist forces in northeast Laos and on the strategic Plaine des Jarres. And we were supporting the Government forces in the Mekong Valley.

The 1962 Geneva Accords

The Soviet Union, however, indicated that it desired an independent and neutral Laos.[37] And we had no wish beyond a free Laos that could live at peace with its neighbors. Subject to a cease-fire we agreed to negotiate. Finally, new accords were signed in Geneva in July 1962.[38]

All participants "solemnly declared" their respect for the sovereignty, neutrality, and territorial integrity of Laos. They agreed, among other things, to: (1) withdraw all foreign troops in the presence of international inspectors; (2) prohibit introduction of military forces in any capacity; (3) withhold any war materiel from Laos except as "the Royal Government of Laos may consider necessary"; (4) not use the territory of Laos to intervene in the internal affairs of other countries.

Responsibility for general supervision of the accords was given to an International Control Commission (ICC) composed of representatives of Canada and Poland with India as chairman.

And all agreed also to support a Government of National Union composed of three factions, with the neutral leader Prince Souvanna Phouma as Premier.

The 14 governments which made these pledges included Communist China and Communist North Viet-Nam as well as the Soviet Union and Poland.

[36] *Documents, 1954,* pp. 283-314.
[37] *Documents, 1962,* p. 283.
[38] Same as note 27 to Document 50.

Record of Communist Aggression and Deception

What happened? The non-Communist nations complied with the agreements. North Viet-Nam and its Pathet Lao puppets did not. We promptly withdrew our 600-man military aid mission. North Viet-Nam kept several thousand troops and military technicians in Laos. North Vietnamese cadres are the backbone of almost every Pathet Lao battalion. This was, and is, of course, a major violation of the Geneva accords.

Later, North Viet-Nam sent additional forces back into Laos—some of them in organized battalions—a second major violation.

The North Vietnamese have continued to use, and improve, the corridor through Laos to reinforce and supply the Viet Cong in South Viet-Nam—a third major violation.

The Communists have continued to ship arms into Laos as well as through it—another major violation.

The Pathet Lao and the North Vietnamese Communists have compounded these international felonies by denials that they were committing them.

But there was another major violation which they could not deny. They barred freedom of access to the areas under their control, both to the Lao Government and to the International Control Commission. The Royal Lao Government, on the other hand, opened the areas under its control to access not only by the ICC but by all Lao factions.

The Communists repeatedly fired at personnel and aircraft on legitimate missions under the authority of the Royal Lao Government. They even fired on ICC helicopters. They repeatedly violated the cease-fire agreement. And this spring they launched an assault on the neutralist forces of General Kong Le, driving them off the Plaine des Jarres, where they had been since early 1961.

This, in bare summary, is the Communist record of aggression, bad faith, and deception in Laos.

A Communist takeover in Laos would be as unacceptable as a Communist takeover in South Viet-Nam. The rest of Southeast Asia would be in jeopardy, and saving it would be much more costly, in blood and treasure, than turning back the aggressors in Laos and South Viet-Nam. The loss of Southeast Asia as a whole to the Communists would be intolerable.

Need for Compliance with Present Agreements

The Communist assault on Laos, like that on South Viet-Nam, involves the larger question of whether anyone is to be permitted to succeed in aggression by terror, guerrilla warfare, and the infiltration of arms and military personnel across national frontiers. If they are allowed to gain from these assaults in Southeast Asia, the Communist advocates of militancy everywhere will feel encouraged.

Also at stake is the fundamental question of whether solemn international contracts are to be performed. All who believe in peace and in building a decent world order and rule of law have an interest in seeing that no government be allowed to gain from breaking its promises.

There is talk of negotiating new political settlements in Southeast Asia. But political settlements were reached in 1954 and 1962. The Geneva accords of 1962 were precisely agreements to neutralize Laos. No new agreements are required. All that is needed is compliance with the agreements already made.

The prescription for peace in Laos and Viet-Nam is simple: Leave your neighbors alone. It is in the vital interest of the free world that Peiping and Hanoi—and all Communists everywhere—learn, once and for all, that they cannot reap rewards from militancy, aggression by seepage, and duplicity. For our part, we certainly do not intend to abandon the peoples of Laos or Viet-Nam or other countries who are trying to remain free from Communist domination.

(53) *Joint Communiqué on Consultations Held at Ventiane, Released June 29, 1964.*[39]

On May 26, 1964 the British Chargé d'Affaires in Vientiane, acting as representative of the British Co-Chairman of the International Conference on the Settlement of the Laotian Question held at Geneva in 1961/62,[40] and in response to a request from the Prime Minister of Laos in a letter of May 19 addressed to the representatives of both Co-Chairmen, [*U.K. and U.S.S.R.*] invited representatives of each of the signatory powers to attend consultations under Article 4 of the Declaration on the Neutrality of Laos, signed at Geneva on July 23, 1962.[41] The consultations

[39] *Department of State Bulletin,* July 20, 1964, pp. 88-91.
[40] Same as note 27 to Document 50.
[41] *Documents, 1962,* p. 287.

opened at the British Embassy in Vientiane on June 2 and the final meeting was held on June 29. They were presided over by the British Chargé d' Affaires.

2. Heads of Mission representing the Governments of Canada, Thailand, the U.S.A. and the Republic of Vietnam took part in the consultations on the basis of this invitation.

3. The Ambassador of India also participated in the consultations on the understanding that:

(A) He regarded the consultations merely as informal consultations among ambassadors of certain Geneva powers in Vientiane;

(B) He did not regard the ambassadors' meetings in Vientiane as consultations envisaged under Article 4 of the Geneva Declaration, nor as a substitute for a 14-power international conference which his Government strongly supported;

(C) His participation would be aimed at, besides an exchange of views on the situation in Laos, the convocation of 14-power consultations under Article 4 of the Geneva Declaration and/or an international conference.

The Ambassador of India was consequently unable to associate himself with any statement in the nature of a finding on the military situation as set out in paragraph 6 below or with any proposal concerning matters of which the I.C.S.C. [International Commission for Supervision and Control in Laos] was or should be seized, in view of India's status as a supervisory power and chairman of the I.C.S.C. He expressed the view that the Commission was the only body charged by the Geneva Conference to make investigations into violations of the cease-fire and to furnish appropriate reports to the Co-Chairmen. He also expressed the view that the Commission should be requested to make a speedy investigation into the present military situation and to report urgently to the Co-Chairmen of the Geneva Conference if it had not already done so.

4. The consultations were intended to provide for an exchange of views between the participating countries aimed at finding ways and means to bring about an improvement in the situation in Laos, and as a means of supporting and strengthening the Government of National Union. The Prime Minister [Prince Souvanna Phouma] held regular and frequent exchanges with the chairman of the consultations and the Laotian Government made available any information requested by the consultants; in this way the Government was associated with the consultations, maintaining contact and showing its continuing interest in the

proceedings. The Prime Minister expressed his satisfaction with the work carried out during the consultations.

5. The representatives agreed that the deteriorating military situation in Laos presented a grave threat to the peace of South-East Asia. They agreed to call on the Co-Chairmen in the way each thought appropriate, to do everything in their power to urge all parties concerned to bring about an immediate cease-fire throughout the Kingdom and withdraw all forces to the positions which they held before the recent fighting. The cease-fire and withdrawal should be controlled and verified by the I.C.S.C.

6. During the meeting a detailed assessment of recent developments in the military situation was made by the representatives of Canada, Thailand, the United Kingdom, the United States and the Republic of Vietnam. (India did not participate in this assessment for the reasons set out in paragraph 3 above.) On the basis of this assessment the five representatives condemned the recent Pathet Lao attacks on the neutralist forces of General Kong Le, attacks clearly made with North Vietnamese assistance, as being in flagrant violation of the Geneva Agreements. In the course of this study evidence was produced concerning the use by North Vietnam of Laos territory to interfere in the internal affairs of the Republic of Vietnam. The conclusions of the assessment and the action which these representatives are recommending in the way each thinks appropriate to the Co-Chairmen are set out in the document annexed to this communique.

7. The representatives were agreed that the Geneva Agreements, if carried out in a constructive spirit, provide the necessary framework to assure the sovereignty, independence, neutrality, unity and territorial integrity of the Kingdom of Laos. They considered, in relation to the work of the I.C.S.C. and the duties imposed on it by the Geneva Protocol, certain recommendations that might be made to the Commission by the Co-Chairmen under Article 8 of the Protocol. They considered in particular recommendations relating to: the resumption of full participation in the work of the Commission by the Polish Commissioner; the importance of the continued and effective functioning of the Commission in full enjoyment of security and immunity for members of the Commission and its personnel; the provision of all facilities to the Commission to move without hindrance in Laos for the purpose of carrying out investigations; and the according of maximum co-operation by the Royal Laotian Government and all political groups in Laos to the Commission in order to enable it to perform its functions under the Geneva Agreements.

8. The representatives looked forward to a stabilization of the political situation in Laos which would ensure the willing co-operation of all the principal political groups in the country and enable the Government of National Union, with Prince Souvanna as Prime Minister, to discharge its responsibility for the execution of the cease-fire as contemplated under Article 9 of the Protocol to the Geneva Declaration on the Neutrality of Laos. To this end they expressed the hope that an early meeting could be held between the leaders of the political parties and urged the Co-Chairmen to use their influence to bring this about.

9. The meeting also discussed on an exploratory basis and without commitment the nature of prior conditions that would be necessary if agreement were ultimately to be reached on the holding of a new international conference on the Laotian question. In this context reference was also made to other proposals for consultations on the Laotian question.

CALL FOR CEASEFIRE AND WITHDRAWAL [42]

The undersigned representatives of the signatories of the Geneva Accords meeting in Vientiane have, at the request of the Prime Minister of Laos, studied recent developments in the military situation in Laos with particular attention to the breaches of the terms of the Geneva declaration on the neutrality of Laos on July 23, 1962 and the protocol to this declaration. They have reached the following conclusions:

(1) There has been a general offensive by Pathet Lao forces in the Plain of Jars area and eastern Xieng Khouang province which started at the beginning of February 1964, culminated in a large scale attack launched on May 16, and is still continuing. This general offensive is in accordance with the pattern of encroachment by Pathet Lao and North Vietnamese forces which has been observed since the signature of the Geneva agreements in July, 1962.

(2) The Neutralist forces of General Kong Le are at present grouped in areas to the west and south of the Plain of Jars, where they are continuing to resist attacks. Pathet Lao propaganda that these forces have been wiped out is thus demonstrably untrue.

(3) Though the Neutralist forces of General Kong Le have suffered some individual desertions, there were no defections of units as claimed by the Pathet Lao.

(4) The so called "true Neutralist" forces of Colonel Deuane are not numerically strong enough nor have they the equipment to have launched unaided an attack of the scale that has taken place against a much larger force, well equipped and supported by artillery, tanks, and attack and transport aircraft of the Royal Laotian Air Force,

[42] Signed on June 29 by representatives of Canada, Thailand, the United Kingdom, the United States, and the Republic of Vietnam.

not to mention causing the displacement of thousands of refugees.

(5) There is therefore no truth in the allegations that the recent fighting has been between different Neutralist factions.

(6) There is indisputable evidence of North Vietnamese involvement in the offensive. This has taken the form of North Vietnamese fighting cadres as well as extensive logistic support. A study of the Pathet Lao forces, the undeveloped area from which they are forced to recruit and the lack of any industrial capability within their territory shows clearly that they have been, and still are, incapable of producing the sophisticated weapons used by them, or the trained technicians or soldiers to serve these weapons. Bearing in mind the growth of the Pathet Lao forces from very small beginnings to their present strength, it is obvious that this could only have taken place with the use of instructors from outside and with the inclusion of foreign cadres within their organisation to ensure their continuous and progressive efficiency. All Pathet Lao road communications run into North Viet Nam and it is self-evident that such cadres and logistic support come from North Viet Nam and are trained North Vietnamese soldiers and technicians.

(7) As a result of their recent operations the Pathet Lao and their allies are in a tactically advantageous position from which to conduct further military operations and are in fact continuing their offensive.

(8) There is furthermore firm evidence of the systematic use of Lao territory by the North Vietnamese for the infiltration of men and arms into South Viet Nam. This evidence concerned frequent occasions between July 23, 1962 and April 1964 on which large parties of North Vietnamese cadres and combatants passed through Laotian territory in breach of Article 2(i) of the Geneva declaration and of Articles 4 and 6 of the protocol to this declaration.

2. In the light of these conclusions and of the great dangers inherent in the present situation for the sovereignty, independence, neutrality, unity and territorial integrity of the Kingdom of Laos and for the peace of South-East Asia as a whole, and acting on behalf of their governments, the representatives call for an immediate end to the fighting throughout Laos.

3. The representatives agreed to invite the co-Chairmen in the way each thought appropriate:

(a) To address an urgent appeal for an immediate ceasefire to all parties in Laos;

(b) To call for a withdrawal of Pathet Lao forces to the positions held on February 1, 1964;

(c) To call all North Vietnamese forces to withdraw from Laotian territory and to desist from any further use of Laotian territory for the purpose of interfering in the internal affairs of the Republic of Viet Nam;

(d) To call on the International Commission for Supervision and Control to submit a report on the situation without delay;

(e) To provide general guidance to the International Commission for Supervision and Control to assist it in its duties to control and verify the ceasefire and withdrawal under (b) and (c) above, and to report to the co-Chairmen on the action it takes (drawing attention to any hindrance encountered in the carrying out [*of*] its duties) on the observance of the ceasefire and on the progress made with and date of completion of the withdrawal;

(f) To call on the Royal Lao Government authorities and on all military commanders and other persons exercising authority in any area of Laos which the Commission judges it necessary to visit in carrying out the request at (e) to give the Commission every assistance in its task.

(54) *Proposal for Reconvening the International Conference on the Settlement of the Laotian Question.*

(a) *Statement by the Soviet Union, July 26, 1964.*[43]

In connection with the continued deterioration of the situation in Laos the Soviet Government, as one of the parties to the Geneva accords [44] on Laos, feels obligated to call the attention of all the states which are parties to the above-mentioned accords to the following.

Lately it has become increasingly obvious that certain states have embarked on a course of flagrant intervention in the internal affairs of Laos and violation of the Geneva accords, which, as is well known, obligate the states which are signatories thereto to respect the independence and neutrality of Laos.

Contrary to the Geneva accords the United States has left its military personnel and various military and semimilitary organizations and services in Laos, continuing to give unilateral military aid to the reactionary forces of the country. With the support of the United States these forces carried out a military coup in Vientiane last April, which brought about an extreme aggravation of the domestic political conditions in the country and paralyzed the operation of the coalition government, the establishment of which was in itself an advance on the road to realization of those principles which are laid down in the Geneva accords. As a result there arose the threat of a complete breakdown of the accords signed at Geneva.

In flagrant violation of the sovereignty of Laos, United States aircraft are conducting reconnaissance flights above the territory of the country [45] and are exposing to bombing and bombardment the areas controlled by the Pathet Lao. The numerous repre-

[43] *Department of State Bulletin,* August 17, 1964, p. 220.
[44] Same as note 27 to Document 50.
[45] Document 51.

sentations made by the Soviet Government, as co-chairman of the Geneva Conference on Laos, to the Government of the U.S.A., with an appeal to discontinue interference in the internal affairs of Laos and violations of the Geneva accords, have not achieved their purpose. In spite of the repeated representations of the co-chairmen, resumption of negotiations between the three political forces of Laos for a peaceful settlement in the country in accordance with the Geneva accords has still not been implemented.

The Soviet Government was the first to support the proposal of [*Prince*] Norodom Sihanouk, Chief of State of Cambodia, for convening a new international conference of 14 states concerning Laos. Considering the tense situation in Laos, the Soviet Government proposed that such a conference be held at Geneva in June 1964. However, the proposal for calling a conference at that time has not met with the support of the U.S.A. and certain other states.

Under various unfounded pretexts the proposal of the Polish People's Republic for conducting consultations with the participation of the three political forces for the purpose of planning a new international conference on Laos has also been rejected.

The Soviet Government can no longer reconcile itself to such a situation when the Geneva accords on Laos are thwarted, when certain states, which have signed the accords, evade the discussion of the dangerous situation in Laos which has been created and which threatens the peace and security not only of that country but of the entire area of Southeast Asia as well. Such a position is also dictated by the fact that in the situation thus created the co-chairmen of the Geneva Conference have been placed in a false position, preventing them from fulfilling the functions imposed upon them.

The Soviet Government therefore addresses a proposal to the governments of all countries which signed the Geneva accords on Laos to convene in August of this year an international conference of 14 states on Laos to discuss urgent measures which would insure a peaceful settlement in Laos in accordance with the Geneva accords of 1962, strict and unswerving fulfillment of these accords by all the states concerned. Such a conference could be held in Geneva or in another city acceptable to all the participants of the conference. This new proposal has been dictated by the sincere desire to contribute to the implementation of the Geneva accords.

For its part, the Soviet Union is prepared, just as before, to contribute to the efforts directed toward expediting the convening of the said international conference. A negative attitude toward this proposal on the part of other states will place the Soviet Government in a position where it will be compelled to consider in general the question of the possibility of fulfillment by the Soviet Union of the functions of co-chairman, since under the conditions of gross and systematic violation of the Geneva accords by certain states, the role of co-chairman loses all useful significance and becomes fictitious.

(b) *Department of State Statement, July 30, 1964.*[46]

The Government of the United States shares the concern of the Government of the Union of Soviet Socialist Republics over the deteriorating situation in Laos, as expressed in the Soviet statement handed to the United States Government on July 26.

As the Soviet Government is aware, the United States Government placed great store in the understandings regarding Laos reached by President Kennedy and Premier Khrushchev at Vienna in June 1961 [47] and the Geneva Agreements on Laos which followed. The United States Government believed that peace could be restored to Laos if foreign interference were ended there and the people of that country were left alone to work out their own destinies on the basis of a policy of neutrality. The Geneva Agreements provided a sound basis for such a policy and placed responsibility upon the International Control Commission and the Co-Chairmen of the Geneva Conference to see to it that the parties lived up to their obligations.

From the very beginning, however, the Pathet Lao and North Viet-Nam, backed by the Chinese Communists, refused to comply with their obligations. North Vietnamese military forces were not withdrawn from Laos under ICC supervision. North Viet-Nam continued to use and, indeed, increased their use of Laotian territory to infiltrate military personnel and supplies into South Viet-Nam. The Pathet Lao, with North Vietnamese support, have repeatedly violated the cease-fire, most recently in their unprovoked attacks against and seizure of neutralist positions on the Plain of Jars, which were the subject of a report to the Co-Chairmen by the International Control Commission dated June 20. The Pathet Lao has refused to cooperate with the International Control Commission and with the Government of National Union.

These repeated violations of the Geneva Agreements have occurred in the face of the special responsibility which Article 8

[46] Department of State Press Release 349, July 31, 1964; text from *Department of State Bulletin,* August 17, 1964, pp. 218-220.
[47] *Documents, 1961,* pp. 136-137.

of the Protocol to the Declaration on the Neutrality of Laos places on the Co-Chairmen to exercise supervision over the observance of the Agreements. At the same time, the International Control Commission has been unable effectively to deal with these violations largely because of the refusal of the Pathet Lao to allow the Commission to exercise free access to areas under Pathet Lao control and also the failure of its Polish member to participate in the Commission's activities in a positive manner.

The Soviet Government's statement makes certain allegations regarding United States activities in Laos which are contrary to fact. The United States withdrew all 666 of its military advisory personnel from Laos under ICC supervision in accordance with Articles 2 and 3 of the Geneva Protocol. In the face of the aggressive attacks launched by the Pathet Lao and North Vietnamese in May on the Plain of Jars in flagrant violation of the Geneva Agreements, the United States responded to Prime Minister Souvanna Phouma's request for assistance by initiating reconnaissance flights. These flights were undertaken to obtain information not otherwise available as to the intentions and dispositions of the attacking forces in view of the forced withdrawal of the International Control Commission from the Plain of Jars and the imminent threat which the attacks posed to the whole of Laos including the Government of National Union and the entire Geneva settlement.

Not only did the United States not support the military coup attempted in April, but it took immediate and effective steps to support the Government of National Union under Prime Minister Souvanna Phouma. The United States Ambassador [*Leonard Unger*] in Vientiane worked in close harmony with the Soviet Ambassador at that time; and the attitude and actions of the United States Government with respect to the attempted coup are well known to the Soviet Government.

The United States continues to exert every effort to resolve the Laotian problem by peaceful means in accordance with the 1962 Agreements. In this connection, the United States Government participated in consultations at Vientiane called for by Prime Minister Souvanna Phouma under paragraph 4 of the Declaration on the Neutrality of Laos.[48] The United States regrets that the Soviet Government did not join in those consultations. In addition, as the Soviet Government will recall, the United States has given its support to the proposal of the Polish Government for diplomatic talks among the Lao parties,

[48] Document 53.

the Co-Chairmen and members of the International Control Commission. The United States Government has been disturbed to note the rejection of these proposals by the Pathet Lao, the North Vietnamese and the Chinese Communists. The United States continues to believe that a preliminary conference of the general type suggested by the Polish Government offers the best hope of dealing with the current problems on the diplomatic level.

The United States Government notes that, in its statement, the Soviet Government proposes the convening of an international conference on Laos in August. As the Soviet Government is undoubtedly aware, Prime Minister Souvanna Phouma, in a communique of May 24, 1964, addressed himself to a similar proposal. In his statement, the Prime Minister expressed a willingness to attend such a conference if, first, a cease-fire were effected in Laos under International Control Commission supervision and the Pathet Lao withdrew from those areas which it illegally occupied by virtue of its May attacks. The United States Government believes the position of the Prime Minister is justified and fully supports this position.

In sum, the United States Government remains of the view that the 1962 Geneva Agreements provide a sound basis for resolution of the Laotian question. What is needed above all is compliance with those Agreements by those who have thus far ignored their commitments. Nevertheless, the United States is prepared to attend a conference such as that proposed by the Soviet Government if Prime Minister Souvanna Phouma's preconditions are met and it is thus demonstrated that there is some reason to believe that such a conference may serve a useful purpose.

D. Cambodia.[49]

(55) *Dispute with South Vietnam and the United States.*

(a) *Statement by United States Representative Adlai E. Stevenson to the United Nations Security Council, May 21, 1964.*[50]

(Excerpts)

The facts about the incidents at issue are relatively simple and clear.

[49] For discussion see *The United States in World Affairs, 1964,* pp. 168-174.
[50] Department of State Press Release 249, May 21, 1964; text from *Department of State Bulletin,* June 8, 1964, pp. 907-913.

The Government of the Republic of Viet-Nam already has confirmed that, in the heat of battle, forces of the Republic of Viet-Nam did, in fact, mistakenly cross an ill-marked frontier between their country and Cambodia in pursuit of armed terrorists on May 7 and May 8, and on earlier occasions. That has been repeated and acknowledged here again today by the representative of Viet-Nam.

The Government of Viet-Nam has expressed its regrets that these incidents occurred with some tragic consequences. It has endeavored to initiate bilateral discussions with the Cambodian Government to remove the causes of these incidents.

But these incidents can only be assessed intelligently in the light of the surrounding facts: namely, the armed conspiracy which seeks to destroy not only the Government of Viet-Nam but the very society of Viet-Nam itself.

Mr. President, it is the people of the Republic of Viet-Nam who are the major victims of armed aggression. It is they who are fighting for their independence against violence directed from outside their borders. It is they who suffer day and night from the terror of the so-called Viet Cong. The prime targets of the Viet Cong for kidnaping, for torture, and for murder have been local officials, schoolteachers, medical workers, priests, agricultural specialists, and any others whose position, profession, or other talents qualified them for service to the people of Viet-Nam—plus, of course, the relatives and children of citizens loyal to their Government.

The chosen military objectives of the Viet Cong—for gunfire or arson or pillage—have been hospitals, schoolhouses, agricultural stations, and various improvement projects by which the Government of Viet-Nam for many years has been raising the living standards of the people. The Government and people of Viet-Nam have been struggling for survival, struggling for years for survival in a war which has been as wicked, as wanton, and as dirty as any waged against an innocent and peaceful people in the whole cruel history of warfare. So there is something ironic in the fact that the victims of this incessant terror are the accused before this Council and are defending themselves in daylight while terrorists perform their dark and dirty work by night throughout their land.

Why the U.S. Is Involved in Viet-Nam

Mr. President, I cannot ignore the fact that at the meeting of this Council 2 days ago, Ambassador [N. T.] Fedorenko, the distinguished representative of the Soviet Union, digressed at great length from the subject before the Council to accuse the United States Government of organizing direct military action against the people of the Indochinese peninsula.

For years—too many years—we have heard these bold and unsupported accusations. I had hoped that these fairy tales would be heard no more. But since the subject has been broached in so fanciful a way, let me set him straight on my Government's policy with respect to Southeast Asia.

First, the United States has no, repeat *no,* national military objective anywhere in Southeast Asia. United States policy for Southeast Asia is very simple. It is the restoration of peace so that the peoples of that area can go about their own independent business in whatever associations they may freely choose for themselves without interference from the outside.

I trust my words have been clear enough on this point.

Second, the United States Government is currently involved in the affairs of the Republic of Viet-Nam for one reason and one reason only: because the Republic of Viet-Nam requested the help of the United states and of other governments to defend itself against armed attack fomented, equipped, and directed from the outside.

This is not the first time that the United States Government has come to the aid of peoples prepared to fight for their freedom and independence against armed aggression sponsored from outside their borders. Nor will it be the last time unless the lesson is learned once and for all by *all* aggressors that armed aggression does not pay—that it no longer works—that it will not be tolerated.

* * *

The Cambodia–Viet-Nam Frontier

Now, Mr. President, if we can return to the more limited issue before this Council today: the security of the frontier between Cambodia and the Republic of Viet-Nam. My Government is in complete sympathy with the concern of the Government of Cambodia for the sanctity of its borders and the security of its people. Indeed, we have been guided for nearly a decade, in this respect, by the words of the final declaration of the Geneva conference of July 21, 1954: [51]

In their relations with Cambodia, Laos and Viet-Nam, each member of the Geneva Conference undertakes to respect the sovereignty,

[51] *Documents, 1954,* p. 314.

the independence, the unity, and the territorial integrity of the above-mentioned states, and to refrain from any interference in their internal affairs.

With respect to the allegations now made against my country,[52] I shall do no more than reiterate what Ambassador [Charles W.] Yost, the United States delegate, said to this Council on Tuesday morning: [53] The United States has expressed regret officially for the tragic results of the border incidents in which an American adviser was present; our careful investigations so far have failed to produce evidence that any Americans were present in the inadvertent crossing of the Cambodian frontier on May 7 and May 8; and there is, of course, no question whatever of either aggression or aggressive intent against Cambodia on the part of my country.

Let me emphasize, Mr. President, that my Government has the greatest regard for Cambodia and its people and its Chief of State, Prince [*Norodom*] Sihanouk, whom I have the privilege of knowing. We believe he has done a great deal for his people and for the independence of his country. We have demonstrated our regard for his effort on behalf of his people in very practical ways over the past decade. We have no doubt that he wants to assure conditions in which his people can live in peace and security. My Government associates itself explicitly with this aim. If the people of Cambodia wish to live in peace and security and independence—and free from external alinement if they so choose—then we want for them precisely what they want for themselves. We have no quarrel whatsoever with the desire of Cambodia to go its own way.

The difficulty, Mr. President, has been that Cambodia has not been in a position to carry out, with its own unaided strength, its own desire to live in peace and tranquillity. Others in the area have not been prepared to leave the people of Cambodia free to pursue their own ends independently and peacefully. The recent difficulties along the frontier which we have been discussing here in the Council are only superficially and accidentally related to the Republic of Viet-Nam. They are deeply and directly related to the fact that the leaders and armed forces of North Viet-Nam, supported by Communist China, have abused the right of Cambodia to live in peace by using Cambodian territory as a passageway, a source of supply, and a sanctuary from counterattack by the forces of South Viet-Nam, which is trying

[52] For text of Cambodian complaint see U.N. Document S/5697, May 13, 1964.
[53] U.S. Delegation Press Release 4391, May 19, 1964.

to maintain its right to live in peace and go its own way, too. Obviously Cambodia cannot be secure, her territorial integrity cannot be assured, her independence cannot be certain, as long as outsiders direct massive violence within the frontiers of her neighboring states. This is the real reason for troubles on the Cambodian border; this is the real reason we are here today.

Now it is suggested that the way to restore security on the Cambodian-Vietnamese border is to reconvene the Geneva conference which 10 years ago reached the solemn agreement which I just read to you.

Mr. President, we can surely do better than that. There is no need for another such conference. A Geneva conference on Cambodia could not be expected to produce an agreement any more effective than the agreements we already have. This Council is seized with a specific issue. The Cambodians have brought a specific complaint to this table. Let us deal with it. There is no need to look elsewhere.

We can make, here and now, a constructive decision to help meet the problem that has been laid before us by the Government of Cambodia—to help keep order on her frontier with Viet-Nam and thus to help eliminate at least one of the sources of tension and violence which afflict the area as a whole.

Let me say, Mr. President, that my Government endorses the statement made by the distinguished representative of Cambodia [Voeunsai Sonn] to the Council on Tuesday when he pointed out that states which are not members of the United Nations are not thereby relieved of responsibility for conducting their affairs in line with the principles of the charter of this organization. We could not agree more fully. Yet the regimes of Peiping and Hanoi, which are not members of this organization, are employing or supporting the use of force against their neighbors. This is why the borders of Cambodia have seen violence. And this is why we are here today. And that is why the United Nations has a duty to do what it can do to maintain order along the frontier between Cambodia and Viet-Nam—to help uphold the principles of the charter in Southeast Asia.

As for the exact action which this Council might take, Mr. President, my Government is prepared to consider several possibilities. We are prepared to discuss any practical and constructive steps to meet the problem before us.

One cannot blame the Vietnamese for concluding that the International Control Commission cannot do an effective job of maintaining frontier security. The "troika" principle of the International Control Commission, which is to say the requirement under article 42 of the Geneva agreement on Viet-Nam [54] that decisions dealing with questions concerning violations which might lead to resumption of hostilities can be taken only by unanimous agreement, has contributed to the frustration of the ICC.

The fact that the situation in South Viet-Nam has reached the crisis stage is itself dramatic testimony of the frustration to which the International Control Commission has been reduced. With the exception of the special report on June 2, 1962,[55] to which I referred, condemning Communist violations of the Geneva accords, the Commission has taken no action with respect to the Communist campaign of aggression and guerrilla warfare against South Viet-Nam.

The representative of Cambodia has suggested that a commission of inquiry investigate whether the Viet Cong has used Cambodian territory. We have no fundamental objection to a committee of inquiry. But we do not believe it addresses itself to the basic problem that exists along the Viet-Nam–Cambodian border. More is needed in order to assure that problems do not continue to arise.

Several practical steps for restoring stability to the frontier have been suggested, and I shall make brief and preliminary general remarks about them. I should like to reiterate what Ambassador Yost said, that we have never rejected any proposal for inspection of Cambodian territory.

One suggestion is that the Council request the two parties directly concerned to establish a substantial military force on a bilateral basis to observe and patrol the frontier and to report to the Secretary-General.

Another suggestion is that such a bilateral force be augmented by the addition of United Nations observers and possibly be placed under United Nations command to provide an impartial third-party element representing the world community. We also could see much merit in this idea.

A third suggestion is to make it an all-United Nations force. This might also be effective. It would involve somewhat larger U.N. expenditures than the other alternatives. But if this method should prove desirable to the members of the Council, the United States will be prepared to contribute.

We would suggest, Mr. President, that whether one of these or some other practical solution is agreed [*upon*], it would be useful to ask the Secretary-General of the United Nations to offer

[54] *Documents, 1954,* p. 298.
[55] For Department of State statement on the report see *Department of State Bulletin,* July 16, 1962, pp. 109-110.

assistance to Cambodia and the Republic of Viet-Nam in clearly marking the frontiers between the two countries. One of the difficulties is that there are places where one does not know whether he stands on one side of the frontier or the other. Certainly it would help reduce the possibility of further incidents if this uncertainty were to be removed.

In conclusion, Mr. President, let me repeat that I am prepared to discuss the policy and the performance of my Government throughout Southeast Asia. But the issue before us is the security of the Cambodian–Viet-Nam border. I have expressed my Government's views on that subject. I hope other members of the Council also will express their views on that subject and that the Council, which is the primary world agency for peace and security, can quickly take effective steps to remedy a situation which could threaten peace and security.

(b) *Resolution of the United Nations Security Council, Adopted June 4, 1964.*[56]

The Security Council,

Considering the complaint by the Royal Government of Cambodia in document S/5697,

Noting the statements made in the Council in regard to this complaint,

Noting with regret the incidents which have occurred on Cambodian territory and the existing situation on the Cambodian-Vietnamese frontier,

Taking note of the apologies and regrets tendered to the Royal Government of Cambodia in regard to these incidents and the loss of life they have entailed,

Noting also the desire of the Governments of the Kingdom of Cambodia and the Republic of Viet-Nam to succeed in restoring their relations to a peaceful and normal state,

1. *Deplores* the incidents caused by the penetration of units of the Army of the Republic of Viet-Nam into Cambodian territory;

2. *Requests* that just and fair compensation should be offered to the Royal Government of Cambodia;

3. *Invites* those responsible to take all appropriate measures to prevent any further violation of the Cambodian frontier;

4. *Requests* all States and Authorities and in particular the members of the Geneva Conference to recognize and respect Cambodia's neutrality and territorial integrity;

5. *Decides* to send three of its members to the two countries

[56] U.N. Document S/5741, June 4, 1964, adopted unanimously.

and to the places where the most recent incidents have occurred in order to consider such measures as may prevent any recurrence of such incidents.[57] They will report to the Security Council within forty-five days.

(56) *The United Nations Mission to Cambodia and Vietnam: Letter from Ambassador Stevenson to the United Nations Security Council, September 9, 1964.*[58]

DEAR MR. PRESIDENT: I have the honor to refer to the report of the Security Council Mission to the Kingdom of Cambodia and the Republic of Vietnam which was submitted to the President of the Security Council on July 27, 1964 (S/5832).

After studying the report with great care and interest, my Government has come to the conclusion that the recommendations made in Part VI—particularly those looking toward the establishment of a group of United Nations observers and the resumption of political relations between Cambodia and Vietnam—offer genuine promise of reducing the incidents which have occurred along the common border between Cambodia and Vietnam and, at the same time, other sources of recent tension between these two countries. My Government believes that the members of the Security Council Mission should be commended for the wisdom they demonstrated in making recommendations which have two great merits: not only do they point in the direction of an improved future, but also they point to practical, albeit modest, ways in which the United Nations can again exercise its fundamental and indispensable peacekeeping responsibilities. My Government has noted with satisfaction that the Republic of Vietnam, one of the two principal parties concerned, has exhibited a forthcoming attitude toward the recommendations of the Security Council Mission.

These recommendations stem from the Security Council resolution of June 4, 1964 (S/5741) [59]—a resolution which was passed in response to a complaint brought before the Council on an urgent basis by the Royal Government of Cambodia. It has been, therefore, a source of both surprise and regret to my Government to note the attitude of the Royal Cambodian Government toward the report of the Security Council Mission. In addi-

[57] U.N. Document S/5749, June 5, 1964; Brazil, the Ivory Coast, and Morocco were appointed by the President of the Security Council to carry out this mission.
[58] U.N. Document S/5955, September 9, 1964; text from *Department of State Bulletin,* October 12, 1964, pp. 527-529.
[59] Document 55b.

tion to casting aspersions upon the independence, objectivity and impartiality of the members of the Security Council Mission, the Royal Cambodian Government has adopted an attitude toward the report which argues, on the one hand, that the Mission's recommendations are not responsive to the Cambodian complaint and, on the other hand, that the United Nations is not competent to judge what steps can be taken to ameliorate a situation brought to the Security Council by the Cambodian Government itself. Faced with this incongruous attitude of the Royal Cambodian Government, my Government has been perplexed in its efforts to discern the motive behind the Cambodian complaint to the Security Council.

My Government has been surprised by a further element of incongruity; namely, despite its contention that United Nations organs are not competent to suggest remedial measures for the unfortunate friction along the Cambodian-Vietnamese border, the Royal Cambodian Government has continued to bring to the attention of the Security Council charges of alleged violations of Cambodian territory or air space by the armed forces of the Republic of Vietnam and the United States. One of these charges constitutes a very serious accusation to be leveled against any country. I am referring, of course, to the Cambodian charge that the Republic of Vietnam and my Government have recently engaged in chemical warfare against the civilian population of Cambodia. This charge was made in a cable to the Security Council President from the Cambodian Foreign Minister (S/5839) [*July 28, 1964*] and has been repeated elsewhere, often with differing details.

My Government has repeatedly and categorically denied this Cambodian charge,[60] as has the Republic of Vietnam. Further, both my Government and the Republic of Vietnam have proposed an impartial international investigation of the Cambodian charge. The Royal Cambodian Government has been unwilling to agree to such an impartial investigation. A letter of August 30 to the Security Council President from Foreign Minister [Huot] Sambath, while reasserting the charge, suggests that the request for an impartial inquiry has come "too late" and is "unacceptable under present circumstances" (S/5940). An earlier official Cambodian statement, a communique from the Ministry of Information on August 16, stated *inter alia* that the assistance of "foreign bureaucrats" was not necessary in

[60] For U.S. letters of August 3 and August 14 see U.N. Documents S/5847 and S/5894; texts in *Department of State Bulletin,* August 24, 1964, pp. 274-275; same, August 31, 1964, p. 319.

counting the number of victims of the chemical warfare allegedly undertaken by the Republic of Vietnam and my Government. This, of course, was not what had been proposed. The proposal was, rather, that a qualified international body be permitted to conduct an impartial inquiry into completely unsubstantiated charges that many Cambodians died as a result of poisonous chemicals spread over Cambodian territory by the Republic of Vietnam and the United States.

Although the reasons for the Cambodian attitude may not be clear, it is apparent that the Royal Cambodian Government is unwilling to subject its charges to the scrutiny of impartial investigation. In this connection, it is worth particular note that two of the occasions on which it is charged that South Vietnamese aircraft dispersed poisonous chemicals over Cambodian territory allegedly took place well before the Security Council Mission had arrived in Cambodia; another occasion allegedly took place while the Mission was visiting the Republic of Vietnam. It is difficult to understand why the Royal Cambodian Government did not bring these alleged incidents to the attention of the Security Council Mission while it was in the area.

In conclusion, Mr. President, I wish to reiterate my Government's belief that the recommendations in the report of the Security Council Mission—assuming arrangements can be agreed on for their implementation—represent practical, although limited, steps by which the United Nations can exercise its peacekeeping responsibilities and contribute to a reduction of tension in Southeast Asia. My Government can only regret that the Royal Cambodian Government does not look upon these recommendations—which stemmed from its own urgent appeal to the Security Council—in a similar light.

I should be grateful if you would have this letter circulated as a Security Council document.

(57) *United States–Cambodian Talks, New Delhi, December 8-17, 1964.*

(a) *Department of State Statement, November 27, 1964.*[61]

Two days ago, on November 25, the United States Government proposed to the Royal Cambodian Government that the U.S.-Cambodian talks which had been originally proposed by the United States on November 16 commence on December 7. As you know, New Delhi has been agreed upon as the site for

[61] *Department of State Bulletin,* December 14, 1964, pp. 856-857.

the discussions. Yesterday the Cambodian Government accepted the proposed date and confirmed that the Cambodian Chief of State [*Prince Norodom Sihanouk*] has designated his Privy Counselor, Mr. Son Sann, as chief Cambodian representative at the talks. He will be assisted by the Cambodian Ambassador to India, Mr. Nong Kimny. President Johnson has designated Ambassador Philip W. Bonsal as his representative at the talks. Mr. Bonsal is former Director of the Office of Southeast Asian Affairs and attended the 1954 Geneva conference on Indochina. The Ambassador joined the Foreign Service in 1938. He has served as Ambassador to Colombia, Bolivia, Cuba, and Morocco. For the past several months he has been serving as a consultant to the Policy Planning Council in the Department.

No agenda has been fixed or announced. Our position on these talks is that they should be aimed at existing differences, that is, resolving those differences between Cambodia and the United States, but each side should be free to introduce any subject relevant to this purpose. We would not consider it appropriate to negotiate on matters involving the interests of third countries without their participation.

(b) *Department of State Statement, December 17, 1964.*[62]

The United States–Cambodian talks which began in New Delhi on December 8 ended today without agreement on major differences. Ambassador Philip W. Bonsal, leader of the U.S. delegation, issued the following statement in New Delhi earlier today:

"In view of the deterioration in Cambodian-United States relations, the United States proposed these talks with the primary object of leaving no stone unturned to ensure that the Royal Cambodian Government understood the position of the United States. This much has been accomplished. It was also our hope to find means to bring about an improvement in relations between us. The Cambodian Government has put forward a number of proposals which will require considerable study by my Government. Accordingly, the U.S. delegation is returning to Washington to report."

[62] *Department of State Bulletin,* January 4, 1965, p. 6.

E. Malaysia and Indonesia.[63]

(58) *Joint Communiqué of President Johnson and Prime Minister Abdul Rahman of Malaysia, Washington, July 23, 1964.*[64]

The President of the United States and the Prime Minister of Malaysia met on July 22 and 23 to discuss matters of mutual interest and recent developments in Southeast Asia.

President Johnson and Prime Minister Tunku Abdul Rahman welcomed this, their first meeting, and the opportunity it presented to become personally acquainted and to review major problems in Southeast Asia. The President and the Prime Minister discussed the Communist threat to and activities in Laos and Vietnam and reaffirmed their support of the cause of freedom in those countries. The President noted with appreciation the contribution Malaysia has made to the common cause in Vietnam by providing equipment, training and advice based on her own experience in combating Communist terrorism. In turn the President made clear that all Southeast Asian countries, including Malaysia, could rely on the firm intent of the United States to resist Communist aggression against free Asian nations.

The Prime Minister reviewed developments in Malaysia with the President and progress made thus far in furthering the economic and social progress of its people. The Prime Minister also expressed appreciation for the contribution of American Peace Corps Volunteers in this task.

The President informed the Prime Minister of his special interest in Malaysia's impressive achievements in the fields of education, economic growth and rural development. The President noted with admiration the Prime Minister's objective of a happy and prosperous nation upholding the principles of justice, freedom and democracy.

The Prime Minister outlined for the President the origins of the Malaysia concept and the history of its formation, and in this context reviewed the current activities by a neighboring state [*Indonesia*] in violation of the territorial integrity of Malaysia.

The Prime Minister recounted his determined and various efforts to seek an amicable and honorable solution to the prob-

[63] For discussion see *The United States in World Affairs, 1964,* pp. 174-185.

[64] White House Press Release, July 23, 1964; text from *Department of State Bulletin,* August 10, 1964, p. 193.

lem including the recent tripartite meeting in Tokyo.[65] He also informed the President of the discussions at the recent Commonwealth Prime Ministers Conference in London.

The President re-affirmed the support of the United States for a free and independent Malaysia, and for Malaysia's effort to maintain her security, preserve her sovereignty and continue her development in peace and harmony.

The President agreed to provide military training in the United States for Malaysian personnel, and to consider promptly and sympathetically credit sales, under existing arrangements, of appropriate military equipment for the defense of Malaysia.

The President expressed his strong hope that a peaceful and honorable way out of the current and dangerous situation could be found, and his appreciation for the earnest endeavors of the Prime Minister to this end. The President and the Prime Minister agreed that, while firmness in self-defense is indispensable, it is better to talk than fight.

The President and the Prime Minister found in the common devotion of the United States and Malaysia to the principles of democratic government and individual freedom a bond of understanding which is certain to bring their two countries into a constantly closer relationship, and agreed to maintain close contact on problems of mutual interest.

(59) *The United States Calls for Negotiation of the Malaysian-Indonesian Dispute: Statement by Ambassador Stevenson to the United Nations Security Council, September 10, 1964.*[66]

My delegation and my Government take a very serious view of the complaint before the Security Council in this case. The Government of Indonesia, a member of the United Nations, has sanctioned the use of force in the pursuit of its quarrel with the sovereign state of Malaysia, which is also a member of the United Nations. The distinguished representative of Indonesia has, indeed, expressed pride in the guerrillas and suggested that his Government will continue to use force until there is a *settlement* of its *quarrel* with Malaysia. And we are all aware of the announced objective of Indonesia to "crush Malaysia"—a fellow member of the United Nations.

[65] The reference is to a meeting of the heads of government of Indonesia, Malaysia, and the Philippines held on June 20, 1964.

[66] U.S. Delegation Press Release 4436, September 10, 1964; text from *Department of State Bulletin,* September 28, 1964, pp. 448-450.

But Indonesia's *quarrel* seems to be with the United Kingdom because it sponsored the independence and federation of its dependent territories in the area and is committed to their defense. And the *settlement* proposed by Indonesia seems to be that Malaysia must change its paternity in a manner satisfactory to Indonesia.

But, Mr. President, this is not a paternity case. This is an accusation by Malaysia that Indonesia has violated its territorial integrity by force. And the fact, which has not been denied, is that on the night of September 2, 1964, an armed band of significant size—equipped and transported by Indonesia and intended for violence—landed on the sovereign territory of Malaysia.

This incursion is the complaint before this Council. And it is this specific act of violence which my delegation specifically deplores.

Malaysia is a member of the United Nations which at the time of its creation voluntarily submitted its territories to examination by the United Nations to make certain that it was indeed the desire of their inhabitants to join the new state. Malaysia is therefore to an unusual degree a child of the United Nations.

Mr. President, the deterioration of relations between Indonesia and Malaysia must be distressing to every member of the United Nations. None is more distressed than my Government.

My Government recognizes both Indonesia and Malaysia as independent nations; we have tried to maintain friendly relations with both—relations based on mutual respect and seeking no more than mutual benefit. The test of our intentions does not depend upon faith in words: It is certified by a long record of useful and cooperative deeds.

We were an active member of the United Nations commission which helped bring about the birth of the Indonesian nation; we welcomed the independence of Malaya in 1957 and the proclamation of Malaysia just over a year ago this month. We welcomed Malaysia's admission to the United Nations just as we earlier welcomed the admission of Indonesia. With both of these ancient peoples we have sought to work in friendly harmony from the very moment they joined the lengthening list of newly independent nations. We have participated with both of them on the tangible tasks of nation building—the construction of roads and industries, the development of university education, the modernization of agriculture, the improvement of health and child welfare, the training of security forces. And we have been proud to be associated with military contingents from both of these nations in U.N. peacekeeping operations in other parts of the world.

Hence we are all the more distressed by the spectacle of one of these countries organizing and employing force as an instrument of its policy toward the other. We have welcomed the efforts of these neighbors, together with the assistance of the Philippines and Thailand, to work out a peaceful resolution of their differences. Our President has even sent out a personal representative [*Attorney General Robert F. Kennedy*] to help bring about a cease-fire, to get the conflict out of the jungles and back to the negotiating table.[67]

My Government has believed from the beginning that if there is any legitimate dispute between these two states, which share common problems and enjoy a close ethnic and cultural affinity, it should be settled by negotiation between themselves, with the assistance of whatever good offices they may find mutually helpful.

Against this background, Mr. President, our attitude on the complaint before us grows directly from the obligation each member of this organization has under the charter.

This Council cannot condone the use of force in international relations outside the framework of the charter.

This Council must try to re-create the conditions of peace and security in the area of conflict, to enable the processes of peaceful settlement to move these two nations away from the precipice of war.

Yesterday the distinguished representative of Indonesia was very frank about the fact that force had in fact been used by his Government. He argued that in dealing with neighbors whose policies Indonesia does not like, the use of force on the territory of those neighbors was justified.

He made all too clear that the announced goal to "crush Malaysia" leads in practice to the arming of military units to operate in the territories of a neighboring nation. This is a new and dangerous doctrine of international law, outside the Charter of the United Nations and foreign to everything that man has learned about the danger of escalation from little wars to big wars and the crucial importance of maintaining the peace.

In the world about us there are, this very afternoon, half a hundred active disputes between neighbors—23 of them in Asia, 10 in Africa, 3 in Europe, and 12 in the Western Hemisphere.

[67] *Department of State Bulletin,* February 17, 1964, pp. 239-243. For discussion see *The United States in World Affairs, 1964,* pp. 183-184.

If other nations involved in these disputes were to take the law into their own hands and drop armed forces on the territory of their neighbors, the precarious peace of our inflammable world would soon go up in smoke.

The distinguished representative of Indonesia said we are faced here with a political problem, not a legal one. But you cannot separate politics and law—and the first law of politics is that there must be some minimum agreement to abide by the rules of the game. The way in which the Indonesian case has been stated here makes it even more necessary that this Council, which is entrusted by the charter with the maintenance of peace and security, clearly identify as inadmissible the armed action of the Indonesian Government against Malaysia on September 2.

The Government of Malaysia, while exercising its inherent right of self-defense also has met its obligation under the charter to bring this matter to the Security Council while there is yet time to escape the fateful consequences of violence and counter-violence.

It is now the duty of this Council to fulfill its obligations to the world community.

Let us focus on the fact that a collision has occurred—a collision which is part of a pattern of hostility which promises to recur and which threatens to expand.

Let us then get on with our duty. And our duty, Mr. President, goes far beyond the angry pointing of a finger at a violation of the charter. Our larger duty is to devise measures to keep these flames from spreading. For it is unmistakably clear that the outer limits of restraint have been reached. And we are face to face with the dread prospect of escalating violence, with unforeseeable consequences for us all.

Mr. President, this Council can do two practical things. I suggest we get right to work on them.

First, the Council should call for the cessation of armed attack on Malaysia.

Second, the Council should help the parties to this dispute establish the condition and climate in which a negotiation on the merits of the disputed issues can be pursued with any prospect of success. This Council and the Secretary-General may well have a role to play in the establishment of such conditions. And the first condition is, of course, compliance with the call of the Security Council to cease hostilities. Once this improved climate has been created, efforts could then be made to resolve the entire dispute by nonviolent means.

Instruments for peaceful settlement are available. Our task

under the charter as members of this Council is to see to it that an agreed instrument is chosen at the earliest possible date and that the parties take steps to pave the way for a return to diplomacy.

The United States delegation has no interest in recriminations about what has happened in the past; we are concerned with the present and the future of peace, and the means of restoring peace and keeping peace in this case. The United States is ready to work constructively and promptly with a deep sense of concern and a sharp sense of urgency for action by the Security Council to put a stop to violence, to create the conditions for peaceful settlement. And I am sure that, as in so many previous cases, there are practical and effective measures available to the United Nations and the Secretary-General to help attain these objectives.

(60) *Action by the United Nations Security Council: Draft Resolution Vetoed by the U.S.S.R., September 17, 1964.*[68]

The Security Council,

Taking note of the complaint of Malaysia contained in document S/5930,

Taking into consideration the statements of the parties and of the members of the Council expressed during the discussion,

Deeply concerned by the fact that the armed incidents which have occurred in that region have seriously aggravated the situation and are likely to endanger peace and security in that region,

Noting with satisfaction the desire of the parties to seek a peaceful solution of the differences between them,

Recalling the relevant provisions of the United Nations Charter,

1. *Regrets* all the incidents which have occurred in the whole region;
2. *Deplores* the incident of 2 September 1964 which forms the basis of the complaint contained in document S/5930;
3. *Requests* the parties concerned to make every effort to avoid the recurrence of such incidents;
4. *Calls upon* the parties to refrain from all threat or use of force and to respect the territorial integrity and political independence of each other, and thus to create a conducive atmosphere for the continuation of their talks;

[68] U.N. Document S/5973, September 15, 1964; defeated by a vote of 9 in favor, 2 opposed (U.S.S.R. and Czechoslovakia).

5. *Recommends* to the Governments concerned thereupon to resume their talks on the basis of the joint communiqué issued by the Heads of Government following the meeting which took place in Tokyo on 20 June 1964. The Reconciliation Commission provided for by that joint communiqué, once established, should keep the Security Council informed concerning the development of the situation.

CHAPTER SEVEN

INTER-AMERICAN AFFAIRS

A. The Alliance for Progress.[1]

(61) *Address by President Johnson to the Pan American Union, Washington, March 16, 1964.*[2]

(Excerpts)

Thirty-one years ago this month Franklin [*D.*] Roosevelt proclaimed the policy of the Good Neighbor. Three years ago this month John [*F.*] Kennedy called for an Alliance for Progress among the American Republics.[3] Today my country rededicates itself to these principles and renews its commitment to the partnership of the hemisphere to carry them forward.

We meet as fellow citizens of a remarkable hemisphere. Here, a century and a half ago, we began the movement for national independence and freedom from foreign rule which is still the most powerful force in all the world. Here, despite occasional conflict, we have peacefully shared our hemisphere to a degree unmatched by any nation, anywhere.

Here, and in this very room, we have helped create a system of international cooperation which Franklin Roosevelt called "the oldest and the most successful association of sovereign governments anywhere in the world." Here are 20 nations who, sharing the traditions and values of Western civilization, are bound together by a common belief in the dignity of man. Here are 20 nations who have no desire to impose a single ideology or system on anyone else, who believe that each country must follow its own path to fulfillment with freedom, who take strength from the richness of their diversity.

So it is on this—this history and this accomplishment, these common values and this common restraint—that we base our

[1] For discussion see *The United States in World Affairs, 1964,* pp. 190-198.

[2] White House Press Release, March 16, 1964; text from *Department of State Bulletin,* April 6, 1964, pp. 535-538.

[3] *Documents, 1961,* pp. 395-401; for text of Charter of Punta del Este establishing the Alliance for Progress see same, pp. 416-435.

hope for our future. Today these hopes center largely on the Alliance for Progress that you are all so interested in.

John F. Kennedy has been taken from us. The alliance remains a source for our faith and a challenge to our capacity. The Alliance for Progress owes much to the vision of President Kennedy. But he understood that it flows from the desires and ideas of those in each of our countries who seek progress with freedom. In its councils, all nations sit as equals. This is the special significance of CIAP [Inter-American Committee on the Alliance for Progress] [4]—the organization that we honor today. Through it, the alliance will now be guided by the advice and wisdom of men from throughout the hemisphere.

It needs and is getting the best leadership our continents have to offer. It has such leadership in Carlos Sanz de Santamaría, one of our most distinguished Americans.

Basic Principles of the Alliance

In the last 3 years we have built a structure of common effort designed to endure for many years. In those years much has been accomplished. Throughout Latin America new schools and factories, housing and hospitals have opened new opportunities. Nations have instituted new measures of land and tax reform, educational expansion, and economic stimulus and discipline.

We are proud of these achievements. But as we take pride in what has thus far been done, our minds turn to the great unfinished business. Only by facing these shortcomings, only by fighting to overcome them, can we make our alliance succeed in the years ahead.

Let me make clear what I believe in. They are not failures of principle or failures of belief. The alliance's basic principles of economic development, of social justice, of human freedom, are not only the right path; they are the only path for those who believe that both the welfare and the dignity of man can advance side by side. To those who prize freedom, there just simply is no alternative.

There is no magic formula to avoid the complex and the sometimes painful and difficult task of basic social reform and economic advance. There is no simple trick that will transform despair into hope, that will turn misery and disease into abundance and health. Those who think that the path of progress in this hemisphere will be easy or painless are arousing false hopes and are inviting disappointment.

[4] For text of resolution creating the CIAP see same, *1963*, pp. 407-413.

The criticism which can give us new vigor and which must guide us is of those who share our beliefs but offer us better ways to move toward better goals. We have learned much about the difficulties and the flaws of our alliance in the past 3 years. We must today profit from this experience. With faith in our principles, with pride in our achievements, with the help of candid and constructive criticism, we are now prepared to move ahead with renewed effort and renewed confidence.

Need for Increased Cooperation

The first area of emphasis is increased cooperation—among ourselves, with other nations, with private and public institutions. We will continue our efforts to protect producing nations against disastrous price changes so harmful to their economies, and consumers against short supply and unfair price rises. We will intensify our cooperation in the use of our resources in the process of development. CIAP itself is an important step in that direction, and CIAP has our full support.

But other institutions as well—the Inter-American and World Banks, the private foundations and cooperatives, the savings institutions and sources of agricultural credit—must in every country focus their energies on the efforts to overcome the massive difficulties of capital shortage and hunger and lack of adequate educational facilities.

So that my own country's participation in this cooperation might receive needed leadership and direction, I have given Secretary [*Thomas C.*] Mann, who enjoys my highest confidence, broad responsibility for our role in the alliance.[5] His appointment reflects my complete determination to meet all the commitments of the United States to the alliance.

Our pledge of substantial external help has been met in the past, and my administration will spare no effort to meet it in the future, and my confidence is reinforced by my knowledge that the people of the United States also support that commitment to our fellow Americans.

We urge and we welcome the constructive contribution of developed nations outside this hemisphere. We believe in diversity in the modern world. We can all learn from one another. Capital, technical know-how, access to markets, fair prices for basic commodities—all of these will contribute to the rapid development which is the goal of all of us.

[5] Thomas C. Mann, the then Assistant Secretary of State for Inter-American Affairs and U.S. Coordinator for the Alliance for Progress.

But public funds are not enough. We must work together to insure the maximum use of private capital, domestic and foreign; without it, growth will certainly fall far behind. Such capital will respond to a stable prospect of fair earnings and a chance to create badly needed industry and business on a responsible and safe and sound basis. Those who destroy the confidence of risk capital, or deny it a chance to offer its energy and talent, endanger the hopes of their people for a more abundant life, because our abundant life flows from that energy and from that talent that we have given a chance.

The Area of Self-Help

The second area of emphasis is the area of self-help. Progress cannot be created by forming international organizations. Progress cannot be imposed by foreign countries. Progress cannot be purchased with large amounts of money or even with large amounts of good will.

Progress in each country depends upon the willingness of that country to mobilize its own resources, to inspire its own people, to create the conditions in which growth can and will flourish, for although help can come from without, success must come only from within. Those who are not willing to do that which is unpopular and that which is difficult will not achieve that which is needed or that which will be lasting. This is as true of my own country's fight against poverty and racial injustice as it is of the fight of others against hunger and disease and illiteracy —the ancient enemies of all mankind.

By broadening education, we can liberate new talents and energy, freeing millions from the bonds of illiteracy. Through land reform aimed at increased production, taking different forms in each country, we can provide those who till the soil with self-respect and increased income, and each country with increased production to feed the hungry and to strengthen their economy.

Fair and progressive taxes, effectively collected, can provide the resources that are needed to improve education and public-health conditions and the social structure that is needed for economic growth. Measures ranging from control of inflation and encouragement of exports to the elimination of deficits in public enterprises can help provide the basis of economic stability and growth on which our alliance can flourish.

The Pursuit of Social Justice

The third area of emphasis is the pursuit of social justice. Development and material progress are not ends in themselves. They are means to a better life and means to an increased opportunity for us all. They are the means for each to contribute his best talents and each to contribute his best desires. They are the means to the full dignity of man, for the Alliance for Progress is a recognition that the claims of the poor and the oppressed are just claims. It is an effort to fulfill those claims while at the same time strengthening democratic society and maintaining the liberty of man.

So, no matter how great our progress, it will lack meaning unless every American from the Indian of the Andes to the impoverished farmer of Appalachia can share in the fruits of change and growth. Land reform, tax changes, education expansion, the fight against disease all contribute to this end. Everything else that we must do must be shaped by these guiding principles. In these areas—cooperation, self-help, social justice—new emphasis can bring us closer to success.

At the same time we must protect the alliance against the efforts of communism to tear down all that we are building. The recent proof of Cuban aggression in Venezuela is only the latest evidence of those intentions. We will soon discuss how best we can meet these threats to the independence of us all. But I now, today, assure you that the full power of the United States is ready to assist any country whose freedom is threatened by forces dictated from beyond the shores of this continent.

* * *

Faith in the Power of Freedom

Those of us who have gathered here today must realize that we are the principal guardians of the Alliance for Progress. But the alliance is not here, and it is not in office buildings; it is not in meeting rooms in presidential mansions throughout the hemisphere. The alliance is in the aspirations of millions of farmers and workers, of men without education, of men without hope, of poverty-stricken families whose homes are the villages and the cities of an entire continent.

They ask simply the opportunity to enter into the world of progress and to share in the growth of the land. From their leaders, from us, they demand concern and compassion and dedicated leadership and dedicated labor.

I am confident that in the days to come we will be able to meet those needs. It will not be an easy task. The barriers are huge. The enemies of our freedom seek to harass us at every turn. We are engaged in a struggle for the destiny of the American Republics, but it was a great poet, William Butler Yeats, who reminded us that there was doubt if any nation can become prosperous unless it has national faith. Our alliance will prosper because, I believe, we do have that faith. It is not idle hope but the same faith that enabled us to nourish a new civilization in these spacious continents, and in that new world we will carry forward our Alliance for Progress in such a way that men in all lands will marvel at the power of freedom to achieve the betterment of man.

(62) *President Johnson Signs Twelve Alliance for Progress Agreements: Remarks by the President, Washington, May 11, 1964.*[6]

(Excerpts)

Ladies and gentlemen: I want to welcome you to the White House this evening. I am slightly tardy because we have just completed an informal review of the Alliance for Progress problems with all of the ambassadors and the distinguished head of CIAP [Inter-American Committee on the Alliance for Progress]. This kind of exchange, we think, strengthens our common aim and our combined ability to advance the alliance.

* * *

I said last November, let us make the Alliance for Progress President Kennedy's living memorial.[7]

Today's agreements are part of our pledge. The United States will provide almost $40 million—the countries of Latin America will provide $60 million—for projects that we are beginning in 13 countries. These projects will help eliminate malaria in Brazil. They will help train farmers in Bolivia. They will establish for the first time three rural electric cooperatives serving 10,000 homes and farms in the countryside of Colombia. They will bring credit and assistance to 21,000 small farms in the land reform and colonization areas of Peru. They will touch the lives and ease the struggles of 23 million people across our hemisphere.

[6] White House Press Release, May 11, 1964; text from *Department of State Bulletin,* June 1, 1964, pp. 854-857.
[7] Cf. *Documents, 1963,* p. 423.

These are only the latest steps in 6 months of very extraordinary effort since I became President. Since last December the United States has extended more than $430 million in assistance. In that 6-month period, we have, by working together, completed more than 52,000 homes, 7,000 new classrooms. We have produced more than a million and a half schoolbooks. We have made more than 25,000 loans to farmers. We have put into operation health programs to care for 4 million people and Food for Peace programs to feed more than 10 million of our fellow Americans. We have built more than 500 miles of roads. We have trained more than 10,000 teachers. We have trained more than 1,000 public administrators. We have established already more than 200 credit unions. If any of you want the address after the meeting, I will be glad to supply it to you. We have 300 water systems that will benefit 10 million people.

In the months to come, we intend to more than double the pace of this action. For this is the time and this is the day and this is an administration of action.

Development, Diversity, and Democracy

Our help is only a small proportion of the resources for growth and the reforms for justice contributed by all of you—you, the countries of Latin America. These are the tangible tokens of the constancy of our cause since the signing of the Charter of Punta del Este.[8] What we believed in then—I should not have to repeat—we stand for now. What we agreed to then, we support now. What we sought and looked forward to then, we seek now.

This is as it must be. Our programs and our policies are not founded on the shifting sands of momentary concern or the passing opinions of any one official or any present official. They are the inescapable issue of the events of our past and the hazards of our present.

When President Kennedy made his first statement to the ambassadors in the dining room of this house on the Alliance for Progress,[9] he said we are going to wage a war on the ancient enemies of mankind—poverty, illiteracy, and disease. We say now, if a peaceful revolution is impossible, a violent revolution is inevitable.

These things are rooted in our devotion to our democratic birthright and dedication to our spiritual values. They are, I want you to know, in short, the only objectives possible to men

[8] Same, *1961*, pp. 416-432.
[9] Same, pp. 395-401.

that seek to retain freedom and protect moral values while pursuing progress in a world that is on the march.

* * *

I have asked the Congress for the funds necessary to meet our obligation under the Alliance for Progress.[10] I will fight for those funds with every resource of my Government. Furthermore, I intend to ask for $250 million this year to replenish the Bank's Fund for Special Operations in accordance with the unanimous vote of the Panama meeting of the Inter-American Bank.[11] That Bank, supported first by President Eisenhower, has become a beacon of hope to the oppressed of our lands.

The principle of diversity stems from President Roosevelt's policy of the Good Neighbor. Within the loose and ample frame of the inter-American system there is room for each nation to order its institutions and to organize its economy so long as it respects the rights of its neighbors. In the councils of the alliance we must guide each other toward the most rewarding course of progress. We do not confuse that duty and that responsibility with any desire or any right to impose those views on unwilling neighbors.

* * *

Our charter charges each American country to seek and to strengthen representative democracy. Without that democracy and without the freedom that it nourishes, material progress is an aimless enterprise, destroying the dignity of the spirit that it is really meant to liberate. So we will continue to join with you to encourage democracy until we build a hemisphere of free nations from the Tierra del Fuego to the Arctic Circle.

A New Hemisphere

But the charter of the alliance is not confined to political democracy. It commands a peaceful, democratic, social revolution across the hemisphere. It calls upon us to throw open the gates of opportunity to the landless and the despised, to throw open the gates of opportunity to the poor and to the oppressed. It asks that unjust privilege be ended and that unfair power be curbed.

The United States signed that charter. We are fulfilling that commitment. We have already begun an all-out war on poverty

10 Cf. Document 4.
11 *Department of State Bulletin,* May 4, 1964, p. 719.

in this country, for a just country cannot permit a class of forsaken in the midst of the affluent and the fortunate. We are also marching forward in our struggle to eliminate racial injustice, to permit every man of every race, of every color, of every belief, to share fully in America's national life.

* * *

I know my country's policies and my country's help are very important to the Alliance for Progress. But in 1961 a new hemisphere began to be born. In that hemisphere, success or failure does not hinge on testing each shifting wind or each new word which comes from our neighbors. Rather, it depends on the courage and the leadership that we can bring to our own people in our own land. I am doing my dead-level best to provide that leadership in my country now.

* * *

(63) *Problems and Objectives of the Alliance for Progress: Address by Assistant Secretary of State for Inter-American Affairs Thomas C. Mann, University of Notre Dame, June 7, 1964.*[12]

(Excerpts)

* * *

. . . I would like briefly to discuss with you today one of the problems of our Latin American foreign policy—the problem of what it is we can do to bring about a more effective exercise of representative democracy in the Western Hemisphere. There is no subject concerning our Latin American foreign policy which has over the years generated more debate or a debate which has generated so much heat and, it seems at times, so little light.

The first point I wish to make is that United States foreign policy is firmly and irrevocably committed to the principle that every individual, no matter in what part of the world he lives, has an inalienable right to his individual freedom and to his individual dignity.

* * *

It has long been, and continues to be, our firm policy to discourage any who conspire to overthrow constitutionally elected governments. But if governments are overthrown, it has long

[12] Department of State Press Release 268, June 5, 1964; text from *Department of State Bulletin,* June 29, 1964, pp. 995-1000.

been our practice, in ways compatible with the sovereignty and the national dignity of others, to encourage the holding of free and fair elections—to encourage a return to constitutional procedures. Other American Republics make equally valuable contributions to building a Western Hemisphere tradition of democracy by their example, by the strength of their moral positions, and by expressions of their principles.

It is understandable that all of us sometimes become impatient with the rate of progress toward making this ideal a reality everywhere. We have not yet reached perfection in our own country. Many American Republics have made great progress in establishing a democratic tradition within the last few decades. In others, democracy seems at times to take two steps forward only to be temporarily pushed back a step. In Cuba the light of democracy has temporarily been extinguished.

But we should not, I think, judge either the rate or degree of hemisphere progress toward democracy solely by the number of coups d'etat which take place. The degree of individual freedom which exists in the hemisphere, the average life span of *de facto* governments, the extent of political repression, the degree of freedom of the press and of peaceful assembly, and the growing number of people in the hemisphere who consistently support the principle of free and periodic elections, are also relevant yardsticks.

If one looks at the forest instead of the trees, he can see that these quiet, unpublicized efforts on the part of the United States and other American Republics have, along with many other factors, contributed to a wider and deeper observance of the forms of representative democracy in this hemisphere and, perhaps even more important, to a growing respect by governments, in deeds as well as words, for the dignity of man and for his basic human rights. I am confident that the general movement will continue to be forward; I hope it can be accelerated.

* * *

U.S. Experience with Intervention

It is sometimes said that since the American community of nations has failed to take effective collective action to eliminate dictatorships in the hemisphere, the United States—unilaterally and alone—should undertake to force all Latin American governments to stay on the path of constitutionality. The United

States has had a rather full experience in attempting, with the best of motives, to impose democracy on other countries.

* * *

Our interventions were, in the Latin American point of view, patronizing in the extreme. By making the United States the sole judge of Latin America's political morality, they were degrading to proud peoples who believed that, in their own wars of independence, they had earned the right to manage their own affairs—to be masters in their own houses. They produced schismatic tendencies in the inter-American family and brought our relations with Latin America to an alltime low.

These historical experiences suggest two things: Unilateral United States interventions in the hemisphere have never succeeded, in themselves, in restoring constitutional government for any appreciable period of time. And they have, in every case, left for our country a legacy of suspicion and resentment which has endured long after our interventions were abandoned as impracticable.

* * *

Latin American Doctrine of Nonintervention

As an answer to the United States interventionist doctrines, Latin Americans developed doctrines of their own. Let there be no mistake: These Latin American counterdoctrines were "tailor-made" for the United States; their purpose was to bring an end to United States interventions. I shall mention only one:

By 1928, when the Sixth International Conference of American States met at Habana, a proposal was introduced which stated the simple proposition that "No state has the right to interfere in the internal affairs of another." After a long and somewhat acrimonious debate the United States managed to prevent adoption of the resolution, but the handwriting was on the wall. In 1933, at the Seventh Conference in Montevideo, the United States accepted the doctrine of nonintervention with qualifications. In 1936, at Buenos Aires, we accepted it unconditionally.

This Latin American doctrine of nonintervention is now written into the Charter of the Organization of American States.[13] It is a treaty obligation. Allow me to read to you articles 15 and 16 of the charter:

[13] *Documents, 1948,* pp. 484-503.

ARTICLE 15. No State or group of States has the right to intervene, directly or indirectly, for any reason whatever, in the internal or external affairs of any other State. The foregoing principle prohibits not only armed force but also any other form of interference or attempted threat against the personality of the State or against its political, economic and cultural elements.

ARTICLE 16. No State may use or encourage the use of coercive measures of an economic or political character in order to force the sovereign will of another State and obtain from it advantages of any kind.

As the scholars Thomas [Ann Thomas and A. J. Thomas, Jr.] point out in their study of *Non-Intervention:*

The essence of intervention is the attempt to compel. . . .

All of this does not mean that we will in the future recognize all governments which come into power in an unconstitutional manner. Each case must be looked at in the light of its own facts. Where the facts warrant it—where the circumstances are such, to use someone else's phrase, as to "outrage the conscience of America"—we reserve our freedom to register our indignation by refusing to recognize or to continue our economic cooperation.

It does mean that, consistent with our treaty obligations, we cannot put ourselves in a doctrinaire straightjacket of automatic application of sanctions to every unconstitutional regime in the hemisphere with the obvious intention of dictating internal political developments in other countries. As the facts amply demonstrate, this is no departure from the practice which has prevailed in the most recent years.

The third point to which I invite your attention is this: Unilateral intervention for the purpose of forcing constitutional changes in another country does not always serve either the cause of democracy or the national security interests of the United States.

* * *

Making the Democratic Ideal a Reality

Against this background, what conclusions are to be drawn? What can we do to help make the democratic ideal a reality in this hemisphere? I offer the following suggestions:

First, we should continue, in our bilateral discussions with other governments, to encourage democracy in the quiet, unpublicized way and on the day-to-day basis that I have already referred to; and we should support parallel efforts of other American states. If there is no intent to force the will of a sovereign government, this tactic is entirely compatible with our commitments and with the dignity and self-respect of others.

Second, we should support appropriate measures for broadening the scope of collective action with the aim of addressing ourselves first to those cases where repression, tyranny, and brutality outrage the conscience of mankind. I can think of no way in which the American community of states can better serve the cause of human dignity, individual and national freedom, and representative democracy than to develop a set of procedures for dealing with this type of problem. The United States has never believed that collective action for such purposes is proscribed by the Charter of the Organization of American States; but if the majority of the member states are of a contrary opinion, then let us amend the charter.

Third, in each case where a government is overthrown by force there should be a careful, dispassionate assessment of each situation in the light of all the surrounding facts and circumstances so that decisions concerning recognition, trade, aid, and other related matters can be made which are consistent with our ideals, with international law, and with our overall national interests. In making this assessment, regard should also be paid to the fact that not only is each American Republic different from all the others but that each *de facto* government is likewise different in its aims, its motives, its policies, and in the kinds of problems it faces.

Fourth, if, as a result of this appraisal, a decision is made not to recognize a regime—and this may well be the case in the future as it has been in the past—then it should be made clear that nonrecognition is based squarely on a failure on the part of another government to abide by the established rules of international conduct.

Fifth, when the decision is made to recognize a regime, it should be clear that there is no basis under international law for equating recognition with United States approval of the internal political policies and practices of another government. Resolution XXXV of the Ninth Inter-American Conference of American States makes this point very clear. It declares:

> That the establishment or maintenance of diplomatic relations with a government does not imply any judgment upon the domestic policy of that government.

Sixth, we should continue our established practice of consulting with other American Republics whenever a question of recognition arises.

Finally, let there be no mistake about our consistent and complete devotion to the principles of human dignity and freedom of the individual. We believe that these principles can only be realized in a democratic political system in which governments are the servants of the people and responsive to their will. They are a central element in our foreign policy toward Latin America. We shall in every way consistent with our obligations continue our efforts to help make democracy a reality throughout the entire hemisphere.

* * *

(64) *The Inter-American Committee on the Alliance for Progress (CIAP): Address by W. W. Rostow, Counselor and Chairman of the Department of State Policy Planning Council, West Point, August 7, 1964.*[14]

(Excerpt)

* * *

The Basis for the Inter-American Committee

I speak to you at a particular moment in the history of the Alliance for Progress. We have passed, I believe, a critical turning point in its affairs.

At São Paulo last November 15 the governments of the hemisphere decided to create in CIAP a kind of steering committee or board of directors for the Alliance for Progress.[15] The Chairman of CIAP is Dr. Carlos Sanz de Santamaría, a distinguished Colombian who, I predict, will emerge in this hemisphere as Mr. Alliance for Progress. Under his chairmanship there are seven members of CIAP. Six are Latin Americans. Each is chosen by a group of Latin American countries. Their job, like mine, is to think in terms of the enterprise as a whole and to set policy for the Alliance for Progress, as defined by the letter and spirit of the Charter of Punta del Este.[16] We are advised by three distinguished Latin American leaders: the Secretary General of the OAS [Organization of American States], Dr. [José] Mora; Dr. Felipe Herrera, President of the Inter-American Bank; and Dr. José Antonio Mayobre, Executive Secretary of

[14] Department of State Press Release 359, August 6, 1964, revised; text from *Department of State Bulletin,* August 31, 1964, pp. 306-311.
[15] Same as note 4 to Document 61.
[16] Same as note 8 to Document 62.

the United Nations Economic Commission for Latin America. In addition, there are the "nine wise men"—mainly Latin American economists of the greatest distinction, who advise the Latin American governments on planning and development policy and participate fully in the deliberations of CIAP.

Behind the creation of CIAP lay these fundamental perceptions shared by our governments.

First, the Alliance for Progress cannot and should not be viewed as a bilateral aid program between individual Latin American countries and the United States. It is, as I said earlier, a common commitment by the governments to their peoples that this is the decade in which we shall all work together to bring about in this hemisphere sustained economic growth under conditions of increasing social justice and political democracy. The Alliance for Progress is, in its essence, therefore, a collective and not a bilateral program.

Second, the primary responsibility for conducting the alliance must lie with the nations and peoples of Latin America themselves. No outside power or international institution can bring about the transformations required to yield sustained economic growth, along the social and political lines desired by a nation. Only the human beings within a nation, working together toward a common goal, building and improving their own institutions, can do the job. Moreover, more than 80 percent of the material resources now being invested in Latin America are the resources of the Latin American nations themselves. President Johnson has made it quite clear that the commitment of the United States to the Alliance for Progress has never been stronger than it is today. And I am confident that this is also true of the international institutions—notably the World Bank, led by Mr. George Woods, and the Inter-American Bank, led by Dr. Felipe Herrera, who contributed so much to the CIAP meetings in Mexico City last month. But all of us working to generate and contribute resources from outside Latin America can only be junior partners in the enterprise. The heart of the task lies in the nations of Latin America themselves.

Third, the Alliance for Progress is a multilateral effort in a different sense. There is a strong impulse in Latin America to break out of the traditional national approaches to development, which have marked the last generation, and to work toward increased economic unity in Latin America. That impulse takes many forms, among them efforts to organize the Central American Common Market, the Latin American Free Trade Area [*LAFTA*], and to carry forward a growing list of development projects which involve more than one country and which would bind the nations of Latin America closer together. There is a desire among the Latin American nations and peoples to give increasing economic substance to the elements of common history, common tradition, and common culture of the region; and there are good technical and economic reasons which support this powerful sentiment.

Finally, those who met at São Paulo and created CIAP also perceived that the Alliance for Progress must be multilateral in the sense that all the agencies committed to assist Latin American development should concert their efforts on a team basis in support of the national and multinational plans, programs, and projects which are its substance.

All these insights and judgments lay behind the decision to multilateralize the Alliance for Progress and to create CIAP as an instrument for this purpose.

There was a second strand of thought present at the São Paulo meetings. Taking stock after some 3 years of practical experience with the Alliance for Progress, our governments had every reason to reaffirm the goals and principles of the Punta del Este Charter. But they felt it was time to identify the specific problems that were delaying forward movement and to attack those problems on a practical basis with great energy. They judged that what was required was machinery to move the whole enterprise forward at a faster pace.

Thus, as the members of CIAP gathered in Mexico City last month at our first meeting, we were inspired and guided by these two principles: first, by the desire of our governments to reaffirm the alliance as a multilateral enterprise and to build it in a framework of true hemispheric partnership; and, second, by the need to get on with the job at an accelerated pace. It was in this collective and pragmatic spirit that we worked and wrote our report.[17]

Tasks Outlined by CIAP

I believe you will find our report a somewhat unusual international document. It does not consist of resolutions. It is a statement of a series of problems, followed by specific assignments of responsibility for dealing with them. It is strictly an action document.

The tasks of the alliance are broken down under four major

17 *Final Report: First Meeting of the Inter-American Committee on the Alliance for Progress (CIAP)*, (Washington: Pan American Union, 1964).

headings: the domestic effort of the Latin American nations; foreign trade; problems of external assistance to Latin America; and Latin American economic integration. Under each heading we tried to isolate quite specific problems which have to be solved if the alliance is to reach its targets. We considered how these problems might be tackled; and we assigned action to those elements, within the whole machinery of the Alliance for Progress, which are most capable of bringing about solutions.

As a result of this method I can tell you we made a lot of work for ourselves, for our governments, and for the various institutions committed to the Alliance for Progress.

Between now and the next meeting of CIAP in October [18] of this year we shall have to address ourselves to more than 20 specific tasks, including an intensive country-by-country review of the state of Alliance for Progress plans and programs. A good many of the problems we posed will, of course, not be finally solved between now and October; but, in the wake of this CIAP meeting, I can report to you that, throughout the hemisphere, in the international institutions of the alliance connected with it, and in the Government of the United States, there is not merely great activity but a fresh determination to grapple with these problems and to get on with the job.

Let me briefly list some of these tasks.

We agreed that we must accelerate the formulation of national development plans and programs. Nine countries of the hemisphere have already completed such plans. It is our hope that in the year ahead all the others will do so. As we indicated in our report, we do not believe that such national programing is a panacea for economic development. We need national plans because they offer a useful and essential method for establishing priorities, for achieving balance in the process of economic growth, for identifying critical bottlenecks, and for providing a clear and rational basis for the allocation of external aid.

We agreed that it was necessary to launch a concerted program in Latin America designed to break down the market barriers between the cities and the countryside. Inefficient marketing arrangements not merely make agricultural products in the cities more expensive than they should be, but they also inhibit that expansion and diversification of agriculture which Latin America urgently requires. Moreover, the sluggishness of Latin American agriculture limits the size of industrial markets and prevents more rapid industrial development.

[18] Cf. Document 65.

We agreed that the governments of Latin America should urgently seek greater efficiency in government-owned corporations. Large deficits in certain of these corporations in certain countries are not merely a drain on public revenues but also a major cause of inflation.

We agreed that, quite aside from the work going forward in the United Nations and other international bodies to expand Latin American trade, CIAP should take a hand, especially, in ironing out trade problems within the hemisphere and, if possible, in helping our colleagues in LAFTA get on with their mission.

We agreed that a major effort should be made to generate more projects for external financing in Latin America; and that both Latin American resources and the resources of the governments and agencies engaged in external assistance should be mobilized for that purpose, since it is a fact that there are more resources available, particularly in the international banking institutions, than are now being fully exploited for the financing of projects.

We examined candidly what all the governments of the hemisphere, including the United States Government, could do to speed the flow of external assistance and streamline the methods for granting such assistance.

We launched a new effort to establish guidelines for the role of foreign private investment in Latin America that would reconcile the legitimate interests of the investor and the country concerned.

We examined a catalog of multinational projects now on the drawing boards, or further advanced, which, if completed, would tend to bind Latin America closer together; and we set up machinery to help push these along.

We made arrangements to refine and complete by October an overall review of Latin American economic requirements and the availability of external resources to meet them for the years 1956-65.

We made arrangements to try to help Costa Rica and Honduras, where, as you know, natural phenomena—the eruption of Irazu in Costa Rica and the forestry plague in Honduras—bear heavily on the economic life of these two nations.

The first CIAP action list is even longer than this. But we are under no illusion that defining problems and assigning men and institutions to work on them automatically insures success. CIAP will be judged by the governments and peoples of the hemisphere—and it should be judged—by the concrete results achieved in the months and years ahead.

What I can tell you now is simply this: Working together as brothers, we approached our task, not as representatives of nations engaged in negotiation or bargaining, but as the board of directors of a great common enterprise. To carry forward that enterprise will require the highest degree of cooperation, not only among the governments of the hemisphere but among the various agencies seeking to assist in Latin American development. Both at the meeting in Mexico City and subsequently there has been heartening evidence of the willingness of all to work together on that team basis to a large common end.

As I said on a public occasion at the end of the CIAP meeting, I believe the Alliance for Progress has grown up; and it has grown up in the only way it could—through the assumption of responsibility and leadership by our Latin American friends.

There are no miracles in economic development. There is no easy way or cheap shortcut to restructuring a society so that it may absorb and apply the fruits of modern science and technology in ways which provide for all the people greater prosperity, greater social justice under conditions of human freedom. It is because the task is so inherently complex that we have always thought of the Alliance for Progress in terms of at least a decade's purposeful common effort.

* * *

(65) *Report of Assistant Secretary of State Mann on Latin American Policy to President Johnson, Made Public October 31, 1964.*[19]

President Franklin Roosevelt laid the cornerstone of our policy toward Latin America when he dedicated this nation "to the policy of the Good Neighbor."

President Truman added economic and social dimensions to our policy in 1949 by announcing his Point Four program.[20]

In the late 1950's, President Eisenhower called for "widespread social progress and economic growth benefiting all the people and achieved within a framework of free institutions."

Beginning in 1961 President Kennedy proposed an Alliance For Progress[21] between the American states dedicated to the more rapid achievement of political democracy, social justice and economic growth. The Alliance came into being as a multi-

[19] *Department of State Bulletin,* November 16, 1964, pp. 706-707.
[20] *Documents, 1949,* p. 10.
[21] Same as note 9 to Document 62.

lateral obligation. A new hope stirred the imagination and the energy of the people of the entire hemisphere.

1964 has been marked by a new unity of purpose in making the Alliance not just a statement of goals but a reality.

Within our own government a new coordination has been achieved between our AID [Agency for International Development] activities and our political and economic policies. As a result, more Alliance For Progress loans were made in the first six months of 1964 than in all of 1963. All of the funds made available by the Congress were committed. More important, the quality of loan programming was improved. Increased emphasis was given to self-help.

In 1964 each American Republic began, for the first time, to discuss in depth with others its problems, its needs and its own self help measures. The new forum is the Inter-American Committee for the Alliance For Progress. In addition to governments, the Inter-American Development Bank, the World Bank, the International Monetary Fund and panels of experts participate in these reviews so that the best talent available in the hemisphere is brought to bear on the complex economic and social problems of our times.

High growth rates in Venezuela, Mexico, Central America and other countries reflect a new confidence in those countries. This is reflected in an increased flow of foreign investments. United States investors, for example, are investing in Latin America at about twice the rate they did in 1963.

There are encouraging signs of accelerated self-help measures throughout the hemisphere. Sixteen countries have adopted improved tax legislation. Twelve countries are working on agrarian reform programs. Latin American education budgets have been increased by twenty-five percent.

Some 900 credit unions have been created, more than 220,000 houses and 23,000 school rooms have been built. Fifteen million more people have been given access to potable water supplies. The diets of millions have been improved by making our surplus agricultural production available in school and family feeding and in food for work programs.

1964 was also a good year for political freedom. The people of Venezuela triumphed over a determined subversive effort by Communists to prevent free elections and a democratic transfer of government.

The people of Brazil achieved a new national consensus and have begun an important program of economic and social reform.

The people of Chile chose freedom in free elections.

Panama and the United States are sitting together at the conference table, as reasonable men should, to resolve their problems.[22]

The water is running again at Guantanamo from a new desalinization plant while the Cuban economy continues to flounder in the sea of Communist mismanagement.

The American Republics imposed strong sanctions against the Castro regime in retaliation for its aggression against Venezuela. And in doing so they collectively served notice that further aggressions would not be tolerated.[23]

Mexico and the United States celebrated the settlement of a long-standing boundary dispute [24] and demonstrated their growing friendship and cooperation.

These are results which people throughout the hemisphere can see and feel and understand. They are developments which open the way for even greater progress in the Alliance against poverty, illiteracy, disease and hunger and for political and economic democracy.

If all of the American Republics do their part, the Alliance For Progress will succeed.

(66) *Third Annual Meeting of the Inter-American Economic and Social Council, Lima, Peru, December 5-11, 1964: Statement by Assistant Secretary of State Mann, December 8, 1964.*[25]

(Excerpts)

* * *

. . . I would like to say a few words about actions—about some of the things the American nations have accomplished together under the alliance since the last meeting of the Inter-American Economic and Social Council 1 year ago.[26]

This year the Inter-American Committee on the Alliance for Progress, which we, too, call CIAP, has not only been constituted under the able and dedicated leadership of Carlos Sanz de Santamaría but it has completed the first cycle of country-by-country studies ever made in our hemisphere. It has examined

[22] Documents 71-74.
[23] Document 70.
[24] The Convention on the settlement of the Chamizal border dispute; entered into force January 14, 1964.
[25] *Department of State Bulletin*, December 28, 1964, pp. 898-901. For discussion see *The United States in World Affairs, 1964*, pp. 196-197.
[26] *Documents, 1963*, pp. 397-413.

national and regional plans, the steps which have been taken to put them into effect, and the efforts which each country is making to carry out its responsibilities under the charter of the alliance. It has recommended specific and concrete courses of action to countries and international organizations on how to accelerate progress.

The report which is a result of this extensive review is before us at this meeting.[27] All of us owe to CIAP and its hardworking subcommittees a vote of thanks. The quality of the work was of course greatly enhanced by the indispensable participation of the Panel of Nine.[28] We owe also a debt of gratitude to the representatives from the Inter-American Development Bank, the World Bank, and the International Monetary Fund who contributed information and valuable counsel during the country reviews. The caliber of the men whom each country sent to discuss its plans and programs was, moreover, impressive. It is not an exaggeration to say that this is the first time that so many able, dedicated people, knowledgeable about hemisphere affairs, have gathered around the same table at the same time in a common multilateral effort to identify specific obstacles and to find concrete solutions to them.

What is needed now is better execution, better performance by all of us in the alliance.

Measures of a self-help nature which are needed vary of course from country to country. They include programs to diversify production and to expand exports. They include the control of inflation and the elimination of the economic and social distortions which inflation creates. They include the reduction of deficits which do not contribute to social or economic progress of the people but which instead drain off budgetary resources needed to expand industry and production and to widen the horizons of social well-being. They include adequate incentives for the sectors of economies which lag behind. They include agricultural, tax, and other reforms which contribute to increased production, economic growth, and social justice. They include the building of institutions for the mobilization and constructive use of savings so that those who need credit most may be able to obtain it on reasonable terms. They include a more equitable distribution of the national product among all the people both directly and indirectly in ways which will contribute to the well-being and dignity of man.

If we can continue to work honestly and sincerely for human

[27] *O.A.S. Report No. CIAP-170* (Washington: Pan American Union, October 1964).
[28] *Documents, 1961,* p. 424.

progress rather than for the short-term personal or political advantage of individuals or groups, we shall see an ever-growing number of countries join those who have already achieved viable and relatively self-sustaining economies capable of meeting both the spiritual and material needs of their peoples. We can then concentrate on building enduring foundations for the great societies which all our people seek instead of spending so much of our energy and resources dealing with crises created by errors of the past.

Increase in Export Earnings

1964 has also been a good year for Latin America's export earnings. Preliminary ECLA [U.N. Economic Commission for Latin America] estimates indicate that the value of Latin America's export earnings will be up about 8 percent over 1963, which in turn showed an increase of 6 percent over 1962.

Much of this increase in earnings was due to price increases in basic products exported by Latin America. Some of the speakers who have preceded me have expressed concern lest prices sag in 1965. There are already signs that the world supply of sugar exceeds demand. But other exports such as coffee, tin, meat, and cotton continue to be firm, and there is reason to hope that they will remain so.

However this may be, greater attention needs to be paid to the diversification and expansion of exports. While Latin America's export earnings will increase by an estimated 8 percent in 1964, the volume of exports will, it appears, increase only by about 1 percent.

Diversification and volume are essential elements in any program to increase export earnings. One of the achievements of 1964 is that this facet of the problem is better understood than before. Our host country, for example, has made particularly noteworthy progress in the export field.

Programs to develop and expand national markets for national industries are also needed. Another of the solid gains in 1964 has been the attention which some countries are giving to the techniques of bringing this about.

Another way of expanding export earnings is to get on with the job of making the Latin American regional trading arrangements more effective. Progress in the Central American Common Market continues to be made. One of my colleagues tells me that the exports of his country to its Central American partners have increased from about 10 percent of total exports to about 50 percent in the last several years. This is a significant achievement.

* * *

Much has been said here about protectionism in the United States. I share your disappointment that our Congress did not pass, in its 1964 session, the implementing legislation to the Coffee Agreement. But I also remind you that the Coffee Agreement itself was ratified[29] and that President Johnson has publicly stated that the enabling legislation will be resubmitted to the next Congress when it convenes next January.

Today, as yesterday, the United States buys about 40 percent of Latin America's total exports. No other country, indeed no other grouping of countries, can match that record. In addition, my country is a principal market for many of the developing countries in other continents which are, as some of the speakers have stressed, associated with Latin America in the group of 77 [the less developed countries in the U.N. Conference on Trade and Development].

* * *

Progress in the Private Sector

There were other solid achievements in 1964 toward the political, economic, and social goals of the alliance. I shall presume on your time only long enough to mention one more—progress in the private sector.

I do not wish even for a minute to minimize the great importance of the public sector in the process of progress. It is not only important; it is indispensable.

But so much has already been said about the public sector that further words from me are unnecessary. I only wish to recall that it is the private sector—principally the domestic private sector—which makes by far the largest investment in job-producing, goods-producing, and tax-producing industries. In this decade of rising populations, all of us need to double as quickly as we can the number of jobs or unemployment will rise. We need rapidly to increase food production, or there will be hunger. The participation of the private sector—and again I am referring principally to the domestic private sector—with its capital and its know-how, and with its unique ability efficiently to make all the day-to-day decisions required in every factory and farm in the increasingly complex society in which we live, is clearly essential to success.

[29] Signed September 28, 1962, entered into force December 27, 1963.

Government policies have a great deal to do with whether the private sector will play its full role—whether it will have fear or confidence, whether it will risk its investment in the hope of making a long-term gain or take flight to what it considers safer havens.

Among the many plus signs of 1964 are indications that both domestic and foreign capital is investing at a higher rate than before.

In conclusion, I should like to repeat that our task is to execute, to put into effect, the plans being developed and improved. We need deeds even more than words. We need continued progress of the kind we have seen in 1964, and we need it at the fastest possible rate.

We will get the job done more quickly if we reason with each other than if we create unnecessary divisions, if we work together for the achievement of the noblest of all goals—the improvement of the spiritual, moral, material, and social sides of the human being.

President Johnson, like President Kennedy before him, has a deep conviction that America—all America—has the will, the courage, and the ability to make the future of this hemisphere as bright and shining as it was in the dreams of Bolívar and Jefferson, of San Martín and of Hidalgo.

B. Cuba.[30]

(67) *United States Policy Toward Cuba: Address by Under-Secretary of State George W. Ball, Roanoke, Virginia, April 23, 1964.*[31]

(Excerpts)

* * *

In my observations to you this evening, I shall try to answer some of the questions that have arisen with regard to our Cuba policy and shall try to clarify some of the confusion that has been apparent in the public debate.

The Nature of the Threat

First, what is the nature of the threat imposed by existence of a Communist regime in Cuba?

[30] For discussion see *The United States in World Affairs, 1964,* pp. 216-220.
[31] Department of State Press Release 180, April 23, 1964; text from *Department of State Bulletin,* May 11, 1964, pp. 738-744.

It is not, in our judgment, a *military* threat to the United States. We shall never permit it to menace our own strategic power, as our actions in October 1962 demonstrated.[32] We are taking constant and effective measures to insure that such a threat does not occur again—and we shall continue to take those measures.

Nor do we regard Cuba as a direct *military* threat to Latin America. The Cuban armed forces are large and equipped with modern weaponry. They are by all odds the most powerful military establishment in Latin America. But Cuba does not possess air- and sealift sufficient to permit it to take offensive action against its neighbors, and, in any event, we maintain overwhelming military forces in the area to prevent Cuba from attacking other American Republics.

The menace of Castro communism to Latin America is of a different and—perhaps I might say—a more modern kind. It is the menace of *subversion,* the undermining of existing governments, the arming of organized Communist minorities, and the mounting of campaigns of sabotage and terror.

* * *

Two Principal Lines of U.S. Strategy

The United States, as the strongest nation in the Western Hemisphere, is faced with a difficult but practical problem. With the existence of a Communist center in Latin America, how do we and our Latin American allies prevent that center from being used as an active center for Communist infection?

The most obvious and direct way to eliminate the Castro regime in Cuba would be by direct military action designed to replace the present government by a non-Communist government friendly to the West. Less direct action might take the form of an enforced blockade—which would still be an act of war.

At the other end of the spectrum from military action is a policy of trying to negotiate with [*Premier Fidel*] Castro. Taking account of the decisions reached within the American system, notably at Punta del Este in January 1962 [33] and later in October 1962,[34] we have consistently maintained that two elements in the Cuban situation are not negotiable. First, Castro's political, economic, and military dependence upon the Soviets; and, sec-

[32] *Documents, 1962,* pp. 367-410.
[33] Same, pp. 336-348.
[34] Same, pp. 370-372

ond, the continuance of Castro's subversive activities in Latin America.

We see no present evidence that Castro is prepared to eliminate these two conditions—and, in fact, the evidence thus far is all the other way.

The limits in which we must erect a Cuban policy are, therefore, well defined and narrow. If, on the one hand, we do not wish to adopt policies that involve an act of war—and even the most vigorous critics of our Cuban policy have rejected this course of action—and, on the other, there seems little sign of a possibility of serious negotiation with the present regime, we are left with two principal lines of strategy for dealing with the menace of Castro's Cuba to Latin America.

First, we must take all possible measures to strengthen the Latin American nations so that they may, through individual and collective means, resist Communist subversion.

Second, we must employ all available instruments of power less than acts of war to limit or reduce the ability of the Cuban government to advance the Communist cause in Latin America through propaganda, sabotage, and subversion.

Cooperative Actions of American States

To the greatest extent possible, we are pursuing both these lines of strategy within the framework of the inter-American system. We have sought to make clear to our Latin American friends that the problem of protecting the continent against the menace of Castro communism must be tackled by the American states as a collective undertaking. The Organization of American States is the principal instrumentality for this purpose, but we are also employing other multilateral groupings within the inter-American family.

* * *

In the long run, however, Latin America will be rendered immune to Communist infection only by an amelioration of the conditions—political, economic, and social—in which subversion flourishes. The United States and the free nations of Latin America have, therefore, through the Alliance for Progress, undertaken a major collective effort. It is directed at the ambitious target of transforming the structure and productive capacity of the Latin American nations so as to bring about not merely an increase but a more equitable distribution of resources. Given the magnitude of this undertaking, it will be years before major results can be achieved. But until such a transformation is accomplished, Latin America will remain a fertile seedbed for Communist subversion.

Program of Economic Denial

By strengthening the Latin American nations through collective political, economic, and military measures we are increasing their ability to resist subversion. But at the same time we must actively pursue measures against Cuba to limit its ability to subvert.

In this effort we are exploiting the propaganda potential to the fullest. But an information program must be regarded primarily as a supplement to substantive policies. Given the present limits of action, we must rely, as our major instrument, on a systematic program of economic denial.

This is the only policy—short of the use of force—that gives promise of having a significant impact on Cuba and its continuance as a Communist base in the Western Hemisphere. Such a program, in our judgment, can and does work effectively to achieve objectives that are in the manifest interest not only of the United States and Latin America but of other free-world nations.

Objectives of Economic Denial Program

In discussing the effectiveness of this program, let me make one point quite clear. We have never contended that a program of economic denial—short of an act of war such as a military blockade that would cut off bloc as well as free-world trade—is likely *by itself* to bring down the present Cuban regime. The objectives which this program can accomplish are more limited. They are four in number:

First, to reduce the will and ability of the present Cuban regime to export subversion and violence to the other American states;

Second, to make plain to the people of Cuba and to elements of the power structure of the regime that the present regime cannot serve their interests;

Third, to demonstrate to the peoples of the American Republics that communism has no future in the Western Hemisphere; and

Fourth, to increase the cost to the Soviet Union of maintaining a Communist outpost in the Western Hemisphere.

Those are the objectives which we seek to achieve by a program of economic denial against Cuba. That program reflects the purpose of the Organization of American States. In our opinion, it is realistically designed to accomplish the limited but nonetheless important objectives toward which it is directed.

* * *

Restrictions on Shipping and on Vital Goods

In order to exploit Cuba's economic vulnerability we have developed programs of common action on two levels:

First, to restrict the availability of free-world shipping to Cuba;

Second, to limit the categories of goods that may be available to Cuba.

In order to make these policies effective, we have sought the cooperation of the other major industrialized countries of the free world, and particularly our NATO allies. We have obtained considerable, although not complete, cooperation.

For example, the number of calls by free-world vessels at Cuban ports dropped 60 percent in 1963 as compared to 1962, and there are reasonable prospects that, over 1964 as a whole, there will be a further drop.

Realistically, we must recognize that the restriction of free-world shipping, while useful, is of only limited utility. Shipping under the control of the bloc could transport the goods that Cuba requires, although at the cost of a considerable reorganization and disruption of schedules and charters.

Much more important is the denial of those categories of goods that are most vital to the operation of the Cuban economy. This includes industrial goods, transport equipment, and critical materials. Not only is Cuba wholly dependent on a large and continuing import of consumer goods if it is to maintain more than a subsistence economy, but its limited industrial plant, including the sugar industry, is based on Western equipment that is rapidly becoming worn out and obsolete and on Western transport equipment that is rapidly falling apart. It is important, therefore, that the West should not bolster the economy by providing spare parts and replacements.

This was the reason, for example, that the administration took such a strong position against the recent sale of 450 buses to the Castro government—400 of which are to be used in Habana. Those 400 additional buses will almost double available public transport in the city that dominates Cuba's economic life. Without those buses the efficiency of the Cuban economy and the level of Cuban morale would be further impaired.

The sale of Western locomotives to Cuba, for instance, would have an even greater impact. Movement of sugar to Cuban ports is almost entirely by rail, and the motive power of the Cuban railroad system is presently in a critical state of disrepair. In a late 1963 description of the "desperate state" of the railroad system, a Cuban official organ estimated that only one-quarter as many locomotives were then in operating condition as in 1959. To replace even a part of this equipment would be a very big boon to the Cuban economy.

* * *

Cuban Economic Failure

In the course of my observations this evening, I have tried to spell out for you the bases for our policy toward Cuba and to explain particularly the reasons why we are seeking—and shall continue to seek—to limit the supply of critical goods to the Cuban economy.

This program is directed at the present Cuban government. It will be continued so long as that government persists in its efforts to subvert and undermine the free societies of Latin America.

Within recent weeks it has become more than ever apparent that our program is succeeding. Cuba under communism is providing a spectacle of economic failure for all to see. Far from offering a better life for the Cuban people, communism is bringing only depression and want.

Today the Cuban economy is in a mess—a mess produced by incompetent management, ideological interference, and the refusal of the United States and many other Western societies to deal with a government that is seeking to undermine its neighbors.

The magnitude of the Cuban economic failure is clearly apparent in the constant complaints of the present Cuban leaders.

But if our program of economic denial is helping to accentuate the failures of the Cuban economy, let me make it quite clear that it is not aimed at the Cuban people. The United States has no quarrel with the people of Cuba. It feels no animosity, only sympathy and sorrow. We have shown our good will by exempting food and medicines from the restrictions imposed on our trade with Cuba. We have never sought in any way to starve the Cuban people.

For we are confident that the people of Cuba will not always be compelled to suffer under Communist tyranny.

Given freedom and democracy, Cuba could develop its high potential for economic and social progress. The Cuban people should not be forced to serve as a vehicle for the intrusion into this hemisphere of an alien way of life that can bring them neither progress nor liberty. Let one final point be clear. We oppose the present Cuban regime not just because its ambitions menace our hemispheric neighbors. We oppose it, above all, because its standards of conduct and its tyrannical practices condemn the people of Cuba to misery and fear.

The people of Cuba deserve better than that.

(68) *The Guantánamo Base Issue.*[35]

(a) *United States Note to the Cuban Government, February 4, 1964.*[36]

On February 2, 1964, units of the United States Coast Guard observed four Cuban fishing boats fishing within the territorial sea of the United States off East Key in the Dry Tortugas.

The United States Coast Guard directed the Cuban vessels to anchor and stand by for boarding and search. The various Cuban vessels complied with this directive, anchoring between 1.5 and 1.9 miles off East Key.

The United States Coast Guard has brought the four Cuban vessels to Key West for interrogation in connection with possible violation of laws of the United States for fishing illegally within the territorial sea (i.e. within the three-mile limit). If it is determined that the Cuban vessels were in fact in violation of law, they will be liable to the penalties prescribed therein.

The Government of the United States protests this unauthorized intrusion into its territorial sea in violation of international law and requests the Government of Cuba to take all the necessary steps to prevent incidents of this nature from recurring in the future.

(b) *Letter from Ambassador Stevenson to the President of United Nations Security Council, February 7, 1964.*[37]

DEAR MR. PRESIDENT: I refer to the letter sent to you by the Permanent Delegation of Cuba on February 4, 1964 (Document

[35] For discussion see *The United States in World Affairs, 1964,* pp. 220-222.
[36] Department of State Press Release 58, February 11, 1964; text from *Department of State Bulletin,* February 24, 1964, p. 276.
[37] U.S. Delegation Press Release 4360; text from *Department of State Bulletin,* February 24, 1964, p. 279.

S/5530) protesting the alleged illegal seizure by the Government of the United States of four Cuban fishing boats in the area of the Dry Tortuga Island. In order that members of the Security Council will be properly informed on this matter, I am addressing this note to you to set forth the facts of the situation.

The facts of the case were communicated by my Government to the Government of Cuba in a note delivered on February 4, 1964, protesting the violation of the territorial sea of the United States by the Cuban fishing boats. The facts communicated and subsequent developments are as follows:

1. On February 2, 1964, four Cuban fishing vessels were observed by units of the United States Coast Guard to be fishing within the territorial sea (i.e., inside the three mile limit) of the United States off East Key in the Dry Tortugas.

2. The United States Coast Guard patrol craft ordered the Cuban vessels to anchor and stand by for boarding and search which they did. When they anchored, the various vessels were between 1.5 and 1.9 miles off East Key. Two of the masters of the fishing boats—Jose Manuel Ventura of the Cardenas No. 14 and Manuel Gomez Barrios of the Lambda No. 8—admitted to United States Coast Guard officials that they were knowingly fishing in United States waters.

3. On the morning of February 3, 1964, following a preliminary search of the vessels and questioning of their masters, the United States Coast Guard vessels brought the Cuban fishing boats to Key West for further investigation and interrogation in connection with violation of Federal law. The boarding, inspection and escort of the boats from East Key to Key West by personnel of the United States Coast Guard was conducted in the normal manner with due regard for the welfare of crews.

4. During this entire procedure and until such time as the four boats were within the naval base at Key West, they had unrestricted use of their radio communications. Clear evidence of this is to be found in the fact that conversations between the boats and Habana were monitored by commercial monitoring services in the Florida area. Once the Cuban vessels had docked at Key West, they were at liberty to communicate with the Czechoslovakian Embassy in Washington, D.C., which is representing Cuban interests in the United States, had they chosen to do so.

5. Federal authorities completed their investigation and interrogation of the crews on February 5, 1964. The authorities concluded that the Cuban vessels were fishing in the territorial waters of the United States contrary to Section 251 of Title 46

of the United States Code. However, as this statute contains no sanctions, prosecution by Federal authorities was not undertaken. At the same time, the Cuban fishing boats were also in probable violation of laws of the state of Florida and thus subject to prosecution by state authorities. State officials formally requested the United States Coast Guard to turn the boats and crews over to the jurisdiction of the state. In accordance with United States law, this was done on February 5, 1964. Legal proceedings before the state courts are pending.

6. Two crews' members have on their own initiative requested political asylum in the United States. This has been granted.

In summary, Mr. President, this is a case involving the unauthorized intrusion into the territorial sea of the United States in violation of international law and the laws of the United States. Those charged with the violation stand before the appropriate court where they will receive a fair trial surrounded by the full guarantees offered by the Constitution and laws of this country. I reject the political motives ascribed by the Cuban Government to the action which has been taken.

As the facts of the case demonstrate, there is absolutely no basis for the intemperate and distorted language in the Cuban letter. I can only conclude that the purpose of the letter was to obscure the fact of the clear violation of international laws and of the laws of the United States.

I respectfully request that you have this letter circulated to the Delegations of all the Member States of the Security Council.

(c) *United States Measures to Guarantee the Security of Guantánamo Base: White House Statement, February 7, 1964.*[38]

When the Cuban Government shut off the water supply to Guantanamo [*February 6, 1964*], it deliberately broke an agreement made in 1938, reasserted in 1947, and personally supported by Fidel Castro in 1958. The United States is determined to guarantee the security of the Guantanamo naval base and does not intend to submit that security or the welfare of the servicemen and their families who live there to further irresponsible actions of the Cuban Government. The President has instructed the Department of Defense to make the Guantanamo base self-sufficient. In response the Secretary of Defense [*Robert S. McNamara*] has issued instructions to:

[38] White House Press Release, February 7, 1964; text from *Department of State Bulletin*, February 24, 1964, p. 281.

1. Assure the base control over its own water supply both by conversion of sea water to fresh water and by the transportation of water by ship.

2. Reduce the employment of Cuban personnel who are subject to the control of the Cuban Government and whose wages contribute to its foreign exchange.

The reckless and irresponsible conduct of the Cuban Government remains a constant threat to the peace of this hemisphere. The consequences of further provocations by Castro should be carefully weighed by all nations.

These matters are being called to the attention of the members of the Organization of American States for consideration in connection with charges now pending against Cuba in that organization.[39] They will also be discussed with the members of the North Atlantic Treaty Organization in order that those governments can take them into account in connection with their determination of their own policies toward the threats to the security of the Western Hemisphere posed by the Castro regime.

(69) *Surveillance Flights over Cuba.*[40]

(a) *Statement by Richard I. Phillips, Director of the Office of News, Department of State, April 20, 1964.*[41]

First, I would recall that the overflights are a substitute for the on-site inspection agreed to by the Soviets in October 1962,[42] but which Fidel Castro refused to permit.

Second, I would point out that the surveillance flights are thoroughly based on the resolution approved by the OAS [Organization of American States] on October 23, 1962.[43]

Third, I would remind you of the various statements made by the late President Kennedy and by Secretary Rusk during the past 15 months on this subject, making it unmistakably clear that we regard the overflights as a necessity to avoid the deception which was practiced against us in 1962.

Fourth, I would recall that Secretary Rusk said, in March a year ago: "If there were any interruption with our surveillance . . . that could create a very dangerous situation." [44]

[39] Same as note 23 to Document 65.
[40] For discussion see *The United States in World Affairs, 1964,* pp. 222-223.
[41] *Department of State Bulletin,* May 11, 1964, p. 744.
[42] *Documents, 1962,* pp. 392-395.
[43] Same, pp. 380-383.
[44] *Department of State Bulletin,* April 1, 1963, p. 472.

Our publicly expressed position on this question remains unchanged.

(b) ***Statement by President Johnson, April 21, 1964.***[45]

I do think that it is essential that we maintain surveillance and know whether any missiles are being shipped into Cuba. We will have to maintain our reconnaissance and our overflights. Any action on their part to stop that would be a very serious action. We have so informed them and informed their friends.

C. The Ninth Meeting of Consultation of Ministers of Foreign Affairs of the American States, Washington, July 21-26, 1964.[46]

(70) *Statement and Final Act.*

(a) ***Statement by Secretary of State Rusk, July 22, 1964.***[47]

(Excerpts)

* * *

Five times in as many years the foreign ministers of the American Republics have met to consider situations affecting the peace of the hemisphere arising in whole or in part from the interventionist activities of the Castro regime. This is a measure of the frequency with which our regional security system has had to act to thwart Castro's aggressive designs.

In the face of continued Cuban aggression the time has now come to make it abundantly clear to the Castro regime that the American governments in complete solidarity will no longer tolerate its efforts to export revolution through the classic Communist techniques of terror and guerrilla warfare and the infiltration of arms and subversive agents.

Origins of Cuban Aggression

The pattern of Cuban aggression emerged soon after the Castro regime came to power in 1959. You will recall the armed expeditions which set forth from Cuban territory against Panama, the Dominican Republic, and Haiti during the first 6 months of that year. When this direct method of overthrowing governments failed, the Cuban government turned to the in-

[45] *Department of State Bulletin,* May 11, 1964, p. 744.
[46] For discussion see *The United States in World Affairs, 1964,* pp. 223-226.
[47] Department of State Press Release 333, July 22, 1964; text from *Department of State Bulletin,* August 10, 1964, pp. 174-179.

direct technique of subversion. From the sending of armed landing parties, Castro shifted to training in subversive techniques, transfer of funds for subversive elements, dissemination of systematic and hostile propaganda, and the clandestine shipment of both arms and men. The new pattern emerged in full bloom last year, when Castro made a major effort to disrupt the democratic elections in Venezuela and, beyond that, to destroy the democratic institutions of that country.

Establishment of Communist Beachhead in Cuba

But it took some time to "tool up" this new mechanism for indirect aggression. Meanwhile, the Castro regime embarked upon another type of assault against the traditions and principles of the American community of nations: the establishment of the Communist system in Cuba itself and the facilitation of military intervention by an extracontinental totalitarian power in this hemisphere.

* * *

The Hemisphere's Initial Response

The response of the American governments to this flagrant challenge to hemisphere security fell short—surely we would have to say now—of the nature of the threat. Neither at the Fifth Meeting of Consultation in 1959 [48] nor the Seventh Meeting in 1960 [49] did the foreign ministers act in a way to make clear to the Castro regime that the transformation of Cuba into a base of operations for international communism would not be tolerated by the American community.

The task of throwing up the hemisphere's defenses devolved on subsequent consultations beginning with the Eighth Meeting of Foreign Ministers in January 1962 at Punta del Este.[50]

* * *

Cuban Intervention in Venezuela

The missile crisis removed whatever doubt remained concerning the Castro regime's status as a pawn of the Soviet bloc. It should have served as a warning to Castro and his followers

[48] Cf. *Documents, 1959*, pp. 482-493.
[49] Cf. Same, *1960*, pp. 495-518.
[50] Same, *1962*, pp. 329-352.

that the American governments were united and firm in their resolve not to permit Cuba to be used as a base for the expansion of communism on this continent and that their patience was running out. Again he did not heed the warning. Instead, he redoubled his subversive offensive against the hemisphere. And he chose Venezuela as a primary target.

I would recall that in the summer of 1963 a Special Committee of the Council of the OAS, under the distinguished leadership of Ambassador [Juan Bautista] de Lavalle of Peru, completed a detailed study of the Cuban effort to promote subversion in our countries.

* * *

The Cuban effort is detailed in the report of the OAS Investigating Committee,[51] which serves as the basis for our action.

The Committee found these to be the chief manifestations of the Castro regime's intervention in Venezuela:

a. A hostile and systematic campaign of propaganda against the Government of Venezuela, as well as the incitement to and support of the communist subversion that is being carried out in that country;

b. Training, in all kinds of subversive activities, of numerous Venezuelan citizens, who traveled to Cuba for that purpose;

c. Remittance of funds through these travelers and other channels, for the purpose of maintaining and increasing subversive activities, and

d. The provision of arms to guerrilla and terrorist groups operating in Venezuela, as shown by the shipment of arms discovered on November 1, 1963, on the Paraguaná Peninsula, and the plan for the capture of the city of Caracas. . . .

The evidence to support these findings is clearly and convincingly set forth in the report. The facts established by the Investigating Committee leave no doubt whatsoever of Cuba's part in this conspiracy against Venezuela.

* * *

Likelihood of Continued Cuban Subversion

By its very nature international communism is aggressive and expansive. We see it at work in all parts of the world, constantly probing and testing for weak spots which it might exploit. In modern dress it marches in the guise of diplomatic relations, trade missions, and cultural exchanges, and peace movements, and youth organizations, and the like. It flies the false ideological

[51] O.A.S. Document OEA/Ser. G/IV, February 18, 1964.

banners of "peaceful coexistence" and "wars of national liberation." But no one should be deceived.

We in the United States are under no illusion as to the designs of the Communists against us and the free world. We know that the Communist menace is deadly serious, that they seek their goals through varied means, and that deceit is a standard element in their tactics.

We are fully aware—and should be—that Moscow, as well as Peiping and Habana, remains committed to the Communist world revolution. Chairman Khrushchev tells us frankly and bluntly that coexistence cannot extend to the ideological sphere, that between us there will be continued competition and conflict. Castro said on July 26 last year that in Latin America the course to follow is violent revolution waged by fighting revolutionaries, that the correlation of forces in the world had changed in favor of those seeking change through armed struggle, and that when revolutionaries in other Latin American countries know how to fulfill their duty they will have the decided support of the Soviet Union and all the socialist camp, including Cuba.

* * *

We should have no illusions about Castro's continuing purpose to export the Cuban revolution. He came to power with the design of converting the Andes into the Sierra Maestra of the Americas. That apparently remains his design. His temperament and ambition, the dynamics of his internal situation, the counsel of those whom he serves and those who serve him—all compel him to promote subversion as a means for breaking out of his insular position.

After years of self-righteous protestations that Cuba exported its revolution by example only, Castro in a recent press interview [52] finally acknowledged that Cuba had been supporting, and will continue to support, subversive groups in other countries. This admission, it is true, adds nothing to what we had already learned through experience. It does serve, however, to underscore Castro's purpose to give the hemisphere no respite in his relentless campaign to foment subversion whenever and wherever conditions permit.

In this interview Castro also tried to put Cuba's subversive activities on the bargaining counter. I wish to make one point very clear: that as far as the United States is concerned, the encouragement and support of subversion by the Castro regime

[52] Cf. *New York Times,* July 6, 1964.

against other countries of this hemisphere is not a subject for bargaining. It simply must stop. And when it does, the hemisphere will know it without the need for discussions with the Castro regime.

Task of This Meeting

As I stated at the outset, I regard our task as being to determine what measures should now be taken to impress on the Castro regime that the hemisphere will no longer permit its subversive acts against the American Republics. In my opinion there are three types of measures which we can take to drive this point home.

One should represent the American community's reaction to Castro's efforts to destroy democracy in Venezuela. Certainly this intervention should not be allowed to go without imposition of sanctions.

I want to make it very clear that the United States considers that the adoption of sanctions by the foreign ministers would be directed exclusively against the Castro regime and not against any other state or people. I hope this can be made clear in the Final Act of this conference. Rather our concern is that we not fail in our obligations to a sister Republic which has been made the victim of aggression and, indeed, which even today continues to spend its blood and treasure to combat Castro Communist subversion and to defend democracy and freedom. To respond to the call of our sister Republic for collective action is our paramount obligation.

The second type of measure would carry the community's clear warning to the Castro regime that if it persists in acts of subversion in other American Republics the full weight of the regional security system will be applied. This should serve as a deterrent, and I trust the Castro regime will heed such a message.

Awareness that subversion, supported by terror, sabotage, and guerrilla action, as practiced by the international Communist movement, is as dangerous a form of aggression as an armed attack has been very slow in developing in this hemisphere, as well as in other parts of the world. I think it is fair to say that until very recently there has been a lack of sufficient understanding of this point everywhere, and this has led to uncertainty in some quarters as to whether our regional security system possesses an adequate mechanism for dealing with Communist subversion.

In the opinion of my Government there is no doubt that the Rio Treaty[53] clearly recognizes multiple forms of aggression and provides effective machinery for defending against them. The preamble states that the treaty is intended, among other things, "to provide for effective reciprocal assistance to meet armed attacks against any American State, and in order to deal with threats of aggression against any of them." Article 3 provides for mutual assistance in meeting an armed attack against any signatory; article 6 specifically recognizes the existence of "aggression which is not an armed attack"; and finally, article 9, while defining unprovoked armed attack and invasion by the armed forces of a state as aggression, opens with the very significant wording: "In addition to other acts which the Organ of Consultation may characterize as aggression. . . ." And thus we feel that the Rio Treaty specifically recognizes the existence of various forms of aggression and, most importantly, recognizes the authority of the Council of the Organization of American States, or the Meeting of Foreign Ministers, to characterize them as such. Article 3 of the Rio Treaty spells out procedures for prompt action in the event of armed attack, and article 6 does the same for a wide variety of situations falling short of armed attack.

A third type of measure should urge our own governments and those of other free-world countries to take appropriate steps in the field of trade with Cuba. This is appropriate because the Communist threat to this hemisphere is a threat also to other parts of the free world.

I close, Mr. Chairman, with one final word, a word I know to be from both the Government and from the people of the United States to our friends throughout the hemisphere, a word on which my fellow countrymen are united, on a nonpartisan basis.

When our Founding Fathers signed our Declaration of Independence, Benjamin Franklin made the famous remark, "We must all hang together, or assuredly we shall all hang separately."

Today it is Venezuela which is under attack. Is there any one of us who can say with assurance, "It cannot be my country tomorrow"? So let's say to our brothers in Venezuela, its government and its brave people, "We are with you in full solidarity and will act with you to insure the safety of your democracy."

And let's say to the Castro regime, "Your interference in the affairs of other countries in this hemisphere must stop—must stop and stop now." This is the basis on which the attitude

[53] *Documents, 1947,* pp. 534-540.

of the United States will rest when we come to the resolutions which will be before us. Thank you, Mr. Chairman.

(b) ***Final Act of the Ninth Meeting of Consultation, July 26, 1964.***[54]

(Excerpts)

FINAL ACT

NINTH MEETING OF CONSULTATION OF MINISTERS OF FOREIGN AFFAIRS, SERVING AS ORGAN OF CONSULTATION IN APPLICATION OF THE INTER-AMERICAN TREATY OF RECIPROCAL ASSISTANCE

The Ninth Meeting of Consultation of Ministers of Foreign Affairs, Serving as Organ of Consultation in Application of the Inter-American Treaty of Reciprocal Assistance, was held at the headquarters of the Organization of American States, the Pan American Union, in Washington, D.C., from July 21 to 26, 1964.

The Council of the Organization of American States convoked the Meeting by a resolution adopted on December 3, 1963, which reads as follows:

WHEREAS:

The Council has taken cognizance of the note of the Ambassador, Representative of Venezuela, by means of which his government requests that, in accordance with Article 6 of the Inter-American Treaty of Reciprocal Assistance, the Organ of Consultation be immediately convoked to consider measures that must be taken to deal with the acts of intervention and aggression on the part of the Cuban Government affecting the territorial integrity and the sovereignty of Venezuela, as well as the operation of its democratic institutions; and

The Ambassador, Representative of Venezuela, has furnished information to substantiate his requests,

The Council of the Organization of American States

RESOLVES:

1. To convoke the Organ of Consultation in accordance with the provisions of the Inter-American Treaty of Reciprocal Assistance, to meet on the date and at the place to be fixed in due time.

2. To constitute itself and act provisionally as Organ of Consultation, in accordance with Article 12 of the aforementioned treaty.

3. To inform the Security Council of the United Nations of the text of this resolution.

[54] *Department of State Bulletin*, August 10, 1964, pp. 179-184.

At the meeting held on the same day, December 3, 1963, the Council of the Organization, acting provisionally as Organ of Consultation, adopted a resolution, whereby a committee was appointed to investigate the acts denounced by Venezuela and to report thereon. The committee, which was composed of representatives of Argentina, Colombia, Costa Rica, the United States of America, and Uruguay, presented its report [55] at the meeting held on February 24, 1964, by the Council, acting provisionally as Organ of Consultation.

With respect to the date and place of the Meeting, the Council of the Organization of American States at its special meeting on June 26, 1964, adopted the following resolution:

WHEREAS:

On December 3, 1963, the Council of the Organization convoked the Organ of Consultation in accordance with the provisions of the Inter-American Treaty of Reciprocal Assistance, stating that it would meet at a place and at a time to be set in due time,

The Council of the Organization of American States

RESOLVES:

1. That the Ninth Meeting of Consultation of Ministers of Foreign Affairs, Serving as Organ of Consultation in Application of the Inter-American Treaty of Reciprocal Assistance, shall be held at the headquarters of the Organization of American States.

2. To set July 21, 1964, as the date for the opening of the meeting.

The organization of the Meeting of Consultation and its deliberations were governed by the Regulations of the Meeting of Consultation of Ministers of Foreign Affairs to Serve as Organ of Consultation in Application of the Inter-American Treaty of Reciprocal Assistance, approved by the Council of the Organization of American States at the meeting held on July 29, 1960.

In accordance with the provisions of Article 15 of the Regulations of the Meeting, a closed preliminary session was held on the morning of July 21. On that occasion, the matters to be dealt with at the opening session were considered, and the order of precedence of the members of this Meeting of Consultation was established by lot, as follows:

CHILE	His Excellency Mr. Julio Philippi Izquierdo Minister of Foreign Affairs

[55] Same as note 51 to Document 70a.

COLOMBIA	His Excellency Mr. Fernando Gómez Martínez Minister of Foreign Affairs
BOLIVIA	His Excellency Mr. Fernando Iturralde Chinel Minister of Foreign Affairs and Worship
GUATEMALA	His Excellency Mr. Alberto Herrarte González Minister of Foreign Affairs
VENEZUELA	His Excellency Mr. Ignacio Iribarren Borges Minister of Foreign Affairs
BRAZIL	His Excellency Mr. Vasco Leitão da Cunha Minister of State for Foreign Affairs
EL SALVADOR	His Excellency Mr. Héctor Escobar Serrano Minister of Foreign Affairs
URUGUAY	His Excellency Mr. Alejandro Zorrilla de San Martín Minister of Foreign Affairs
DOMINICAN REPUBLIC	His Excellency Mr. José A. Bonilla Atiles Special Delegate
ECUADOR	His Excellency Mr. Gonzalo Escudero Minister of Foreign Affairs
COSTA RICA	His Excellency Mr. Daniel Oduber Quirós Minister of Foreign Affairs
PARAGUAY	His Excellency Mr. Raúl Sapena Pastor Minister of Foreign Affairs
HAITI	His Excellency Mr. René Chalmers Secretary of State for Foreign Affairs and Worship
NICARAGUA	His Excellency Mr. Alfonso Ortega Urbina Minister of Foreign Affairs
PANAMA	His Excellency Mr. Galileo Solís Minister of Foreign Affairs
MEXICO	His Excellency Mr. Vicente Sánchez Gavito Special Delegate
PERU	His Excellency Mr. Fernando Schwalb López-Aldana Minister of Foreign Affairs
UNITED STATES OF AMERICA	His Excellency Mr. Dean Rusk Secretary of State
ARGENTINA	His Excellency Mr. Miguel Angel Zavala Ortiz Minister of Foreign Affairs and Worship

HONDURAS His Excellency Mr. Jorge Fidel Durón
Minister of Foreign Affairs

His Excellency, Dr. José A. Mora, Secretary General of the Organization of American States also participated in the Meeting.

Finding it necessary to return to his country, the Minister of Foreign Affairs of Peru, by note dated July 23, 1964, addressed to the Secretary General of the Meeting, appointed Mr. Celso Pastor de la Torre, Peruvian Ambassador to the United States of America, as Special Delegate to the Meeting.

Mr. José Rolz-Bennett also attended the Meeting as representative of the Secretary-General of the United Nations.

In accordance with Article 27 of the Regulations, on July 21, the Secretary General of the Organization of American States, Mr. José A. Mora, installed the opening session, at which His Excellency Mr. Vasco Leitão da Cunha, Minister of State for Foreign Affairs of Brazil, was elected President of the Meeting. At the same session, His Excellency Mr. Galileo Solís, Minister of Foreign Affairs of Panama, was elected Vice President of the Meeting. In accordance with the same article, Mr. William Sanders, Secretary of the Council of the Organization of American States, acted as Secretary General of the Meeting. Mr. Santiago Ortiz, Director of the Office of Council and Conference Secretariat Services, acted as Assistant Secretary General.

His Excellency Mr. Vasco Leitão da Cunha, Minister of State for Foreign Affairs of Brazil, and His Excellency Mr. Alejandro Zorrilla de San Martín, Minister of Foreign Affairs of Uruguay, addressed the inaugural session held on the same date.

In accordance with the Regulations, the Meeting appointed a Credentials Committee composed of the Foreign Ministers of Peru, Urguay, and Nicaragua. It also appointed a Style Committee composed of representatives of Colombia, Brazil, Haiti, and the United States of America.

In accordance with the provisions of Article 20 of the Regulations, a General Committee was formed, composed of all the members and charged with considering the topics and submitting their conclusions to a plenary session of the Meeting for approval. His Excellency Mr. Fernando Gómez Martínez, Minister of Foreign Affairs of Colombia, and His Excellency Mr. Miguel Angel Zavala Ortiz, Minister of Foreign Affairs of Argentina, were designated as Chairman and Rapporteur of the General Committee, respectively.

This Final Act was signed at the closing session held on July 26. His Excellency Mr. Gonzalo Escudero, Minister of Foreign Affairs of Ecuador, and His Excellency Mr. Vasco Leitão da Cunha, Minister of State for Foreign Affairs of Brazil, President of the Meeting, addressed the same session.

As the result of its deliberations, the Ninth Meeting of Consultation of Ministers of Foreign Affairs, Serving as Organ of Consultation in Application of the Inter-American Treaty of Reciprocal Assistance, approved the following resolutions and declarations:

I

APPLICATION OF MEASURES TO THE PRESENT GOVERNMENT OF CUBA [56]

The Ninth Meeting of Consultation of Ministers of Foreign Affairs, Serving as Organ of Consultation in Application of the Inter-American Treaty of Reciprocal Assistance.

HAVING SEEN the report of the Investigating Committee designated on December 3, 1963, by the Council of the Organization of American States, acting provisionally as Organ of Consultation, and

CONSIDERING:

That the said report establishes among its conclusions that "the Republic of Venezuela has been the target of a series of actions sponsored and directed by the Government of Cuba, openly intended to subvert Venezuelan institutions and to overthrow the democratic Government of Venezuela through terrorism, sabotage, assult, and guerrilla warfare," and

That the aforementioned acts, like all acts of intervention and aggression, conflict with the principles and aims of the inter-American system.

RESOLVES:

1. To declare that the acts verified by the Investigating Committee constitute an aggression and an intervention on the part of the Government of Cuba in the internal affairs of Venezuela, which affects all of the member states.

2. To condemn emphatically the present Government of Cuba for its acts of aggression and of intervention against the territorial inviolability, the sovereignty, and the political independence of Venezuela.

[56] Adopted by a vote of 15-4 (Bolivia, Chile, Mexico, Uruguay). Venezuela was not eligible to vote.

3. To apply, in accordance with the provisions of Articles 6 and 8 of the Inter-American Treaty of Reciprocal Assistance, the following measures:

a. That the governments of the American states not maintain diplomatic or consular relations with the Government of Cuba;

b. That the governments of the American states suspend all their trade, whether direct or indirect, with Cuba, except in foodstuffs, medicines, and medical equipment that may be sent to Cuba for humanitarian reasons; and

c. That the governments of the American states suspend all sea transportation between their countries and Cuba, except for such transportation as may be necessary for reasons of a humanitarian nature.

4. To authorize the Council of the Organization of American States, by an affirmative vote of two thirds of its members, to discontinue the measures adopted in the present resolution at such time as the Government of Cuba shall have ceased to constitute a danger to the peace and security of the hemisphere.

5. To warn the Government of Cuba that if it should persist in carrying out acts that possess characteristics of aggression and intervention against one or more of the member states of the Organization, the member states shall preserve their essential rights as sovereign states by the use of self-defense in either individual or collective form, which could go so far as resort to armed force, until such time as the Organ of Consultation takes measures to guarantee the peace and security of the hemisphere.

6. To urge those states not members of the Organization of American States that are animated by the same ideals as the inter-American system to examine the possibility of effectively demonstrating their solidarity in achieving the purposes of this resolution.

7. To instruct the Secretary General of the Organization of American States to transmit to the United Nations Security Council the text of the present resolution, in accordance with the provisions of Article 54 of the United Nations Charter.

II

DECLARATION TO THE PEOPLE OF CUBA [57]

WHEREAS:

The preamble to the Charter of the Organization of American States declares that, "the historic mission of America is to offer to man a land of liberty, and a favorable environment for

[57] Adopted by a vote of 16-0 with 3 abstentions (Bolivia, Chile, Mexico).

the development of his personality and the realization of his just aspirations"; and that "the true significance of American solidarity and good neighborliness can only mean the consolidation on this continent, within the framework of democratic institutions, of a system of individual liberty and social justice based on respect for the essential rights of man"; [58]

The Charter of the Organization declares that the solidarity of the American states and the high purposes toward which it is dedicated demand that the political organization of these states be based on the effective exercise of representative democracy;

The Charter also proclaims "the fundamental rights of the individual" and reaffirms that the "education of peoples should be directed toward justice, freedom, and peace";

The Declaration of Santiago, Chile,[59] adopted by the Fifth Meeting of Consultation of Ministers of Foreign Affairs and signed by the present Cuban Government, proclaimed that the faith of peoples of America in the effective exercise of representative democracy is the best vehicle for the promotion of their social and political progress (Resolution XCV of the Tenth Inter-American Conference), while well-planned and intensive development of the economies of the American countries and improvement in the standard of living of their peoples represent the best and firmest foundation on which the practical exercise of democracy and the stabilization of their institutions can be established;

The Ninth International Conference of American States condemned "the methods of every system tending to suppress political and civil rights and liberties, and in particular the action of international communism or any other totalitarian doctrine";

The present Government of Cuba, identifying itself with the principles of Marxist-Leninist ideology, has established a political, economic, and social system alien to the democratic and Christian traditions of the American family of nations and contrary to the principles of juridical organization upon which rest the security and peaceful harmonious relations of the peoples of the hemisphere; and

The exclusion of the present Government of Cuba from participation in the inter-American system, by virtue of the provisions of Resolution VI [60] of the Eighth Meeting of Con-

[58] *Documents, 1948,* pp. 484-485.
[59] Same, *1959,* pp. 490-492.
[60] Same, *1962,* pp. 344-346.

sultation of Ministers of Foreign Affairs, by no means signifies any intention to deny the Cuban people their rightful place in the community of American peoples;

The Ninth Meeting of Consultation of Ministers of Foreign Affairs, Serving as Organ of Consultation in Application of the Inter-American Treaty of Reciprocal Assistance,

DECLARES:

That the free peoples of the Americas are convinced that the inter-American system offers to the Cuban people unequaled conditions for the realization of their ideals of peace, liberty, and social and economic progress;

That the peoples belonging to the inter-American system are in complete sympathy with the Cuban people in all their sufferings, in the face of the total loss of their liberty both in the spirtual domain and in the social and economic field, the denial of their most elementary human rights, the burden of their persecutions, and the destruction of a legal system that was open to improvement and that offered the possibility of stability; and

That, within this spirit of solidarity, the free peoples of America cannot and must not remain indifferent to or uninterested in the fate of the noble Cuban people, which is oppressed by a dictatorship that renounces the Christian and democratic traditions of the American peoples; and in consequence

EXPRESSES:

1. Its profound concern for the fate of the brother people of Cuba.

2. Its deepest hope that the Cuban people, strengthened by confidence in the solidarity with them of the other American peoples and governments, will be able, by their own endeavor, very soon to liberate themselves from the tyranny of the Communist regime that oppresses them and to establish in that country a government freely elected by the will of the people that will assure respect for fundamental human rights.

3. Its firm conviction that the emphatic condemnation of the policy of the present Cuban Government of aggression and intervention against Venezuela will be taken by the people of Cuba as a renewed stimulus for its hope there will come to prevail in that country a climate of freedom that will offer to man in Cuba a favorable environment for the development of his personality and the realization of his just aspirations.

III

REGIONAL AND INTERNATIONAL ECONOMIC COORDINATION [61]

WHEREAS:

The objectives of liberty and democracy that inspire the inter-American system, threatened as they are by communist subversion, cannot be fully attained if the peoples of the states that compose it lack adequate and sufficient means for bringing about vigorous social progress and better standards of living;

The persistence of a situation in which the world is divided into areas of poverty and plenty is a serious obstacle to any possibility that may present itself in the American hemisphere for achieving an economically more just society;

Harmonious and decisive action is indispensable, in both the regional and the international spheres, to combat the causes of economic underdevelopment and social backwardness, since prosperity and world peace based on the freedom of man cannot be achieved unless all the American countries attain equality in the economic and social field;

In particular, the continued existence of such a state of underdevelopment and poverty among large sectors of mankind, which becomes more acute in spite of the world increase in wealth and the advance of science and technology from which these sectors cannot derive full benefit, encourages the subversive action of international communism;

The countries of Latin America expressed their aspirations in the Charter of Alta Gracia and declared their determined intention to work together to build a better world in which there will be a more equitable distribution of income;

The Conference on Trade and Development, held recently in Geneva,[62] provided a forum for a full discussion of the problems of international economics and established the basis for adequate solutions to problems arising in the fields of raw materials, manufactured products, and international financing; and

The instruments adopted at the two aforementioned meetings supplement and perfect those signed at the Special Meeting of the Inter-American Economic and Social Council held at Punta del Este in August 1961, and especially, the Charter of Punta del Este,[63]

The Ninth Meeting of Consultation of Ministers of Foreign

[61] Adopted by a vote of 19-0.
[62] Document 97.
[63] Same as note 8 to Document 62.

Affairs, Serving as Organ of Consultation in Application of the Inter-American Treaty of Reciprocal Assistance,

DECLARES:

That the aims of unity and peace with liberty and democracy pursued in the struggle against international communism, which threatens the stability of the institutions of the inter-American system and of the countries that compose it, must be achieved by eliminating those obstacles that hinder social progress and economic development, and

RESOLVES:

1. To reaffirm the determined will of their peoples to work, in the regional and international spheres, for the achievement of the objectives expressed in the Charter of Alta Gracia and at the Conference on Trade and Development, which are in line with the aims and purposes of the Alliance for Progress.

2. To request the Inter-American Economic and Social Council to continue the necessary studies in order to find adequate solutions to the problems involved.

IV

DIPLOMATIC RELATIONS AMONG THE MEMBER STATES [64]

The Ninth Meeting of Consultation of Ministers of Foreign Affairs, Serving as Organ of Consultation in Application of the Inter-American Treaty of Reciprocal Assistance,

RESOLVES:

To transmit to the Council of the Organization of American States the draft resolution "Diplomatic Relations Among the Member States," presented by the Delegation of Argentina (OEA/Ser.F/II.9/Doc. No. 30, Rev. 2).

[*Resolutions V and VI, a Vote of Recognition and a Vote of Thanks respectively, follow.*]

* * *

STATEMENTS

STATEMENT OF CHILE

The Delegation of Chile abstained from voting on paragraphs 1 and 2 of the operative part of Resolution I, because of its

[64] Adopted by a vote of 19-0.

doubts regarding the legality of the use of the term "aggression" in describing the acts. It voted negatively on paragraph 3, because it is firmly convinced that the measures agreed to are not appropriate to the particular case that has brought about the application of the Inter-American Treaty of Reciprocal Assistance. It also voted against paragraph 5, because it believes that there are discrepancies between the provisions of that paragraph and those of Article 51 of the Charter of the United Nations and of Article 3 of the Rio Treaty. With reference to its abstention on paragraph 6, its attitude is consistent with the attitude taken with respect to the measures called for in paragraph 3.

The Delegation of Chile abstained from voting on the Declaration to the People of Cuba since, although agreeing with its basic content, it maintains relations with the Republic of Cuba and since it believes precisely in the principle of nonintervention, it has deemed it preferable not to give positive support to this resolution.

STATEMENT OF MEXICO

The Delegation of Mexico wishes to make it a matter of record in the Final Act, that the Government of Mexico:

1. Is convinced that the measures provided for in the third paragraph of the operative part of Resolution I (which the Delegation of Mexico voted against) lack foundation inasmuch as the Inter-American Treaty of Reciprocal Assistance does not envisage, in any part, the application of such measures in situations of the kind and nature dealt with by this Meeting of Consultation.

2. Makes a specific reservation to the fifth paragraph of the operative part of the same resolution since it endeavors to extend, in such a way as to be incompatible with the provisions of Articles 3 and 10 of the Inter-American Treaty of Reciprocal Assistance, the right to individual or collective self-defense.

3. Reiterates without reservations its "will to cooperate permanently in the fulfillment of the principles and purposes of a policy of peace," to which "is essentially related" the "obligation of mutual assistance and common defense of the American Republics," in accordance with the provisions of paragraph five of the Preamble of the Inter-American Treaty of Reciprocal Assistance.

IN WITNESS WHEREOF, the Ministers of Foreign Affairs sign the present Final Act.

DONE in the Pan American Union, Washington, D.C., United

States of America, in the four official languages of the Organization, on July twenty-six, nineteen hundred sixty-four. The Secretary General shall deposit the original of the Final Act in the archives of the Pan American Union, which will transmit the authenticated copies thereof to the governments of the American republics.

D. The Panama Crisis.[65]

(71) *Note of the Panamanian Government to the United States, January 10, 1964.*[66]

In the name of the Government and people of Panama, I present to your excellency a formal protest for the unmerciful acts of aggression carried out by the armed forces of the United States of America stationed in the Canal Zone against the territorial integrity of the republic and its undefended civil population during last night and this morning.

The unjustifiable aggression to which I have referred, without parallel in the history of relations between our two countries, has brought to us Panamanians, up to now, a tragic toll of 17 deaths and more than 200 injured. In addition, the buildings and property situated in certain sectors of the City of Panama adjacent to the Canal Zone have suffered damage of major consequence as a result of the controllable acts of aggression by the North American forces.

The inhuman actions—such as that of the police of the Canal Zone, and later the North American armed forces that attacked a group of young students of both sexes that totaled no more than 50, which attempted to display in a calm manner the national flag in that strip of Panamanian territory—are lacking in any justification.

This incomparable incident has revived chapters of the past that we believed would never again occur in American lands.

The acts of violence that motivate this note cannot be ignored nor tolerated by Panama. My Government, conscious of its responsibility, will make use of all measures at its disposal, of those of the American regional system and international organizations, with an end to achieve a just indemnification for the dead and for the injured and for the property destroyed.

My Government seeks the application of sanctions for those responsible for such damages and the guarantee that in the fu-

[65] For discussion see *The United States in World Affairs, 1964,* pp. 226-234.
[66] Unofficial translation from *New York Times,* January 11, 1964.

ture neither the armed forces stationed in the Canal Zone nor the civilian North American population residing in that section of national territory will ever again unloose similar actions of aggression against a weak and unarmed people anxious to come to the defense of its inalienable rights.

Finally, I desire to inform your excellency, that due to the events to which I have referred, the Government of Panama considers its diplomatic relations with your illustrious Government broken, and as a result has issued instructions to its Ambassador, Augusto G. Arango, for his immediate return to his country.

I take this opportunity to manifest to your excellency the guarantee of my highest consideration.

(72) *The Inter-American Peace Committee Steps In.*

(a) *White House Statement, January 14, 1964.*[67]

The President received a full report on the situation in Panama from Mr. Mann. Mr. Mann emphasized that United States forces have behaved admirably under extreme provocation by mobs and snipers attacking the Canal Zone. The President continues to believe that the first essential is the maintenance of peace. For this reason, the United States welcomes the establishment of the Joint Cooperation Committee through the Inter-American Peace Committee.

The United States tries to live by the policy of the good neighbor and expects others to do the same. The United States cannot allow the security of the Panama Canal to be imperiled. We have a recognized obligation to operate the Canal efficiently and securely. And we intend to honor that obligation in the interests of all who depend on it. The United States continues to believe that when order is fully restored it should be possible to have direct and candid discussions between the two governments.

(b) *Communiqué of the Inter-American Peace Committee, January 15, 1964.*[68]

The Inter-American Peace Committee, based on its statutes which authorize it to offer its good offices to the states requesting them, has carried on conversations with representatives of the Republic of Panama and the United States and notes with satisfaction the re-establishment of peace which is an indispensa-

[67] *Department of State Bulletin,* February 3, 1964, p. 152.
[68] Same, p. 156.

ble condition for understanding and negotiation between the parties.

As a consequence, the Inter-American Peace Committee has invited the parties to re-establish their diplomatic relations as quickly as possible. The parties have agreed to accept this invitation and as a consequence thereof have agreed to begin discussions which will be initiated thirty days after diplomatic relations are re-established by means of representatives who will have sufficient powers to discuss without limitations all existing matters of any nature which may affect the relations between the United States and Panama.[69]

(c) *Statement by President Johnson, January 23, 1964.*[70]

I want to take this opportunity to restate our position on Panama and the Canal Zone. No purpose is served by rehashing either recent or ancient events. There have been excesses and errors on the part of both Americans and Panamanians. Earlier this month actions of imprudent students from both countries played into the hands of agitators seeking to divide us. What followed was a needless and tragic loss of life on both sides.

Our own forces were confronted with sniper fire and mob attack. Their role was one of resisting aggression and not committing it. At all times they remained inside the Canal Zone, and they took only those defensive actions required to maintain law and order and to protect lives and property within the canal itself. Our obligation to safeguard the canal against riots and vandals and sabotage and other interference rests on the precepts of international law, the requirements of international commerce, and the needs of free-world security.

These obligations cannot be abandoned. But the security of the Panama Canal is not inconsistent with the interests of the Republic of Panama. Both of these objectives can and should be assured by the actions and the agreement of Panama and the United States. This Government has long recognized that our operation of the canal across Panama poses special problems for both countries. It is necessary, therefore, that our relations be given constant attention.

Over the past few years we have taken a number of actions to remove inequities and irritants. We recognize that there are things to be done, and we are prepared to talk about the ways

[69] A disagreement regarding the Spanish translation of the communiqué arose after it was issued, and relations between Panama and the United States were not reestablished.

[70] White House Press Release, January 23, 1964; text from *Department of State Bulletin,* February 10, 1964, pp. 195-196.

and means of doing them. But violence is never justified and is never a basis for talks. Consequently, the first item of business has been the restoration of public order. The Inter-American Peace Committee, which I met this morning, deserves the thanks of us all not only for helping to restore order but for its good offices. For the future, we have stated our willingness to engage without limitation or delay in a full and frank review and reconsideration of all issues between our two countries.

We have set no preconditions to the resumption of peaceful discussions. We are bound by no preconceptions of what they will produce. And we hope that Panama can take the same approach. In the meantime, we expect neither country to either foster or yield to any kind of pressure with respect to such discussions. We are prepared, 30 days after relations are restored, to sit in conference with Panamanian officials to seek concrete solutions to all problems dividing our countries. Each Government will be free to raise any issue and to take any position. And our Government will consider all practical solutions to practical problems that are offered in good faith.

Certainly solutions can be found which are compatible with the dignity and the security of both countries as well as the needs of world commerce. And certainly Panama and the United States can remain, as they should remain, good friends and good neighbors.

(73) *Action by the Organization of American States.*

(a) *Statement by Ellsworth Bunker, United States Representative to the Council of the Organization of American States, January 31, 1964.*[71]

The Government of the United States regrets that the Government of Panama has chosen to break off not only diplomatic relations and direct talks but discussions which were going on through the Inter-American Peace Committee, and to take instead the course of bringing this matter before the Council to level charges of aggression against the United States.

Both the U.S. Government and our people were profoundly saddened by the unfortunate events which transpired in Panama on January 9, 1964, and on the days immediately following.[72] These events, which have left a tragic balance of dead and wounded on both sides, cannot in any way be considered to have served the best interests of either the United States or

[71] *Department of State Bulletin*, February 24, 1964, pp. 300-302.
[72] Documents 71 and 72.

Panama but rather have redounded to the sole benefit of those who seek the breakdown of the inter-American system, of those who would sow the seeds of discord among the sister Republics of the New World, of those who seek to reap the bitter harvest that would result from internecine strife in the Americas.

I want to reiterate that the United states remains ready at all times to try to resolve our differences around the conference table. We do not think that violence is the way to settle disputes, nor, may I add, is emotion. This is a time for calm and reason.

The record will show that the Peace Committee has worked tirelessly and selflessly, literally day and night, in Panama and in Washington, and always in the spirit of utmost impartiality and helpfulness in its efforts to bring the two parties together. My Government wishes to express its deep gratification to the Inter-American Peace Committee, and individually to the distinguished members who make it up, for their significant contribution to the peacekeeping tradition of our organization. I shall have occasion to refer again to the Inter-American Peace Committee, Mr. Chairman, but I now wish to turn to the specific charges which have brought us together today.

U.S. Welcomes Investigation

The truth is that the United States has at no time committed any act of aggression against the Government or the people of Panama. There is no basis in fact for the charges which have been made. Since we have not committed aggression, we are obviously not responsible for the damages and injuries to which Panama alludes.

The United States therefore welcomes a full investigation of the charges which have been made by an appropriate body of the Organization of American States and will, of course, cooperate fully in such an investigation.

If an investigation is made it will demonstrate that the civil police and the United States military forces in the Canal Zone never made any attempt to enter Panama itself and, indeed, that they only attempted to protect lives and property in the zone. It will show that, as a result of the attacks which were made on the zone, there were more than 100 American casualties, both civilian and military, including 4 killed. It will show continuous sniping with rifle fire from buildings and the roofs of buildings in Panama City into the zone and great restraint on the part of United States forces notwithstanding these attacks. It will show that violent mobs, infiltrated and led by extremists, including persons trained in Communist countries for political action of the kind that took place, assaulted the zone on a wide perimeter, setting fire to buildings inside the zone and attacking with incendiary bombs and rocks the people who were inside. It will show that the Government of Panama, instead of attempting to restore order, was, through a controlled press, television, and radio, inciting the people to attack and to violence. It will show a delay for some 36 hours on the part of the Government of Panama in restoring order. It will show looting and burning by violent mobs in Panama City itself. And it will show that no small proportion of the Panamanian casualties were caused by Panamanians themselves, including those who died of fire and suffocation in buildings and in automobiles which were set on fire.

Mr. Chairman, I reserve the right at a future meeting to make specific comments on these details of alleged happenings to which the distinguished representative of Panama referred, which unfortunately do not correspond with the facts.

We also think it important that any investigation include the full story of the efforts of the IAPC in the last 20 days. For we are confident that that will demonstrate that the United States has gone more than halfway in seeking to resolve this matter.

As to the most appropriate mechanism by which such an investigation might be undertaken, my delegation believes that there are several possibilities which might be explored, and certainly it would be essential to have a full investigation before seeking or implying any judgment on the charges. In addition to the present proposal to invoke the Rio Treaty,[73] it is possible, and in the view of my Government would be quite appropriate, for the IAPC itself to undertake an investigation. This has the advantage that its members are thoroughly familiar with so much of the situation. Alternatively, the U.S. would be willing to undertake a joint investigation with representatives of Panama under the chairmanship of a representative of the Council. Perhaps, as an initial step before taking final action on the current proposal, the Council might request one of its own committees to gather the necessary information and evidence.

The U.S. Objective

In determining what action should be taken, however, it seems to me important to bear in mind the principal stumbling

[73] Same as note 53 to Document 70a.

block at the moment which has divided the United States and Panama and the real *objective* which we seek. This point was well stated by the distinguished delegate of Panama himself when he said, if I heard him right, that "Since it has not been possible to attain an express manifestation of the intention of the Government of the United States to initiate negotiations for the conclusion of a new treaty . . . the Government of Panama finds itself under the painful necessity of presenting its case to the Council of the OAS."

Whether the Rio Treaty is the proper instrument to seek to force a revision of existing treaties is a question which the Council will, of course, want to consider. However, the most important consideration which guides our deliberations and action is the objective which we seek. So far as the United States is concerned, our consistently held objective remains to restore diplomatic and friendly relations with the Government and people of Panama and to sit down together with them at the conference table to seek to resolve all outstanding issues.

As President Johnson has said,[74]

> Our obligation to safeguard the canal against riots and vandals and sabotage and other interference rests on the precepts of international law, the requirements of international commerce, and the needs of free-world security.
>
> These obligations cannot be abandoned. But the security of the Panama Canal is not inconsistent with the interests of the Republic of Panama. Both of these objectives can and should be assured by the actions and the agreement of Panama and the United States.

We have taken the position that, while we cannot agree to preconditions which impair existing treaties in advance of discussion and agreement, we are prepared to engage in a full and frank review and reconsideration of all issues—may I repeat, *all* issues between the two countries—including those arising from the canal and from the treaties relating to it, in an effort to find practical solutions to practical problems and to eliminate the cause of tension.

We have made it abundantly clear that in the discussions which we propose, each Government would be free to raise any matters it wished and that each Government must be equally free to take any position it deems necessary on any issue raised by the other.

In short, Mr. Chairman, the United States rejects all charges of aggression.

[74] Document 72c.

The United States reiterates its appreciation for the work of the Inter-American Peace Committee and its conviction that the instrumentalities of the OAS are competent to deal with this problem.

The United States is prepared to cooperate in a full investigation of the facts if that is desired.

The United States urges that the Council issue a call to prevent any further violence.

The United States feels that the principal stumbling block at the moment is the insistence of one of the parties on a precondition of treaty revision.

The United States maintains its objective of resuming talks on all issues.

The United States is willing to do this on the basis of the communique of January 15.[75] It is willing to accept the wording of the draft communique which was discussed in the sessions of the Inter-American Peace Committee. In any event the United States is prepared to resume meetings with the Peace Committee and with the representatives of Panama to seek to work out a new solution.

And finally, the United States Government and people continue to extend the hand of friendship to Panama and to the Panamanian people.

(b) *Resolution of the Council of the Organization of American States, Adopted February 7, 1964.*[76]

WHEREAS:

Article 4 of the Charter of the Organization of American States [77] proclaims the following as the first two essential purposes of the Organization: "To strengthen the peace and security of the continent" and "To prevent possible causes of difficulties and to ensure the pacific settlement of disputes that may arise among the member states";

The Inter-American Treaty of Reciprocal Assistance recognizes the pre-eminent position within the inter-American system of the procedures for the pacific settlement of controversies, and explicitly and especially mentions the principles set forth in the preamble and declarations of the Act of Chapultepec; [78] and

At the special meetings of the Council held on January 31 and

[75] Document 72b.
[76] Adopted by a vote of 15-0 with 2 abstentions (Chile, Colombia); text in *Department of State Bulletin,* February 24, 1964, p. 304.
[77] Same as note 58 to Document 70b.
[78] *Documents, 1944-1945,* pp. 717-720.

February 4, 1964, both the Representative of the Government of Panama and the Representative of the United States Government expressed a desire that the tragic events that occurred in Panama last January 9 and 10 be fully investigated,

THE COUNCIL OF THE ORGANIZATION OF AMERICAN STATES ACTING PROVISIONALLY AS ORGAN OF CONSULTATION

RESOLVES:

1. To urge both governments to abstain from committing any act that might result in violating the peace in Panama.

2. To establish a general committee composed of all the members of the Council, acting provisionally as Organ of Consultation, with the exception of the Representatives of the parties in conflict.

3. The general committee shall:

a. Investigate, fully and at once, the acts that occurred in Panama on January 9 and 10, 1964, and thereafter, and submit a report to the Organ of Consultation on the matter and on the efforts exerted by the governments of the United States and Panama during subsequent days to find a solution to the dispute;

b. Propose to the parties procedures intended to ensure that the peace will not be violated while an effort is being made to find a solution to the dispute between them;

c. Bearing in mind the causes of the dispute, to assist the parties in their search for a fair solution thereof and to submit a report to the Organ of Consultation on this phase of the subject; and

d. Create the special committees that it deems necessary for the fulfillment of its task.

4. To request the American governments and the Secretary General of the Organization to furnish full cooperation in order to facilitate the work of the general committee.

(c) ***Statement by President Johnson, March 21, 1964.***[79]

The present inability to resolve our differences with Panama is a source of deep regret.

Our two countries are not linked by only a single agreement or a single interest. We are bound together in an inter-American system whose objective is, in the words of the charter, ". . . through their mutual understanding and respect for the sovereignty of each one, to provide for the betterment of all. . . ."

[79] White House Press Release, March 21, 1964; text from *Department of State Bulletin*, April 6, 1964, pp. 533-539.

Under the many treaties and declarations which form the fabric of that system, we have long been allies in the struggle to strengthen democracy and enhance the welfare of our people.

Our history is witness to this essential unity of interest and belief. Panama has unhesitatingly come to our side, twice in this century, when we were threatened by aggression. On December 7, 1941, Panama declared war on our attackers even before our own Congress had time to act. Since that war, Panama has wholeheartedly joined with us, and our sister Republics, in shaping the agreements and goals of this continent.

We have also had a special relationship with Panama, for they have shared with us the benefits, the burdens and trust of maintaining the Panama Canal as a lifeline of defense and a keystone of hemispheric prosperity. All free nations are grateful for the effort they have given to this task.

As circumstances change, as history shapes new attitudes and expectations, we have reviewed periodically this special relationship.

We are well aware that the claims of the Government of Panama, and of the majority of the Panamanian people, do not spring from malice or hatred of America. They are based on a deeply felt sense of the honest and fair needs of Panama. It is, therefore, our obligation as allies and partners to review these claims and to meet them, when meeting them is both just and possible.

We are ready to do this.

We are prepared to review every issue which now divides us, and every problem which the Panama Government wishes to raise.

We are prepared to do this at any time and at any place.

As soon as he is invited by the Government of Panama, our Ambassador will be on his way. We shall also designate a special representative. He will arrive with full authority to discuss every difficulty. He will be charged with the responsibility of seeking a solution which recognizes the fair claims of Panama and protects the interests of all the American nations in the canal. We cannot determine, even before our meeting, what form that solution might best take. But his instructions will not prohibit any solution which is fair, and subject to the appropriate constitutional processes of both our Governments.

I hope that on this basis we can begin to resolve our problems and move ahead to confront the real enemies of this hemisphere—the enemies of hunger and ignorance, disease and injustice. I know President [*Roberto F.*] Chiari shares this hope. For, despite today's disagreements, the common values and interests which unite us are far stronger and more enduring than the differences which now divide us.

(74) *The United States and Panama Resume Diplomatic Relations: Announcement by the Council of the Organization of American States, April 3, 1964.*[80]

(Excerpts)

The Chairman of the General Committee of the Council of the Organization of American States acting provisionally as Organ of Consultation is pleased to announce that the duly authorized Representatives of the governments of the Republic of Panama and of the United States of America have agreed, on behalf of their governments, to a Joint Declaration which in the English and Spanish languages reads as follows:

JOINT DECLARATION

In accordance with the friendly declarations of the Presidents of the United States of America and of the Republic of Panama of the 21st and 24th of March, 1964, respectively, annexed hereto,[81] which are in agreement in a sincere desire to resolve favorably all the differences between the two countries;

Meeting under the Chairmanship of the President of the Council and recognizing the important cooperation offered by the Organization of American States through the Inter-American Peace Committee and the Delegation of the General Committee of the Organ of Consultation, the Representatives of both governments have agreed:

1. To re-establish diplomatic relations.
2. To designate without delay Special Ambassadors with sufficient powers to seek the prompt elimination of the causes of conflict between the two countries, without limitations or preconditions of any kind.
3. That therefore, the Ambassadors designated will begin immediately the necessary procedures with the objective of reaching a just and fair agreement which would be subject to the constitutional processes of each country.

WASHINGTON, D.C.,
April 3, 1964

[80] *Department of State Bulletin*, April 27, 1964, p. 656.
[81] Not printed here. For text of President Johnson's statement see Document 73c.

DECLARACIÓN CONJUNTA

[*The Joint Declaration in Spanish follows.*]

* * *

The Chairman of the General Committee of the Council of the Organization of American States acting provisionally as Organ of Consultation records that the parties agree that both texts are equally authentic and that the words "agreement" in the English version and "convenio" in the Spanish version cover all possible forms of international engagements.

(75) *Proposal for a New Sea-Level Canal and for a New Treaty on the Panama Canal: Statement by President Johnson, December 18, 1964.*[82]

This Government has completed an intensive review of policy toward the present and the future of the Panama Canal. On the basis of this review I have reached two decisions.

First, I have decided that the United States should press forward with Panama and other interested governments in plans and preparations for a sea-level canal in this area.

Second, I have decided to propose to the Government of Panama the negotiation of an entirely new treaty on the existing Panama Canal.

These decisions reflect the unanimous judgment of the Secretary of State, the Secretary of Defense, the Joint Chiefs of Staff. They are based on the recommendations of Ambassador Robert Anderson, Secretary [of the Army] Stephen Ailes, Secretary Thomas Mann [Assistant Secretary of State for Inter-American Affairs], and our Ambassador in Panama, Ambassador Jack Vaughn. They have the full support of Mr. Truman and General Eisenhower. They have been reported to, and in most instances sympathetically received by, the leadership of the Congress.

These two steps, I think, are needed now—needed for the protection and the promotion of peaceful trade—for the welfare of the hemisphere—in the true interests of the United States—and in fairness and justice to all.

For 50 years the Panama Canal has carried ships of all nations in peaceful trade between the two great oceans—on terms of entire equality and at no profit to this country. The canal has

[82] White House Press Release, December 18, 1964; text from *Department of State Bulletin,* January 4, 1965, pp. 5-6.

also served the cause of peace and freedom in two world wars. It has brought great economic contributions to Panama. For the rest of its life the canal will continue to serve trade, and peace, and the people of Panama.

But that life is now limited. The canal is growing old, and so are the treaties for its management, which go back to 1903.

The Panama Canal, with its limiting locks and channels, will soon be inadequate to the needs of our world commerce. Already more than 300 ships built or building are too big to go through with full loads. Many of them—like our own modern aircraft carriers—cannot even go through at all.

So I think it is time to plan in earnest for a sea-level canal. Such a canal will be more modern, more economical, and will be far easier to defend. It will be free of complex, costly, vulnerable locks and seaways. It will serve the future as the Panama Canal we know has served the past and the present.

The Congress has already authorized $17 million for studies of possible sites and of the other practical problems of a sea-level canal.[83] There seem to be four possible routes—two in Panama, one in Colombia, and one which goes through Nicaragua and possibly Costa Rica as well.

I have asked the Secretary of State to begin discussions immediately with all the governments concerned with these possible new routes. In these discussions we will be prepared to work on the terms and the conditions of building and operating a new canal, and if preliminary arrangements can be reached, we will be ready to go ahead with selected site surveys.

Last January there was violence in Panama. As I said then, ". . . violence is never justified and is never a basis for talks." [84]

But while the people of the United States have never made concessions to force, they have always supported fair play and full respect for the rights of others. So from the very first day, as your President, I made it clear that we were ready to sit down and to seek answers, to reason together, and to try to find the answers that would be just, fair, and right, without precondition or without precommitment on either side.

On that basis, relations between our two countries—negotiations—were resumed in April,[85] and on that basis I chose Mr. Robert Anderson, the distinguished former Secretary of the Treasury under President Eisenhower, to be my special ambassador on this problem. Since then Ambassador Anderson has

[83] Public Law 88-609, approved September 22, 1964.
[84] Document 72c.
[85] Document 74.

been working with the American Ambassador, Mr. Vaughn, with the Secretary of the Army, Mr. Ailes, and with Secretary Mann of the State Department. They have recommended that we should propose a new treaty for the existing canal. After careful review with my senior advisers, I have accepted this recommendation.

Today we have informed the Government of Panama that we are ready to negotiate a new treaty. In such a treaty we must retain the rights which are necessary for the effective operation and the protection of the canal and the administration of the areas that are necessary for these purposes. Such a treaty would replace the treaty of 1903 and its amendments. It should recognize the sovereignty of Panama. It should provide for its own termination when a sea-level canal comes into operation. It should provide for effective discharge of our common responsibilities for hemispheric defense. Until a new agreement is reached, of course, the present treaties will remain in effect.

In these new proposals we will take every possible step to deal fairly and helpfully with the citizens of both Panama and the United States who have served so faithfully through the years in operating and maintaining the canal.

These changes are necessary not because of failure but because of success; not because of backwardness but because of progress. The age before us is an age of larger, faster ships. It is an age of friendly partnership among the nations concerned with the traffic between the oceans. This new age requires new arrangements.

The strength of our American system is that we have always tried to understand and meet the needs of the future. We have been at our best when we have been both bold and prudent in moving forward. The planning of a new canal and the negotiation of a new treaty are just such bold and prudent steps. So let us today in friendship take them together.

E. United States-Mexican Relations.

(76) *Joint Communiqué of President Johnson and President Adolfo López Mateos, Palm Springs, February 22, 1964.*[86]

President Adolfo López Mateos and President Lyndon B. Johnson had a number of talks at Palm Springs on February 21

[86] White House Press Release, February 22, 1964; text from *Department of State Bulletin,* March 16, 1964, pp. 396-398. For discussion see *The United States in World Affairs, 1964,* pp. 234-236.

and 22, which gave them an opportunity to renew their personal friendship and to examine, in a spirit of cordiality and good neighborliness, matters of common interest to the two countries.

The two Presidents noted with satisfaction the high level of understanding and cooperation established in recent years in the relations between Mexico and the United States and announced their decision to continue working toward the attainment of the goals set forth in the joint communique of June 30, 1962,[87] issued following the conversations President Adolfo López Mateos and President John F. Kennedy had in Mexico City. In that connection, the two Chiefs of State expressed their profound sorrow at the premature, tragic death of President Kennedy.

The two Presidents reaffirmed their adherence to the principle enunciated by the Mexican patriot Benito Juárez more than a hundred years ago: "Respect for the rights of others is peace." The two Presidents are determined to abide scrupulously by this principle in the conduct of their relations with each other and with other nations and to make energetic efforts to see that it also serves as a principle for all members of the international community, both large and small.

The two Presidents also reaffirmed their support of the principle of self-determination of all peoples and of its corollary, non-intervention. They agreed that they would endeavor at every suitable opportunity to promote the acceptance of such principles, not only with words but with deeds, in the Americas and throughout the world. They expressed their faith in representative democracy, and in that connection they pointed out with special satisfaction that their peoples will have the opportunity within a few months freely to elect those who are to govern them.

The two Presidents reiterated the devotion of their peoples to the ideals of human liberty and the dignity of the individual and their decision to work for the protection and strengthening of those ideals by every adequate means, and in particular by supporting the efforts that are being made through the Alliance for Progress. They recognized, in fact, that it will not be possible to realize those ideals completely in the Americas if, in the cities, workers do not have an opportunity for productive employment; if, in the rural areas, farmers and farm laborers do not have land and the resources to make it productive; if families cannot find decent housing; if education is not within the

[87] *Department of State Bulletin,* July 23, 1962, pp. 135-137.

reach of all; or if sickness and hunger undermine the vitality of people.

The two Chiefs of State examined the trade relations between Mexico and the United States and noted with satisfaction the higher levels they have reached. Geographic proximity, ease of communications, and the development of their economies make the two countries natural markets for each other's products. They agreed that as a general rule it is in the interest of both countries to try to maintain their access to each other's markets and to expand it whenever possible.

The two Presidents emphasized the essential role of exports in the economy of the developing nations and the great contributions that the developed nations can make to the attainment of the Alliance for Progress goals by providing stable, expanding markets for the products of the developing nations. In examining this topic, the Presidents took into account the talks that have taken place between officials of the two countries with respect to sugar, lead and zinc, cattle, meats, and textiles.

The two Chiefs of State expressed satisfaction that the international coffee agreement, which is so important to the Latin American economy, has entered into force.[88] As for cotton, they agreed that the system of consultation that has existed between the authorities of the two countries in the past five years should be continued, since the United States and Mexico are the largest exporters of this fiber.

The two Presidents pointed out again, in a more general way, the need for intensifying the efforts that their governments have been making in the various international organizations to reach higher trade levels and, in particular, to eliminate discriminatory and restrictive practices regarding the exports of their respective countries throughout the world. They emphasized in this connection the special importance to the Latin American countries, and to Mexico in particular, of the elimination of such practices with respect to their basic commodities, in order to create a broader, more stable market for these products that will lead to an increase in their income from exports. On this point, President López Mateos expressed his interest in seeing that industrial workers and farm laborers obtain a fair share of such income, in order to enable them to improve their standard of living.

President López Mateos reaffirmed his purpose of continuing the policy of promoting economic development at rates greater

88 On December 27, 1963.

than the population growth rate within a framework of monetary stability, which is so important for protecting the income of the greatest number of people. President Johnson, for his part, expressed his satisfaction at the cooperation which his Government was able to give Mexico through the recent renewal of the agreements in force between the financial authorities of the two countries.

The two Chiefs of State agreed on the need to strengthen the Organization of American States still further and to give it greater authority as an instrument of the American Republics for the maintenance of peace in the Hemisphere and the promotion of their common interests. With regard to the United Nations, they reiterated their desire to strengthen it by working together, and with its other members who are animated by the same desire, toward a realization of the principles and aims of the San Francisco Charter.

Both Presidents noted with satisfaction that on January 14 last their governments exchanged the instruments of ratification of the convention which provides for the full settlement of the Chamizal problem.[89] After the legislation necessary for implementing the convention has been enacted,[90] they agreed to hold a fitting ceremony in Chamizal to mark symbolically the new course of the Rio Grande between Ciudad Juarez and El Paso.[91] They agreed that the two governments must continue to work through the International Boundary and Water Commission, the United States and Mexico, with a view to making the Rio Grande once again the boundary between the two countries. To that end they will instruct their respective Commissioners to submit studies as soon as possible of cases relating to any portions of land that may have become separated from the country to which they belong through changes in the Rio Grande and to recommend the action that ought to be taken.

The two Presidents noted the progress that has been made with regard to the construction of the second large Rio Grande dam—the Amistad Dam at Ciudad Acuna and Del Rio—which promises great benefits for both countries in the use of the water, flood control, and the generation of electric power. President López Mateos recalled that President Johnson, when still in the Senate, played an outstanding role in obtaining

[89] Text of Convention in *Department of State Bulletin,* September 23, 1963, pp. 480-484.

[90] Public Law 88-300, approved April 29, 1964.

[91] The ceremony was held on September 25, 1964. For President Johnson's address see *Department of State Bulletin,* October 19, 1964, pp. 545-549.

approval in the United States Congress of the legislation needed for the construction of that dam. Both Presidents voiced their satisfaction at the progress made in the initial construction phase and the fact that the building of the dam itself will soon be under way.

President López Mateos recalled his talks in June 1962 with President Kennedy on the problem of the salinity of the waters of the Colorado River. On that occasion the Presidents expressed "their determination, with the scientific studies as a basis, to reach a permanent and effective solution at the earliest possible time with the aim of preventing the recurrence of this problem after October 1963." President López Mateos observed that the Government of Mexico and Mexican public opinion consider that this problem is the only serious one between the two countries and emphasized the importance of finding a permanent solution as soon as possible. After presenting the United States' point of view, President Johnson described the experimental construction which is now being actively carried out in order to find an adequate permanent solution which he would recommend to the Congress. On the basis of this exchange, the Presidents confirmed that the mutual and friendly understanding contained in the Joint Communique of June 1962 is still in effect and that adequate provisional measures will be taken pending a final solution.

The two Presidents expressed their satisfaction at the measures recently taken by the two Governments to improve control over the illegal traffic in drugs and were in agreement on permanently strengthening cooperation between the two countries in order to put a stop to this criminal activity.

The Presidents concluded their talks in complete agreement that they will devote their best efforts to maintaining the close, friendly relations that happily exist between their two countries and to settling any problems that may exist between them, now or in the future, in the same spirit that animated the mutually beneficial solution of the Chamizal case. They reaffirmed the determination of their countries to work jointly in order to promote international understanding and peaceful relations among all nations.

F. The Problem of Overthrow of Elected Governments.

(77) *Message from President Johnson to Interim President Ranieri Mazzilli of Brazil, April 2, 1964.*[92]

Please accept my warmest good wishes on your installation as President of the United States of Brazil. The American people have watched with anxiety the political and economic difficulties through which your great nation has been passing, and have admired the resolute will of the Brazilian community to resolve these difficulties within a framework of constitutional democracy and without civil strife.

The relations of friendship and cooperation between our two governments and peoples are a great historical legacy for us both and a precious asset in the interests of peace and prosperity and liberty in this hemisphere and in the whole world. I look forward to the continued strengthening of those relations and to our intensified cooperation in the interests of economic progress and social justice for all and of hemispheric and world peace.

(78) *The United States Renews Normal Relations with Bolivia: Department of State Statement, December 7, 1964.*[93]

The Department of State has instructed our Ambassador in La Paz, Douglas Henderson, to acknowledge the note of the Foreign Minister of Bolivia [Joaquín Zenteno Anaya], dated November 7, 1964.[94] By means of this acknowledgment the United States is renewing normal relations with Bolivia under the Military Junta of Government, which is presided over by Gen. René Barrientos Ortuño.

The United States Government has ascertained that the Military Junta is in effective control of the government and the country, and that it has pledged itself to fulfill Bolivia's international obligations. The United States Government has noted the declaration of the President of the Junta that elections

92 White House Press Release, April 2, 1964; text from *Department of State Bulletin,* April 20, 1964, p. 609. For discussion see *The United States in World Affairs, 1964,* pp. 201-207.

93 Department of State Press Release 515, December 7, 1964; text from *Department of State Bulletin,* December 28, 1964, p. 901. For discussion see *The United States in World Affairs, 1964,* pp. 209-211.

94 Not printed here.

would be held soon, looking toward the early restoration of constitutional government, and that the Junta has now fixed definite dates for both.

The United States decision was taken after consultation with other governments of this hemisphere and elsewhere and following similar action by a number of them.

CHAPTER EIGHT

THE MIDDLE EAST AND SOUTH ASIA

A. The United States and the Middle East.[1]

(79) *American Policy in the Near East: Address by Deputy Under-Secretary of State for Political Affairs U. Alexis Johnson, Washington, January 20, 1964.*[2]

(Excerpt)

* * *

We recognize of course that the Near East belongs to the people of the Near East and that American interests and objectives must be consistent with those of the people of the area. In this imperfect world, where no man and no state ever gets exactly what he wants, we sincerely believe that American interests and objectives are consistent with those of the Near Eastern peoples. By pursuit of our own objectives we aim to buttress their peace and independence and prosperity, for we see this to be in our own interest. But it is not enough for us or other outside states to be interested in the well-being of the Near East. The people themselves, the region as a whole, must contribute to the efforts that will be needed.

Our objectives in the Middle East are clear and can be briefly stated.

First, as a fundamental contribution to world peace, we are deeply concerned with helping to create political stability, to advancing economic development, and to modernizing the social systems of the area. Our concern is both for the sake of the peoples involved and for strengthening the free world against expansion by those hostile to it.

Second, we are concerned to limit hostile Soviet influence in the area. Arab experience with the Soviet Union since 1955 has tended to increase awareness that the Near East in fact shares in larger measure mutual interests with the West.

[1] For discussion see *The United States in World Affairs, 1964,* pp. 243-253.

[2] Department of State Press Release 20, January 20, 1964; text from *Department of State Bulletin,* February 10, 1964, pp. 208-211.

Third, there should be an accommodation between Israel and its Arab neighbors, which we believe is the only way in which the area as a whole can develop political stability, self-sustained economic growth, and, thus, true independence. We know this is difficult, but we also know it is important to our national security interests and to the attainment of our objectives in the area.

Fourth, the continued flow of oil at economically reasonable rates to Western Europe is of great importance. Europe's economic strength, so essential to free-world strength, relies on an elastic supply of Near Eastern oil at reasonable cost. The oil-producing states, conversely, have an interest in Western markets.

Fifth, access to the air and sea routes to and through the Near East is important to us commercially and militarily.

Forces and Factors Affecting U.S. Policy

In trying to achieve these objectives, we face certain forces and factors that may enhance or hinder our efforts. Among the more important are:

1. *Arab nationalism.* On its positive side, the drive for Arab unity and national dignity is based on the dream of a national, unified, and prosperous Arab future. Although Arab nationalism has a large component of neutralism, it is also one of the strongest forces resisting Soviet expansionism in the area.

Negatively, Arab nationalism contains the strains of resentment and suspicion engendered by the colonial past and by the frustrations of the mid-20th century. In the past year ideological and practical differences between various Arab national groups have even been the cause of regrettable violence, governmental upsets, and continued instability. We are not opposed to Arab unity. We do believe, however, that all the peoples of the area have a right to determine how and when it will be realized.

2. *The historical gap in social, cultural, and political understanding* poses serious difficulties of communication between us and the peoples and governments of the area. Bridging this gap is in itself a continuing major challenge to our Government, for without a bridge our efforts to be helpful may be misunderstood and stultified.

3. *The Soviet drive for domination* is demonstrated by the continued Soviet efforts to create dissension and undermine any trends toward peace and stability in the area. The Soviet position and Communist potential in the Near East have markedly declined in the past few years, but the Communists have by no means given up their objectives.

4. The Near East is important to us in its own right, but we live in one world. Our Near Eastern interests must be fitted into and sometimes must necessarily be modified by our *worldwide security and strategic concerns.* At times what we would *like* to do in the Near East may be obstructed by what we *must* do elsewhere in the world.

Those are the main forces and factors constituting the policy environment in which we seek to attain our Near Eastern objectives. In that policy environment we are faced constantly with choices. Practically speaking, we are faced with such questions as:

1. How can we deal with a single Arab state without alienating other Arab states temporarily at odds with it? Or—

2. How can we maintain constructive relations with the more conservative and traditional states without stifling modernist democratic forces in the area? Or—

3. How can we act to insure the security and integrity of the individual states of the area, including Israel, without becoming directly involved in their disputes and losing our ability to act as a moderating influence in area disputes? How can we most effectively pursue our bilateral relationships with individual Arab states without appearing to stand in the way of the attainment of Arab unity?

Over the years we have found that an essential element in a workable Near Eastern policy is to avoid taking sides in regional disputes. This does not mean that we will stand idly by if aggression is committed. We have shown we will not. Nor does it mean that we will not use appropriate occasions to be helpful to disputing parties or to discuss frankly possible solutions to issues and problems as we see them. We do this constantly. Whenever possible, we also do it quietly. We have an interest in the independence and well-being of all the states of the Near East. Instability, uncertainty, and insecurity in one Near Eastern state may quickly spread into the region as a whole. We cannot afford to pick and choose. We must maintain constructive and balanced relationships with the area as a whole. This we have endeavored to do. It was in this spirit that last May 8 President Kennedy publicly reiterated our general policy. He said in part: [3]

> The United States supports social and economic and political progress in the Middle East. We support the security of both Israel and her neighbors. . . . We strongly oppose the use of force or the threat of force in the Near East, and we also seek to limit the spread of com-

[3] *Documents, 1963,* p. 268.

munism in the Middle East which would, of course, destroy the independence of the people.

The President also said that in the event of direct or indirect aggression we would support appropriate courses of action in the United Nations or on our own to prevent or put a stop to such aggression.

I believe that what the President said on May 8, 1963, contains no ambiguity and lends itself to no misinterpretation. Any intended victim of any would-be aggressor can count on our support. In so saying we do not threaten or cajole. We underline our commitment to our objectives. It may be that some believe they do not need our help, but we are certain all states are aware of our intentions and commitments and of our capability if need be to carry them out. Those who wish our help can count on it when they need it.

Our policy in recent years has been predicated on a greater awareness of the aspirations of the Near Eastern peoples, *their* accomplishments and *their* potential. It is perhaps mainly this awareness that has brought us whatever successes we may have achieved in the Near East. It is perhaps when we have lacked this awareness that we have had our failures.

In the coming months many of our policies will be put to the test. I would not pretend to you that we believe the decisions we reach and the actions we believe we must take will always meet with full approval on the part of the Arab states or of Israel. We will seek their understanding and will value their approval. We will always endeavor to act in such a way as not to damage their interests. But in the final analysis our policies will be based on the United States interest as we see it. Since we sincerely believe there is no incompatibility between our interests and those of the peoples of the Near East, we shall pursue our policies in the full confidence that they are right and fair for all concerned.

B. Yemen.[4]

(80) *Resolution of the United Nations Security Council, Adopted April 9, 1964.*[5]

The Security Council,

Having considered the complaint of the Yemen Arab Republic regarding the British air attack on Yemeni Territory on 28 March 1964 (S/5635),

[4] For discussion see *The United States in World Affairs, 1964,* pp. 256-262.
[5] U.N. Document S/5650, April 9, 1964; adopted by a vote of 9-0-2 (United States and United Kingdom).

Deeply concerned at the serious situation prevailing in the area,

Recalling Article 2, paragraphs 3 and 4 of the Charter of the United Nations,

Having heard the statements made in the Security Council on this matter:

1. *Condemns* reprisals as incompatible with the purposes and principles of the United Nations;

2. *Deplores* the British military action at Harib on 28 March 1964;

3. *Deplores* all attacks and incidents which have occurred in the area;

4. *Calls upon* the Yemen Arab Republic and the United Kingdom to exercise the maximum restraint in order to avoid further incidents and to restore peace in the area;

5. *Requests* the Secretary-General to use his good offices to try to settle outstanding issues, in agreement with the two parties.

C. Jordan.

(81) *Joint Communiqué of President Johnson and King Hussein, Washington, April 15, 1964.*[6]

King Hussein of Jordan and President Johnson have completed two days of discussions on matters of mutual interest and concern. Both welcomed the opportunity presented by the King's visit at the invitation of the President for a full exchange of views.

The President presented the views of the United States on various world problems, including those of the Middle East. He emphasized the strong desire of the United States for friendly relations with all Arab states, and its devotion to peace in the area. King Hussein put forward the views of Jordan and the other Arab states on various Middle East problems and their impact on relations between the two nations. Cordiality, good will and candor marked the discussions. A common concern for preserving and strengthening a just peace in the area was evident throughout the talks.

The two leaders declared their firm determination to make every effort to increase the broad area of understanding which already exists between Jordan and the United States and agreed that His Majesty's visit advanced this objective.

[6] White House Press Release, April 15, 1964; text from *Department of State Bulletin,* May 4, 1964, pp. 697-698. For discussion see *The United States in World Affairs, 1964,* pp. 248-249.

The President expressed the intention of the Government of the United States to continue to support Jordanian efforts to attain a viable and self-sustaining economy.

His Majesty and his party will spend a few days travelling in the United States before returning home.

D. Israel.[7]

(82) *Joint Communiqué of President Johnson and Prime Minister Levi Eshkol, Washington, June 2, 1964.*[8]

Prime Minister Eshkol and President Johnson have completed two days of discussions on matters of mutual interest and concern. Both welcomed the opportunity presented by the Prime Minister's visit at the invitation of the President for a full exchange of views.

The President presented the views of the United States on various world problems, including those of the Near East. He emphasized the strong desire of the United States for friendly relations with all nations of the Near East, and its devotion to peace in the area and to peaceful economic and social development of all countries in the area. He congratulated Prime Minister Eshkol on the progress made by Israel since 1948 in the economic, technical, social and cultural fields. He noted the example provided by Israel in economic growth and human development in conditions of freedom.

Prime Minister Eshkol expressed deep appreciation for the consistent interest and sympathy shown by the U.S. and for the generous economic assistance rendered by the U.S. Government and the American people to Israel over the years. He was confident that Israel's development would continue unabated towards the rapid achievement of a self-sustaining economy. It was his deep conviction that peace and the maintenance of the territorial integrity and national independence of all countries in the Near East is of vital interest to the region and to the world.

The President welcomed assurances of Israel's deep concern, which the United States shares, for peace in the area. He reiterated to Prime Minister Eshkol U.S. support for the territorial integrity and political independence of all countries in the Near East and emphasized the firm opposition of the U.S. to aggression and the use of force or the threat of force against any country. In this connection, both leaders expressed their concern

[7] For discussion see *The United States in World Affairs, 1964,* pp. 249-250.
[8] White House Press Release, June 2, 1964; text from *Department of State Bulletin,* June 22, 1964, pp. 959-960.

at the diversion of vitally important resources from development to armaments.

The two leaders declared their firm determination to make every effort to increase the broad area of understanding which already exists between Israel and the United States and agreed that the Prime Minister's visit advanced this objective.

The agreement reached to undertake joint studies on problems of desalting [9] provided concrete evidence of the desire of the United States to continue to assist Israel in its efforts to solve remaining economic problems. Both countries view this as part of the world-wide cooperative effort being undertaken to solve the problem of scarcity of water and hope for rapid progress toward large-scale desalting in Israel. The knowledge and experience obtained from the joint effort will be available to all countries with water deficiencies.

In conclusion, the President and Prime Minister expressed their conviction that their peoples shared common values and were dedicated to the advancement of man, to individual freedom, and to human dignity.

(83) *United States–Israeli Agreement on Desalting.*

(a) *Memorandum of Understanding, October 14, 1964.*[10]

Having examined the recommendations of the Joint Israeli-United States desalting team, the undersigned affirm the following Principles of Understanding:

1. That an invitation for proposals for the undertaking of a detailed feasibility study by a consulting engineering firm should be issued promptly by the Governments;
2. That, based upon review of the proposals, and interviews if necessary, an engineer be selected and an appropriate contract acceptable to both Governments be executed;
3. That the cost of the engineering study be shared equally by the two Governments;
4. That a Joint Board, consisting of an equal number of representatives from each of the Governments (with a representative of the International Atomic Energy Agency as an observer), be appointed to prepare the invitation, make recommendations for selection of the engineer and the terms of the contract, and to perform such other functions in relation to the engineering

[9] Cf. Document 83.
[10] Department of State Press Release 450, October 15, 1964; text from *Department of State Bulletin*, November 16, 1964, p. 724.

contract as will later be defined by the Governments, and to make recommendations to the two Governments.

Done at Washington in duplicate this fourteenth day of October, 1964.

KENNETH HOLUM
Acting Secretary
United States Department of the Interior
GLENN T. SEABORG
Chairman
United States Atomic Energy Commission
AVRAHAM HARMAN
Ambassador of Israel
General ZVI ZUR
Prime Minister of Israel's Coordinator of the Water Desalting Project

(b) ***Statement by President Johnson, October 15, 1964.***[11]

I am pleased to announce that the Governments of the United States and Israel have agreed to a second step toward the solution of Israel's critical water needs.

The first step was taken last June when Prime Minister Eshkol and I established a joint United States–Israeli study team to conduct technical surveys.[12] These have already been completed.

Now we have agreed that our Governments will share equally in the cost of a detailed engineering study for a large water desalting project to meet Israel's pressing demands for more fresh water.

Both Governments will promptly issue invitations to American engineering consulting firms to participate in the second step. A joint board, with each Government equally represented, will assist in making the selection and will oversee the effort.

E. The Syria-Israel Dispute.

(84) ***Action in the United Nations Security Council: United States–United Kingdom Draft Resolution Vetoed by the U.S.S.R., December 21, 1964.***[13]

The Security Council,

Having heard the statements of the representatives of Israel and the Syrian Arab Republic,

[11] White House Press Release, October 15, 1964; text in same.
[12] Document 82; see also *Department of State Bulletin,* June 29, 1964, p. 1001 and same, August 17, 1964, pp. 230-231.
[13] U.N. Document S/6113, December 17, 1964; defeated by a vote of 8 in

Taking into consideration the report of the Secretary-General of 24 November 1964,

1. *Deplores* the renewal of military action on the Israel-Syria Armistice Demarcation Line on 13 November 1964 and *deeply regrets* the loss of life on both sides;

2. *Takes special note* in the report of the Secretary-General of the observations of the Chief of Staff in paragraphs 24 through 27, and in the light of these observations, *recommends specifically:*

(a) That Israel and Syria co-operate fully with the Chairman of the Mixed Armistice Commission in his efforts to maintain peace in the area;

(b) That the parties co-operate promptly in the continuation of the work begun in 1963, of survey and demarcation as suggested in paragraph 45 of document S/5401, commencing in the area of Tel El Qadi, and proceeding thereafter to completion, in fulfilment of the recommendations of the Chief of Staff's reports of 24 August 1963 and 24 November 1964;

(c) That the parties participate fully in the meetings of the Mixed Armistice Commission;

3. *Requests* the Secretary-General to inform the Council by 31 March of the progress that has been made toward implementing these suggestions.

F. India and Pakistan.[14]

(85) *The Problem of Kashmir: Statement by United States Representative Adlai E. Stevenson to the United Nations Security Council, February 14, 1964.*[15]

So much has been said on the Kashmir case in this Council over the past 16 years that I shall not impose on your patience by reviewing the case again.

It is a matter of greatest regret to my Government, as it is to so many governments here represented, that India and Pakistan have been unable to reach a settlement either through mechanism[*s*] set up by the Security Council or in bilateral talks, and that this dispute continues to occupy so much time of the international community. We are also profoundly concerned with

favor, 3 opposed (U.S.S.R., Czechoslovakia, Morocco) and no abstentions. For discussion see *The United States in World Affairs, 1964*, pp. 251-253.

[14] For discussion see *The United States in World Affairs, 1964*, pp. 262-272.

[15] U.S. Delegation Press Release 4362; text from *Department of State Bulletin*, March 16, 1964, pp. 425-426.

the recurring communal disturbances in India and Pakistan which have caused such appalling loss of life, destruction of property, and displacement of peoples and human misery. It is hard for us to understand why these two countries have not found it possible during all of these years of bloodshed and of violence to take joint action to calm this situation and to allay the suffering, to stem the panic and migration of thousands of frightened human beings. Until there is a far greater effort to resolve these problems, they will continue to threaten the integrity and the prosperity of both countries.

I should like today to review just the essentials of the approach which my Government has taken and continues to take toward this everlasting question of Kashmir.

The origin of the dispute is complicated and deeply buried in the history of the great subcontinent. But in 1948 India and Pakistan agreed to the UNCIP [United Nations Commission for India and Pakistan] resolutions [16] as a political compromise of the difficulties which followed from the partition of the subcontinent into two countries and the ensuing dispute over the status of Kashmir. The essence of this compromise was that the people of Jammu and Kashmir should have the right to determine their future without coercion or intimidation from the military forces of either country. Our support of the United Nations resolutions is based on this principle of self-determination. The political compromise has not been fulfilled, and so we have seen no progress, only further embitterment of relations between these two great countries.

Throughout the history of this issue it has been the desire of the United States to do what it could to compose the differences between the two friends. In doing so, we have started from the point of agreement between them because it was an equitable compromise based upon the sound principle that the people whose political affiliation and national status was subject to dispute have the right to express their will. We continue to support this principle as providing a sound basis upon which a political compromise of the dispute between India and Pakistan can be achieved through peaceful means.

If India and Pakistan are genuinely desirous of composing their differences, which is a prior condition of any political compromise, a fresh attempt must be made in light of today's realities to see how the basic principles can be applied to achieve

[16] U.N. Documents S/726, April 22, 1948 and S/955, August 13, 1948.

such a political settlement. India, and indeed part of the very area in dispute, is under threat of Chinese Communist military attack. For this reason, as well as because of our longstanding concern that the Kashmir question be peacefully resolved, we urged bilateral talks between the parties last year. While these talks did not bring an agreement, neither were they useless. Exploration of disputes through negotiation is a fundamental principle of the United Nations. It is the only way agreement can be achieved short of imposition by force. An agreement cannot be imposed from outside.

We recognize that the legitimate security interests of both India and Pakistan involve intricate internal problems of law and order and political consent. However, the international community has a right to expect that these two great and ancient countries—a right to expect of them what we expect of all members of the United Nations community, and that is to say a diligent and unrelenting effort to resolve their differences peacefully through negotiations. It must be recognized by both countries that the problem of Kashmir cannot be settled unilaterally by either party. It can only be settled, as I say, by agreement and by compromise, taking into account the free expression of the will of the people concerned. The United Nations was created to assist member states in this regard, and its resources are available to help the parties in the search for a solution. Friends of both countries also stand ready to help.

Given the history of efforts to resolve the issues between India and Pakistan in the past, my Government believes that the two countries should consider the possibility of recourse to the good offices of a country or a person of their choice to assist them in bringing about the resumption of negotiations and in mediating their differences. My Government also suggests that the Secretary-General might be of assistance to the two countries in exploring the possibility of such third-party mediation.

There has already been some progress toward bilateral talks on the communal and migration questions. I hope that the two nations may now resume their efforts to agree upon this first step toward finding a firmer basis for communal harmony and dealing with the problem of refugees.

These suggestions, Mr. President, are accompanied by the earnest hope of stimulating these two members of the United Nations to make a new approach in a new and urgent effort to resolve their differences. These problems are not susceptible of quick solution, we know only too well. My Government has no illusions on that score. But a fresh start must be made, and Pakistan and India have, we believe, a responsibility to their own people, to the people of Kashmir, and to the world community to set these issues on the road to final solution for the sake of humanity and of peace.

CHAPTER NINE

THE UNITED STATES AND AFRICA

A. United States Policy in Africa.

(86) *Address by G. Mennen Williams, Assistant Secretary of State for African Affairs, Rochester, March 1, 1964.*[1]

(Excerpt)

* * *

In terms of national self-interest, we have an important strategic interest in Africa. That continent faces the much-traveled Atlantic, Mediterranean, and Indian Ocean shipping lanes, and it shares control of such key passages as Gibraltar, Suez, and Aden. A friendly Africa provides a protective flank to Europe and is important to the success of the Atlantic alliance. Its important airfields have great strategic value, and the Communists have given evidence of how much they would like to have access to them.

Africa is important for economic reasons. It is a wealthy continent, and one day its full potential will be realized. Africa already produces nearly all the world's diamonds, more than half of its gold and cobalt, and a fifth of its copper. It produces such rare metals as tantalite and germanium, which are critical to the advance of modern technology. In addition, its countries are major exporters of coffee, cocoa, hides, skins, and vegetable oils. U.S. trade with Africa and our investments there are rising each year.

We also are interested in Africa because of its growing importance in world affairs. Africa's 35 independent countries constitute nearly one-third of the membership of the United Nations, and the United States has diplomatic relations with each of them.

In view of our expanding relations with Africa, I feel it imperative for Americans to be better informed about African

[1] Department of State Press Release 91, February 29, 1964; text from *Department of State Bulletin,* March 30, 1964, pp. 501-506.

affairs. For that reason I have chosen to speak tonight on Africa's problems and progress. I am sure Americans are increasingly aware of Africa's problems, but I am less confident that the average American knows as much about the political, economic, and social progress modern Africa is making.

A prominent young African statesman recently wrote: "Africa, in these last five years, has been cutting new trails. Anyone who has hacked his way through a forest undergrowth knows that you cannot go far without some scratches and even some blood on your legs."

Certainly, recent headlines from Africa bear out the truth of that statement. There have been—and still are—quite a few troubles in Africa during this period of transition. And if the history of developing countries is a true guide, one can predict that there will be more disturbances, both in independent Africa and in yet-to-be-independent Africa.

In the last few months we have read about revolts in Zanzibar and Gabon. There has been fighting between Algeria and Morocco and between Ethiopia and Somalia over border issues. There have been troop mutinies in Tanganyika, Uganda, and Kenya. There have been uprisings in Congo and Rwanda. There have been anti-American demonstrations in Ghana. And there are such potential trouble spots as Southern Rhodesia, South Africa, and the Portuguese territories of Angola and Mozambique, all of which have a long way to go to resolve important issues between blacks and whites.

These trouble spots pose serious threats to peace and stability in that part of the world, and some of them have overtones that could lead to worldwide problems if they are not resolved quickly.

At the same time, I do not think we should seize upon present unrest in parts of Africa as a valid excuse to denounce Africans generally as unable to govern themselves. Africans, I might point out, have not generally condemned the more developed nations as unfit to govern themselves, even though the Western World perpetrated such practices as segregation, genocide, and colonialism. Instead of reaching quick conclusions on Africa, it would be more productive if more of us in the United States and the free world took a greater interest in the causes of Africa's problems and sought additional ways to help Africa move forward in true independence. The desire to make rapid progress is Africa's most cherished aspiration.

As we view Africa today, what is needed more than anything else is perspective—the ability to see the continent as a whole; to explore the causes fundamental to African unrest; to measure Africa's progress as well as its problems; and, finally, to see clearly how best to cope with the longrun challenge of Africa. Too often we view Africa as do blind men gathered around an elephant to examine it, and we get only part of the truth. We think of Africa in terms of a trunk, a leg, or a tail, and we fail to get an overall picture of what is happening throughout that continent.

Basic Problems of African Leaders

What are some of the basic problems causing African unrest? Let me answer that by asking you to think as an African. If you were the leader of a young African nation today, what issues would be foremost in your mind?

Certainly you would be concerned with the problem of preserving your country's freedom and protecting your national interests. At the same time, your people would urge you to be concerned with progress toward independence in still-dependent Africa, and you would encourage all steps directed toward obtaining self-government for all peoples on the continent.

As an African leader, you would have to explore every possible avenue—governmental and private—that showed promise of helping your country and its people make economic and social advances. You would be fully aware of the serious difficulties Africa faces: an average annual income of only $120 for the continent as a whole; a 15-percent literacy rate; a low life expectancy—one out of every five Africans dies before reaching puberty; a low agricultural productivity rate—the world's second largest landmass accounts for only 5 percent of the world's agricultural products; massive problems of malnutrition and disease; inadequate transportation and communications facilities. When you gathered your human and material resources to tackle these problems, you would discover a shortage of investment capital; a lack of trained technicians, professional people, and administrators; all too few businessmen, large or small; a serious shortage of industrial production upon which to build.

You are conscious of young students returned from Paris, London, Moscow, or the United States, who haven't yet faced the hard realities of national development and who think there's an easier, quicker way to solve your country's problems. You know you have to move fast enough to get them on your side, and you must show results. You can't seem to be following a "conservative" program.

But despite these problems, pressures are upon you to provide progress because your people saw independence as a passport to rapid improvement. And, as a political leader, you realize your political opponents will never permit the people to forget that you promised or implied that your administration would provide this better life.

Obviously, you need help, but to whom do you turn? You can turn to your fellow African leaders and work out some cooperative endeavors, but for the most part they face the same difficulties as you. If you take a really objective view, you are aware that the long-term prospects of your cooperative endeavors are not sufficient to produce the needed results. All of you are starting with approximately the same handicaps.

In the light of these monumental problems faced by Africa's developing nations and their leaders, it is remarkable that there have been so few troubles thus far. Of the 31 new nations that have attained sovereignty in Africa since the end of 1951, only the Congo and Algeria had any serious difficulties during the transfer of power. Not only was Africa's overall record good while the new states were gaining their freedom; they have made a considerable amount of progress in the early years of independence.

Regional and Economic Cooperation in Africa

A heartening degree of progress has been achieved in the political sphere, and Africans can take great pride that the preponderant share of this progress is being made without foreign help.

There has been important regional and economic cooperation in Africa. One highly significant forward step is the successful formation of the Organization of African Unity. This body came into being last May at the historic African heads-of-state conference at Addis Ababa. It is now a 34-member, Africa-wide organization, embracing all independent states except South Africa. The OAU has already begun to function as a vehicle of continental political, economic, social, and cultural cooperation.

Of particular importance is the fact that the OAU is helping Africa over some of the rough spots encountered by all new nations. It does so by providing a forum in which Africans can work out inter-African problems without outside help or interference. African leaders are deeply concerned with their continent's troubles and are determined to use their own resources to solve their problems. This determination was well illustrated last week by Nigeria's Prime Minister [*Sir Abubakar Tafawa*] Balewa in his welcoming address to the Lagos meeting of the OAU Council of Ministers, when he said:

> Africa has in recent months had its moments of trial and is likely to continue to have them for some time yet. . . . The task before you is to devise ways and means of resolving these crises within our organization without resorting to outside help, with all its complicating consequences. . . . We now appreciate more than in the past that we are our brother's keeper and that whatever affects one of us, affects us all.

Although the OAU was formed when most new African governments were less than 4 years old—and the organization itself has not yet reached its first birthday—it has recorded a number of remarkable accomplishments. It played a significant role in stopping last fall's hostilities between Algeria and Morocco and helped to work out the peace agreement just reached between the two countries. It recently helped arrange a cease-fire between Ethiopia and Somalia. It has approved steps that Tanganyika may employ to draw upon the military forces of other African countries to assist it in maintaining internal order. This is a remarkable record for an organization less than a year old. It is all the more impressive when we remember that it has been accomplished by relatively new nations.

In the economic field, the pace of developments in recent months has overshadowed the slow rate of change that took place over many decades of the past century. But, as is true in our own country, quiet and steady improvement is much less newsworthy than the latest crisis. Nevertheless, demonstrable progress has been made by individual countries and by the continent as a whole.

Nigeria, which has about one-fifth of Africa's total population, is a case in point. That country's gross national product has risen at an average annual rate of 3.8 percent since 1950—a slightly higher rate than our own for the same years. In total agricultural production, which is the basis of most African economies, its 1961 level was 23 percent above that for the 1952-54 period. It increased its electric power production ninefold between 1947 and 1962—from 86 million to 750 million kilowatt hours. In cement production, Nigeria's output rose from 113,000 metric tons in 1958 to 426,000 tons in 1962—an increase of almost fourfold in 4 years.

At the risk of your displeasure, let me cite brief statistics from just a few other countries. Although not a lively topic, I think evidence of Africa's economic progress is important for us to recognize.

Between 1958 and 1962, Ethiopia's manufacturing index rose from 100 to 156 and its power production nearly doubled, rising from 79 million to 151 million kilowatt hours. In the same years, Ethiopia's neighbor, Sudan, increased its cotton production from 125,000 to 185,000 metric tons, its total exports from $125 million to $227 million.

In East Africa, between 1958 and 1962, Tanganyikan cement production rose from 346 million to 398 million metric tons; its meat production rose 24 percent, from 125,000 to 155,000 metric tons; and its diamond exports were up 25 percent from 515,000 to 647,000 carats. Tanganyika's neighbor, Uganda, raised its electrical output 65 percent during the same period, from 278 million to 454 million kilowatt hours; and its coffee production went up 50 percent from 92,000 to 138,000 metric tons.

Let me also give you one example of educational progress. In the West African country of Liberia, between 1950 and 1963, the number of schools rose from 270 to 800; the number of teachers from 684 to 2,594; the number of pupils from 24,000 to more than 77,000; and the money put into education rose from $410,000 to $4.5 million.

Africa is also demonstrating progress in its international trade. Excluding South Africa, the continent's exports increased by some 30 percent from the mid-1950's to 1962. The 1953-55 average of African exports was about $4.2 billion annually, while in 1962 that figure rose to nearly $5.5 billion. This, in turn, has enabled Africa to buy more abroad for development purposes.

New Relationships with Europe

African states have entered into a variety of new relationships with the former European metropoles, relationships which preserve valuable cultural ties and common economic interests while recognizing the sovereignty of the new nations. Nigeria, Ghana, and the other major former British dependencies are now full members of the Commonwealth of Nations and continue to share in the Commonwealth trade preference system and sterling bloc financial arrangements. Similarly, many French-speaking African states share preferential trading arrangements and the franc zone with metropolitan France. These are voluntary relationships from which African states can withdraw if they feel it is in their interests—and some have done so.

In addition, 18 African states have forged new economic ties with the six European members of the European Economic Community—the Common Market. In their special status as Associated Overseas Countries of the EEC, these African states share in reciprocal reduction of import duties and benefit from substantial economic assistance extended by all the European member states through a European Development Fund.

The Economic Commission for Africa, a U.N. body operating under able African leadership and largely staffed by Africans, has begun to have a vital role in Africa's economic planning. In particular, it is building a philosophy of regional economic growth and a program of regional projects to discourage narrow, nationalistic economic enterprises which would waste scarce African resources and capital.

A new African Development Bank has recently been established under stimulus of the Economic Commission for Africa, and its authorized capital of $250 million will be subscribed by the African nations themselves. Here, again, emphasis will be on economic projects that transcend national boundaries, such as river valley development and international transportation and communications.

The recent International Coffee Council meeting in London is another example of the ability of a number of African countries to work effectively together and with Latin American coffee producers. The Council was able to reach an agreement on sales quota increases that meets the needs of both consuming and producing nations. Furthermore, it is hoped that increased sales of coffee by African and other nations will arrest the recent rapid increase in coffee prices.

This is a somewhat extended catalog of facts and figures, but it shows that solid progress is being made in Africa. It demonstrates why I can conclude these remarks with a vote of confidence in Africa.

Africa has a promising future, one, I believe, that will be fulfilled despite shortrun setbacks and disappointments. It is a continent of great potential, and its people have high aspirations and are willing to work to attain them.

American foreign policy in Africa is predicated upon a long-range view of African developments. Running through it is the philosophy that politically and economically strong and independent countries in Africa are not only in the best interests of that continent but also in the best interests of the United States. While we have moral and humanitarian desires to help less fortunate nations, the improvement of their economic and political stability protects American interests as well.

This is true because as African countries increase their ability to protect their independence, they become truly nonalined.

Consequently, seeking their own destinies, they will reject subordination by a foreign dynamism, which communism demands.

In his first state of the Union message,[2] President Johnson recognized that fact when he said we must help free nations develop their independence and raise their standard of living. This is what American policy is designed to do in Africa, and we are pleased to be contributing to the promising progress African nations are making today. I am confident those nations will cope with their problems and continue to make impressive progress in the future. We all have a stake in such progress.

B. East Africa.[3]

(87) *United States Recognition of the Government of Zanzibar: Department of State Statement, February 23, 1964.*[4]

The United States today (Sunday, February 23) announced its recognition of the Government of Zanzibar headed by President Abeid Amani Karume.

The Commonwealth Governments of Great Britain, Canada, Australia, New Zealand, Malaysia, and India have also recognized the Karume government.

Prior to this action by the United States, consultations were held with a number of governments including those African governments most immediately concerned. Recognition of the new Zanzibar Government has already been announced by the following African states: Tanganyika, Kenya, Uganda, Ethiopia, Ghana, and the United Arab Republic.

Instructions have been sent by the United States to Mr. Frank Carlucci, a career Foreign Service officer, who has been designated to be the Chargé of Embassy in Zanzibar, to convey to the Karume regime the decision of the United States to recognize the new government and to establish diplomatic relations.

Ambassador William Leonhart, Jr., in Dar-es-Salaam, accompanied by Mr. Carlucci, on February 20 went to Zanzibar and conferred with President Karume and members of his Cabinet concerning the question of recognition. Also present at the Cabinet meeting was Mr. Donald K. Petterson, who has been acting as officer in charge since the departure from Zanzibar of the previous officer in charge, Frederick P. Picard.

Ambassador Leonhart told Mr. Karume of the desire of the

[2] Document 1.
[3] For discussion see *The United States in World Affairs, 1964,* pp. 277-283.
[4] Department of State Press Release 80, February 23, 1964; text from *Department of State Bulletin,* March 16, 1964, p. 424.

United States to maintain and strengthen its ties of friendship and good relations with the people of Zanzibar. President Karume and the Cabinet at that time made known their desire to establish friendly relations with the United States. He declared that the Zanzibar Government would welcome the presence of Mr. Carlucci and Mr. Petterson as soon as diplomatic relations were established.

The United States has consistently affirmed its policy of supporting the efforts of the peoples of Africa to attain their national aspirations for freedom and self-determination. In their actions with respect to recognition and the establishment of diplomatic relations both Governments are affirming their mutual responsibilities as sovereign states under international law including their rights and obligations under the Charter of the United Nations.

The United States hopes that the Zanzibar Government, as have other African governments, will follow a policy of nonalinement as they carry forward their efforts to establish their own unique African institutions which will enable them to improve the standard of living and welfare of their people.

C. The Democratic Republic of the Congo (Leopoldville).[5]

(88) *Resolution of the Organization of African Unity, Adopted September 10, 1964.*[6]

The Council of Ministers of the Organization of African Unity meeting for its Third Extra-ordinary Session in Addis Ababa from 5 to 10 September 1964, to examine the Congolese problem, its repercussions on the neighbouring states and on the African scene at large;

Having studied the messages addressed to it by several African Heads of State and Government, especially that of President [*Joseph*] Kasavubu expressing his conviction that the solution to the Congolese problem should be found within the Organization of African Unity;

Having noted the invitations of the Governments of the Democratic Republic of the Congo, the Republic of Congo (Brazzaville) and the Kingdom of Burundi to the OAU to send a fact-finding and goodwill mission to their countries to seek means of restoring normal relations between the Democratic Republic of [*the*] Congo and the Republic of Congo (Brazzaville) and be-

[5] For discussion see *The United States in World Affairs, 1964,* pp. 296-310.
[6] Organization of African Unity Document, ECM/Res. 5 (III), September 10, 1964.

tween the Democratic Republic of [*the*] Congo and the Kingdom of Burundi;

Taking note of the statement by the Prime Minister [*Moïse Tshombé*] of the Democratic Republic of [*the*] Congo indicating his efforts and desire to bring about national reconciliation in his country;

Deeply concerned by the deteriorating situation in the Democratic Republic of [*the*] Congo resulting from foreign intervention as well as use of mercenaries principally recruited from the racist countries of South Africa and Southern Rhodesia;

Reaffirming the resolutions of the Organization of African Unity inviting all African states to abstain from any relationship whatsoever with the Government of South Africa because of its policy of *apartheid;*

Considering that foreign intervention and the use of mercenaries has unfortunate effects on the neighbouring independent states as well as on the struggle for national liberation in Angola, Southern Rhodesia, Mozambique and the other territories in the region which are still under colonial domination, and constitutes a serious threat to peace in the African continent;

Convinced that the solution to the Congolese problem although essentially political, depends on the pursuit of national reconciliation and the restoration of order, so as to permit stability, economic development of the Congo, as well as the safeguarding of its territorial integrity;

Deeply conscious of the responsibilities and of the competence of the Organization of African Unity to find a peaceful solution to all the problems and differences which affect peace and security in the African continent;

1. *Appeals* to the Government of the Democratic Republic of the Congo to stop immediately the recruitment of mercenaries and to expel as soon as possible all mercenaries of whatever origin who are already in the Congo so as to facilitate an African solution.
2. *Notes* the solemn undertaking of the Prime Minister of the Democratic Republic of the Congo to guarantee the security of combatants who lay down their arms.
3. *Requests* especially all those now fighting to cease hostilities so as to seek, with the help of the Organization of African Unity, a solution that would make possible national reconciliation and the restoration of order in the Congo.
4. *Appeals* to all the political leaders of the Democratic Republic of the Congo to seek, by all appropriate means, to restore and consolidate national reconciliation.

5. *Decides* to set up and to send immediately to the Democratic Republic of the Congo, the Republic of Congo (Brazzaville) and the Kingdom of Burundi an *ad hoc* Commission consisting of Cameroun, Ethiopia, Ghana, Guinea, Nigeria, Somalia, Tunisia, U.A.R., Upper Volta and placed under the effective Chairmanship of H. E. Jomo Kenyatta Prime Minister of Kenya, which will have the following mandate:
   a) to help and encourage the efforts of the Government of the Democratic Republic of the Congo in the restoration of national reconciliation in conformity with paragraphs 2 and 3 above.
   b) to seek by all possible means to bring about normal relations between the Democratic Republic of the Congo and its neighbours, especially the Kingdom of Burundi and the Republic of Congo (Brazzaville).
6. *Invites* this Commission to submit its report to the Administrative Secretary-General, for immediate distribution to all Member States.
7. *Appeals* strongly to all powers at present intervening in the internal affairs of the Democratic Republic of the Congo to cease their interference. The Member States are further invited to give instructions to their diplomatic missions accredited to these powers with the view of impressing upon them this appeal.
8. *Requests* all Member States to refrain from any action that might aggravate the situation in the Democratic Republic of the Congo, or worsen the relationship between the Democratic Republic of the Congo and its neighbours.
9. *Requests* the Administrative Secretary-General to provide the Commission with all the necessary assistance to accomplish its mission.

(89) *Visit to the United States of the* Ad Hoc *Commission on the Congo of the Organization of African Unity, September 25-30, 1964.*[7]

(a) *Department of State Statement, September 23, 1964.*[8]

The United States has been informed that a delegation representing the Congo reconciliation commission of the Organization of African Unity intends to come to the United States to discuss

[7] For discussion see *The United States in World Affairs, 1964,* pp. 303-304.
[8] *Department of State Bulletin,* October 19, 1964, p. 553.

American military assistance to the Congo. We have instructed our Ambassador in Nairobi [Kenya], William Attwood, to make clear to the OAU Commission that we are anxious to cooperate with the OAU in every appropriate way. We attach great importance to the success of its efforts to contribute to a solution of the Congo problem.

However, we could not agree to discuss our aid to the Congo without the participation by the Congo Government, at whose request our aid is being given. We have, therefore, asked our Ambassador to indicate to the Commission that, if the Government of the Congo is willing to participate in such discussions, U.S. representatives will be prepared to meet with representatives of the Government of the Congo and the OAU Commission at a mutually agreed time and place and on the basis of a previously agreed agenda.

Limited U.S. military assistance to the Congo is at the request of the sovereign Government of the Congo to assist it in maintaining law and order. For a number of years we have been providing assistance to the Congo through the United Nations and also on a bilateral basis. The United States has given similar assistance to other African nations at their request.

(b) *Joint Press Communiqué, September 30, 1964.*[9]

The Special Delegation sent to Washington by the *Ad Hoc* Commission on the Congo and composed of the following members:

Mr. Joseph Murumbi, Minister of State, Government of Kenya and Head of the Delegation;

Mr. Kojo Botsio, Minister of Foreign Affairs, Republic of Ghana;

Mr. Louis Lansana Beavogui, Minister of Foreign Affairs, Republic of Guinea;

H. E. Dr. Mostafa Kamel, Ambassador of the United Arab Republic; and

Mr. Gratien Pognon, Assistant Secretary-General, Organization of African Unity,

met with Mr. Dean Rusk, United States Secretary of State, together with the Assistant Secretary of State for African Affairs, Mr. G. Mennen Williams, and discussed the plans of the O.A.U. Commission to support and encourage the efforts of the Government of the Democratic Republic of the Congo in the restoration of national reconciliation.

[9] Department of State Press Release 424, September 30, 1964; text from *Department of State Bulletin,* October 19, 1964, pp. 553-554.

The Delegation stated that it had come to the United States on a goodwill mission. It also made it clear that it was not the Commission's intention to raise with the United States matters affecting the sovereignty of the Democratic Republic of the Congo.

In welcoming these assurances, the Secretary of State asked the Delegation to convey to the Chairman of the Commission, Mr. Jomo Kenyatta, Prime Minister of Kenya, the sympathetic understanding of the United States Government that he is engaged in a most significant undertaking in the service of Africa, to the success of which the United States attaches great importance. The Secretary of State stated that, with this in mind, the Chairman of the *Ad Hoc* Commission should be assured of the desire of the Government of the United States to cooperate with the Commission in every appropriate way in carrying out the mission entrusted to it by the O.A.U.

The Delegation welcomed these assurances of cooperation from the Government of the United States.

The Delegation and the Secretary of State agreed that their discussions have been helpful in clarifying the views of the Commission and of the United States Government and in establishing a general framework for cooperation between them.

The Delegation on behalf of the Chairman of the Commission expressed its appreciation to the Secretary of State for the cordial atmosphere in which the talks were conducted and for the spirit animating the United States Government in its relations with the O.A.U.

(90) *The Rescue of Hostages from the Congo.*

(a) *Message from Secretary of State Rusk to Chairman of the* Ad Hoc *Commission of the Congo Prime Minister Jomo Kenyatta, November 16, 1964.*[10]

Rebel leaders in Stanleyville have announced that they will today execute an American missionary doctor, Dr. Paul Carlson, who has been falsely accused of espionage and of being a major in the United States Army. The United States Government declares unequivocally that Dr. Carlson is not in any way connected with the U.S. military and has been engaged only in his activities as a medical missionary. Dr. Carlson is a man of peace who has served the Congolese people with dedication and faith for 3½ years, taking care of the sick and wounded, including members of the rebel forces. His execution on charges which are patently

[10] *Department of State Bulletin,* December 14, 1964, pp. 838-839.

false would be an outrageous violation of international law and of accepted standards of humanitarian conduct. My Government holds the rebel leaders directly responsible for the safety of Dr. Carlson and all other American citizens in areas under rebel control.

It is now clear from this case as well as other information coming out of Stanleyville that the situation in Stanleyville is rapidly collapsing into anarchy. Under these circumstances, the world—and most particularly those nations whose citizens are directly threatened by the lawlessness and violence in Stanleyville—must look to the OAU [*Organization of African Unity*] as well as the Congolese Government to take rapid and effective action to protect the lives of innocent civilians, Congolese and foreigners, in Stanleyville.

Most immediately, I urge you to bring all of your influence to bear to prevent this act of atrocity against an innocent human being and to intervene at once with the rebel authorities to permit the entry into Stanleyville of the International Red Cross to assure the safety of all foreigners in rebel-held territory. I strongly urge as well that representatives of the OAU *Ad Hoc* Commission accompany the ICRC. I have asked that this appeal be supported by member governments of the OAU *Ad Hoc* Commission.

(b) ***Letter from United States Representative Adlai E. Stevenson to the President of the United Nations Security Council, November 21, 1964.***[11]

For many weeks a situation of extreme danger to the lives of innocent civilians has prevailed in Stanleyville and surrounding areas in the Congo. Many innocent Congolese and foreigners have been mistreated and killed. Threats have been made and are currently in effect against the lives of others.

Appeals have been made by the Congolese Government, by the *Ad Hoc* Commission of the Organization of African Unity, by various Governments, and today jointly from thirteen Governments, that the lives of these hostages be spared. The International Committee of the Red Cross has for many weeks also sought in vain permission to carry out its recognized responsibilities. The lives of citizens of at least eighteen Member nations of the United Nations are involved.

On 20 November the United States Government received a

[11] U.N. Document S/6056, November 23, 1964; text from *Department of State Bulletin*, December 14, 1964, p. 840.

message from Christophe Gbenye [12] suggesting preliminary discussions in Nairobi and asking that the United States fix a time for these discussions. The United States immediately accepted this suggestion and Ambassador [*William*] Attwood in Nairobi proposed a meeting with Prime Minister Kenyatta, Chairman of the Conciliation Commission of the Organization of African Unity, Mr. Gbenye's representative, Mr. Thomas Kanza, and such other persons as they desired for mid-day in Nairobi on 21 November. Ambassador Attwood did meet with Mr. Kenyatta and Organization of African Unity Secretary General Diallo Telli. However, it is not known where Mr. Kanza is and no meeting with him has taken place thus far.

Inasmuch as at least one execution threat has only been held in abeyance until Monday, we believe that the Security Council needs to be informed of the situation in case it proves necessary for the Council to take steps to help protect the lives of the innocent people involved. The United States Government therefore fully associates itself with the letter of today's date from the Government of Belgium to the President of the Security Council.[13]

I should appreciate it if you would circulate this letter as a document of the Security Council.

(c) ***Department of State Statement, November 24, 1964.***[14]

The U.S. Government has just received confirmation that a short time ago—early morning of November 24 in the Congo—a unit of Belgian paratroopers carried by United States military transport planes landed at Stanleyville in the Congo. This landing has been made (1) with the authorization of the Government of the Congo,[15] (2) in conformity with our adherence to the Geneva Conventions, and (3) in exercise of our clear responsibility to protect U.S. citizens under the circumstances existing in the Stanleyville area.

The purpose of this action is to save the lives of innocent men, women, and children, both Congolese and citizens of at least 18 foreign countries. More than 1,000 civilians have been held as hostages by the Congolese rebels. They have been threatened repeatedly with death by their captors. The decision to send in a rescue force was taken only after the most careful

[12] Text in same, p. 839.
[13] U.N. Document S/6055, November 21, 1964.
[14] Department of State Press Release 499, November 24, 1964; text from *Department of State Bulletin,* December 14, 1964, pp. 841-842.
[15] Text of letter of November 21, 1964 from Prime Minister Tshombé to Ambassador G. McMurtrie Godley in same, p. 843.

deliberation and when every other avenue to secure the safety of these innocent people was closed by rebel intransigence. This decision was made jointly by the United States and Belgian Governments with the full knowledge and agreement of the legal Government of the Congo. The immediate mission is the rescue of innocent civilians and the evacuation of those who wish to leave the area. When this mission is accomplished, the rescue force will be withdrawn promptly.

The rebel authorities revealed in late August that they were holding foreign civilians as hostages. Late in October the rebel leaders issued statements that the safety of these civilians could not be guaranteed.

Thousands of innocent civilians, Congolese and foreign, have been subjected in recent months to inhumane and unlawful treatment by rebel forces in the Congo. Some have been killed; others have been tortured. Missionaries and other individuals whose lives have been devoted to unselfish service to the Congolese people have been maligned and mistreated. Some have been tried in "courts" that have no legal standing, deprived of competent advice of counsel, and found guilty of spurious charges. In some cases, when rebel troops have evacuated an area, organized gangs and uncontrolled mobs have carried out mass killings of Congolese and some foreigners.

The safety of the civilians in the Stanleyville area is a matter of wide international concern. In addition to Congolese nationals, citizens of Argentina, Austria, Belgium, Canada, Cyprus, France, Germany, Greece, Haiti, India, Ireland, Italy, the Netherlands, Pakistan, the Sudan, Switzerland, the United Kingdom, and the United States are in Stanleyville. Citizens of other countries are probably also present.

The rebels' action in holding and threatening hostages is in direct violation of the Geneva Conventions and accepted humanitarian principles. Moreover, the harassment and mistreatment of civilians have continued in rebel-held areas despite repeated protests and appeals from international organizations and interested governments. The efforts of the International Committee of the Red Cross to carry out its traditional humanitarian role in such circumstances have been repeatedly frustrated by the rebel leaders. Proposals for evacuation of foreigners from Stanleyville under United Nations and ICRC auspices have been rejected. Appeals from the Organization of African Unity and from a concilium of 16 signatories of the Geneva Conventions have also proved fruitless.

We agreed to discuss with rebel representatives arrangements for release of the American hostages. Our Ambassador in Nairobi undertook these discussions. However, it quickly became clear that the rebel representative was not concerned with the safety of the hostages or other humanitarian considerations but rather sought to use the lives of these civilians for political purposes. We therefore have informed the rebel representative through Prime Minister Kenyatta that under these circumstances we cannot continue these talks.

In order to protect the lives of innocent civilians in the Stanleyville area the Government of the Congo has authorized external help in rescuing them. Accordingly, the Government of Belgium dispatched a contingent of paratroops to accomplish the rescue and the United States Government supplied transport aircraft.

This operation is humanitarian—not military. It is designed to avoid bloodshed—not to engage the rebel forces in combat. Its purpose is to accomplish its task quickly and withdraw—not to seize or hold territory. Personnel engaged are under orders to use force only in their own defense or in the defense of the foreign and Congolese civilians. They will depart from the scene as soon as their evacuation mission is accomplished.

We are informing the United Nations and the OAU *Ad Hoc* Commission of the purely humanitarian purpose of this action and of the regrettable circumstances that made it necessary.

(d) ***Department of State Statement, November 26, 1964.***[16]

The rescue mission within Stanleyville has now been completed and the paratroop force withdrawn to the Stanleyville airport area. Only limited search activity continues in outlying areas around Stanleyville for the few remaining possible evacuees.

In the last 24 hours, however, it has become clear that rebel groups have collected a large number of hostages 225 miles to the north at or near Paulis. Reports indicate that this group, comprising perhaps several hundred foreign civilians—men, women, and children, including seven Americans—is in imminent peril.

In order to complete the evacuation mission as rapidly as possible and minimize further loss of life, a part of the paratroop force has therefore been flown to Paulis. This unit arrived at Paulis at 11 p.m. and will complete its evacuation mission as rapidly as possible. In keeping with its purpose, the rescue

[16] Same, pp. 844-845.

force will complete its humanitarian mission and withdraw from the Congo promptly.

(e) *News Conference Statement by President Johnson, LBJ Ranch, Johnson City, November 28, 1964.*[17]

Let me add here this statement voluntarily before I submit for questions, a word about the Congo and about Africa, which has engaged our very special attention, as you know, this week. This terrible experience, this reign of terror and disorder, these innocent lives sacrificed in political reprisals, constitute a tragedy for Africa and for the Congo as well as for the rest of the world.

What has happened in Stanleyville has happened far too often to Congolese and foreigners alike on both sides for various conflicts in the Congo in recent years. The Congo has suffered through more than 4 years of violence and bloodshed and disunity. It has been an arena of power struggles and ideological wars. I hope now that it can have at last a chance for peace and order and economic recovery, so that the ordinary people of the Congo can hope for improvement in their lot and for protection against the daily threat of violent death.

I have wired the relatives of our citizens who lost their lives there my feelings and expressed my great sympathy for them in this hour. We lost three Americans. Undoubtedly we would have lost dozens more had we not acted promptly and decisively in cooperation with the Belgian paratroopers. As you know, more than 4,000 Congolese themselves, most of whom were people with education—more than 4,000 Congolese in recent months have lost their lives because of these disorders.

I would like to stress to those of you here at the ranch this morning that the United States has no political goals to impose upon the Congo. We have no narrow interest. We have no economic gain to be served in the Congo. We seek to impose no political solution, neither our own nor that of some other outsider. We have tried only to meet our obligations to the legitimate government and to its efforts to achieve unity and stability and reconciliation in the Congo. So we hope now that everyone who has had a part in this 4-year agony of the Congo will bury past differences and try to work together in a spirit of compassion, to help reach these goals of unity and stability and reconciliation. If this could happen, perhaps the hundreds of innocent lives, Congolese and foreign, that have been sacrificed will not have been sacrificed in vain. We were necessarily a party to the decisions, and I assume full responsibility for those made for

[17] Same, pp. 845-846.

our planes to carry the paratroopers in there in this humanitarian venture. We had to act and act promptly in order to keep hundreds and even thousands of people from being massacred. And we did act in time.

The paratroop force that we moved in there will be moved out tonight, and it will be moved out of the Congo to Ascension Island in the South Atlantic Ocean.

(91) *Action in the United Nations Security Council.*

(a) *Statement by Ambassador Stevenson, December 14, 1964.*[18]

(Excerpts)

* * *

In the last few days the United States has been variously accused, and I quote, of "wanton aggression"; of "premeditated aggression"; of plotting a humanitarian mission as a "pretext" for military intervention; of a "nefarious action" designed "to exterminate the black inhabitants"; of "inhumanitarianism"; of a "wanton and deliberate massacre of Congolese people"; of a "murderous operation"; of a "premeditated and coldblooded act"; of "not being truly concerned with the lives of the hostages"; of a "crude subterfuge"; of "massive cannibalism"; of having killed [*Patrice*] Lumumba "with cynicism and premeditation"; of genocide against an entire people; of being caught "redhanded"; of using the United Nations as a "Trojan horse"; of a racist attack to kill thousands of "blacks," an operation which, in the words of one of the speakers, proved to him that a "white, if his name is Carlson, or if he is an American, a Belgian, or an Englishman, is worth thousands upon thousands of blacks."

And that's not all! We have heard words in this chamber either charging or implying that the United States Government was an accomplice to the death of Dag Hammarskjold—and even the assassination of President Kennedy!

I have served in the United Nations from its inception off and on for 7 years. But never before have I heard such irrational, irresponsible, insulting, and repugnant language in these chambers—and used to contemptuously impugn and slander a gallant and successful effort to save human lives of many nationalities and colors.

[18] U.S. Delegation Press Release 4479, December 14, 1964; text from *Department of State Bulletin,* January 4, 1965, pp. 15-24.

But even such a torrent of abuse of my country is of no consequence compared to the specter of racial antagonism and conflict raised in this chamber. I need no credentials as a spokesman for racial equality and social justice in this country, and the Government of this country needs none in the world. Yet at a time when all responsible men and governments are trying to erase every vestige of racial antagonism, when racism has become an ugly word in all nations, we hear its ominous undertones—in the United Nations.

Racial hatred, racial strife, has cursed the world for too long. I make no defense of the sins of the white race in this respect. But the antidote for white racism is not black racism. Racism in any form by anybody is an offense to the conscience of mankind and to the Charter of the United Nations, which enjoins us to promote and encourage "respect for human rights and for fundamental freedoms for all without distinction as to race, sex, language, or religion."

* * *

Facts About U.S.-Belgian Rescue Mission

The Council has heard the sober, factual account of that operation by the Foreign Minister [*Paul-Henri Spaak*] of Belgium. In fact, only a very small number of rebels were killed as a consequence of that operation and these only in self-defense or because they were at the moment resisting the attempts to rescue the hostages.

The grim story of thousands of innocent civilians—many of them foreign—illegally seized, brutalized, and threatened, and many murdered by rebels against the Congo Government, has already been related to this Council. Every means—legal, moral, and humane, including the United Nations—was exhausted to protect their lives and secure their release, all without avail. When it became apparent that there was no hope, the Belgian and American Governments, with the cooperation of the Government of the United Kingdom and with the express authorization of the sovereign Government of the Democratic Republic of the Congo, undertook an emergency rescue mission to save the lives of those innocent people.

The operation was carried out with restraint, courage, discipline, and dispatch. In 4 days 2,000 people—Europeans, Americans, Africans, and Asians—were rescued and evacuated to safe territory. These included Americans, Britons, and Belgians; Pakistanis, Indians, Congolese, Greeks, French, Dutch, Germans, Canadians, Spaniards, Portuguese, Swiss, and Italians; as well as citizens of Ghana, Uganda, Ethiopia, and the United Arab Republic.

The mission lasted 4 days from first to last and left the Stanleyville area the day its task ended; it returned immediately to Belgium; the episode is finished.

Yet the memorandum [19] from certain African states supporting the request for this meeting charges that the United States and Belgium, in defiance of article 52 of the charter and as a deliberate affront to the Organization of African Unity, launched military operations in Stanleyville and other parts of the Congo with the concurrence of the United Kingdom and that these actions constituted intervention in African affairs, a flagrant violation of the charter, and a threat to the peace and security of the African Continent.

It makes no mention whatever of the repeated and repulsive threats made by those controlling Stanleyville, of the solely merciful objectives of the rescue mission, of its authorization by the Government of the Congo, of the fact that the mission withdrew as soon as it had evacuated the foreign hostages and other civilians who wished to escape, nor of the fact that some of the signatories of the letter are themselves intervening in the Congo against its Government, or of other relevant facts known to the members of this Council—and to the world at large.

The United States emphatically denies the charges made in this memorandum and in the debate. We have no apologies to make to any state appearing before this Council. We are proud of our part in saving human lives imperiled by the civil war in the Congo.

The United States took part in no operation with military purposes in the Congo.

We violated no provision of the United Nations Charter.

Our action was no threat to peace and security; it was not an affront—deliberate or otherwise—to the OAU; and it constituted no intervention in Congolese or African affairs.

This mission was exactly what we said it was when we notified this Council at the beginning—nothing more and nothing less than a mission to save the lives of innocent people of diverse nationalities, many of whom were teachers, doctors, and missionaries who have devoted their careers to selfless service to the Congolese people. To anyone willing to consider the facts—in good faith—that must be clear. To anyone who will face the

[19] U.N. Document S/6076, December 1, 1964.

facts, unobstructed by hatred for [*Prime Minister Moïse*] Tshombe or the Congo or Belgium or the United States and Great Britain, that must be clear.

While our primary obligation was to protect the lives of American citizens, we are proud that the mission rescued so many innocent people of 18 other nationalities from their dreadful predicament. We mourn the thousands of others—Congolese and foreign—already sacrificed in the preceding months of their horrible civil strife in this tortured country. And we urge all nations to appeal for the safety of those who remain in danger.

No amount of detail—and certainly no extraneous issues—can obscure the stark outlines of that story. Yet questions have been raised—harsh statements have been made—about the motivations involved in launching the rescue mission. Let me therefore speak to that point.

Why the Mission Was Launched

For months before the rescue mission was undertaken, diplomatic efforts had been pursued through every conceivable channel to persuade the rebels to release the hostages.

Conscious of the legal and humanitarian issues at stake, the Secretary-General [*U Thant*] of the United Nations, the International Committee of the Red Cross, the *Ad Hoc* Commission of the Organization of African Unity, the Government of the Congo, and various other governments, including African governments, made repeated efforts to secure the rights and release of the hostages for three long, anxious, and frustrating months.

Every available avenue was tried; every approach was ignored or in effect rejected by the rebels; and in the process the Red Cross, the World Health Organization, and the United Nations were vilified by the military leaders of the rebels "as espionage organizations in the service of the neo-colonialists." These are the exact words used by the so-called General Olenga in a message on September 3, 1964. This accusation was also repeatedly broadcast by Stanleyville.

For some days before November 23 it was difficult to be sure who was in charge in Stanleyville—or indeed whether *anyone* was in control. It was impossible to know whether any agreement that might be made with any alleged representative of the rebels could in fact be carried out.

Nonetheless, when the possibility arose, through the good offices of the chairman [*Jomo Kenyatta*] of the *Ad Hoc* Commission of the Organization of African Unity, of a meeting with a representative of the rebels in Nairobi on November 21, my Government immediately named its Ambassador to Kenya, Mr. William Attwood, to represent it for the purpose of discussing the safety of the hostages.

Mr. Thomas Kanza, who was said to represent the rebels, did not appear. Instead, on that day, November 21, the Stanleyville Radio, mouthpiece of the rebel forces, suggested that the hostages be burned alive or massacred with machetes and "devoured."

On the following day, November 22, the rebel representative belatedly did appear in Nairobi, and a meeting was subsequently held with Ambassador Attwood on November 23. The rebel spokesman, however, refused to address the problem of the release of the hostages on its humanitarian merits; he persisted in callous efforts to barter their lives for political and military concessions from the Government of the Congo.

It must be obvious that my Government could neither legally nor morally accept this as a satisfactory basis for discussion. Legally, we could not concede what lies within the competence of another sovereign government. Morally, we could not agree that our citizens could be illegally held for ransom.

* * *

By the time the Belgian paratroopers arrived in Stanleyville, and before the outlaws even knew of their impending arrival, the total of those thus already cruelly tortured and slaughtered amounted to 35 foreigners, including 19 Belgians, 2 Americans, 2 Indians, 2 Greeks, 1 Italian, 2 Portuguese, 2 Togolese, and 4 Dutch, and 1 English, many of them missionaries who had spent their lives to help the Congolese people. That, at least, is the verified number. God alone knows how many others, long missing and out of touch with the outside world, had met a similar fate.

During this period of many months before the rescue mission arrived in Stanleyville, the rebels not only murdered these foreigners but systematically slaughtered local Congolese officials, police, teachers, intellectuals, members of opposing political groups, labor leaders, and rank-and-file members of labor unions who were considered unreliable or even undesirable by their captors. The exact number of Congolese so liquidated may never be known, but it had reached thousands long before November 24.

In case there is still any doubt in your minds that the rescue of the hostages was a matter of life and death, members of the

Council might find of interest this photostat of a telegram from General Olenga to Major Tshenda in Kindu, dated September 30, 1964. It says: "Major Tshenda Oscar, Kindu: Reference your unnumbered telegram, Americans Belgians must be held in a secure place stop In case of bombing region, exterminate all without requesting further orders. signed General Olenga."

* * *

Let me now put the position of the United States into context. It has been consistent since independence day in the Congo, on June 30, 1960.

From the beginning the United States has been opposed to any breakup of the Congo by secessionist movements—secessions based in Elisabethville, in Kasai, in Stanleyville, or anywhere else.

From the beginning the United States has favored responsible efforts for political reconciliation of dissident groups in the Congo through compromise and consensus.

And from the beginning we have been opposed—and remain opposed—to foreign intervention in the internal affairs of the sovereign and independent state of the Congo.

In July 1960 the Government of the Congo—faced with a mutiny in its security forces and with a collapse of order and essential services—formally requested the United States to lend military assistance in restoring order. The request was declined by the United States Government in favor of a United Nations effort. The United States Government supported in principle and in practice—including very large financial and material contributions—United Nations aid to the Congo precisely for the reason that any other course might have brought international conflict to the heart of Africa, with dangerous consequences not only for the Congo itself but for the whole continent.

The accomplishments of the United Nations are a matter of history. Law and order were maintained, secession was crushed, some advance toward political stability was made, massive economic and technical aid was supplied from all over the world.

But unfortunately the United Nations—largely because some members of the U.N. refused to pay their assessments for the Congo operation—was unable to remain long enough to finish the task it had undertaken. It had to withdraw despite sober warnings that withdrawal was premature.

Well before the United Nations left, new insurrections broke out, encouraged from neighboring countries where enemies of the Congo Government found comfort and aid through the embassies of a non-African power. Ever since that time both the [*Cyrille*] Adoula government and the present government have been afflicted by insurgents aided and supported from outside. Prime Minister Adoula repeatedly sought help from Africa, but, with one or two notable exceptions, his plea for help was unheeded. In those circumstances he sought military aid from the United States and Belgium.

Aid Given at Request of Congolese Government

It has been charged in this Council that, quite apart from the rescue mission, the United States has intervened militarily in the Congo.

I reject this charge. These are the facts:

As I have stated, Prime Minister Adoula earlier this year requested—and the United States provided—some military materiel and training assistance to the Congo. This is exactly what all other African states have done or are doing. There is not one of them that does not obtain military equipment or training or both from outside Africa in the exercise of its own sovereign right.

When, in accordance with the constitution of the Congo, President [*Joseph*] Kasavubu selected Prime Minister Tshombe to succeed Prime Minister Adoula, who had resigned, the United States continued this program. It did so upon specific affirmation by Prime Minister Tshombe that the Government of the Congo desired that the program be continued. As the need arose, the United States, at the request of the Government of the Congo, provided additional equipment and transport. It was not requested to, and did not, undertake military operations in the Congo.

Mr. President, statements have been made here which seem to add up to the astounding proposition that the United States has no right to provide assistance to the Congolese Government and that that Government has no right to accept it because the aid comes from outside Africa. I repeat that there is hardly an African state which has not requested and received military aid, in the form of arms or training or both, from outside Africa. Certainly Algeria, for example, has received and is receiving massive foreign military aid in both these categories.

Is this sovereign right to be exercised by some and denied to others? Would other states in Africa who receive arms and military assistance from outside the continent relinquish this equipment or assistance, or ask for its withdrawal, in the unhappy event that rebellion broke out within their boundaries? I very much doubt that they would or that anyone here really believes they should.

It is perhaps necessary to repeat that the United States furnished military assistance to the Congo in the form of transport and communications equipment, in the first instance to the government of Mr. Adoula, when it became quite apparent that the United Nations would be unable to undertake the necessary reorganization of the Congolese army. Our assistance was continued when it became clear that the U.N. operation was about to be terminated for lack of funds, after a rebellion fomented from abroad had broken out in the Congo and after Mr. Adoula had appealed to other African states for aid to maintain peace and security in his country.

Would any African country which has spoken at this table deny that, under similar circumstances, it would have urgently appealed for and gratefully accepted military aid from outside Africa? And, I must add, if these countries sincerely wish the Government of the Congo not to seek such aid, let them scrupulously refrain from stirring up rebellion and aiding the insurgents. If they demand that the Government cease to defend itself with the only means at its disposal, while at the same time themselves refusing aid to the Government and granting it to the rebels, what confidence in their good faith can anyone have? On what grounds and for what purpose do they appeal to a Council the duty of which is to maintain international peace and security? If the practice of supporting rebellion against a government which is disliked by other governments becomes prevalent in Africa, what security will any African government have?

Let us not be hypocritical. Either each government recognizes the right of other governments to exist and refrains from attempting to overthrow them, or we revert to a primitive state of anarchy in which each conspires against its neighbor. The golden rule is do unto others as you would have them do unto you.

The world has made some progress, and military invasions of one another's territory are diminishing, thanks in large measure to the United Nations. But a new practice has developed, or rather an old practice has developed new momentum—the more or less hidden intervention by nations in the internal affairs of their neighbors. Most of the fighting and killing that still goes on can be traced to outside interventions designed to undermine or overthrow governments.

In Africa nearly every country wants and needs the help of outsiders in achieving those "better standards of life in larger freedom" which are the goal of their rising expectations and the promise of their political independence. So outsiders are bound to be involved to some extent in their internal affairs. The question therefore is: Under what rules will the outsiders operate on the inside? Over the years, more through the practice of nations than the teachings of scholars, have we not developed some general principles to guide this widespread practice of mutual involvement? Where the government, recognized diplomatically by other states as the responsible government, exercises its sovereign right to ask for outside help, then it would seem that the response and the involvement of outsiders is all right.

But I concede that it is not an easy line to draw. The principle that outsiders should be invited and not crash the party is far from an infallible guide to good conduct. But still, the principle of permission is certainly the best one yet developed to prevent a reversion to imperialism and foreign domination. For if the outsiders, not the insiders, decide when intervention is right, the fragile fabric of nationhood will come apart at the seams in a score of new African nations.

Every nation has its dissidents, its internal struggle for power, its internal arguments about who should be in charge and how the country should be run. But if every internal rivalry is to become a Spanish Civil War, with each faction drawing in other Africans and great powers from other continents, the history of independent Africa in this century will be bloody and shameful and the aspirations of Africa's wonderful peoples will be cruelly postponed.

That is why we supported the United Nations Operation in the Congo and were sorry that it had to be withdrawn, its mission incomplete, because of the United Nations financial difficulties. And that is why we oppose unsolicited foreign intervention in the Congo.

Illegal Intervention

Contrast the aid that has been supplied to successive governments of the Congo upon request with the current intervention in the internal affairs of the Congo—in support of rebellion against the legitimate government. These outside elements have included foreign countries as far away as Peiping and Moscow, as near as Burundi and the neighboring Congo. They have included admissions as flagrant as the public statement by the President [*Ahmed Ben Bella*] of Algeria:

> It is not enough to demonstrate. What we are now doing is sending arms, rifles, and volunteers. We say that we are sending and we will continue indefinitely to send arms and men.

Last week Algerian military aircraft flew into Juba in the Sudan near the border of the Congo. They transferred cargo to trucks which then departed toward the Congolese frontier. We received reports of Algerian personnel in transit at the airport at Khartoum; of Ghanaian aircraft transferring cargoes of rifles to Egyptian aircraft at Khartoum for shipment to Juba; of rebel leaders being received in Khartoum and Cairo; of mortars, machineguns, and ammunition from Communist China used by the rebels; of Soviet encouragement and offers to replace arms given to the rebels by the United Arab Republic and Algeria.

The representative of Algeria has so far not commented on these charges, although very liberal in his criticisms of my country's long effort to assist the Congo to preserve its independence, integrity, and unity. At the same time the Government of Ghana states only that it does "not know the veracity of this allegation" that it has supplied arms to the enemies of the Government of the Congo.

* * *

If there should be any question about illegal interference in the Congo, let me point out that earlier this week [*Christophe*] Gbenye himself stated that the rebels were receiving foreign military assistance. He declared that an unspecified number of Congolese who have been trained in Communist China are en route to join the rebels and that Russian and Chinese weapons, food, and medicines had already been received. He declared that Presidents [*Kwame*] Nkrumah, [*Gamal Abdel*] Nasser, and Ben Bella had promised to send arms and volunteers and that African states would provide aircraft.

The rebel leader further stated that the operational plan is being held up pending Security Council action. He added that the center for the buildup of rebel strength would be Brazzaville and that the object is to assemble outside assistance, including volunteers and supplies, from which a drive would then be launched to take Léopoldville.

Let us understand what is happening. What is happening is that outside governments are claiming that *they*—not the Government of the Congo—shall decide whether that Government can be assisted or whether its enemies shall be assisted to overthrow it.

Obligation of the Security Council

I submit, Mr. President, that this is the proper and urgent business of this Council—not the complaint against a 4-day effort to save innocent lives which has long since ended. *This* is intervention in gross violation of the United Nations Charter and of repeated resolutions of this Council concerning the Congo.

On July 22, 1960, by unanimous vote the Security Council passed a resolution [20] which requested "all States to refrain from any action which might tend to impede the restoration of law and order and the exercise by the Government of the Congo of its authority and also to refrain from any action which might undermine the territorial integrity and the political independence of the Republic of the Congo."

On November 24, 1961, this Council voted another resolution [21] which urged "all Member States to lend their support, according to their national procedures, to the Central Government of the Republic of the Congo, in conformity with the Charter and the decisions of the United Nations."

These resolutions are in full force today. In his last report on the Congo to the Security Council dated June 29, 1964,[22] the Secretary-General explicitly states: ". . . the resolutions of the Security Council concerning the Congo continue to be applicable, since they have no terminal date."

Obviously all states are *not* refraining from actions which "impede the restoration of law and order and the exercise by the Government of the Congo of its authority." Obviously all states are *not* refraining from actions which "undermine the territorial integrity and the political independence of the Republic of the Congo." And obviously all states are *not* lending their support to the Government of the Congo "in conformity with the Charter and the decisions of the United Nations."

It is now up to the Council to see to it that these prior decisions are enforced—that the flagrant violations of the 1960 and 1961 resolutions are stopped.

The danger of foreign intervention in the internal affairs of

[20] *Documents, 1960,* p. 360.
[21] Same, *1961,* pp. 350-352.
[22] U.N. Document S/5784.

the Congo is no less today—to the Congo, to Africa, and to all the world—than it was in 1960. It is no less a danger when certain of those who intervene are themselves Africans. And the responsibility of the United Nations is no less clear than it was then.

My delegation therefore urges the Council to reaffirm its support of the unity and territorial integrity of the Congo and call on all states to refrain from any action which would impede the restoration of law and order and the exercise by the Government of the Congo of its authority, and to consider, as an urgent matter, the establishment of an inspection and investigation group to proceed to the Congo and to report to this Council so that outside intervention in the affairs of the Government of the Congo can be brought to an end at the earliest possible moment.

But, Mr. President, it is not enough that we should merely call upon members of this organization to refrain from hostile and illegal acts against the Government of the Congo. The Security Council has a solemn obligation to propose constructive and positive solutions to the problems which the Congo faces and to do so rationally and responsibly, without malice or emotion, or political or ideological self-interest. Our obligation is to protect and assure the integrity and independence of the Congo; it is to enable the people of the Congo to select their own government and create their own institutions.

Basis for Solution of Congo Problem

The principles required for a viable solution to the Congo are not difficult to identify; they have been inherent in the problem from the beginning and have formed the basis of repeated Security Council resolutions on the Congo problem. What are these principles?

First, that the unity, territorial integrity, and political independence of the Congo should be respected and strengthened by all states;

Second, that all states should refrain from any action which might impede the restoration of law and order and the exercise by the Government of the Congo of its authority;

Third, that secession, civil war, tribal rivalries, and acts of defiance of the authority of the Central Government of the Congo should be deplored, as they consistently have been deplored by the Security Council since 1960;

Fourth, that a heavy responsibility lies in the hands of the Government of the Congo to bring about a speedy resolution of internal conflicts within the country and to hasten the process of national reconciliation of responsible elements within the nation, in order that the Congo may realize its great potential as a strong and free nation of Africa and member of the international community.

In this connection, I would like to remind the Council that the present Government of the Congo was appointed by President Kasavubu under the transitional provisions of the new constitution, which charges it with the responsibility of preparing for national elections to be held early next year. I am sure that all member states will agree that it is in the interests of the Congo, of Africa, and of the world community that this government should be given every opportunity—and every encouragement—to create the conditions for full and free elections which will permit the Congolese people to make their own free choice of their own leaders.

These principles, Mr. President, provide a basis on which to build constructively and responsibly. But they are, after all, principles and have value only as they are translated into action. This in turn imposes a heavy obligation on all states who are in a position to help the Government of the Congo—and whose assistance that Government desires to redouble their efforts to bring about a viable solution to the stubborn and debilitating problems that plague that country.

Let me say a few words about those who are in a position to help. No country is more aware than my own that the Congo is an African country. In the interrelated world of today, it should be clear that the Congo problem must be solved in an African context. It is for this reason that my Government viewed both with sympathy and hope the constructive initiative which the Council of Ministers of the Organization of African Unity took at Addis Ababa in September in its efforts to contribute to a solution of the Congo problems.[23] The fact that its efforts to achieve the objectives set forth in the resolution which it passed at that time have not yet yielded the desired results should not be cause for despair; it is, instead, a reason for reaffirmation of the sound principles which were expressed in that resolution, and to try to find new ways of applying them so as to assist the Democratic Republic of the Congo in achieving a rapid, peaceful solution of its problems.

[23] Document 88.

Given the special responsibility of the members of the Organization of African Unity to assist the Government of the Congo, the United Nations also bears a continuing heavy responsibility to help. This obligation arises not only out of the history of its past efforts to assist that country but also out of its continuing mandate to promote world peace and stability. Although, for reasons we are all aware of, the United Nations has steadily reduced its role in the Congo, it nevertheless continues to play a most important and constructive part in the rehabilitation of the country's economic and social system.

Again, my delegation is strongly of the opinion that it is timely now for the United Nations to reexamine both what it is doing and what more it could do to assist the Government of the Democratic Republic of the Congo with the solution of its problems. In saying this, I am not suggesting vast new programs or dramatic new forms of international assistance to the Congo. What I am suggesting is that the United Nations, the Organization of African Unity, and perhaps such other organs as the Economic Commission for Africa, could severally or jointly reexamine with the Government of the Democratic Republic of the Congo the problems which the latter faces and thereby bring their combined wisdom and their combined efforts to bear on the solution of the Congo's urgent difficulties.

At our last meeting, Mr. [Paul-Henri] Spaak, the distinguished Foreign Minister of Belgium, expressed the strong conviction that the problems of the Congo cannot be solved by military means alone. My Government wholeheartedly concurs in this judgment. We hope to see an early end to the rebellion in a manner which will assure that all of the Congo's responsible political, economic, and social resources are effectively and peacefully mobilized in tackling the great tasks of national rehabilitation and national building. Toward this end, Mr. President, I wish to pledge the wholehearted support of my Government to cooperate with any and all responsible efforts by this organization, by the OAU, and by other appropriate international organizations.

With good will, with imagination, and with a disinterested sense of our international responsibilities, the continuing difficulties in the Congo, as with so many of the other stubborn problems which this organization has had to face throughout its history, will yield to the combined wisdom and urgent efforts of those who are dedicated to responsible and constructive solutions.

(b) ***Resolution of the United Nations Security Council, Adopted December 30, 1964.***[24]

The Security Council,

Noting with concern the aggravation of the situation in the Democratic Republic of the Congo,

Deploring the recent events in the Democratic Republic of the Congo,

Convinced that the solution of the Congolese problem depends on national reconciliation and the restoration of public order,

Recalling the pertinent resolutions of the General Assembly and the Security Council,

Reaffirming the sovereignty and territorial integrity of the Democratic Republic of the Congo,

Taking into consideration the resolution of the Organization of African Unity dated 10 September,[25] in particular paragraph 4 relating to the mercenaries,

Convinced that the Organization of African Unity should be able, in the context of Article 52 of the Charter, to help find a peaceful solution to all the problems and disputes affecting peace and security in the continent of Africa,

Having in mind the efforts of the Organization of African Unity to help the Government of the Democratic Republic of the Congo and the other political factions in the Congo to find a peaceful solution to their dispute,

1. *Requests* all States to refrain or desist from intervening in the domestic affairs of the Congo;

2. *Appeals* for a cease-fire in the Congo in accordance with the Organization of African Unity's resolution dated 10 September 1964;

3. *Considers,* in accordance with the Organization of African Unity's resolution dated 10 September 1964, that the mercenaries should as a matter of urgency be withdrawn from the Congo;

4. *Encourages* the Organization of African Unity to pursue its efforts to help the Government of the Democratic Republic of the Congo to achieve national reconciliation in accordance with resolution CM/Resolution 5 (III) dated 10 September 1964 of the Organization of African Unity;

5. *Requests* all States to assist the Organization of African Unity in the attainment of these objectives;

6. *Requests* the Organization of African Unity, in accordance

[24] U.N. Document S/6129, December 30, 1964; adopted by a vote of 10-0-1 (France).

[25] See note 23 to Document 91a.

with Article 54 of the Charter, to keep the Security Council fully informed of any action it may take under this resolution;

7. *Requests* the Secretary-General of the United Nations to follow the situation in the Congo, and to report to the Security Council at the appropriate time.

D. The Problem of *Apartheid* in the Republic of South Africa.

(92) *Consideration by the United Nations Security Council.*

(a) *Statement by Ambassador Stevenson, June 16, 1964.*[26]

(Excerpts)

I want to express the appreciation of my delegation to the distinguished Ambassador of Norway [*Sivert A. Nielsen*] and to the other conferees who have produced the resolution [27] that has just been introduced after prolonged and careful consideration. Pending the introduction of a resolution, we have refrained from speaking at this session of the Security Council on the subject of *apartheid*. However, now that a resolution is before the Council for action, I should like to take the liberty of expressing the views of my Government on the subject of racial discrimination in the Republic of South Africa and on the resolution that has been introduced.

The *apartheid* policies of the Government of South Africa not only offend the principles set forth in the charter; they challenge our determination to uphold these principles, and they challenge the ability of the United Nations to find the best means of influencing the course of South African history toward peaceful change.

South Africa's racial policies have forced upon the United Nations the task of trying to persuade a member state to alter a course of action which affects not only its own peoples but the racial situation in the world at large. The United Nations' task is not only to help the majority of the peoples of South Africa to fulfill their legitimate aspirations but also to avoid a racial conflict which could seriously trouble peace and progress in Africa and throughout the world.

Ever since the seventh session in 1952, the Assembly first, and then the Security Council, have sought to express the United Nations' convictions and impress its influence upon a situation

[26] U.S. Delegation Press Release 4415 and Corr. 1; text from *Department of State Bulletin*, July 6, 1964, pp. 29-32.
[27] Document 92b.

which, because it involves violations of the charter and because it may become even more serious, is a situation of international concern.

* * *

New Developments in South Africa

Since last the Security Council turned its attention to the question of *apartheid,*[28] new developments in South Africa have increased our concern. Just last week we learned with profound regret of the life sentences imposed on eight of the defendants in the Rivonia trials, including some of the most prominent leaders in the struggle against *apartheid,* although we were, of course, relieved that death sentences were not imposed. The sentences and the actions that led to them are yet another distressing sign of the tragic interaction between repression and violence which in South Africa today continues to frustrate any progress toward conciliation and negotiation. The basic philosophy of the laws under which the defendants were charged, the law under which persons are detained for the purpose of providing evidence, and the whole legislative and administrative machinery which takes away the rights of all in trying to preserve them for a minority, is cause for deep concern.

Since the Security Council last considered *apartheid,* the promulgation of new laws of the kind described in the report of the Special Committee on Apartheid, the further additions to the military forces of South Africa that might be used for internal suppression, and the passage by the South African Parliament of the discriminatory Bantu Laws Amendment bill, all these indications give us little hope that the Government is changing its view of the status of nonwhites in South Africa.

There is no doubt in our minds that seeds of violence are planted by each one of these repressive acts based upon the repugnant philosophy of *apartheid.* There is an increasingly dangerous interaction between repression and violence, and time is running out in which to turn the spiral down—toward a peaceful solution. The moving statement of Nelson Mandela, spoken in his defense at the Rivonia trial, presented to the world the anguish and frustration of those struggling against the injustices of South Africa's racial policies.

Since the adoption of the Security Council's resolution of 4 December,[29] the Council has received two reports from the

[28] Cf. *Documents, 1963,* pp. 348-361.
[29] Same, pp. 357-359.

Special Committee on Apartheid [30] and the report of the Secretary-General [31] which contained the report of the group of experts which he appointed under the terms of that resolution. We have examined the various conclusions and recommendations of these bodies with care. While we have a number of reservations about certain aspects of these reports, and in particular do not subscribe to the recommendations in paragraph 121 of the report of the group of experts, we share the intense concern which they reflect.

We very much regret that the South African Government did not choose to afford the group of experts an opportunity to visit South Africa and thus to enhance the objectivity and accuracy of their report. Such a visit would, we think, have facilitated the group's task.

Their report places particular emphasis on the need for what they term a "National Convention" to help to bring about a peaceful resolution of the situation. The United States has consistently held that the ultimate solution in South Africa must be worked out by the peoples of South Africa themselves, worked out on the basis of a free and equal exchange of views between all segments of the population, worked out on the basis of give and take.

The first link in such consultation must be the establishment of communication. We would hope the South African Government for its part would respond favorably to such a concept, would cooperate with the United Nations, and would seek such assistance, both within and outside the United Nations, as might be useful.

We also see merit in the concept of a special training and education program for South Africans to be established under the auspices of the United Nations. Such a program would afford to those South Africans who have chosen to leave their country, or who have little access to higher education within their country, a chance to pursue their studies elsewhere. The United States is prepared to examine opportunities to contribute to such a program, both financially and in terms of scholarship and other facilities at American educational institutions. There is much interest throughout the world in such a program and much willingness to help in providing educational opportunities for South Africans. In the past, however, there has been some difficulty in finding the best way of applying offers of assistance. We would envisage that such a program, if established,

[30] U.N. Documents S/5621, March 25, 1964 and S/5717, May 25, 1964.
[31] U.N. Document S/5658 and Corr. 1, May 5, 1964.

would provide a useful central point for administering effectively educational assistance for South Africans.

U.S. Position Concerning Sanctions

Much has been said here in the Council and elsewhere on the question of sanctions. My Government continues to believe that the situation in South Africa, though charged with somber and dangerous implications, does not today provide a basis under the charter for the application by the Security Council of coercive measures. Nor can we support the concept of an ultimatum to the South African Government which could be interpreted as threatening the application of coercive measures in the situation now prevailing, since in our view the charter clearly does not empower the Security Council to apply coercive measures in such a situation.

However, the group of experts has suggested that a study of sanctions be undertaken. My Government has given this proposal serious and prolonged consideration and would be prepared to support the initiation of a properly designed study and to participate in it. But—and let me be explicit—our willingness to see such a study go forward under certain circumstances or our willingness to participate in such a study represents in no way an advance commitment on the part of my Government to support at any specific time the application under the charter of coercive measures with regard to the South African situation or any other situation; nor should this position be interpreted as relating to our view of the situation in South Africa today or what it may become tomorrow. We do feel that such a study, if agreed to by the Security Council, could make a contribution to a fuller understanding on the part of the Council. While our support for such a study, and agreement to participate in it, is without any commitments or implications as to our future actions, we think that if and when a situation arose in which sanctions might be appropriately considered under the charter—a situation which does not today exist—the availability of a detailed, practical, and expert study would have considerable utility.

Mr. President, like other members of the United Nations, we continue to search for practical means of bringing about in South Africa the changes we all seek. In a spirit of fairness we must search for means and steps which would have a practical and beneficial effect on the present situation. This has been the spirit of the resolutions adopted by the Council last August[32] and December, and we believe that it is the spirit of the resolution just introduced by the distinguished representative of Norway. Needless to say, we will continue to adhere to the past resolutions of the Security Council, and we will continue to search for ways of impressing upon the Government of South Africa the conviction of our Government and people that only through a policy of justice and equity for all its peoples can it look forward to a peaceful future.

(b) *Resolution of the United Nations Security Council, Adopted June 18, 1964.*[33]

The Security Council,

Having considered the question of race conflict in South Africa resulting from the policies, of *apartheid* of the Government of the Republic of South Africa, brought to the attention of the Security Council by fifty-eight Member States in their letter of 27 April 1964,[34]

Being gravely concerned with the situation in South Africa arising out of the policies of *apartheid* which are contrary to the principles and purposes of the Charter of the United Nations and inconsistent with the provisions of the Universal Declaration of Human Rights[35] as well as South Africa's obligations under the Charter,

Taking note with appreciation of the reports of the Special Committee on the Policies of *Apartheid* of the Government of the Republic of South Africa and the report of the Group of Experts appointed by the Secretary-General pursuant to the Security Council resolution of 4 December 1963 (S/5471),

Recalling the resolutions of the Security Council of 7 August 1963 (S/5386), 4 December 1963 (S/5471) and 9 June 1964 (S/5761),

Convinced that the situation in South Africa is continuing seriously to disturb international peace and security,

Deploring the refusal of the Government of the Republic of South Africa to comply with pertinent Security Council resolutions,

Taking into account the recommendations and conclusions of the Group of Experts,

[32] *Documents, 1963,* pp. 355-356.
[33] U.N. Document S/5773, June 18, 1964; adopted by a vote of 8-0-3 (Czechoslovakia, France, U.S.S.R.).
[34] U.N. Document S/5674.
[35] *Documents, 1948,* pp. 430-438.

1. *Condemns* the *apartheid* policies of the Government of the Republic of South Africa and the legislation supporting these policies, such as the General Law Amendment Act, and in particular its ninety-day detention clause;

2. *Urgently reiterates* its appeal to the Government of the Republic of South Africa to liberate all persons imprisoned, interned or subjected to other restrictions for having opposed the policies of *apartheid;*

3. *Notes* the recommendations and the conclusions in the Report of the Group of Experts;

4. *Urgently appeals* to the Government of the Republic of South Africa to:

(a) renounce the execution of any persons sentenced to death for their opposition to the policy of *apartheid;*

(b) grant immediate amnesty to all persons detained or on trial, as well as clemency to all persons sentenced for their opposition to the Government's racial policies;

(c) abolish the practice of imprisonment without charges, without access to counsel or without the right of prompt trial;

5. *Endorses* and subscribes in particular to the main conclusion of the Group of Experts that "all the people of South Africa should be brought into consultation and should thus be enabled to decide the future of their country at the national level";

6. *Requests* the Secretary-General to consider what assistance the United Nations may offer to facilitate such consultations among representatives of all elements of the population in South Africa;

7. *Invites* the Government of the Republic of South Africa to accept the main conclusion of the Group of Experts referred to in paragraph 5 above and to co-operate with the Secretary-General and to submit its views to him with respect to such consultations by 30 November 1964;

8. *Decides* to establish an Expert Committee, composed of representatives of each present member of the Security Council, to undertake a technical and practical study, and report to the Security Council as to the feasibility, effectiveness, and implications of measures which could, as appropriate, be taken by the Security Council under the United Nations Charter;

9. *Requests* the Secretary-General to provide to the Expert Committee the Secretariat's material on the subjects to be studied by the Committee, and to co-operate with the Committee as requested by it;

10. *Authorizes* the Expert Committee to request all United

Nations Members to co-operate with it and to submit their views on such measures to the Committee no later than 30 November 1964, and the Committee to complete its report not later than three months thereafter;

11. *Invites* the Secretary-General in consultation with appropriate United Nations specialized agencies to establish an educational and training programme for the purpose of arranging for education and training abroad for South Africans;

12. *Reaffirms* its call upon all States to cease forthwith the sale and shipment to South Africa of arms, ammunition of all types, military vehicles, and equipment and materials for the manufacture and maintenance of arms and ammunition in South Africa;

13. *Requests* all Member States to take such steps as they deem appropriate to persuade the Government of the Republic of South Africa to comply with this resolution.

CHAPTER TEN

THE UNITED NATIONS AT A CROSSROAD

A. The United Nations in the Mid-Sixties.

(93) *The United States and the United Nations: Address by Secretary of State Rusk, New York, January 10, 1964.*[1]

(Excerpts)

* * *

The U.N. a Necessity for Our Times

Let me begin by observing that it means little to study the performance of an institution against abstract standards without reference to the realities—and even the illusions—of the total environment in which it must operate. In that context the first thing that strikes one about the United Nations is that international organization is a plain necessity of our times. This is so for both technical and political reasons.

The technical reasons stem, of course, from the headlong rush of scientific discovery and technological advance. That process has overrun the hypothetical question as to whether there is to be an international community that requires organization. It has left us with the practical question of *what kind* of international community we have the wit to organize around the scientific and technical imperatives of our time.

* * *

World community is a fact

—because instantaneous international communication is a fact;

—because fast international transport is a fact;

1 Department of State Press Release 11; text from *Department of State Bulletin*, January 27, 1964, pp. 112-119. For discussion see *The United States in World Affairs, 1964*, pp. 318-321.

—because matters ranging from the control of communicable disease to weather reporting and forecasting demand international organization;
—because the transfer of technology essential to the spread of industrialization and the modernization of agriculture can be assisted by international organizations;
—because modern economics engage nations in a web of commercial, financial, and technical arrangements at the international level.

The advance of science, and the technology that follows, create an insistent demand to build international technical and regulatory institutions which lend substance to world community. Few people seem to realize just how far this movement has gone. The United States is now a member of 53 international organizations. We contribute to 22 international operating programs, mostly sponsored by these same organizations. And last year we attended 547 international intergovernmental conferences, mostly on technical subjects. We do these things because they are always helpful and often downright essential to the conduct of our national and international affairs.

It is obvious that in the 1970's we shall require more effective international organization—making for a more substantial world community—than we have today. We already know that in the next decade we shall become accustomed to international communication, including television, via satellites in outer space. We shall travel in aircraft that fly at speeds above a thousand and perhaps above two thousand miles per hour. Industrialization will pursue its relentless course. Cities and their suburbs will keep on growing. The world economy will become increasingly interdependent. And science will rush ahead, leaving to us the task of fashioning institutions—increasingly on the international level—to administer its benefits and circumscribe its dangers.

So, while nations may cling to national values and ideas and ambitions and prerogatives, science has created a functional international society, whether we like it or not. And that society, like any other, must be organized.

Anyone who questions the *need* for international technical organizations like the United Nations agencies dealing with maritime matters, civil aviation, telecommunications, atomic energy, and meteorology simply does not recognize the times in which we live.

In a world caught up in an urgent drive to modernize areas containing two-thirds of the human race, there is need also for the United Nations specialized agencies dealing with health, agriculture, labor standards, education, and other subjects related to national development and human welfare. A massive effort to transfer and adapt modern technology from the more to the less advanced areas is a part of the great drama of our age. This sometimes can be done best through, or with the help of, the institutions of the international community.

And the international organizations concerned with trade and monetary and financial affairs are important to the expanding prosperity of the world economy.

Adjustment to Reality of Political World

The need for political organs at the international level is just as plain as the need for technical agencies.

You will recall that the decision to try to form a new international organization to preserve peace grew out of the agonies of the Second World War. The United States took the lead in this enterprise. President Franklin D. Roosevelt and Secretary of State Cordell Hull sought to avoid repeating what many believed to have been mistakes in political tactics which kept the United States from joining the League of Nations. They consulted at every stage the leaders of both political parties in both Houses of Congress. They insisted that the formation of this organization should be accomplished, if possible, *before* the end of the war.

Most of our allies readily endorsed this objective and cooperated in achieving it. You will recall that the charter conference at San Francisco convened before the end of the war against Hitler and that the United States Senate consented to ratification of the charter in July 1945, before the end of the war in the Pacific. The vote in the Senate was 89 to 2, reflecting a national consensus bordering on unanimity. The significance of that solemn action was especially appreciated by those of us who were in uniform.

The commitment of the United States to the United Nations was wholehearted. We threw our best efforts and some of our best men into getting it organized and moving. We set about binding the wounds of war. We demobilized our armed forces and drastically reduced our military budget. We proposed—not only proposed but worked hard to obtain agreement—that atomic energy should be put under control of an agency of the United Nations, that it should be devoted solely to peaceful purposes, that nuclear weapons should be abolished and forever forbidden.

What happened? Stalin refused to cooperate. Even before the guns were silent, he set in motion a program of imperialistic expansion, in violation of his pledges to the Western Allies and in contravention of the principles of the United Nations.

You will recall that the United Nations was designed on the assumption that the great powers in the alliance destined to be victors in the Second World War would remain united to maintain the future peace of the world. The United Nations would be the instrument through which these powers, in cooperation with others, of course, would give effect to their mutual determination to keep the peace against any threats that might arise from some future Mussolini or Hitler. World peace was to be enforced by international forces carrying the flag of the United Nations but called into action and directed by agreement among the major powers. Action without big-power agreement was not ruled out by the charter, but such agreement was assumed to be the prior condition of an effective peace organization. Indeed, it was stated repeatedly by early supporters of the United Nations that the organization could not possibly work unless the wartime Allies joined in collective action within the United Nations to exert their combined power to make it work.

That view of the postwar world rapidly turned out to be an illusory hope. One might well have expected—as many good people did—that when the conceptual basis for the United Nations fell to the ground, the organization would fall down beside it.

But all great institutions are flexible. The United Nations adjusted gradually to the political and power realities of the quite different world that came into being. In the absence of major-power agreement in the Security Council, it drew on the charter's authority to balance that weakness with a greater reliance upon the General Assembly.

By adapting to political reality the United Nations lived and grew in effectiveness, in prestige, and in relevance. It could not act in some of the ways the founding fathers intended it to act, but it went on to do many things that the founding fathers never envisaged as being necessary. The most dramatic reversal of its intended role is seen in the fact that, while the United Nations could not bring the great powers together, it could on occasion keep them apart by getting between them—by becoming the "man in the middle"—as it did in differing ways in the Middle East and in the Congo.

In short, the political organs of the United Nations survived and did effective work under the shadow of a nuclear arms race of awesome proportions, despite the so-called cold war between the major powers whose unity was once presumed to be its foundation.

This was not bound to happen. It is evident that in the political environment of the second half of the 20th century both technical and political reasons dictate the need for large-scale and diversified international organizations. But it does not necessarily follow that the United Nations was destined to work in practice—or even to survive. Indeed, its very survival may be more of an achievement than it seems at first blush. That it has steadily grown in its capacity to act is even more remarkable.

It has survived and grown in effectiveness because a great majority of the nations of the world have been determined to make it work. They have repulsed those who sought to wreck or paralyze it. They have remained determined not only to keep it alive but to improve and strengthen it. To this we owe in part the peace of the world.

Preserver and Repairer of World Peace

Indeed, it is difficult to avoid the conclusion that the existence of the General Assembly and the Security Council these past 18 years was a plain necessity for the preservation and repair of world peace. The failures would still have been failures, but without the U.N. some of the successes might not have been possible.

In the world of today any breach of the peace could lead to the destruction of civilization. In the thermonuclear age any instrumentality with a potential for deterring war can hardly be described as less than indispensable to mankind. In 18 brief years the United Nations has helped to deter or to terminate warfare in Iran and Greece, in Kashmir and Korea, in the Congo and the Caribbean, and twice in the Middle East and twice in the Western Pacific. It is not fanciful to speculate that any or all of us may owe our lives to the fact that these dangers were contained, with the active and persistent help of the processes of the United Nations.

With half a dozen international disputes chronically or repeatedly at the flash point, with forces of change bordering on violence loose in the world, our very instinct to survival informs us that we must keep building the peacekeeping machinery of the United Nations—and keep it lubricated with funds and logistical support.

And if we are to entertain rational hopes for general disarmament, we know that the U.N. must develop a reliable system for reconciling international conflict without resort to force. For peace in the world community—like peace in smaller communities—means not an end of conflict but an accepted system of dealing with conflict and with change through nonviolent means.

"Switchboard for Bilateral Diplomacy"

Traditional bilateral diplomacy—of the quiet kind—has a heavier task today than at any time in history. But with the annual agenda of urgent international business growing apace, with the birth of more than half a hundred new nations in less than two decades, an institution that can serve as an annual diplomatic conference becomes almost a necessity. As a general manager of our own nation's diplomatic establishment, I cannot imagine how we could conduct or coordinate our foreign affairs if we were limited to dealing directly through bilateral channels with the 114 nations with which we have diplomatic relations tonight.

At the last General Assembly representatives of 111 countries met for more than 3 months to discuss, negotiate, and debate. Two more countries became U.N. members, to make it 113. When the tumult and the shouting had died, the General Assembly had adopted, curiously enough, 113 resolutions. This is what we have come to call parliamentary diplomacy.

But outside the formal agenda the General Assembly also has become the world's greatest switchboard for bilateral diplomacy. For many of the young and small nations, lacking a fully developed diplomatic service, the United Nations is the main, sometimes the only, general mechanism available for the conduct of their diplomacy.

Without formal decision the opening of each new Assembly has turned into something like an informal conference of the foreign ministers of the world community. In New York last fall, in a period of 11 days, I conferred with the foreign ministers or heads of government of 54 nations.

I believe that too many items are placed on the agenda of the General Assembly. Too many issues are debated and not enough are negotiated. I feel strongly that members should take more seriously article 33 of the charter which pledges them to seek solutions to their disputes "first of all . . . by negotiation, enquiry, mediation, conciliation, arbitration, judicial settlement, resort to regional agencies or arrangements, or other peaceful means of their own choice" before bringing disputes to the U.N. at all.

But the point here is that it is hard to imagine the conduct of diplomacy throughout the year without a meeting of the General Assembly to deal in one forum and, in a more or less systematic manner, with subjects which demand widespread diplomatic attention among the members of the world community.

The need for an annual diplomatic conference, the need for a peacekeeping deterrent to wars large and small, and the need for an international monitor of peaceful change are plain enough. They seem to me to warrant the conclusion that the political organs as well as the technical organs of the United Nations have been very useful to the world at large for the past decade and a half. Common sense informs us that they can be even more useful in the years ahead.

Recognizing the Peacekeeping Capacity of U.N.

I suspect that the near future will witness another period of adjustment for the United Nations. Some adjustments are, indeed, required—because the political environment is changing and so is the structure of the U.N. itself.

For one thing the cobweb syndrome, the illusion that one nation or bloc of nations could, by coercion, weave the world into a single pattern directed from a single center of power, is fading into limbo. That other illusion, the bipolar theory, of a world divided permanently between two overwhelming centers of power with most other nations clustered about them, is fading too. The reality of a world of great diversity with many centers of power and influence is coming into better focus.

Meanwhile, a first brake has been placed on the nuclear arms race,[2] and the major powers are searching for other agreements in areas of common interest. One is entitled to hope that the major power conflicts which so often have characterized U.N. proceedings in the past will yield more and more to great-power cooperation; indeed, there was some evidence to sustain such a hope in the actions of the 18th General Assembly.

As long as a member possessing great power was intent on promoting conflict and upheaval—the better to coerce the world into its own image—that member might well regard the United Nations as a threat to its own ambitions. But suppose it is agreed that all members, despite their deep differences, share a

[2] Text of the nuclear test-ban treaty of August 5, 1963 in *Documents, 1963,* pp. 130-132.

common interest in survival and therefore a common interest in preventing resort to force anywhere in the world. Then the peacekeeping capacity of the United Nations can be seen realistically for what it is: an indispensable service potentially in the national interest of all members—in the common interest of even rival states.

If this reality is grasped by the responsible leaders of all the large powers, then the peacekeeping capacity of the United Nations will find some degree of support from all sides, not as a rival system of order but as contributor to, and sometimes guarantor of, the common interest in survival.

It would be a great service to peace if there could develop common recognition of a common interest in the peacekeeping capacity of the United Nations. That recognition is far from common now. My belief that it will dawn is based on the fact that it would serve the national interests of all nations, large and small, and because sooner or later nations can be expected to act in line with their national interests.

Peace will not be achieved by repeating worn-out propaganda themes or resetting rusty old traps. But if our Soviet friends are prepared to act on what Chairman Khrushchev says in part of his New Year's message [3]—that war over territorial questions is unacceptable, that nations should not be the targets of direct or indirect aggression, that we should use the United Nations and every other means of peaceful settlement—then let us together build up the peacekeeping machinery of the United Nations to prevent even small wars in our flammable world.

For small wars could too easily, too quickly, lead to nuclear war, and nuclear war can too easily, too quickly, prove fatal to friend and foe alike.

Problems Affected by Growth

Meanwhile the internal structure of the United Nations has been changing radically over the past several years. The United Nations began life with 51 members. When its headquarters building was designed, United Nations officials believed they were foresighted in planning for an eventual membership of 75. This year major alterations will be undertaken to make room for the present 113 members and more. It is a fair guess that membership of the U.N. will level off during the next decade at 125 to 130 members.

[3] Document 35a.

This more than doubling of the U.N.'s membership is proud testament to the tidal sweep through the old colonial areas of the doctrine of self-determination of peoples. It is a triumph of largely peaceful change. It is a tribute to those advanced countries which have helped bring dependent areas to self-government and independence and made possible their free choice of their own destiny. It is a striking and welcome result of the greatest wave of national liberation in all time. It also has important implications for all U.N. members—the new members and the older members too—and for the U.N. itself.

The most prosaic—but nonetheless important—implication is for methods of work in the General Assembly. With more than twice as many voices to be heard, views to be reconciled, and votes to be cast and counted, on a swelling agenda of business, there is obvious danger that the General Assembly will be swamped.

I already have suggested that the agenda may be unnecessarily bloated, that in many cases private discourse and real progress are preferable to public debate and symbolic resolution and that the U.N. might well be used more as a court of last resort and less as a forum of original jurisdiction.

But I think still more needs to be done. If the expanded Assembly is to work with reasonable proficiency, it must find ways of delegating some of its work to units less cumbersome than committees of 113 members. The General Assembly is the only parliamentary body in the world that tries to do most of its business in committees-of-the-whole. The Assembly has, in fact, moved to establish several subcommittees, including one to consider financing peacekeeping operations, and perhaps more thought should now be given to the future role of such committees in the work of the organization.

The radical expansion of the membership raises problems for the newer and smaller nations. They rightly feel that they are under-represented on some organs—notably the Security Council and the Economic and Social Council—whose membership was based on the U.N.'s original size and composition.

The growth of membership also raises problems for the middle-range powers, who were early members and have reason to feel that they are next in line for a larger voice.

And it raises problems—or potential problems—for the larger powers too.

The rapid and radical expansion of the General Assembly may require some adaptation of procedures if the U.N. is to remain relevant to the real world and therefore effective in that world.

Theoretically, a two-thirds majority of the General Assembly could now be formed by nations with only 10 percent of the world's population, or who contribute, altogether, 5 percent of the assessed budget. In practice, of course, this does not happen, and I do not share the dread expressed by some that the General Assembly will be taken over by its "swirling majorities."

But even the theoretical possibility that a two-thirds majority, made up primarily of smaller states, could recommend a course of action for which other nations would bear the primary responsibility and burden is one that requires thoughtful attention.

There are two extreme views of how national influence should be expressed in the work of the United Nations. At one extreme is the contention that no action at all should be taken by the United Nations without the unanimous approval of the permanent members of the Security Council. This is a prescription for chronic paralysis. The United Nations was never intended to be kept in such a box. The rights and duties of the General Assembly are inherent in the charter. The United Nations has been able to develop its capacity to act precisely because those rights were not blocked by the requirement of big-power unanimity.

At the other extreme are those few who feel that nothing should matter except the number of votes that can be mustered—that what a majority wants done must be done regardless of what states make up the majority. This notion flies in the face of common sense. The plain fact of the matter is that the United Nations simply cannot take significant action without the support of the members who supply it with resources and have the capacity to act.

Some have suggested that all General Assembly votes should be weighted to reflect population, or wealth, or level of contributions, or some combination of these or other factors. I do not believe that so far-reaching an answer would be realistic or practical. The equal vote in the General Assembly for each member—however unequal in size, wealth, experience, technology, or other criterion—is rooted in the idea of "sovereign equality." And that idea is not one which any nation, large or small, is eager to abandon.

I do not pretend to have the final answer, nor is it timely or appropriate for any member to formulate the answer without wide and careful consultations with others in the world community. However, extended discussions lie ahead on such questions as expanding the councils, scales of payment for peacekeeping, and procedures for authorizing peacekeeping operations.

I shall not discuss U.N. finances in detail tonight. But let me say that the first principle of a healthy organization is that all its members take part in its work and contribute their proper shares to its financial support. Two years ago more than half the U.N. members were behind in their dues—some because of political objections but many simply because they were not paying. I am glad to see that most members are now beginning to act on the principle of collective financial responsibility. But there remains a serious problem of large nations that have not been willing to pay for peacekeeping operations.

I would hope that the discussions which lie ahead will not only strengthen the financial underpinnings of the U.N. but, among other things, develop an acceptable way for the General Assembly to take account of capacity to act, of responsibility for the consequences, and of actual contributions to the work of the U.N. Such a way must be found if the United Nations machinery is to be relevant to the tasks that lie ahead—in peacekeeping, in nation building, and in the expansion of human rights.

All adjustment is difficult. Adaptation of the U.N. to recent changes in the environment may take time. It will require a shift away from some hardened ideas and some rigid patterns of action and reaction—perhaps on all sides. It will require—to come back to [*Dag*] Hammarskjold's words—"perseverance and patience, a firm grip on realities, careful but imaginative planning, a clear awareness of the dangers. . . ."

To ask all this may seem to be asking a great deal. But I am inclined toward confidence because the U.N. already has demonstrated a capacity to adapt under the flexible provisions of the charter to the realities of international politics.

I am further persuaded that all, or most, of the smaller members are realistic enough to know:

—that their own national interests lie with, not against, an effective United Nations;

—that the U.N. can be effective only if it has the backing of those who have the means to make it effective;

—that the U.N. is made less, not more, effective by ritualistic passage of symbolic resolutions with no practical influence on the real world;

—that only responsible use of voting power is effective use of voting power;
—that true progress on behalf of the world community lies along the path on which the weak and the strong find ways to walk together.

The Greatest Goal—Extending Human Rights

These are some of the reasons, derived from analysis of the current state of world affairs, why I expect the United Nations to evolve and to grow in executive capacity to act in support of its goals.

And apart from the issue of human survival, the greatest of these goals is, of course, the steady extension of human rights. Dedication to the principle of the universality of fundamental human rights collides in practice with dedication to the principle of national sovereignty. For most violations of human rights are committed within the confines of national societies, often by the very governments that have ratified the charter's prescription for "fundamental freedoms for all." Yet securing equal rights for all individual members of the human race is the ultimate goal of world community—and the ultimate challenge to the United Nations as the elementary but principal expression of that community. Somehow the United Nations must learn how to increase respect for the rights of the human person throughout the world.

It is here that we sense the permanent value and the final force of the basic principles of a charter which dares to speak for "We the peoples of the United Nations." Sometimes I feel that we talk too much about the universality and brotherhood of man and too little about the valuable and interesting differences that distinguish all brothers. But the lessons of recorded history, and the teachings of the world's great teachers, make clear the basic wants of mankind.

Men and women everywhere want a decent standard of material welfare for themselves and their children. They want to live in conditions of personal security. They want social justice. They want to experience a sense of achievement, for themselves and for the groups with which they identify themselves.

But men and women everywhere want more. They want personal freedom and human dignity.

Individuals and societies place differing values on these aspirations. But surely these are universal desires, shared by all races in all lands, interpreted by all religions, and given concrete form—or lipservice—by leaders and spokesmen for every kind of political, economic, and social system.

Peace and security, achievement and welfare, freedom and dignity—these are the goals of the United Nations for all peoples. And any nation which questions for long *whether* we should seek these aims is destined to become a pariah of the world community.

Because the kind of world projected in the charter is the kind of world we want, the United Nations—despite its quarrels and its shortcomings—commands our continuing support. As President Johnson said to the General Assembly on December 17:[4] ". . . more than ever we support the United Nations as the best instrument yet devised to promote the peace of the world and to promote the well-being of mankind."

And because the kind of world projected in the charter is the kind most people everywhere want, I believe that others will join with us in improving and strengthening the United Nations. That is why I am confident that the executive capacity of the United Nations—its machinery for keeping peace, building nations, and promoting human rights—will be greater on its 25th birthday than on its 18th.

(94) *Introduction to the Annual Report on the Work of the Organization by United Nations Secretary-General U Thant, November 18, 1964.*[5]

(Excerpts)

I

The introduction to the annual report has been delayed considerably this year in view of the postponement of the General Assembly. I have taken advantage of the delay to bring the introduction up to date, although the annual report covers only the period up to 15 June 1964.

Since the last introduction, which was dated 20 August 1963,[6] there has been some progress in disarmament, and also in our activities in the field of outer space. In the Congo, the military phase of the operations came to an end on 30 June 1964. How-

[4] *Documents, 1963,* p. 451.
[5] *Introduction to the Annual Report of the Secretary-General on the Work of the Organization, 15 June 1963—15 June 1964,* General Assembly, *Official Records,* Nineteenth Session, Supplement No. 1A (A/5801/Add. 1).
[6] Text in *U.N. Review,* February 1963, pp. 14-17.

ever, the technical assistance and civilian operations still continue.

The major peace-keeping operation undertaken by the Organization during the period under review has, of course, been in Cyprus.[7] Recent developments encourage me to hope that our efforts may assist in bringing about a peaceful solution of the various problems of this troubled island.

The most important event of the year in the economic field was the convening of the United Nations Conference on Trade and Development.[8] The interest generated by this historic conference overshadowed all other developments in the economic field. I may point in this connexion to the progress we have been making towards the merging of the Expanded Programme of Technical Assistance and the Special Fund in a United Nations Development Programme. I hope that the General Assembly will, before long, approve the establishment of this new unified programme.

During recent months the financial crisis of the United Nations has been one of my major preoccupations, and I have no doubt this is true of delegations also. My detailed comments on the financial crisis are to be found elsewhere in the introduction. All Member Governments seem to me to be agreed on the common objective of strengthening the effectiveness of the United Nations. If this objective is to be realized, I must reiterate that the financial solvency of the world Organization should be reestablished on a firmer and more stable footing.

II

Questions relating to disarmament continue to command serious attention and to have high priority on the international agenda. Although the expectations of the eighteenth session of the General Assembly have not been realized, the fact remains that more significant progress in achieving some measure of disarmament has taken place since the summer of 1963 than in all the years since the founding of the United Nations.

The partial test ban treaty,[9] the establishment of the direct communications link between Moscow and Washington,[10] the the resolution of the General Assembly to ban nuclear and other weapons of mass destruction from outer space,[11] the unilateral reductions of the military budgets of the Soviet Union and the

[7] Cf. Documents 23 and 25.
[8] Cf. Documents 96 and 97.
[9] Same as note 2 to Document 93.
[10] *Documents, 1963,* pp. 115-116.
[11] Same, p. 157.

United States, and the mutual cut-backs in production of fissionable material for military purposes by these two countries and the United Kingdom, are all indications that a start may finally have been made to grapple successfully with the many difficult problems involved in putting an end to the arms race.

These first steps demonstrate the importance of using simultaneously a variety of diplomatic instruments and techniques. They include direct discussions through diplomatic channels, deliberations in regional and other conferences, detailed negotiations in the Conference of the Eighteen-Nation Committee on Disarmament, and the annual review in the General Assembly which provides support and guidance to these discussions and negotiations. The utilization of all these channels and organs provides an opportunity for a thorough consideration of the many political and technical problems of disarmament, encourages the great Powers to bring to bear their major responsibilities on this field and enables the other countries, all of which are vitally interested, to make their contributions towards finding solutions.

This past year has also seen the development of a new institutional approach or procedure, which involves what may be called "reciprocal unilateral action" or the "policy of mutual example". This avenue of progress permits the Powers chiefly concerned to take new steps by independent or co-ordinated unilateral actions.

Despite these favourable developments, however, the year 1964 has not fulfilled the hopes generated by the partial test ban treaty and the general improvement in international relations in 1963. The resolutions on disarmament adopted at the eighteenth session either by acclamation or by overwhelming majorities have remained unimplemented in important respects.

Although the Eighteen-Nation Committee met for more than six months in 1964 in a good atmosphere, with several new and interesting proposals emerging from the discussions,[12] it failed to make any concrete substantive progress. Despite a detailed discussion of a long list of collateral measures and an intensive debate on general and complete disarmament, the Committee reported that it had thus far not been able to reach any specific agreement.

The treaty banning nuclear weapon tests in the atmosphere, in outer space and under water remains neither universal nor comprehensive. Although more than one hundred States have

[12] Cf. Documents 36, 37 and 39.

become parties to the treaty, some States are conspicuous by their absence from the list of signatories. No progress has been made towards an agreement to ban underground tests, nor do the negotiations give the impression of having been conducted with the sense of urgency called for by the General Assembly. If it is agreed that both national and international security depend not on technical developments from continued underground nuclear testing, but on political and military restraint and the progressive curtailment and reversal of the arms race, a comprehensive test ban would be a logical next step. In this connexion, the joint memorandum of the eight non-aligned members of the Eighteen-Nation Committee [13] may point the way to a practical solution.

Another area where progress is most urgent is in the prevention of the spread of nuclear weapons. It is almost three years since the General Assembly unanimously adopted a resolution calling on both nuclear and non-nuclear States to enter into an international agreement to prevent the wider dissemination of nuclear weapons.[14] The dangers of dissemination have markedly increased during this time, with one more country [*Communist China*] joining the "nuclear club", and the failure to implement the Assembly resolution gives cause for genuine and growing concern. I am hopeful that all States will give this problem their most careful attention. This is an area where each country may make a specific contribution.

One measure which seemed to hold out some promise of agreement is the destruction of bomber aircraft. This question was discussed for the first time by the Eighteen-Nation Committee during the current year and specific proposals were made by both the Soviet Union and the United States.[15] Each of these Powers has also indicated that there is some flexibility in its position and that it wishes to continue negotiations on the subject. It is hardly necessary to underline the fact that if an agreement could be reached on any concrete measure of real disarmament, even if only modest to begin with, it would symbolize the intentions of the great Powers in the field of disarmament and would have most beneficial political, psychological and moral results.

The reduction and elimination of vehicles for the delivery of nuclear weapons continues to be the key issue of general and complete disarmament. The Eighteen-Nation Committee broke new ground by its concentrated effort to find an agreed basis for

[13] Conference Document ENDC/145, September 14, 1964 (annex to U.N. Document A/5731 (DC/209), September 22, 1964).
[14] Resolution 1665 (XVI), December 4, 1961.
[15] Documents 36 and 37.

a working group to study the elimination of vehicles for the delivery of nuclear weapons. The Committee has for the first time come within reach of an agreement on a procedure to examine jointly the technical and strategic problems associated with this vitally important measure, and I feel certain that Members will wish to encourage the mutual accommodation necessary for agreement on such new exploratory machinery.

Although both the Soviet Union and the United States favoured each of the foregoing measures, as indeed did all of the participants in the Conference of the Eighteen-Nation Committee, the disagreement between them on how to attain the desired objectives reflected a fundamental divergence in their approach to the respective measures. The efforts of the other participants to find mutually acceptable compromises did not succeed during the past session. Nevertheless, the intensive discussions at the Conference once again served to clarify positions and to indicate in what areas and in what ways progress might be possible. By exploring the various problems in depth, the Conference has also made it easier for the main parties to reach agreement more quickly when the requisite political decisions are taken by one or both sides.

That such further steps are necessary and that the time is ripe is, I believe, hardly open to question. Such steps would not only impose further limitations on the arms race, but would help to strengthen the agreements already achieved. They would also have a positive and far-reaching effect on the international political climate in general. Without such additional agreements, the momentum initiated by the partial test ban treaty might be lost. Accordingly, I consider it to be of the highest importance that what was not achieved during the past few months be yet achieved at the forthcoming session of the General Assembly and during the next round of talks in the Eighteen-Nation Committee in 1965. In addition, I hope consideration will also be given to the possibility of a dialogue among the five nuclear Powers.

III

Since the last introduction, there has been renewed progress in international co-operation in the peaceful uses of outer space. The long deadlock in legal issues in the Committee on the Peaceful Uses of Outer Space was broken in November 1963 with the submission to the General Assembly of an agreed draft declaration of legal principles governing the activities of States in the exploration and use of outer space. The nine principles were unanimously approved by the General Assembly in resolution 1962 (XVIII).[16]

* * *

IV

During 1964, United Nations activities in the economic and social field were carried forward in the perspective and spirit of the United Nations Development Decade. This has meant more than expansion. During the year, there have been a greater awareness of the implications and requirements of target setting for economic development, and greater efforts to increase the momentum of development. Major issues have been elucidated, and progress has been made in combining greater concentration on these issues with better integration of the vast array of United Nations activities.

The year 1964 has witnessed the deliberations of the United Nations Conference on Trade and Development, the largest inter-governmental conference ever assembled, with representatives of 119 States participating in it. It was only natural that the comprehensive review which this great gathering undertook should deal with policy issues in the broad field of international trade and development, for these are of the very essence of international co-operation. The Conference has already been recognized as an event of historic importance likely to have a significant impact on international co-operation for decades to come. The Final Act of the Conference[17] represents the culmination of efforts and discussions over almost two decades, during which new political forces and ideas of international economic co-operation were gradually taking shape within the United Nations.

In its nineteen years of existence, the United Nations has developed, both at Headquarters and in the regional centres, conference techniques which permit great gatherings of almost universal scope to be welded into instruments of organized and planned co-operation. Even the best conference techniques would, however, have been of little avail if many of the concepts underlying international economic relations had not been ripe for change, and if the spread of new ideas had not coincided with the emergence of new political forces in the world. It was the combination of these factors which rendered possible the success of the Conference on Trade and Development and

[16] *Documents, 1963,* pp. 465-467.
[17] Document 97.

made of it one of the most important events since the establishment of the United Nations. The significance of the Conference was discussed in detail by its Secretary-General, Dr. Raúl Prebisch, in a report to me.[18] I have decided to publish that report since it represents, to my mind, an authoritative Secretariat evaluation of the Conference, the Final Act and report of which are before the General Assembly.

The Conference has recommended action by the Assembly with a view, above all, to attaining two goals: to enlarge the role of the United Nations in the field of international trade, and to add to the broad concepts of negotiation and co-operation inherent in the Charter new conciliation procedures which are essential to carry out decisions whose ultimate purpose is to change the existing international division of labour.

* * *

Apart from its political impact, the United Nations Conference on Trade and Development achieved, in the course of twelve weeks, what would have been considered over-ambitious only a few years ago. Its Final Act covered, both in the preamble and in detailed specific recommendations, almost every point which had been the subject of earlier debates and recommendations on trade and development, and listed additional subjects for study and action; it dealt with economic co-operation among all groups of countries, irrespective of their economic and social systems and levels of development, and sought maximum co-operation and trade for the benefit of the whole community of nations; thus the Final Act can be viewed as a successful attempt at a further advancement and codification of the many efforts which in past years have gone into the development and implementation of Chapter IX of the Charter entitled "International economic and social co-operation".

* * *

Let us hope that the Conference will be followed by concrete and universally acceptable steps which will help to bring about appropriate changes in the policies of all trading nations.

* * *

As we approach the half-way mark in the United Nations Development Decade, the Organization finds itself, in the economic and social field, not only increasingly involved in the

[18] U.N. Document E/Conf. 46/3, February 12, 1964.

search for ways and means to accelerate growth and change, but also more insistently called upon to help in the provision of the elements necessary to policy makers for mapping out sound development strategies at the national and international levels. This is evidenced by the increasing emphasis laid in 1964 on development planning, an area of work in which more studies and field operations are needed to promote effectively the transfer, adaptation and improvement of methods and techniques. A promising start has been made in this respect with the establishment of United Nations regional development and planning institutes, and development planning accounts for a growing number of Secretariat activities at Headquarters and in the regions. During the year, projections, which are now widely recognized as indispensable for the formulation and execution of meaningful plans and programmes, have also been the subject of increased attention. The population projections prepared during the year bring into relief a most challenging problem, when compared with those relating to food production. This problem has been highlighted by the findings of the Asian Population Conference held in December 1963 under the auspices of the United Nations, and it is likely to receive special attention next year at the Second United Nations World Population Conference.

* * *

VI

On 29 June 1964, I submitted a report to the Security Council[19] which dealt with the withdrawal of the United Nations Force in the Congo, which had then just been completed, and the continuation of United Nations civilian assistance in the Congo. Little needs to be added here to what was said in that report beyond the observation that, immediately following the withdrawal of the United Nations Force, some of our worst fears for the Congo began to be realized and our apprehensions about that country's future were very great.

In view of the serious deterioration in the internal security situation in the Congo since the withdrawal of the Force, it is only natural that the question should be asked why the Force was withdrawn in the first place, since the course of events that might be expected to follow the withdrawal of the Force could have been anticipated. The answer is that there was no decision by the competent organs of the United Nations to extend the

[19] U.N. Document S/5784 and Corr. 1, 2.

mandate of the Force, and there was no request from the Government of the Congo for any extension of the Force beyond the end of June 1964.[20] Without such a request there could be no basis for any United Nations action involving the continued presence of the United Nations Force in the Congo after last June. The Force was sent to the Congo in the first place in answer to the urgent appeal of the Congolese Government; it remained there for almost four years at the desire of that Government; it could not remain there after 30 June without a further request from the Government. Indeed, after December 1963 there was never any intimation from the Government of the Congo of any wish to have the United Nations Force stay on after June 1964.

I cannot say, of course, how the United Nations would have responded had there been a request from the Government for a continuance of the United Nations Force in the Congo beyond June 1964 up to which date funds had been sanctioned by the General Assembly; but such a request most certainly would have been given serious consideration. There was, however, an evident feeling in some quarters that the United Nations could not maintain an armed force in the Congo indefinitely, and that far too much had already been expended for this purpose.

Much of the disorder in the Congo thus far has been due basically to the spectacular failure of the Congolese National Army. There are other factors, of course, especially the lack of preparation of the Congolese people for independence in 1960. It will be recalled, however, that a major event influencing the future of the Congo occurred when, within a few days following the country's independence, the Congolese National Army—one of the largest and best armed armies of Africa—mutinied and ceased to be a positive factor for security, law and order in the country. This led to the reappearance of Belgian troops, and started the chain of events which caused the Government, then headed by Mr. [*Joseph*] Kasavubu and Mr. [*Patrice*] Lumumba, to appeal to the United Nations for military and other assistance. The United Nations could not ignore that appeal without losing the confidence of most of the world. In responding to it, the United Nations served the interests of the peace of Africa and of the world, as well as those of the Congo, by preventing a power vacuum in the very heart of Africa which would have been extremely grave, with the inevitable risk of East-West confrontation as well as inter-African rivalry and conflict.

[20] Resolution 1885 (XVIII), October 18, 1963.

As I have reported previously, recognizing how vital it would be to the future of the Congo to have its Army made effective and dependable through retraining and reorganization in order that it might regain a reasonable measure of discipline and morale, repeated efforts were made by the United Nations to induce the Government of the Congo to accept United Nations assistance in the retraining and reorganization of the Army. Indeed, at one stage the personal approval of Prime Minister [*Cyrille*] Adoula was given to me directly for the United Nations training plan, based mainly on assistance to be provided by other African countries—and we proceeded to make arrangements and even recruit personnel for that purpose—but I understand that the Prime Minister was unable to obtain the approval of the Commander of the Army, General [*Joseph D.*] Mobutu, for the project.

It would seem advisable also to clear up one more misconception about the Congo, which concerns the often falsely reported attitude of the United Nations towards Mr. Moïse Tshombé, who is now the Prime Minister. The United Nations Operation in the Congo, having been directed by the Security Council to seek, among other things, to preserve the territorial integrity of the country, to prevent civil war and to eliminate mercenaries, was inevitably opposed to the attempted secession of Katanga. While sparing no effort to achieve a peaceful solution, it did what it could, in collaboration with the Government of the Congo, to prevent the attempted secession from becoming an accomplished fact. It succeeded in its objective. The attempted secession of Katanga was led by Mr. Tshombé, as President of that Province. Although the United Nations operation thwarted the Katanga secessionist effort, it never failed to recognize Mr. Tshombé as President of the Province of Katanga, a position to which he had been duly elected.

The Government of the Congo has recently turned to the Organization of African Unity for assistance in helping it to re-establish peace, law and order in the Congo. That organization acted on this appeal by setting up an *ad hoc* committee, under the chairmanship of the Prime Minister of Kenya, Mr. Jomo Kenyatta, with a view to assisting the Congo (Leopoldville) to normalize its relations with its neighbours, the Congo (Brazzaville) and Burundi in particular, and to exercising its good offices in an effort to secure a solution to the problem of the Congo by means of conciliation.[21] I hope that this effort will prove helpful.

[21] Document 88.

Although the prevailing picture of the Congo may be dark and unpromising, that country has demonstrated remarkable resilience throughout the troubles which have beset it since its independence. The resources of the country are rich. Surprises are frequent in the Congo, and it should not be excluded that the country, realizing that it no longer has a United Nations Force to depend upon for internal security, will in time muster the will and the ability to attain both security and political stability. For the sake of the Congo and its people, for the sake of the continent of Africa and for the cause of peace, I most earnestly hope that this will be so.

Meanwhile, it is worth recalling that, in its four years in the Congo, the United Nations operation reduced to a minimum the risk of East-West conflict there; it prevented the country from being engulfed in civil war, of tribal or other origins; it greatly helped to preserve the territorial integrity of the country; it was mainly responsible for restoring some semblance of law and order throughout the country; it eliminated completely the mercenaries of Katanga, some of whom have now reappeared in Leopoldville; and it provided, and continues to provide, a great amount of technical assistance. These are certainly achievements of lasting value.

It is sometimes forgotten that, although the United Nations Force has withdrawn from the Congo, the largest United Nations Technical Assistance/Special Fund operation anywhere in the world, at present consisting of approximately 2,000 persons, is still found in that country. The main reason for the comparatively large size of this programme is that the voluntary Congo fund, and various funds in trust, have made it possible until now to finance substantial extra-budgetary assistance programmes under the aegis of the United Nations civilian operations in the Congo. Even though there have been some indications that a few countries might be prepared to make voluntary contributions to the Congo fund on a matching basis for the year 1965-1966, I do not intend, in view of the generally disappointing response to my appeal in 1964, to make a further general appeal to Member States to contribute to the fund in 1965.

* * *

VII

Since last March, the United Nations peace-keeping effort in Cyprus has been a major concern of the Organization, and I have been reporting on it in detail to the Security Council from time to time. The United Nations Force in Cyprus has already served two three-month terms in the island and its mandate was extended for a third three-month term by the Security Council on 25 September 1964.[22]

The mandate of the United Nations Force in Cyprus has been to prevent a recurrence of fighting and to contribute to the maintenance and restoration of law and order, and to a return to normal conditions there. The Force has done much more than might have been expected of it towards the fulfillment of that mandate. The Commanders of the Force, General [*P. S.*] Gyani and later General [*K. S.*] Thimayya, the officers and men of the national contingents and the civilian members of the United Nations Secretariat associated with them have, in most difficult and complex conditions, performed their duties with signal devotion and effectiveness. I should also like to pay tribute to the valuable services of my Special Representatives, first Mr. [*Pier P.*] Spinelli, then Mr. Galo Plaza [*Lasso*], and now Mr. [*Carlos Alfredo*] Bernardes.

The situation in Cyprus is, by any measure, a grim and formidable one, and it is sufficient here to recall that, in spite of the highly inflammable state of affairs which prevails in the island, there have been so far, while the Force has been in Cyprus, only two outbreaks of serious fighting, both of which were quickly contained and halted, the first of these in the St. Hilarion area in late April, and the second in the Kokkina area in early August.

Despite the great obstacles to a return to normal conditions in the island, and, indeed, to any quick solution of the problems of Cyprus, some progress has been made in reducing the dangers and discomforts under which some parts of the population of Cyprus have been living, and it is to be hoped that this progress will continue, with increasingly beneficial results.

As regards the efforts to resolve the long-term problems of Cyprus through the United Nations Mediator, it is not possible at this stage to report any significant advance. The work of Ambassador [*Sakari S.*] Tuomioja, the first Mediator, whose tragic death interrupted his painstaking and persistent attempts to find an acceptable solution, is now carried on by Mr. Galo Plaza, who brings to the task of Mediator valuable first-hand experience of the situation in Cyprus from his service as my Special Representative there. It is certain that Mr. Plaza will spare no effort in seeking a peaceful solution, taking advantage

[22] U.N. Document S/5987. U.N. Document S/6121, adopted December 18, 1964, provided for a fourth three-month extension until March 26, 1965.

of the relative quiet which the presence of the Force has produced.

The financial arrangements to support the Force, in accordance with paragraph 6 of the resolution adopted by the Security Council on 4 March 1964,[23] have proved to be far from satisfactory. As I had occasion to state to the Council in my reports on the conduct of the Cyprus operation, the method of financing the Force has been inadequate and funds have been received in such manner, as regards both pledges and payment of pledges, as seriously to hamper the planning, efficiency and economical running of the Force.

* * *

IX

One mission in the peace-keeping sphere, the United Nations Yemen Observation Mission, has come to an end. It had been set up in mid-1963[24] to observe the implementation of an agreement between Saudi Arabia and the United Arab Republic under which they had undertaken to disengage from their direct and indirect interventions in the prevailing civil war in Yemen. During its fourteen-month period of activities, the Mission was restricted by the terms of its mandate to observation alone and was able to report only a limited measure of disengagement. It was terminated on 4 September 1964, when the two States concerned, which had met the full costs of the operation, informed me, one that it was not prepared to continue to do so, and the other that it had no objection to the termination of the Mission. Despite its weak and inadequate mandate and its limited results, the Mission did contribute to a reduction of international tension in the region of its operation and to some improvement in the internal security situation in Yemen. Moreover, it helped to keep the door open for further highest level discussions between the Saudi Arabian and United Arab Republic Governments on the Yemen problem, which have finally, in fact, taken place with encouraging results.

X

In the introduction to last year's report, I referred briefly to the fact that I had sent a team of United Nations officials to carry out certain tasks as envisaged by the Governments of the Federation of Malaya, the Republic of Indonesia and the Re-

[23] Document 25b.
[24] U.N. Document S/5331, June 11, 1963, in *Documents, 1963,* pp. 263-264.

public of the Philippines. On 5 August 1963, these Governments had requested me to ascertain, prior to the establishment of Malaysia, the views of the people of Sabah (North Borneo) and Sarawak within the context of General Assembly resolution 1541 (XV), principle IX of the annex, "by a fresh approach which in the opinion of the Secretary-General is necessary to ensure complete compliance with the principle of self-determination within the requirements embodied in principle IX". From the very beginning of 1963, I had observed with concern the rising tension in South-East Asia on account of the difference of opinion among the countries most directly interested in the Malaysia issue. It was in the hope that some form of United Nations participation might help to reduce tensions in the area and among the parties that I agreed to respond positively to the request made by the three Governments.

As is well known, the United Nations Malaysia Mission expressed the opinion that "the participation of the two territories in the proposed Federation, having been approved by their legislative bodies, as well as by a large majority of the people through free and impartially conducted elections in which the question of Malaysia was a major issue, the significance of which was appreciated by the electorate, may be regarded as the result of the freely expressed wishes of the territory's peoples acting with full knowledge of the change in their status, their wishes having been expressed through informed and democratic processes, impartially conducted and based on universal adult suffrage". I accepted this view of the Mission in my conclusions.

Unfortunately, the hope I had expressed that the participation of the United Nations might help to reduce tension has not been fulfilled. There have been continued incidents in the area, and accusations and counter-accusations have been exchanged, culminating in the complaint by Malaysia to the Security Council in September 1964.[25] After a number of meetings, the Security Council was unable to adopt a resolution on this issue.[26] Tension in the area, especially between Indonesia and Malaysia, continues to be a source of concern to me. I wish to express the hope that the endeavours of statesmen of the area to solve this difficult question peacefully will be steadfastly continued, and that the leaders of the countries involved will spare no effort to bring about a peaceful settlement of their differences.

[25] U.N. Document S/5967.
[26] Document 60.

XI

In the course of the year 1963-1964, a number of Member States have offered military units to the United Nations on a standby basis, that is, to be available to the United Nations when an acceptable demand is made by the Organization. Some other Member States have evinced interest in pursuing a similar course. I have welcomed the offers, but have been in no position to do much more than this, in the absence of any authorizing action by an appropriate organ of the United Nations, even though no expense to the Organization would be involved until a contingent was called into actual United Nations service.

There is much that could be done and needs to be done in the way of advance selection, training and other preparations which would make the offered contingents more effective and which would in general ensure better, more efficient and more economical peace-keeping operations in the future. It may be useful to have this question studied comprehensively in all its aspects, including manpower, logistics and financing. Such a study may yield recommendations for consideration by the competent organs which may then authorize the Secretary-General to proceed along such lines as may be generally approved. I would accordingly welcome appropriate action by a competent United Nations organ which would authorize the undertaking of such a study.

XII

Decolonization continued to be one of the most important questions engaging the attention of the United Nations. Debates on this question in the General Assembly as well as in the other bodies concerned were held in the context of the Declaration on the Granting of Independence to Colonial Countries and Peoples, embodied in General Assembly resolution 1514 (XV).[27]

During the eighteenth session of the General Assembly, several delegations expressed concern at the delay in the implementation of the Declaration. The Assembly then requested the Special Committee on the Situation with regard to the Implementation of the Declaration on the Granting of Independence to Colonial Countries and Peoples to continue to seek the most effective and expeditious means for the immediate implementation of the Declaration in all territories which had not yet attained independence.[28] The Assembly also transferred to the Special

[27] *Documents, 1960,* pp. 575-577.
[28] Same, *1963,* pp. 464-465.

Committee the functions previously performed by the former Committee on Information from Non-Self-Governing Territories.[29] With the disbanding of the Committee on Information, the Special Committee is now the only body responsible for matters relating to dependent territories, with the exception of the three remaining Trust Territories, for which the Trusteeship Council is responsible.

As in the two previous years, the Special Committee has been studying conditions in various dependent territories in order to determine the extent to which the administering Powers are implementing the Declaration. In a document prepared in April 1963, the Special Committee listed sixty-four territories to which the Declaration is applicable. While I share the concern of Member States with regard to the delay in the implementation of the Declaration, especially in relation to some of the larger territories in Africa, it is gratifying to note that Kenya, Zanzibar, Malawi (Nyasaland), Malta and Zambia (Northern Rhodesia) have become independent sovereign States.

In spite of the many efforts that have been made to persuade Portugal to accept the principle of self-determination for the peoples of the territories under its administration, it continues to insist that the territories are parts of its "overseas provinces", and that the peoples of the territories have already been accorded "self-determination". The Portuguese concept of self-determination has been rejected by the General Assembly as anachronistic, and it also conflicts with the concept of that term as defined in the Charter.

As the Mandatory Power for South West Africa, South Africa not only has continued to ignore the resolutions of the General Assembly, but also refuses to co-operate with those agencies of the Organization that have sought to render assistance to South West Africa. During the year the Special Committee considered the Odendaal Commission report, which was released by the South African Government. The Committee's view is that the recommendations of the Odendaal Commission are inconsistent with the responsibilities of the South African Government as the Mandatory Power for the Territory and that they should not be implemented.

The situation in Southern Rhodesia continues to give much cause for anxiety. The replacement of Mr. Winston Field by Mr. Ian Smith as Prime Minister in April 1964 reflected the ascendancy of those members of the Rhodesian Front who favour a unilateral declaration of independence. Although in June 1964

[29] Resolution 1970 (XVIII), December 16, 1963.

Mr. Smith announced that there would be no unilateral declaration of independence, he continues to demand independence for Southern Rhodesia on the basis of the existing constitution and restricted franchise.

With a view to demonstrating to the United Kingdom Government that this demand had the support of the majority of the population, his Government proceeded to conduct a test of public opinion by means of consultation with local chiefs and headmen, in addition to a referendum of all registered voters; this method was rejected by the United Kingdom Government as incapable of revealing satisfactory evidence of the wishes of the African population.

The United Kingdom Government, in a statement issued on 27 October, made clear to the Southern Rhodesian Government the serious consequences of a unilateral declaration of independence. The statement has helped to clear any doubt as to the position of the United Kingdom Government and has, at least for the time being, averted what would most certainly have been a crisis in Southern Rhodesia. The dangers still persist; and there is no evidence that the Southern Rhodesian Government is prepared to accept the principles enunciated in various General Assembly resolutions concerning Southern Rhodesia. Nor is there any indication that the Southern Rhodesian Government proposes to establish full democratic freedom and equality of political rights, and to convene a constitutional conference of all parties in Southern Rhodesia for the drafting of a new constitution based on the principle of "one man, one vote" and to prepare for an early independence of the territory.

* * *

XIII

The period under review did not witness any improvement in the situation arising from the racial policies of the Government of the Republic of South Africa. On the contrary, the trend has been in the reverse direction and has been a source of heightened concern during the year, particularly in view of new legislative measures and the detention and trial of large numbers of persons for their opposition to the policies of *apartheid.* The Security Council devoted more time and attention to this problem than ever before and adopted four resolutions aimed at bringing about racial harmony based on equal rights and fundamental freedoms for all the people of South Africa.

In pursuance of the Security Council resolution of 4 December 1963,[30] a Group of Experts was set up to examine methods of resolving the present situation in South Africa through full, peaceful and orderly application of human rights and fundamental freedoms to all inhabitants of the territory as a whole, regardless of race, colour or creed, and to consider what part the United Nations might play in the achievement of that end. This Group, under the chairmanship of Mrs. Alva Myrdal, made a number of recommendations based on the essential principle that all the people of South Africa should be brought into consultation to decide the future of their country in free discussion at the national level. This principle was endorsed by the Security Council in June 1964.[31]

Taking account of the composition of the population of South Africa and the present international context, there is a great danger that a continuation of the efforts to impose policies decided by one racial group in South Africa and the closing up of possibilities for a peaceful change may increasingly lead to violence which is likely to have widespread international repercussions. I can only reiterate the hope that the Government of South Africa will heed world opinion and the recommendations and decisions of United Nations organs, and take early steps to achieve racial harmony based on free consultations and respect for the human rights and fundamental freedoms of all the people of the country. I also believe the United Nations should persevere in its efforts to persuade the South African Government and people to seek a peaceful solution to the long-standing problem and thus reverse the unfortunate trends of recent years.

XIV

In May 1963, the General Assembly met in special session to consider, *inter alia,* the financial situation of the Organization in the light of a report of the Working Group on the Examination of the Administrative and Budgetary Procedures of the United Nations. At the end of the session, on 27 June 1963, it adopted a resolution [32] in which it noted with concern the financial situation resulting from the non-payment of a substantial portion of past assessments for the Special Account for the United Nations Emergency Force and the *Ad Hoc* Account for the United Nations Operation in the Congo, and appealed to Member States in arrears in respect of these accounts to pay

[30] *Documents, 1963,* pp. 357-359.
[31] U.N. Document S/5761, June 9, 1964. For text of U.N. Document S/5773 of June 18, 1964 see Document 92b.
[32] *Documents, 1963,* pp. 438-439.

their arrears, disregarding other factors, as soon as their respective constitutional and financial arrangements would permit.

At that time, the arrears to the peace-keeping accounts totalled $99.7 million, the Organization had cash resources totalling $57.9 million and its deficit was some $114 million.

Fifteen months later, on 30 September 1964, the arrears for the two accounts totalled $112.3 million, the Organization's cash resources totalled $24.8 million and its deficit was $113.3 million.

Thus, over a fifteen-month period, there has been virtually no improvement in the deficit position although in that period the Organization was able to apply in settlement of its debts approximately $50 million of non-recurring income which derived from the sale of United Nations bonds and from the collection of assessments and voluntary contributions to the *Ad Hoc* Account for the United Nations Operation in the Congo.

While a further $15 million may be received for United Nations bonds, the present prospect in respect of the over-all financial position is that unless the deficit is to be further increased the Organization's cash resources will practically disappear within the next six months.

In this situation I found it necessary to say in my statement to the Working Group in September:[33] ". . . I am convinced by the experience of the past three years that a policy of drift, of improvisation, of *ad hoc* solutions, of reliance on the generosity of the few rather than the collective responsibility of all, cannot much longer endure. In fact, time, if I may say so, is rapidly running out. It is imperative, therefore, that your efforts in the weeks that remain between now and the nineteenth session of the General Assembly be crowned with success".

Since I addressed the Working Group in September, it has been decided further to postpone the opening of the nineteenth session to 1 December 1964. Meanwhile valiant efforts have been and are being made, both within and outside the Working Group, to find a solution for the financial crisis which may be acceptable to all sides. I would like to express my deep appreciation for these efforts, and I can only hope that such a solution may be found before the General Assembly meets.

XV

By resolutions 1991 A and B (XVIII),[34] the General Assembly adopted amendments to Articles 23, 27 and 61 of the Charter to increase the number of non-permanent members of the Secu-

[33] U.N. Document A/AC.113/29, September 9, 1964.
[34] *Documents, 1963,* pp. 471-473.

rity Council and to enlarge the membership of the Economic and Social Council. These amendments have so far been ratified by only thirty-two Members. They will come into force only when they have been ratified by two-thirds of the Members, including all the permanent members of the Security Council. As of today, none of the permanent members of the Security Council has done so. I sincerely hope that there will be greater progress in the ratification of these amendments in the near future, and that we may see the membership of both these principal organs expanded in 1965. I am sure that such expansion, which will make it possible to secure more adequate geographical representation in the two Councils, will contribute to the greater effectiveness of both bodies.

* * *

B. The United Nations Crisis.

(95) *The Peace-Keeping Issue.*[35]

(a) *United States Working Paper on Financing United Nations Peace-Keeping Operations, September 14, 1964.*[36]

The United States delegation has the honour to present to the Working Group of Twenty-One the attached Working Paper containing suggestions for changes in the arrangements and methods for initiating and financing United Nations peace-keeping operations involving the use of military forces.

Last March, as members of the Working Group are aware, the United States and United Kingdom delegations indicated that they were prepared to explore with other Members of the United Nations, in the first instance those represented in the Working Group of Twenty-One, ways to reinforce the capacity of the United Nations to undertake and finance such peace-keeping operations in the future. Accordingly the United States and United Kingdom delegations at that time suggested certain ideas for discussion, and explored those ideas, informally and in broad outline, with various members of the Working Group, including the Soviet delegation.

The attached Working Paper embodies the main lines of these ideas and the salient features of the suggestions then made, as modified by subsequent discussions. It is now submitted by

[35] For discussion see *The United States in World Affairs, 1964,* pp. 321-329.
[36] U.N. Document A/AC.113/30, September 14, 1964; text from *Department of State Bulletin,* October 5, 1964, pp. 485-489.

the United States for consideration and discussion in the Working Group.

These suggestions presuppose settlement in some manner of arrears for past peacekeeping operations. Such payments may take any number of possible forms so long as they conform to the United Nations Charter and Financial Regulations.

ARRANGEMENTS AND METHODS FOR INITIATING AND FINANCING UNITED NATIONS PEACEKEEPING OPERATIONS INVOLVING THE USE OF MILITARY FORCES

A. To preserve and reinforce the peacekeeping capacity of the United Nations, it is in the interest of the entire membership of the Organization that there be established, within the framework prescribed by the Charter, generally acceptable new procedures and methods for the future initiation of United Nations peacekeeping operations involving the use of military forces and the obtaining of necessary financing for such operations.

These procedures and methods must safeguard the capacity of the United Nations to undertake and carry on successfully such future peacekeeping operations. Within the scope of this objective, they should also take account of the interests and capacities of all Member States and the special status under the Charter of certain of them.

B. In establishing such procedures and methods, particular consideration should be given to the following principles:

1. Any new arrangements should make it possible to take due account of the interests and capacities of all Member States, but must not permit any State to obstruct the United Nations in the discharge of its peacekeeping responsibilities.

2. The Security Council has primary responsibility under the Charter for the initiation of peacekeeping operations involving the use of military forces.

3. The General Assembly may recommend such peacekeeping operations, in the event that the Security Council is unable to act.

4. All Member States have a responsibility under the Charter to contribute to expenses of such United Nations peacekeeping operations when assessed by the General Assembly under Article 17.

5. In apportioning expenses, account should be taken of any excessive burden which the cost of expensive operations might impose on the economies of developing countries.

6. United Nations procedures should be adapted to take into

account the interests of those Members, including Permanent Members of the Security Council, that bear special responsibilities. Member States making large financial contributions for such peacekeeping operations should have an appropriate voice in the determination of methods of financing such operations.

C. Arrangements for embodying these considerations in the initiation and financing of United Nations peacekeeping operations involving the use of military forces would include the following interdependent elements:

1. All proposals to initiate such peacekeeping operations would be considered first in the Security Council. The General Assembly would not authorize or assume control of such peacekeeping operations unless the Council had demonstrated that it was unable to take action.

2. The General Assembly would establish a standing special finance committee. The composition of this committee should be similar to that of the present Working Group of Twenty-One: that is, it would include the Permanent Members of the Security Council and a relatively high percentage of those Member States in each geographical area that are large financial contributors to the United Nations. It would be constituted under and governed by firm rules of procedure of the General Assembly.

3. In apportioning expenses for such peacekeeping operations, the General Assembly would act only on a recommendation from the committee passed by a two-thirds majority of the committee's membership.

4. In making recommendations, the committee would consider various alternative methods of financing, including direct financing by countries involved in a dispute, voluntary contributions, and assessed contributions. In the event that the Assembly did not accept a particular recommendation, the committee would resume consideration of the matter with a view to recommending an acceptable alternative.

5. One of the available methods of assessment for peacekeeping operations involving the use of military forces would be a special scale of assessments in which, over a specified amount, States having greater ability to pay would be allocated higher percentages, and States having less ability to pay would be allocated smaller percentages than in the regular scale of assessments.

6. Pending action by the General Assembly on financial arrangements for such a peacekeeping operation initiated by the Security Council or General Assembly, the Secretary-General would continue to be authorized under the provisions of the

annual resolution on unforeseen and extraordinary expenditures, to commit up to $2 million (and with the concurrence of the Advisory Committee on Administrative and Budgetary Questions up to $10 million) to finance the initial stage of an operation. Commitments and expenditures above this initial amount could be made by the Secretary-General only after the General Assembly had adopted a financing resolution on the basis of a recommendation of the special finance committee.

(b) *United States Memorandum on the United Nations Financial Crisis and Ambassador Stevenson's Letter of Transmittal to Secretary-General Thant, October 8, 1964.*[37]

(Excerpts)

EXCELLENCY: I have the honor to enclose a Memorandum by the United States of America, dated October 8, 1964, concerning "The United Nations Financial Crisis." I would appreciate it if you would arrange to have the Memorandum circulated as an official document of the General Assembly.

The Memorandum deals with the serious extent of the financial issue facing the Organization, the law on the issue as established by the International Court of Justice and the General Assembly, and the implications which a breach of the Charter on the question would entail.

* * *

A. The Financial Crisis

* * *

The crisis is painfully clear. The UN has a net deficit of $134 million.

On June 30 the UN had on its books unpaid obligations owed to governments and other outsiders totaling some $117 million. In addition, it owed to its own Working Capital Fund—which it is supposed to have on hand in order to keep afloat and solvent pending the receipt of assessments—$40 million. Other internal accounts were owed $27 million. Against this total of $183 million of obligations it had $49 million in cash resources, or a net deficit of $134 million.

What does this mean?

[37] U.N. Document A/5739, October 8, 1964; text from *Department of State Bulletin,* November 9, 1964, pp. 681-690.

It means that the UN does not have the money to pay its debts, and that it would be bankrupt today if it were not for the forbearance of the Member Governments to which it owes those debts.

It means that, unless something is done, the United Nations will have to default on its obligations to Member Governments which, in good faith and in reliance on the UN's promises and good faith, have furnished troops and supplies and services to the UN, at its request, for the safeguarding of the peace. In so doing, these Governments incurred substantial additional and extraordinary expenditures which the UN agreed to reimburse —an agreement which the Secretary General referred to in his statement at the opening session of the Working Group of 21 on September 9 (Doc. A/AC.113/29, p. 5) as "the commitment which the Organization has accepted, in its collective capacity, towards those of its Members who have furnished the men and material for its successive peace-keeping operations."

Which are those Governments?

The UN owes significant amounts to Argentina, Austria, Brazil, Canada, Denmark, Ethiopia, Ghana, Indonesia, India, Iran, Ireland, Italy, Liberia, Malaysia, Mali, Morocco, Netherlands, Nigeria, Norway, Pakistan, Philippines, Sierra Leone, Sudan, Sweden, Tunisia, UAR, the United Kingdom, Yugoslavia, and the United States. It is to be noted that 19 of these 29 countries are developing countries.

* * *

These 29 countries will suffer if the UN is forced, by the default of the Members which owe it, into defaulting to those which it owes; the entire organization will suffer if it does not honor its just obligations and becomes morally bankrupt.

The 29 Members would suffer by a default, but the real sufferer would be the UN itself. How could an enfeebled and creditless defaulter maintain peace and security? Indeed, how could any institution that had committed such a breach of faith hope long to survive as a credit-worthy and effective organization?

As the Secretary General said at the opening session of the Working Group of 21, "failure to take care of the past may not leave us with much of a future."

What has caused this crisis?

The crisis has been thrust upon the United Nations by those Members which have refused to pay the assessments for the

Middle East (UNEF) and Congo (ONUC) operations as voted by the General Assembly in accordance with the Charter.

It is worthwhile recalling exactly how those operations were authorized and exactly what they were.

B. The Middle East Operation—UNEF

UNEF grew out of the Suez crisis of 1956. The Security Council found itself unable to act because of vetoes by certain of the Permanent Members. Yugoslavia then, on October 31, 1956, introduced the following Resolution (S/3719):

"The Security Council,

"*Considering* that a grave situation has been created by action undertaken against Egypt,

"*Taking into account* that the lack of unanimity of its permanent members at the 749th and 750th meetings of the Security Council has prevented it from exercising its primary responsibility for the maintenance of international peace and security,

"*Decides* to call an emergency special session of the General Assembly, as provided in General Assembly resolution 377A (V) of 3 November 1950 [*Note:* The Uniting for Peace Resolution] [38] in order to make appropriate recommendations."

The Yugoslav Resolution was adopted 7–2–2, and the Soviet Union voted *for* the Resolution.

Thus the Soviet Union *supported* the referral by the Security Council of the crisis to the General Assembly for "appropriate recommendations" under the very Uniting for Peace Resolution which the Soviet Union now tries to discredit.

* * *

Yet now the Soviet Union contends that there was something illegal about an operation (a) which was recommended by the General Assembly pursuant to a referral by the Security Council voted for by the Soviets themselves, (b) which involved no enforcement or military action whatsoever but merely the securing and supervising of a previously agreed to cease-fire, (c) which was consented to by the government concerned, and (d) which was authorized by the Assembly without a negative vote by anyone.[39]

Rejecting the Soviet contentions, the International Court of

[38] *Documents, 1950,* pp. 182-186.

[39] Resolution 1000 (ES-I), November 5, 1956, in same, *1956,* pp. 354-355. The Soviet Union abstained.

Justice held (see under heading D 1 below) that UNEF was properly authorized by the Assembly.

C. The Congo Operation—ONUC

The United Nations operation in the Congo was authorized by the Security Council on July 14, 1960, by Resolution S/4387,[40] reading in part as follows:

"The Security Council, . . .

"2. *Decides* to authorize the Secretary-General to take the necessary steps, in consultation with the Government of the Republic of the Congo, to provide the Government with such military assistance, as may be necessary, until, through the efforts of the Congolese Government with the technical assistance of the United Nations, the national security forces may be able, in the opinion of the Government, to meet fully their tasks;"

The Soviet Union voted *for* the Resolution, which clearly gave the Secretary General discretionary authority, in consultation with the Congolese Government, to determine the make-up of ONUC.

On July 18, 1960, the Secretary General presented to the Security Council his first report (S/4389) in which he recited the steps taken by him to invite Member States to furnish forces for ONUC.

On July 22, 1960, the Security Council adopted Resolution S/4405,[41] reading in part as follows:

"The Security Council, . . .

* * *

"3. *Commends* the Secretary-General for the prompt action he has taken to carry out Resolution S/4387 of the Security Council and his first report;"

The Soviet Union voted *for* the resolution.

In the face of this record, it is difficult to understand the Soviet Union's present claim (Soviet Memorandum of September 11, 1964, p. 5)[42] that it was improper for the Secretary General to invite States to take part in ONUC—when he did so pursuant to direct Security Council authorization and approval,

[40] *Documents, 1960,* p. 353.
[41] Same, p. 360.
[42] U.N. Document A/5729.

twice voted for by the Soviet Union itself. There was no "by-passing" of the Security Council (Soviet Memorandum, p. 5); on the contrary the Secretary General did exactly what the Council authorized him to do and commended him for having done!

On August 9, 1960, the Security Council adopted Resolution S/4426,[43] confirming the authority given to the Secretary General by the two prior Resolutions and requesting him to continue to carry out his responsibility. The Soviet Union voted *for* that Resolution too.

Furthermore, six months later, the Security Council on February 21, 1961, adopted Resolution S/4741 [44] which broadened ONUC's mandate and reaffirmed the three earlier Security Council Resolutions and an intervening General Assembly Resolution.[45] The Soviet Union abstained.

Finally, the Security Council on November 24, 1961, nine months later, adopted Resolution S/5002,[46] which in effect again reauthorized the ONUC operation, recalling the earlier Security Council Resolutions (and intervening General Assembly Resolutions), and again broadened ONUC's mandate. The Soviet Union voted *for* the Resolution.

Against this record of Security Council authorization and repeated reauthorization, it is difficult to understand how the Soviet Union can now contend that the operation was not legal and was not validly authorized.

As for the Soviet contention that ONUC was not conducted in accordance with the five Security Council Resolutions, it is enough to point out that ONUC was reauthorized by the Security Council's Resolutions of February 21, 1961, and November 24, 1961—six months and fifteen months, respectively, after its inception.

If the Security Council had felt that ONUC was not being properly conducted in accordance with its Resolutions, it could at any time have changed or given further explicit instructions. No such instructions were ever given or even suggested by the Security Council, and the record of Security Council authorization and reauthorization, and reaffirmation, of the ONUC operation, remains unchallenged.

The International Court of Justice accordingly held (see under heading D below) that ONUC *was* properly authorized.

[43] *Documents, 1960,* pp. 362-363.
[44] *Documents, 1961,* pp. 341-343.
[45] Resolution 1474 (ES-IV), September 20, 1960, in same, *1960,* pp. 378-379.
[46] Same, *1961,* pp. 350-352.

D. Soviet Legal Arguments

* * *

It should first be noted that every one of the arguments put forward by the Soviet Union in its memorandum of September 11, 1964, and elsewhere, was made by the Soviet Representative in his submission and argument before the International Court of Justice in the summer of 1962, when the Court considered the question of whether the UNEF and ONUC assessments voted by the General Assembly were "expenses of the Organization" within the meaning of Article 17, paragraph 2, of the Charter, and therefore binding obligations of the Members.

Every single one of those arguments was specifically rejected in the Court's Advisory Opinion of July 20, 1962.[47] That Opinion was accepted on December 19, 1962, by the General Assembly by the overwhelming vote of 76–17–8,[48] after the Assembly had decisively defeated an amendment which would merely have taken note of the Opinion.

Nevertheless, it may be useful to deal briefly with the Soviet contentions.

1. *The Claimed "Exclusive" Peacekeeping Rights of the Security Council*

The Soviet position is that the Security Council, and *only* the Security Council, has *any* right to take any action whatsoever with respect to the keeping of the peace, and that the General Assembly has no rights whatsoever in that area.

It should first be noted that this argument has nothing to do with ONUC, which was authorized and reauthorized by the Security Council by repeated Resolutions, four out of five of which were voted *for* by the Soviet Union—it abstained on the fourth. Further, it will be remembered that UNEF was recommended by the General Assembly pursuant to the Security Council's referral of the problem to the General Assembly for its recommendations, by a resolution which the Soviet Union voted *for*.

In any event, there is no basis for the contention that the Security Council has exclusive rights as to peacekeeping, and

[47] International Court of Justice, "Certain expenses of the United Nations (Article 17, Paragraph 2 of the Charter), Advisory Opinion of 20 July 1962": *I.C.J. Reports 1962*.
[48] *Documents, 1962*, pp. 470-471.

the General Assembly none. Article 24 of the Charter gives the Security Council "*primary* responsibility for the maintenance of international peace and security," but not *exclusive* authority.

The Charter provisions set forth unequivocally the authority of the General Assembly in this regard. Subject only to Article 12, paragraph 1,[49]

–Article 10 authorizes the General Assembly to discuss and make recommendations on any questions or matters within the scope of the Charter;

–Article 11, paragraph 2, authorizes the General Assembly to discuss and make recommendations with regard to any questions relating to the maintenance of international peace and security (except that any question on which "action" is necessary shall be referred to the Security Council);

–Article 14 authorizes the General Assembly to recommend measures for the peaceful adjustment of any situation likely to impair the general welfare or friendly relations among nations, including situations resulting from a violation of the purposes and principles of the United Nations; and

–Article 35 provides that any dispute or situation which might lead to international friction or give rise to a dispute may be brought to the attention of the Security Council or of the General Assembly, whose proceedings are to be subject to Articles 11 and 12.

The word "action" in the exception to Article 11, paragraph 2, clearly applies only to coercive or enforcement action, and therefore not to recommendations by the General Assembly. So the International Court of Justice held in its Advisory Opinion of July 20, 1962, saying at pages 164-165:

"The Court considers that the kind of action referred to in Article 11, paragraph 2, is coercive or enforcement action. This paragraph, which applies not merely to general questions relating to peace and security, but also to specific cases brought before the General Assembly by a State under Article 35, in its first sentence empowers the General Assembly, by means of recommendations to States or to the Security Council, or to both, to organize peacekeeping operations, at the request, or with the consent, of the States concerned. This power of the

[49] That paragraph reads: "While the Security Council is exercising in respect of any dispute or situation the functions assigned to it in the present charter, the General Assembly shall not make any recommendation with regard to that dispute or situation unless the Security Council so requests." [Footnote in original.]

General Assembly is a special power which in no way derogates from its general powers under Article 10 or Article 14, except as limited by the last sentence of Article 11, paragraph 2. This last sentence says that when 'action' is necessary the General Assembly shall refer the question to the Security Council. The word 'action' must mean such action as is solely within the province of the Security Council. It cannot refer to recommendations which the Security Council might make, as for instance under Article 38, because the General Assembly under Article 11 has a comparable power. The 'action' which is solely within the province of the Security Council is that which is indicated by the title of Chapter VII of the Charter, namely 'Action with respect to threats to the peace, breaches of the peace, and acts of aggression.' If the word 'action' in Article 11, paragraph 2, were interpreted to mean that the General Assembly could make recommendations only of a general character affecting peace and security in the abstract, and not in relation to specific cases, the paragraph would not have provided that the General Assembly may make recommendations on questions brought before it by States or by the Security Council. Accordingly, the last sentence of Article 11, paragraph 2, has no application where the necessary action is not enforcement action."

The Security Council *does* have the sole authority, under Chapter VII, to make binding decisions, obligatory and compulsory on all Members, for *coercive* or *enforcement* action, but that does not mean that the General Assembly cannot make *recommendations* (as opposed to binding decisions) as to the preservation of the peace.

UNEF, as shown by the Secretary General's report and on the face of the Resolutions which authorized it (see . . . above), involved no enforcement action, and was clearly within the recommendatory power of the General Assembly as regards a situation turned over to it by the Security Council by a Resolution voted for by the Soviet Union.

ONUC *was* authorized by the Security Council, and reauthorized by the Security Council, and no valid objection can be raised to that authorization.

Few Members of the United Nations would ever agree that, if the Security Council proves itself unable to act in the face of an international emergency, the General Assembly can only stand by, motionless and powerless to take any step for the preservation of the peace.

Certainly the record of recent years shows that the General Assembly can take and has taken appropriate measures in the interest of international peace, and that it has done so with the support of the overwhelming majority of the Members, who believe that such measures are fully within the letter and the spirit of the Charter.

2. *The Claimed "Exclusive" Rights of the Security Council as to Peacekeeping Expenses*

The Soviet Union also contends that the Security Council has *sole* authority to determine the expenses of a peacekeeping operation, and to assess them on the membership, and that the General Assembly has no such right.

We think it unlikely that many Members would ever agree that the 11 Members of the Security Council should be able to assess the other 101 Members without any consent or action on their part—surely taxation without representation.

There is not the slightest justification in the Charter for any such contention. The only reference in the Charter to the Organization's expenses is in Article 17, paragraph 2, which provides that "the expenses of the Organization shall be borne by the Members as apportioned by the General Assembly." The Security Council is never mentioned in the Charter in connection with any UN expenses.

3. *The Claimed "Non-Includability" of Peacekeeping Expenses under Article 17*

Article 17 of the Charter reads:

"1. The General Assembly shall consider and approve the budget of the Organization.

"2. The expenses of the Organization *shall* be borne by the Members as apportioned by the General Assembly." (emphasis supplied)

It is clear that if the expenses of UNEF and ONUC, as apportioned by the General Assembly, are "expenses of the Organization," they are obligatory on the Members and must be paid.

This is precisely the question which was decided in the affirmative by the International Court of Justice in its Advisory Opinion of July 20, 1962, accepted by the General Assembly.

* * *

The Soviet memorandum contends (pp. 9, 10) that the fact that the General Assembly set up separate accounts for UNEF and ONUC expenses, apart from the regular budget, and, in certain cases, apportioned and assessed those expenses in a manner different from that used in the case of regular budget expenses, took UNEF and ONUC expenses out of the category of "expenses of the Organization" as found in Article 17, paragraph 2.

The International Court of Justice in its Advisory Opinion of July 20, 1962 decisively rejected this contention.

* * *

The clear conclusion is that the UNEF and ONUC expenses *are* "expenses of the Organization" as referred to in Article 17, paragraph 2, and, as duly apportioned by the General Assembly, "*shall* be borne by the Members" as obligatory obligations.

4. *The Claimed "Non-Applicability" of Article 19*

* * *

The Soviet Memorandum of September 11, 1964, states (p. 11) that the arrears to which Article 19 refers are arrears in the payment of expenses under Article 17. This is of course true.

But the Memorandum contends (pp. 10, 11) that since, according to the Soviet claim, UNEF and ONUC expenses are solely within the competence of the Security Council and are not "expenses of the Organization" under Article 17, they cannot be included in the calculation of arrears under Article 19.

But, as the International Court of Justice has held and as the General Assembly confirmed (see heading D 3 above), UNEF and ONUC expenses *are* "expenses of the Organization" under Article 17 and *were* properly apportioned under that Article by the General Assembly. Therefore they *are* to be included in any calculation of arrears under Article 19.

* * *

E. The Attitude of the UN Membership

From the foregoing it is clear that UNEF and ONUC arrears are legal and binding obligations of Members. Furthermore, it is the overwhelming conviction of the U.N. Membership that they *should* be paid, and that all Members have a collective responsibility for the financing of such operations.

* * *

On June 27, 1963, by the vote of 79–12–17, the General Assembly adopted Resolution 1877 (S/IV), reading in part as follows:

"*Noting* with concern the present financial situation of the Organization resulting from the non-payment of a substantial portion of past assessments for the United Nations Emergency Force Special Account and the *ad hoc* Account for the United Nations Operation in the Congo,

"*Believing* that it is essential that all assessments for these Accounts be paid as soon as possible,

"1. *Appeals* to Member States which continue to be in arrears in respect of their assessed contributions for payment to the United Nations Emergency Force Special Account and the *ad hoc* Account for the United Nations Operation in the Congo to pay their arrears, disregarding other factors, as soon as their respective constitutional and financial arrangements can be processed, and, pending such arrangements, to make an announcement of their intention to do so:

"2. *Expresses its conviction* that Member States which are in arrears and object on political and juridical grounds to paying their assessments on these accounts nevertheless will, without prejudice to their respective positions, make a special effort towards solving the financial difficulties of the United Nations by making these payments;"

Despite the overwhelming support for the *legal* conclusion of the International Court of Justice that UNEF and ONUC expenses are legally binding obligations, and for the *political* conclusion that these expenses *should* be paid, regardless of legal dissent, to keep the UN solvent, the United Nations is still faced with refusals by certain States to pay their shares of these expenses.

F. Article 19

November 10 is the opening of the General Assembly,[50] and November 10 presents the inevitable and inescapable issue of Article 19 unless requisite payments are made before that opening. Article 19 reads as follows:

"A Member of the United Nations which is in arrears in the payment of its financial contributions to the Organization shall have no vote in the General Assembly if the amount of its arrears equals or exceeds the amount of the contributions due from it for the preceding two full years. The General Assembly

[50] On October 23, 41 members requested postponement of the Nineteenth Session. Following a polling of all members by Secretary-General Thant, the opening session was postponed to December 1, 1964.

may, nevertheless, permit such a Member to vote if it is satisfied that the failure to pay is due to conditions beyond the control of the Member."

The first sentence of Article 19 says in simple and clear terms that a Member subject to its provisions *shall have* no vote in the General Assembly. It does not say that the General Assembly has any discretion with respect to such a Member; it does not say that the General Assembly shall *vote* as to whether the delinquent shall have no vote; it simply says that the delinquent *shall* have no vote. The first sentence of Article 19 in the French text is even more emphatic: it says the delinquent Member *cannot* vote—"ne peut participer au vote."

The second sentence of Article 19 *does* provide for a vote; a delinquent Member whose failure to pay is due to conditions beyond its control *may* be permitted by the General Assembly to vote. But there is no discretion as to a delinquent Member whose failure to pay is *not* due to conditions beyond its control, no discretion as to a Member which *refuses* to pay.

The United States hopes that those Members about to be confronted by Article 19 will take the action necessary to avoid the confrontation.

The way to avoid the confrontation is for those subject to the terms of Article 19 to make the necessary payments.

The United States does not seek the confrontation—but if on November 10 the plain and explicit terms of Article 19 do become applicable, there is no alternative to its application.

It is not only that Article 19 means what it says—that the Member shall have no vote—it is that failure to apply the Article would be a violation of the Charter which would have far-reaching consequences.

Failure to apply the Article would break faith with the overwhelming majority of Members who are paying their peacekeeping assessments—often at great sacrifice—as obligations binding under the Charter.

Failure to apply the Article would be a repudiation of the International Court of Justice and of that rule of international law whose continued growth is vital for progress toward peace and disarmament.

Failure to apply the Article would mean the discarding of the *only* sanction which the United Nations has in support of its capacity to collect what its Members owe it.

Failure to apply the Article would undermine the only mandatory power the General Assembly has—the power under Article 17 to assess the expenses of the Organization on the Members.

Failure to apply the Article would tempt Members to pick and choose, with impunity, from among their obligations to the United Nations, refusing to pay for items they dislike even though those items were authorized by the overwhelming vote of the Members. Indeed, the Soviet Union has already said that it will not pay for certain items in the regular budgets. How could any organization function on such a fiscal quicksand?

Failure to apply the Article to a great power simply because it is a great power would undermine the constitutional integrity of the United Nations, and could sharply affect the attitude toward the Organization of those who have always been its strongest supporters.

Failure to apply the Article could seriously jeopardize the support of United Nations operations and programs, not only for the keeping of the peace but for economic and social development.

The consequences of not applying Article 19 would thus be far worse than any conjectured consequences of applying it.

We believe that it is the desire of most Members of the United Nations that the situation *not* arise which makes Article 19 applicable, and therefore we believe that it is up to the Membership to see to it that the confrontation is avoided through the means available under the Charter for avoiding it—the making of the necessary payments.

G. The Fundamental Issue

The United Nations' financial crisis is not an adversary issue between individual Members; it is an issue between those who refuse to pay and the Organization itself, the Organization as a whole. It is an issue which involves the future capacity of the United Nations as an effective institution. If the United Nations cannot collect what is due from its Members, it cannot pay what it owes; if it cannot collect what is due from its Members, it will have no means of effectively carrying on its peacekeeping functions and its economic and social programs will be jeopardized.

The issue is one which vitally affects *all* Members of the United Nations.

The United Nations is of particular importance to its developing Members. It is not only a free and open forum where all can defend what they think and urge what they want, it is an institution which, in response to the interests of all—both large and small—can *act*. But it cannot act unless it has the funds to support its acts. And if it cannot get from its Members the funds to support its acts, *all* would be the losers. So it is to *all* countries that the United Nations must look for a solution.

It has sometimes been said that somehow the United States should work out with the Soviet Union a compromise on some of the fundamental issues.

Could the United States—or should it—agree that Member States which are not members of the Security Council should have nothing at all to say about peacekeeping, even in cases in which the Security Council cannot act? And nothing to say about peacekeeping expenses or their assessment?

Could the United States—or should it—agree that Article 19, despite its plain terms, should not be applied against a great power in support of General Assembly assessments, simply because it is a great power?

The United States does not see how, without violating the Charter, anyone could or should agree to any of these propositions.

H. United States Efforts to Find Solutions

* * *

On March 6 of this year the United States proposed to the Soviet Delegation certain ideas as to the initiation, conduct and financing of future peacekeeping operations which it was hoped —without sacrificing the rights of the General Assembly—would emphasize the *primary* role of the Security Council in peacekeeping and the desirability of according full weight to the views and positions of the Permanent Members of the Security Council and other major contributors to peacekeeping expenses. The United States hope was that agreement as to *future* peacekeeping operations would facilitate the solution of the present problem.

However, despite frequent inquiries as to when a reply to the United States suggestions could be expected, four months went by without any answer. Then in early July, the Soviet Union circulated a memorandum, dated July 10, 1964 (Doc. S/5811), which merely repeated the familiar Soviet thesis that only the Security Council has any rights under the Charter with respect to peacekeeping operations, and that the General Assembly and the Secretary General have none. There was no mention of the arrears problem or of any of the ideas the United States had suggested for discussion.

On receipt of that memorandum, and later, the United States

Delegation again endeavored to enter into a discussion with the Soviet Delegation as to the United States suggestions. Unfortunately the unvarying answer was that the uncompromising Soviet memorandum of July 10 was the only reply to be expected.

This sincere effort to enter into a dialogue with the Soviet Delegation was in the hope that adjustments as to the arrangements for the initiation and financing of future peacekeeping operations could make it easier to reach some solution as to the present and the past. Unfortunately, there has been no Soviet willingness to enter into that dialogue.

It is common knowledge that representatives of other Member States also have sought to initiate discussions with the Soviet Union on this subject and also have been met with a reiteration of past Soviet contentions.

Nonetheless, the United States has not given up hope, and it intends to continue its attempts to work out new arrangements in the hope that solutions for the future may make it easier for those in arrears on UNEF and ONUC assessments to clear up in some manner these past arrears. The United States intends to continue its efforts in the Working Group of 21, now meeting under the chairmanship of Chief [*S. O.*] Adebo of Nigeria, and the United States hopes that all other Members of the Group will join in this attempt.

Accordingly, the United States has tabled in the Working Group, as a basis for discussion, a Working Paper. . . .[51]

* * *

I. What Other States Have Done

It is recognized that the Soviet Union and certain other States in arrears for UNEF and ONUC have strongly-held views against paying these arrears. However, the example of what other States have done when in a similar position indicates that loyalty to the Organization, respect for the International Court of Justice and the rule of law, and consideration for the overwhelming views of Members, should be overriding.

* * *

In insisting that Member States, including great powers . . . find some way to make the necessary payments, all must be prepared to be flexible with regard to the modalities of payment. The only vitally essential ingredient in any solution is that the funds be made available to the United Nations. Most Member

[51] Document 95a.

States are undoubtedly prepared to be flexible in approach to such a solution, are inclined to be considerate of the interests and prestige of States which have thus far found difficulty in payment, and are ready to negotiate on any reasonable basis consistent with the relevant provisions of the United Nations Charter and Financial Regulations.

* * *

(c) *The "By Acclamation" Procedure in the General Assembly: Statement by Ambassador Stevenson, December 1, 1964.*[52]

Our hope right along has been to get started on talks about how the United Nations can clean up its financial situation and arrange about the management and financing of future peacekeeping operations.[53] It now looks as if all parties are prepared to talk about these important constitutional matters, and we share the general hope that these consultations can proceed very rapidly.

It is of course necessary that, while the constitutional discussions are going on, the basic issues involved should not be prejudiced by having votes in the General Assembly. The no-voting agreement that was arrived at today therefore seems sensible to us.

C. The United Nations Conference on Trade and Development (UNCTAD), Geneva, March 23-June 16, 1964.[54]

(96) *Statement by Under-Secretary of State George W. Ball, March 25, 1964.*[55]

(Excerpts)

Within the past few years the world has focused great attention on the relations between what we have come to call the developed and the developing nations. There has been a wide acceptance of the proposition that 20th-century concepts of humanity require that all the world's peoples have the opportunity to secure a decent standard of living. There has also

[52] U.S. Delegation Press Release 4472, December 1, 1964; text in *Department of State Bulletin,* December 21, 1964, p. 891.
[53] Cf. Document 95b.
[54] For discussion see *The United States in World Affairs, 1964,* pp. 330-339.
[55] Department of State Press Release 133, March 25, 1964; text from *Department of State Bulletin,* April 20, 1964, pp. 634-640.

been recognition of the fact that, until this goal is secured, the world will not attain the stability essential to the maintenance of peace.

The tasks of development are familiar to all nations, no matter what may be their average levels of income.

* * *

We have had many conferences to discuss separate aspects of this general subject. This Conference is, I think, unique. It is organized on a world scale, and it is addressed to the whole problem in its full dimensions.

The general frame of our discussions in the next few weeks must inevitably be the relations between the industrial and the developing countries, but this Conference should reduce those relations to practical terms. It should consider all of the means by which the developing countries can obtain capital—and particularly foreign exchange—necessary for development, whether through the transfer of public resources in the form of foreign aid, through external private investment, through the enlargement of internal markets, or through the expansion of external trade. And all of these questions must be considered in the context of a world environment that is compatible with our larger objectives.

In the careful and imaginative papers that have been drafted in preparation for this Conference, the problem facing the developing countries has been expressed in terms of a trade gap. I think none of us—least of all, our distinguished Secretary General [Raúl Prebisch]—believes in a mechanistic approach to this question. I am sure he would agree with me that the trade gap should be regarded not so much as an arithmetical statement but as a figure of speech broadly suggesting the scale and the challenge of the problem of development.

I know he would agree also that there are no single or easy or even independent solutions to this problem. It is the responsibility of this Conference to consider all the feasible ways of expanding our efforts in all relevant fields.

Of necessity, therefore, the Conference must grapple with a series of interdependent issues. It is altogether proper that the major focus for this Conference should be on the means for making trade a more effective instrument for development. But these possibilities cannot be considered in isolation. We must also explore the means of increasing and making more effective use of the flow of foreign capital and technical assistance—both public and private; the economic merits of forming or expanding regional economic groupings; and generally the full range of internal policies that are critical to the mobilization and use of capital and that will necessarily shape the contribution that the external environment can make to development.

Given the magnitude of the development problem, there is ample room for imagination and fresh ideas. At the same time, we must be wary of approaches that do not closely reflect the economic or political realities—approaches that begin and end in discussion and thus obscure the actions really needed for progress.

* * *

I wish to comment briefly on the broad questions before the Conference—not as separate issues but in terms of how they fit into the requirements for an effective development strategy.

Responsibilities of Industrial Countries

I shall begin with the central assumption of this meeting—an assumption in which, I am sure, we all concur—that if the developing countries are to achieve self-sustaining growth, they must be able to earn a growing volume of foreign exchange in world markets. To do this, they must develop expanding markets for their raw materials at reasonably stable and equitable prices. They must also find growing world outlets for the products of their nascent manufacturing industries. This will not happen automatically. The expansion of trading opportunities involves difficult problems of policy and decision for both the industrial countries and the developing countries.

Let me begin by reviewing the contributions that the industrial countries can make to the trade prospects of the developing countries and, at the same time, to the more effective use of world resources which expanding trade can promote.

First, and in my view most important, is the need for industrial countries to achieve and maintain full employment and a high rate of economic growth. These conditions will improve both demand and prices for the exports of the developing countries. For example, sustained economic recovery in the United States and Canada and continued high growth in Western Europe and Japan were largely responsible for the recent sharp turnaround in prices for industrial materials. They also contributed to a stronger market for some tropical products. This improvement in demand and prices, if sustained, will make a difference of at least $1 billion on an annual basis in the export earnings of the developing countries.

Full employment in the industrial countries is also necessary to create a favorable climate for the structural readjustments that accompany trade liberalization. We must devise ways and means of cushioning sudden and sharp disruptions in the markets of importing countries. On the basic issues, however, we in the industrial countries need more education in trade—both to deflate the mythology that still surrounds competition from the so-called low-wage countries and to produce a better understanding of the large potential for gains from freer trade. Such education can best be conducted in an atmosphere of full employment.

Second, the industrial countries as a group must be prepared to reduce tariffs and other barriers to the imports of primary products, semiprocessed materials, and manufactured goods of special interest to the developing countries. The industrial countries have done much in recent years to reduce these barriers. More can be achieved by deep, across-the-board tariff cuts in the Kennedy Round,[56] and we are prepared to have these benefits accorded to the developing countries without asking reciprocity. Such tariff cuts can be of immediate help to the developing countries. But even more important, they can provide an environment that will make it possible for them to build productive export industries. It is at this point that the present Conference and the GATT [General Agreement on Tariffs and Trade] Conference, which is to follow, so strongly complement each other.

Third, the industrial countries should be prepared to cooperate, wherever and whenever feasible, in perfecting arrangements that would reduce instabilities associated with trade in commodities and thus enhance development.

We have made some progress in cushioning the effects of fluctuations in commodity prices through the new drawing rights in the International Monetary Fund.

We also support efforts to stabilize prices of specific commodities in chronic oversupply at levels consistent both with market forces and development requirements. These problems can be usefully approached only on a commodity-by-commodity basis, and the arrangements we work out must be designed both to deal with the underlying supply imbalances and to promote development. There is no grand design for the myriad of indi-

[56] Document 25.

vidual commodity situations and problems. We should frankly recognize that such agreements, important as they may be for some commodities, are feasible for only a small number.

Principles of Nondiscriminatory Trade

* * *

In the postwar world there have been two competing concepts as to how the industrial and developing countries might most usefully organize their relations. In principle, my Government has assumed that all industrial countries should accept a responsibility to advance the economic well-being of all developing countries. But the view has also been advanced—sometimes more by way of emphasis than as an assertion of discrete principle—that it would be better to organize these relationships on the basis of special responsibilities between individual industrial countries or groups of countries and individual developing countries or groups of countries.

I do not think that we can fully resolve this major conceptual question in the course of this Conference. But I do feel that, in discussing proposals for special trading relationships between the industrial and developing countries, we must be quite clear whether they fall within one pattern or the other. Moreover, we should conduct our discussions during the coming weeks in full awareness that special trading arrangements have historically evolved in the context of special political relationships and that special responsibilities in the area of trade are likely to carry with them special responsibilities in the areas of politics and even of defense.

I do not make these points to support either one approach or the other but rather to point out that serious departures from the principles of nondiscriminatory trade—particularly in relation to trading arrangements between the industrial and the developing countries—inevitably involve the question as to how key relations among nations should be organized.

Improving Home Markets

I have mentioned certain measures that industrial countries can take to improve access to their markets and to expand their demand for imports from the developing countries. Simply stated, the more access, the more trade—and the United States strongly favors lower tariffs and greater market access.

But tariffs have become less of a barrier to exports, and this will be true all the more after the Kennedy Round. To exploit the opportunities that stem from greater market access for their manufactures, the developing countries must be able to compete not merely with other exporting countries but with the domestic industries of the importing countries.

It is essential, therefore, for the developing countries to market their manufactures on a competitive basis. This, in turn, will often depend on their ability to develop mass national markets—or, where necessary, regional markets.

It is in such markets that the economies of scale originate. This fundamental point is well documented in the history of countries going through the process of development. Apart from a very few special cases, manufactures have been sold massively abroad only after they have been produced for an extensive market at home.

Under these circumstances, we might all give more consideration and support to ways of expanding internal markets in the developing countries. In most cases this will require actions in both the rural and urban areas and the use, in combination, of private and public capital—domestic and foreign.

In rural areas higher priority might well be accorded to raising agricultural productivity and modernizing systems of marketing. In urban areas more could be done to break away from the traditional and restrictive marketing patterns that characterize many of the narrowly based industries in the developing countries and to aim at larger scale and lower cost production for the home market.

These two lines of action could reinforce each other and result in a rise in productivity, a reduction in costs, and an increase in demand. In these ways production for a large domestic market could help the developing countries produce and sell manufactured goods competitively on the world market.

Economic Cooperation on Regional Basis

Many countries, of course, are too small to provide domestic mass markets. The benefits of such a market may be achieved by economic cooperation on a regional basis.

Unquestionably the postwar dismantling of colonial arrangements and the birth of 51 new countries has involved some serious economic costs. As our Secretary General has pointed out, nearly 100 of the nations represented at this Conference have populations of less than 15 million. Of these, two-thirds have populations of less than 5 million.

The integration of national markets into regional markets offers possibilities for recouping these economic costs—and much more. Manufacturing industries based on the larger internal needs of a regional market will reach a competitive position in international markets much earlier and much more effectively.

The United States supports further efforts in this field. We favor changing the GATT rules to give developing countries more flexibility to pursue various forms of economic integration—partial or comprehensive. But the industrial countries should continue to be subject to strict standards in this regard.

This is, in other words, a case where special trade preferences among groups of developing countries could make a contribution to economic growth large enough to outweigh the costs of a departure from nondiscriminatory trading principles.

But let us have no illusions as to the underlying requirement for real progress through integration. The economic advantages of such a course depend on the degree to which competitive principles are permitted to guide the use and movement of labor, capital, and materials within an economic union or trading group. This requires that the participating nations put aside considerations of political prestige and advantage and that they commit themselves from the outset to a full line of action. Thus, each step forward will make it that much more difficult to reverse the entire process.

Need for Private Foreign Investment

When we talk of a development gap, we are talking in large measure of the need of the developing countries to be able to draw on greater capital resources for investment. Part of these capital resources must be used to finance the import of equipment and other materials from abroad. All these capital resources are required to enable a nation to use its human and material resources more effectively and to gain access to the benefits of the constantly widening revolution in technology.

Private foreign investment can itself provide a major source of such capital. In addition, it can stimulate the mobilization of domestic capital in the developing countries. Finally, it normally brings with it technological skills and a knowledge of foreign markets that can facilitate the efforts of developing countries to expand their export industries.

However, the data on the flow of private investment in recent years are very disturbing. In 1956 the net flow of private capital from all member countries of the Development Assistance Committee to the developing countries amounted to $2.4 billion, or 43 percent of the total flow of foreign capital moving to those countries. By 1962 the contribution of private capital was still $2.4 billion, but it represented only 29 percent of the total capital flow.

Over the past two or three decades standards of conduct in international business have undergone drastic change for the better. Yet many developing countries are, I fear, still influenced by the clichés of the past. Would it not be useful to examine carefully the experience of countries that have been attracting a flow of private foreign investment? Would it not also be useful to study the new techniques, new attitudes, and new procedures that have arisen in this field in response to the conditions of this century?

In raising these questions I do not wish to be misunderstood. My country, while itself committed to free enterprise, does not seek to dictate the form or shape of the economic systems of others. I recognize that there are internal political and emotional pressures that may create opposition to the investment of external capital in many countries. I am well aware of differences in conditions and outlook among the nations of the world that require diversity in business as well as in other forms of social organization. I am aware also that even the facilities and organizational modes for providing such capital require adjustment to changing conditions. They have evolved in the past, and further evolution is in progress.

But nations must make their choices of national policy with full awareness of inescapable economic facts. Nations that elect to pursue policies that tend to eliminate the private sector or discriminate against outside investment should be aware that they are denying themselves a source of capital that could otherwise greatly speed their own economic development.

I suggest, therefore, that in the course of these proceedings we reexamine the possibilities of expanding the flow of external private investment capital.

Private capital admittedly cannot be more than one element in an interrelated approach to development. Yet, with regard to this question as to so many others, the developing countries have it within their own hands to determine how fast they will move in achieving growth. Their attitudes and their laws and their procedures will, in most cases, determine whether the flow of external private capital and technology takes place. Experience gives us no limits on how far the process can carry.

Role of Foreign Aid

I turn finally to the question of foreign aid—bilateral and multilateral. Clearly this is neither the least important nor the residual element in the package. But economic assistance is made more—or less—effective by what happens in the other fields we have discussed.

My Government believes that foreign aid should assist developing countries with a supplemental source of capital. This capital can contribute to development in the following specific ways:

First, as a supplemental source of long-term capital for certain projects that will not produce immediate returns but which are a necessary base for other projects and a stimulant to the development process as a whole;

Second, as a source of capital to finance imports of materials and equipment that could otherwise become serious production bottlenecks in a situation of foreign exchange stringency;

Third, as a source of seed capital that can stimulate the mobilization and effective use of capital from internal sources.

We believe, in short, that foreign aid will play an essential role if it exercises the catalytic effect it is designed to produce. This, in turn, will depend on cooperation between donor and recipient countries.

We are looking forward to an extensive and frank discussion at the Conference of the requirements for aid and the functions aid can perform. At this point such a discussion could serve a healthy purpose. Almost without exception the industrial countries now command the resources that enable them to participate in supplying foreign assistance. Yet more and more of the donor countries are becoming concerned over whether their efforts are producing the results for which they had hoped. In allocating capital assistance they sometimes find a shortage of what they consider to be soundly conceived projects. The developing countries, on the other hand, have now acquired the experience to speak with some assurance on how they themselves can contribute to the process.

A constructive exchange of views can resolve misunderstanding. It can lead to the time when industrial countries, in speaking of the need for self-help, and developing countries, in emphasizing their requirements for foreign capital, will not be talking at cross purposes. In fact, at the working level where development decisions are made from day to day, there is already a wider common basis of concepts, vocabulary, and experience than is generally understood. I believe this Conference can enlarge these understandings among us.

Collective Obligations and Responsibilities

There are, it seems to me, a few general comments that we should bear in mind during our discussions.

First, the economic growth of any nation is a mixture of interrelated elements. We can emphasize one element or another at this Conference, but it would be unwise for us to focus on any single element to the exclusion of the others.

Second, economic development should not be studied simply in terms of aggregates. It is a phenomenon of individual countries. It is not the summation on a world basis of unrequited needs but the reflection of individual country programs, carefully drawn up, faithfully executed, and reflecting a national purpose.

Third, economic development is an intricate and difficult process. It has proved difficult for the industrial countries who have gone through it in the past, and it will be so for the newer countries that are going through it now. The developing countries of today, however, have the advantages of today's technology and of close international cooperation. These advantages can accelerate the process of growth.

These three propositions could, I think, set the tone for the Conference. After all, this is no adversary proceeding between the industrial and developing countries. The distinction between the two groups is not a clear one, and the differences within the two groups are very large.

We are here to solve problems we accept as common problems—not to debate. We are here to draw nations standing at different points along the historic paths of growth closer together—not to divide them.

The progress of the developing countries requires the cooperation of all, and it is futile to test proposals on the assumption that what one gains the other must necessarily lose.

All of us—the industrial and developing countries—have unfilled aspirations at home. But we are also part of an interdependent world with collective obligations and responsibilities. We each have vested interests in the other's welfare.

My country believes strongly in this kind of interdependence and in these kinds of vested interests. We have been, and continue to be, committed to help those who wish to help themselves, and we undertake this commitment, as President Kennedy said in his inaugural address, for one reason only: "because it is right."[57]

(97) *Preamble and Recommendations of the Final Act of UNCTAD, Adopted June 15, 1964.*[58]

(Excerpts)

FIRST PART—PREAMBLE

The United Nations Conference on Trade and Development has adopted this Final Act.

Section I

BACKGROUND

1. The States participating in the Conference are determined to achieve the high purposes embodied in the United Nations Charter "to promote social progress and better standards of life in larger freedom"; [59] to seek a better and more effective system of international economic co-operation, whereby the division of the world into areas of poverty and plenty may be banished and prosperity achieved by all; and to find ways by which the human and material resources of the world may be harnessed for the abolition of poverty everywhere. In an age when scientific progress has put unprecedented abundance within man's reach, it is essential that the flows of world trade should help to eliminate the wide economic disparities among nations. The international community must combine its efforts to ensure that all countries—regardless of size, of wealth, of economic and social system—enjoy the benefits of international trade for their economic development and social progress.

2. Recognizing that universal peace and prosperity are closely linked and that the economic growth of the developing countries will also contribute to the economic growth of the developed countries, realizing the dangers of a widening gulf in living

[57] *Documents, 1961,* p. 13.
[58] *Proceedings of the United Nations Conference on Trade and Development: Final Act and Report,* U.N. Document E/Conf. 46/141, Vol. I (New York: United Nations, 1964).
[59] Preamble to the Charter of the United Nations. [Footnote in original.]

standards between peoples, and convinced of the benefits of international co-operation with a view to helping the developing countries to reach a higher standard of life, the States signatories of this Final Act are resolved, in a sense of human solidarity, "to employ international machinery for the promotion of the economic and social advancement of all peoples." [60]

3. In endorsing the decision to convene the United Nations Conference on Trade and Development, the General Assembly of the United Nations was motivated by certain basic considerations.[61] Economic and social progress throughout the world depends in large measure on a steady expansion in international trade. The extensive development of equitable and mutually advantageous international trade creates a good basis for the establishment of neighbourly relations between States, helps to strengthen peace and an atmosphere of mutual confidence and understanding among nations, and promotes higher living standards and more rapid economic progress in all countries of the world. Finally, the accelerated economic development of the developing countries depends largely on a substantial increase in their share in international trade.

4. The task of development, which implies a complex of structural changes in the economic and social environment in which men live, is for the benefit of the people as a whole. The developing countries are already engaged in a determined attempt to achieve, by their own efforts, a breakthrough into self-sustaining economic growth which furthers social progress. These efforts must continue and be enlarged. Economic and social progress should go together. If privilege, extremes of wealth and poverty, and social injustice persist, then the goal of development is lost. If the social and cultural dimension of development is ignored, economic advance alone can bring no abiding benefit.

5. The developing countries recognize that they have the primary responsibility to raise the living standards of their peoples; but their national exertions to this end will be greatly impaired if not supplemented and strengthened by constructive international action based on respect for national sovereignty. An essential element of such action is that international policies in the field of trade and development should result in a modified international division of labour, which is more rational and equitable and is accompanied by the necessary adjustments in world production and trade. The resultant increase in pro-

60 Same.

61 Resolution 1785 (XVII), December 8, 1962.

ductivity and purchasing power of the developing countries will contribute to the economic growth of the industrialized countries as well, and thus become a means to world-wide prosperity.

6. The issues before the Conference have been at once challenging and urgent. While there are varying degrees of development, the joint income of the developing countries, with two-thirds of the world's population, is not much more than one-tenth of that of the industrialized countries. Moreover, the dramatic increase in the population of the developing countries multiplies the difficulties they face in assuring to their peoples even the simplest elements of a decent human life. The aim must be to create, jointly, new trade and new wealth, so as to share a common prosperity, and thereby avoid the waste and other unfavourable consequences of closed paths to development. The international community is called upon to join in a constructive and universal policy of co-operation for trade and development which will further economic progress throughout the world.

7. The designation of the nineteen-sixties as the United Nations Development Decade [62] was a recognition of deep world-wide concern with the urgent necessity of raising the standard of living of the developing countries and an earnest of the resolve of the United Nations, working together, to accomplish this task. Wide concern has been expressed regarding the inadequacy of the Decade's objective of a minimum rate of growth of aggregate national income of 5 per cent per annum by 1970. To attain even this rate of growth it is essential that measures and action be taken by both the developing and the developed countries, including measures to raise the level and accelerate the rate of growth of earnings of the developing countries from trade, as a means of helping them to overcome their persistent external imbalance.

8. The United Nations Conference on Trade and Development was convened in order to provide, by means of international co-operation, appropriate solutions to the problems of world trade in the interest of all peoples and particularly to the urgent trade and development problems of the developing countries. In a period when their need for imports of development goods and for technical knowledge has been increasing, developing countries have been faced with a situation in which their export earnings and capacity to import goods and services

[62] Resolution 1710 (XVI), December 19, 1961, in *Documents, 1961,* pp. 535-538.

have been inadequate. The growth in import requirements has not been matched by a commensurate expansion in export earnings. The resultant trade gap, which gold and foreign exchange reserves have been inadequate to bridge, has had to be filled very largely by capital imports. This, in itself, cannot provide a complete or permanent solution, and indeed, the servicing of external debts and the outgoings on other "invisible" items themselves present severe burdens for developing countries. Moreover, the terms of trade have operated to the disadvantage of the developing countries. In recent years many developing countries have been faced with declining prices for their exports of primary commodities, at a time when prices of their imports of manufactured goods, particularly capital equipment, have increased. This, together with the heavy dependence of individual developing countries on primary commodity exports has reduced their capacity to import. Unless these and other unfavourable trends are changed in the near future, the efforts of the developing countries to develop, diversify and industrialize their economies will be seriously hampered.

9. Deeply conscious of the urgency of the problems with which the Conference has dealt, the States participating in this Conference, taking note of the recommendations of the Conference, are determined to do their utmost to lay the foundations of a better world economic order.

[*Section II, "Constitution and Proceedings," and Section III, "Findings," follow.*]

* * *

Section IV

REASONS AND CONSIDERATIONS

In drawing up its recommendations, the Conference has been guided by the following essential reasons and considerations:

31. The development of equitable and mutually advantageous trade can promote higher standards of living, full employment and rapid economic progress in all countries of the world.

32. The fundamental problems of developing countries are well identified and what is now required is a universal readiness to act and generally to adopt practical measures aimed at increasing exports and export earnings of developing countries and accelerating their economic development.

33. At the root of the foreign trade difficulties facing the developing countries and other countries highly dependent on a narrow range of primary commodities are the slow rate of growth of demand for their exports of primary commodities, accounting for 90 per cent of their exports, the increasing participation of developed countries in world trade in primary commodities, and the deterioration in the terms of trade of developing countries from 1950 to 1962.

34. During the period of structural readjustments of their economies, the developing countries will remain heavily dependent on commodity exports to meet growing import needs involved in the process of industrialization and diversification.

35. Because of the outstanding importance of commodity trade for economic development, particularly of the developing countries, and the special difficulties affecting trade in primary commodities, it is important and urgent that action be taken over a wide front and on dynamic and comprehensive lines so as to conduct a concerted attack on international commodity problems.

36. There is accordingly a need for a deliberate effort on the part of all industrialized countries to remedy the adverse tendencies in question.

37. This comprehensive action should include international commodity arrangements as one of the means of stimulating a dynamic and steady growth of the real export earnings of the developing countries so as to provide them with expanding resources for their economic and social development and of securing over-all stabilization in primary commodity markets. It is also necessary to accelerate the removal of existing obstacles and to forestall the creation of new obstacles to commodity trade.

38. Compensatory financing is an appropriate solution to meet the serious residual problems caused by short-term fluctuations in the prices of and earnings from primary commodity exports. For residual long-term problems, financial solutions should be sought.

39. The developing countries should not rely merely on the expansion of traditional exports of primary products and raw materials. Promotion of industries with an export potential in developing countries is essential. Diversification and expansion of exports of manufactured and semi-manufactured goods are among the important means to assist the developing countries to achieve, in time, a balance in their external accounts.

40. The establishment and expansion, in developing coun-

tries, of industries with an export potential call for a whole series of interrelated measures and action on the part of the developing countries within the framework of over-all planning, as well as by developed countries and appropriate international organizations.

41. The role of the public sector in the economic development of developing countries is recognized, as well as the role of private capital, domestic and foreign.

42. Developing countries face obstacles and difficulties in marketing their manufactures and semi-manufactures in the developed countries. In order to facilitate the industrial exports of developing countries, their products should have freer access, particularly to the markets of the developed countries, but also to the markets of other developing countries.

43. Easier access to markets should be provided, not only for existing and traditional exports of manufactures and semi-manufactures, but also for a wider range of products in order to improve the opportunities for the establishment, in the developing countries, of a wider range of industries more technically evolved and producing industrial goods of higher degrees of complexity.

44. Substantial imports of manufactures and semi-manufactures may involve some readjustment in the industrial structures of the developed countries.

45. A lowering of trade barriers would improve the competitive position of the developing countries relative to that of domestic producers in the market of each developed country, but it would not improve their competitive position in that market in relation to exports from other developed countries. Special measures in favour of exports from the developing countries would be needed to bring about the required expansion of such exports.

46. In addition to the expansion of exports of manufactures to developed countries, the expansion of such trade among the developing countries themselves would contribute towards solving the dilemma posed by the economic and technological requirements of modern industry, on the one hand, and the limited domestic markets of individual countries on the other. Because of the many forms which economic co-operation might have in various cases and the problems which they might cause, it is considered that a certain flexibility is needed.

47. The Conference has considered the general targets on which the international community might focus in dealing with the problems of development through trade and international

co-operation. A number of principles and criteria, aimed at providing constructive guidelines for policies in the various areas of international financial and technical co-operation, have been formulated. The major questions identified are as follows:

(*a*) The need for higher growth rates for developing countries; measures to be taken by developed and developing countries, including measures to increase foreign exchange availabilities.

(*b*) Guidelines for international financial and technical co-operation; terms and conditions of aid, and the relation of trade and aid to maintain the continuity of sound development plans or programmes.

(*c*) External debt problems.

(*d*) The need and means for increasing the flow of financial resources to the developing countries.

(*e*) Compensatory finance; supplementary financial measures.

(*f*) Aspects of shipping and all other invisible items.

(*g*) The need for periodic reviews.

48. There is wide recognition of the importance and gravity of the problem posed by the financing of development, in all its many complex aspects, and this recognition should form the basis for continuing reviews and action in this field.

49. There is also recognition of the need for greater and more systematic efforts by all parties involved, with a fair division of responsibilities among developed and developing countries, in order to engender the necessary co-operative efforts at the national, regional and international levels.

50. More specifically, there is wide agreement in some key areas which, though necessarily limited in scope, constituted forward steps. These areas include measures for accelerated growth in developing countries and increase in foreign exchange availabilities; guidelines for international financial and technical co-operation, compensatory financing and supplementary financial measures, and for dealing with external debt problems; and some aspects of shipping in relation to the trade of developing countries.

51. Finally, in some other areas, there is also agreement that specific measures, which have been proposed, should be given further consideration or should be studied by the appropriate international organizations.

52. In approaching the problem of institutional arrangements, the Conference has taken into account the fact that sustained

efforts are necessary to raise standards of living in all countries and to accelerate the economic growth of developing countries, and that international trade is an important instrument for economic development. The Conference has provided a unique opportunity to make a comprehensive review of the problems of trade and of trade in relation to economic development, particularly those problems affecting the developing countries. It has recognized that adequate and effectively functioning organizational arrangements are essential if the full contribution of international trade to the accelerated growth of the developing countries is to be successfully achieved through the formulation and implementation of the necessary policies.

53. To this end, the Conference has examined the operation of existing international institutions and has recognized both their contributions and their limitations in dealing with all the problems of trade and related problems of development. It believes that participating Governments should make the most effective use of institutions and arrangements to which they are or may become parties, and is convinced, at the same time, that there should be a further review of both the present and the proposed institutional arrangements, in the light of the experience of their work and activities. The Conference has further taken note of the widespread desire among developing countries for a comprehensive trade organization, and has recognized that further institutional arrangements are necessary in order to continue the work initiated by this Conference and to implement its recommendations and conclusions.

SECOND PART—A CONSOLIDATION OF THE RECOMMENDATIONS OF THE CONFERENCE [63]

Section I

PRINCIPLES

54. The Conference has recommended the following General Principles to govern international trade relations and trade policies conducive to development: (see Annex A.I.1)

General Principle One

Economic relations between countries, including trade relations, shall be based on respect for the principle of sovereign

[63] The results of the voting on the Principles and Recommendations adopted by the Conference appear in Annex A. Observations and reservations appear in Annex B. [Footnote in original.]

equality of States, self-determination of peoples, and non-interference in the internal affairs of other countries.

General Principle Two

There shall be no discrimination on the basis of differences in socio-economic systems. Adaptation of trading methods shall be consistent with this principle.

General Principle Three

Every country has the sovereign right freely to trade with other countries, and freely to dispose of its natural resources in the interest of the economic development and well-being of its own people.

General Principle Four

Economic development and social progress should be the common concern of the whole international community and should, by increasing economic prosperity and well-being, help strengthen peaceful relations and co-operation among nations. Accordingly, all countries pledge themselves to pursue internal and external economic policies designed to accelerate economic growth throughout the world, and in particular to help promote, in developing countries, a rate of growth consistent with the need to bring about a substantial and steady increase in average income, in order to narrow the gap between the standard of living in developing countries and that in the developed countries.

General Principle Five

National and international economic policies should be directed towards the attainment of an international division of labour in harmony with the needs and interests of developing countries in particular, and of the world as a whole. Developed countries should assist the developing countries in their efforts to speed up their economic and social progress, should co-operate in measures taken by developing countries for diversifying their economies, and should encourage appropriate adjustments in their own economies to this end.

General Principle Six

International trade is one of the most important factors in economic development. It should be governed by such rules as are consistent with the attainment of economic and social progress and should not be hampered by measures incompatible therewith. All countries should co-operate in creating conditions of international trade conducive, in particular, to the achievement of a rapid increase in the export earnings of developing countries and, in general, to the promotion of an expansion and diversification of trade between all countries, whether at similar levels of development, at different levels of development, or having different economic and social systems.

General Principle Seven

The expansion and diversification of international trade depends upon increasing access to markets, and upon remunerative prices for the exports of primary products. Developed countries shall progressively reduce and eliminate barriers and other restrictions that hinder trade and consumption of products from developing countries and take positive measures such as will create and increase markets for the exports of developing countries. All countries should co-operate through suitable international arrangements, on an orderly basis, in implementing measures designed to increase and stabilize primary commodity export earnings, particularly of developing countries, at equitable and remunerative prices and to maintain a mutually acceptable relationship between the prices of manufactured goods and those of primary products.

General Principle Eight

International trade should be conducted to mutual advantage on the basis of the most-favoured-nation treatment and should be free from measures detrimental to the trading interests of other countries. However, developed countries should grant concessions to all developing countries and extend to developing countries all concessions they grant to one another and should not, in granting these or other concessions, require any concessions in return from developing countries. New preferential concessions, both tariff and non-tariff, should be made to developing countries as a whole and such preferences should not be extended to developed countries. Developing countries need not extend to developed countries preferential treatment in operation amongst them. Special preferences at present enjoyed by certain developing countries in certain developed countries should be regarded as transitional and subject to progressive reduction. They should be eliminated as and when effective international measures guaranteeing at least equivalent advantages to the countries concerned come into operation.

General Principle Nine

Developed countries participating in regional economic groupings should do their utmost to ensure that their economic integration does not cause injury to, or otherwise adversely affect, the expansion of their imports from third countries, and, in particular, from developing countries, either individually or collectively.

General Principle Ten

Regional economic groupings, integration or other forms of economic co-operation should be promoted among developing countries as a means of expanding their intra-regional and extra-regional trade and encouraging their economic growth and their industrial and agricultural diversification, with due regard to the special features of development of the various countries concerned, as well as their economic and social systems. It will be necessary to ensure that such co-operation makes an effective contribution to the economic development of these countries, and does not inhibit the economic development of other developing countries outside such groupings.

General Principle Eleven

International institutions and developed countries should provide an increasing net flow of international financial, technical and economic assistance to support and reinforce, by supplementing the export earnings of developing countries, the efforts made by them to accelerate their economic growth through diversification, industrialization and increase of productivity, on the basis of their national policies, plans and programmes of economic development. Such assistance should not be subject to any political or military conditions. This assistance, whatever its form and from whatever source, including foreign public and private loans and capital, should flow to developing countries on terms fully in keeping with their trade and development needs. International financial and monetary policies should be designed to take full account of the trade and development needs of developing countries.

General Principle Twelve

All countries recognize that a significant portion of resources released in successive stages as a result of the conclusion of an agreement on general and complete disarmament under effective international control should be allocated to the promotion of economic development in developing countries.

General Principle Thirteen

The Conference decided to include, as a separate part of the Principles adopted by the Conference, the Principles relating to the transit trade of land-locked countries set forth in Annex A.I.2 below.

General Principle Fourteen

Complete decolonization, in compliance with the United Nations Declaration on the Granting of Independence to Colonial Countries and Peoples and the liquidation of the remnants of colonialism in all its forms,[64] is a necessary condition for economic development and the exercise of sovereign rights over natural resources.

General Principle Fifteen

The adoption of international policies and measures for the economic development of the developing countries shall take into account the individual characteristics and different stages of development of the developing countries, special attention being paid to the less developed among them, as an effective means of ensuring sustained growth with equitable opportunity for each developing country.

55. The Conference has recommended a number of Special Principles to govern international trade relations and trade policies conducive to development (see Annex A.I.1).

56. The Conference has adopted the following recommendation on Principles relating to the transit trade of land-locked countries (see Annex A.I.2).

The Conference,

Having regard to the various aspects of the problem of transit trade of land-locked States,

Considering that, for the promotion of the economic development of the land-locked States, it is essential to provide facilities to enable them to overcome the effects of their land-locked position on their trade,

Adopts the following principles together with the Interpretative Note:

[64] Resolution 1514 (XV), December 14, 1960, in *Documents, 1960,* pp. 575-577.

[*These eight principles follow.*]

* * *

57. In the light of its adoption of principles governing international trade relations and trade policies conducive to development, the Conference has recognized the necessity of achieving the broadest possible measure of agreement at the earliest possible moment on a set of Principles, and has recommended that the institutional machinery proposed by the Conference should continue efforts to that end (see Annex A.I.3).

Section II

INTERNATIONAL COMMODITY PROBLEMS

58. In order to deal with the problems facing the primary commodity trade of developing countries, the Conference has recommended that the provisions outlined below should be considered as means of increasing the export earnings of the developing countries by general measures as well as by specific measures related to individual commodities and, that, to this end, practical steps should be taken by Governments concerned to implement, at the earliest possible date, those of the following provisions which are applicable in the light of certain considerations (see Annex A.II.1), as solutions of the urgent problems of developing countries:

(*a*) Provisions for international commodity arrangements, with a basic objective of stimulating a dynamic and steady growth and ensuring reasonable predictability in the real export earnings of the developing countries so as to provide them with expanding resources for their economic and social development, while taking into account the interests of consumers in importing countries, through remunerative, equitable and stable prices for primary commodities, having due regard to their import purchasing power, assured satisfactory access and increased imports and consumption, as well as co-ordination of production and marketing policies (see Annexes A.II.1 and A.II.2);

(*b*) Provisions for a programme of measures and actions for the removal of obstacles (tariff, non-tariff and other) and discriminatory practices and for expansion of market opportunities for primary commodity exports and for increases in their consumption and imports in developed countries (see Annexes A.II.1 and A.II.2).

The Conference has given general approval to the establishment of a Commission on Commodity Arrangements and Policies within the framework of the continuing institutional machinery which will be established following the United Nations Conference on Trade and Development. The Conference has also generally formulated terms of reference for the new commission and requested that they be given prompt and favourable consideration by the continuing institutional machinery (see Annex A.II.1).

60. The Conference has also adopted recommendations for active measures to promote market opportunities for primary commodity exports and for increases in consumption and imports in both developed and developing countries. It has expressed the belief that food aid should become an integral and continuing part of international aid under the United Nations and the Food and Agriculture Organization of the United Nations. It has also recommended special action, both national and international, to deal with cases where natural products exported by developing countries face competition from synthetics and other substitutes. It has also recommended, *inter alia,* the study and preparation of a programme of action for the organization of commodity trade (see Annexes A.II.3, A.II.4, A.II.5, A.II.6, A.II.7 and A.II.8).

61. The Conference has noted the heavy dependence of some developing countries on foreign exchange earnings from the export of minerals and fuels, and has recommended that the developed countries should effectively reduce and/or eliminate barriers and discrimination against the trade and consumption of those products, particularly internal taxation, with a view to increasing the real income of the developing countries from these exports. It has also recommended action to provide the developing countries producing minerals and fuels with an appreciable increase in the revenues which accrue to them as a result of the export of these natural resources (see Annex A.II.9).

Section III

TRADE IN MANUFACTURES AND SEMI-MANUFACTURES

62. The Conference recognizes the urgent need for the diversification and expansion of the export trade of developing countries in manufactures and semi-manufactures, as a means of accelerating their economic development and raising their standards of living. It considers that individual and joint action by

both developed and developing countries is necessary to enable the latter to obtain increased participation, commensurate with the needs of their development, in the growth of international trade in manufactured and semi-manufactured products.

63. The Conference has adopted a series of recommendations designed to help in the promotion of industries with an export potential and in the expansion of their export trade in manufactures and semi-manufactures. These recommendations deal with the following questions:

(*a*) Industrial development (see Annex A.III.1), dealing with the creation of a specialized agency for industrial development;

(*b*) Industrial branch agreements on partial division of labour (see Annex A.III.2);

(*c*) The establishment and expansion of industries with an export potential (see Annex A.III.3).

64. The Conference has recommended the adoption by Governments participating in the Conference of certain guidelines in their foreign trade and assistance policies and programmes providing for increased access, in the largest possible measure, to markets for manufactured and semi-manufactured products of interest to developing countries, so as to enable these countries to increase and diversify their exports of these products on a stable and lasting basis. These guidelines also include appropriate provision by developing and developed countries for cooperation between Governments and private groups to build up export production in developing countries (see Annexes A.III.4, and A.III.6).

65. The Conference has noted both the agreement, signified by all developing countries and a great majority of the developed countries, with the principle of assisting the industrial development of developing countries, by the extension of preferences in their favour, and the opposition to this principle expressed by some developed countries. The Conference has recommended that the Secretary-General of the United Nations establish a committee of governmental representatives to consider the matter with a view to working out the best method of implementing such preferences on the basis of non-reciprocity from the developing countries, as well as to discuss further the differences of principle involved (see Annex A.III.5).

66. The Conference has adopted a recommendation based on the readiness of the centrally planned economies to take action with a view to increasing through appropriate measures, the im-

port of manufactures and semi-manufactures from the developing countries (see Annex A.III.7).

67. The Conference has adopted a recommendation outlining practical measures for the promotion of trade in manufactures and semi-manufactures among developing countries (see Annex A.III.8).

68. The Conference has also adopted a recommendation calling on developed countries to take certain measures, *inter alia,* on import promotion and industrial adjustment (see Annex A.III.6).

Section IV

FINANCING FOR AN EXPANSION OF INTERNATIONAL TRADE AND IMPROVEMENT OF THE INVISIBLE TRADE OF DEVELOPING COUNTRIES

69. On the main issues before the Conference on the financing of development, trade and invisible transactions, a large consensus of agreement was reached, though complete agreement was not always achieved.

70. The Conference recognizes the wide concern expressed regarding the inadequacy of the growth target of 5 per cent per annum set for the United Nations Development Decade. The Conference acknowledges the need for steps to be taken, by both developing and developed countries, to mobilize domestic and international resources for accelerated growth in developing countries at rates even higher than that envisaged for the Development Decade where feasible; and that the economic situations, policies and plans of individual developing countries be examined for this purpose with the consent of the country concerned. The Conference also recognizes in this connexion, that the import capacity of developing countries, resulting from the combined total of export proceeds, invisible earnings and capital inflow, and taking into account the evolution of prices, should rise sufficiently, and the measures taken by the developing countries themselves should be adequate, so as to enable these higher rates of growth to be achieved; and that all countries, developed and developing, should undertake, individually and in co-operation, such measures as may be necessary to ensure this. The Conference has also recommended that each economically advanced country should endeavour to supply, in the light of principles set forth in Annex A.IV.1, financial resources to the developing countries of a minimum net amount approaching as nearly as possible to 1 per cent of its national income, having

regard, however, to the special position of certain countries which are net importers of capital (see Annex A.IV.2). The Conference has also adopted a recommendation providing, *inter alia,* that the rate of interest on government loans to the developing countries should not normally exceed 3 per cent (see Annex A.IV.3).

71. The Conference has adopted recommendations concerning terms and conditions of financial and technical co-operation provided by industrialized countries through bilateral and multilateral programmes of assistance to developing countries (see Annexes A.IV.1, A.IV.3 and A.IV.4).

72. The Conference has proposed certain measures to deal with the increasing burden of accumulated debt and service payments in developing countries, with the objective of facilitating, whenever warranted and under appropriate conditions, the re-scheduling or consolidation of debts, with appropriate periods of grace and amortization, and reasonable rates of interest (see Annexes A.IV.1 and A.IV.5). It has also approved the possibility of deliveries on credit of industrial equipment reimbursable in goods (see Annex A.IV.6).

73. The Conference has adopted the following recommendations proposing measures and studies concerning an increase in the volume or an improvement in the terms of financing for developing countries:

(*a*) Recommendations concerning a United Nations Capital Development Fund (see Annex A.IV.7), and the gradual transformation of the United Nations Special Fund (see Annex A.IV.8);

(*b*) The provision of aid for development on a regional basis (see Annexes A.IV.9 and A.IV.10);

(*c*) The promotion of the flow of public and private capital both to the public and private sectors in developing countries (see Annexes A.IV.11, A.IV.12 and A.IV.13);

(*d*) Review of the use and terms of credit, export financing and marketing, and credit insurance (see Annexes A.IV.14, A.IV.15 and A.IV.16).

74. The Conference has recognized, further, that adverse movements in the export proceeds of developing countries can be disruptive of development. The Conference has, therefore, recommended that, as regards payments difficulties caused by temporary export shortfalls, members of the International Monetary Fund should study certain measures with a view to liberalizing the terms of the compensatory credit system operated by

the Fund since February 1963 (see Annex A.IV.17). As regards longer-term problems, the Conference has recommended (see Annex A.IV.18):

(*a*) That the International Bank for Reconstruction and Development be invited to study the feasibility of a scheme that would provide supplementary financial resources to developing countries experiencing shortfalls in export proceeds from reasonable expectations. The relevant economic circumstances for consideration would include the adverse effects of significant increases in import prices.

(*b*) That the continuing machinery recommended by this Conference be invited to study and organize further discussion of concepts and proposals for compensatory financing put forward by the delegations of developing countries at the Conference, taking into account the effect of shortfalls in export earnings and adverse movements in the terms of trade.

75. The Conference has also recommended a study of the international monetary issues relating to problems of trade and development with special reference to the objectives and decisions of this Conference (see Annex A.IV.19). It has also approved a recommendation on the participation of nationals of developing countries in the process of policy formulation in international financial and monetary agencies (see Annex A.IV. 20).

76. The Conference has agreed on a draft text containing a Common Measure of Understanding on shipping questions, and has recommended that appropriate intergovernmental procedures, including any committee that might be deemed necessary, be established to promote understanding and co-operation in the field of shipping, and to study and report on its economic aspects (see Annexes A.IV.21 and A.IV.22).

77. The Conference has also considered and recommended measures on insurance, tourism, technical assistance and transfer of technology, taking into account the need to improve the invisible trade of developing countries (see Annexes A.IV.23, A.IV. 24, A.IV.25 and A.IV.26).

Section V

INSTITUTIONAL ARRANGEMENTS

78. The Conference has recommended to the United Nations General Assembly that it adopt, at its nineteenth session, the following provisions, *inter alia:*

(*a*) The present United Nations Conference on Trade and Development should be established as an organ of the General Assembly to be convened at intervals of not more than three years and with a membership comprising those States which are members of the United Nations, the specialized agencies, or the International Atomic Energy Agency.[65]

(*b*) The principal functions of the Conference shall be:

(i) To promote international trade, especially with a view to accelerating economic development, particularly trade between countries at different stages of development, between developing countries and between countries with different systems of economic and social organization, taking into account the functions performed by existing international organizations;

(ii) To formulate principles and policies on international trade and related problems of economic development;

(iii) To make proposals for putting the said principles and policies into effect and to take such other steps within its competence as may be relevant to this end, having regard to differences in economic systems and stages of development;

(iv) Generally, to review and facilitate the co-ordination of activities of other institutions within the United Nations system in the field of international trade and related problems of economic development, and in this regard to co-operate with the General Assembly and the Economic and Social Council in respect to the performance of their Charter responsibilities for co-ordination;

(v) To initiate action, where appropriate, in co-operation with the competent organs of the United Nations for the negotiation and adoption of multilateral legal instruments in the field of trade, with due regard to the adequacy of existing organs of negotiation and without duplication of their activities;

(vi) To be available as a centre for harmonizing the trade and related development policies of Governments and regional economic groupings in pursuance of Article 1 of the United Nations Charter; and

(vii) To deal with any other matters within the scope of its competence.

(*c*) A permanent organ of the Conference, to be known as

[65] On December 30, 1964 the General Assembly adopted without objection a resolution establishing the United Nations Conference on Trade and Development as an organ of the General Assembly.

the Trade and Development Board, should be established as part of the United Nations machinery in the economic field, consisting of fifty-five members elected by the Conference from among its membership, with full regard for both equitable geographical distribution and the desirability of continuing representation for the principal trading States.

(*d*) For the effective discharge of its functions, the Board should establish such subsidiary organs as may be necessary, and in particular three committees—on commodities, manufactures, and invisibles and financing related to trade.

(*e*) Each State represented at the Conference should have one vote. Subject to provisions to be determined by the General Assembly at its nineteenth session after consideration by it of a report and proposals to be made by a Special Committee to be appointed by the Secretary-General of the United Nations, decisions of the Conference on matters of substance should be taken by a two-thirds majority of the representatives present and voting, and decisions of the Board by simple majority. The task of the Special Committee shall be to prepare proposals for procedures, within the continuing machinery, designed to establish a process of conciliation to take place before voting, and to provide an adequate basis for the adoption of recommendations with regard to proposals of a specific nature for action substantially affecting the economic or financial interests of particular countries.

(*f*) Arrangements should be made, in accordance with Article 101 of the Charter, for the immediate establishment of an adequate, permanent and full-time secretariat within the United Nations Secretariat for the proper servicing of the Conference, the Board and its subsidiary bodies.

(*g*) The Conference should review, in the light of experience, the effectiveness and further evolution of institutional arrangements with a view to recommending such changes and improvements as might be necessary. To this end it should study all relevant subjects including matters relating to the establishment of a comprehensive organization based on the entire membership of the United Nations system of organizations to deal with trade and with trade in relation to development (see Annex A.V.1).

79. The Conference has also recommended action concerning interim institutional arrangements, and the terms of reference of subsidiary organs of the Trade and Development Board (see Annexes A.V.2 and A.V.3).

[*Section VI, "Special Problems," and Section VII, "Programme of Work," follow.*]

* * *

D. The Third United Nations International Conference on the Peaceful Uses of Atomic Energy, Geneva, August 31-September 9, 1964.

(98) *Remarks by President Johnson, August 30, 1964.*[66]

I would like to extend my best wishes to all the delegates at this Third International Conference on the Peaceful Uses of Atomic Energy.

A great challenge confronts you. You can hasten the day when the atom will be harnessed to hard labor for man's welfare. You can reduce the risk that the atom will be used for man's destruction.

We stand at the threshold of the age of nuclear power, but whether nuclear power will meet our needs tomorrow depends on our work and our wisdom today.

In the United States we have been working and learning. We have now learned how to build large-scale reactors whose electric power will be economically competitive in many parts of our country and the world.

Our utility companies now aim to build or purchase reactors producing electricity at between 4 and 6 mils per kilowatt hour. This achievement has come from 15 years of concentrated research and development. The United States Government has spent more than $1.6 billion on this effort. American private enterprise has spent an additional $500 million.

These expenditures are an investment of our people and an investment in the future of all mankind. Through our Government and through private enterprise we are prepared to use this vast new technology to help other countries meet their energy needs.

At present the large-scale reactor offers the best hope of economic production of electricity. Not every country and not every community will use this large size, but our rapid rate of progress should soon lead to economic production in smaller reactors, too.

A further application of nuclear energy will be large-scale desalting of water. The time is coming when a single desalting

[66] White House Press Release, August 30, 1964; text from *Department of State Bulletin,* September 21, 1964, pp. 411-412.

plant powered by nuclear energy will produce hundreds of millions of dollars' worth of precious water and large amounts of electricity every day.

Our Government is proceeding with an aggressive program of nuclear desalting. What we learn in this program will be shared with other nations. Already we have begun cooperative exchanges with Mexico, with Israel,[67] and with the Soviet Union.[68]

Today I invite all of you to join with us in this enterprise. As we move ahead we look to the International Atomic Energy Agency to play an ever larger role in these peaceful efforts. Already it has set standards for the care and for the keeping of nuclear materials. This achievement has raised our hopes for a workable system of world law on nuclear energy.

For almost 20 years we have known the atom's terror as a weapon of war. Today we begin to know its hope as a powerhouse of peace. Today at last we really have good reason for believing that the atom can be made the servant and not the scourge of mankind.

[67] Document 83.
[68] Document 31.

INDEX

The Numbers in this index refer to pages rather than to documents.

COUNCIL ON FOREIGN RELATIONS

PUBLICATIONS

FOREIGN AFFAIRS (quarterly), edited by Hamilton Fish Armstrong.

THE UNITED STATES IN WORLD AFFAIRS (annual). Volumes for 1931, 1932 and 1933, by Walter Lippmann and William O. Scroggs; for 1934-1935, 1936, 1937, 1938, 1939 and 1940, by Whitney H. Shepardson and William O. Scroggs; for 1945-1947, 1947-1948 and 1948-1949, by John C. Campbell; for 1949, 1950, 1951, 1952, 1953 and 1954, by Richard P. Stebbins; for 1955, by Hollis W. Barber; for 1956, 1957, 1958, 1959, 1960, 1961, 1962 and 1963, by Richard P. Stebbins.

DOCUMENTS ON AMERICAN FOREIGN RELATIONS (annual). Volume for 1952 edited by Clarence W. Baier and Richard P. Stebbins; for 1953 and 1954, edited by Peter V. Curl; for 1955, 1956, 1957, 1958 and 1959, edited by Paul E. Zinner; for 1960, 1961, 1962 and 1963, edited by Richard P. Stebbins.

POLITICAL HANDBOOK AND ATLAS OF THE WORLD (annual), edited by Walter H. Mallory.

AFRICAN BATTLELINE: American Policy Choices in Southern Africa, by Waldemar A. Nielsen (1965).

NATO in Transition: The Future of the Atlantic Alliance, by Timothy W. Stanley (1965).

Alternative to Partition: For a Broader Conception of America's Role in Europe, by Zbigniew Brzezinski (1965).

The Troubled Partnership: A Re-Appraisal of the Atlantic Alliance, by Henry A. Kissinger (1965).

Remnants of Empire: The United Nations and the End of Colonialism, by David W. Wainhouse (1965).

The European Community and American Trade: A Study in Atlantic Economics and Policy, by Randall Hinshaw (1964).

The Fourth Dimension of Foreign Policy: Educational and Cultural Affairs, by Philip H. Coombs (1964).

American Agencies Interested in International Affairs (Fifth Edition), compiled by Donald Wasson (1964).

Japan and the United States in World Trade, by Warren S. Hunsberger (1964).

Foreign Affairs Bibliography, 1952-1962, by Henry L. Roberts (1964).

The Dollar in World Affairs: An Essay in International Financial Policy, by Henry G. Aubrey (1964).

On Dealing with the Communist World, by George F. Kennan (1964).

Foreign Aid and Foreign Policy, by Edward S. Mason (1964).

The Scientific Revolution and World Politics, by Caryl P. Haskins (1964).

Africa: A Foreign Affairs Reader, edited by Philip W. Quigg (1964).

The Philippines and the United States: Problems of Partnership, by George E. Taylor (1964).

Southeast Asia in United States Policy, by Russell H. Fifield (1963).

UNESCO: Assessment and Promise, by George N. Shuster (1963).

The Peaceful Atom in Foreign Policy, by Arnold Kramish (1963).

The Arabs and the World: Nasser's Arab Nationalist Policy, by Charles D. Cremeans (1963).

Toward an Atlantic Community, by Christian A. Herter (1963).

The Soviet Union, 1922-1962: A Foreign Affairs Reader, edited by Philip E. Mosely (1963).

The Politics of Foreign Aid: American Experience in Southeast Asia, by John D. Montgomery (1962).

Spearheads of Democracy: Labor in the Developing Countries, by George C. Lodge (1962).

Latin America: Diplomacy and Reality, by Adolf A. Berle (1962).

The Organization of American States and the Hemisphere Crisis, by John C. Dreier (1962).

The United Nations: Structure for Peace, by Ernest A. Gross (1962).

The Long Polar Watch: Canada and the Defense of North America, by Melvin Conant (1962).

Arms and Politics in Latin America (Revised Edition), by Edwin Lieuwen (1961).

The Future of Underdeveloped Countries: Political Implications of Economic Development (Revised Edition), by Eugene Staley (1961).

Spain and Defense of the West: Ally and Liability, by Arthur P. Whitaker (1961).

Social Change in Latin America Today: Its Implications for United States Policy, by Richard N. Adams, John P. Gillin, Allan R. Holmberg, Oscar Lewis, Richard W. Patch, and Charles W. Wagley (1961).

Foreign Policy: The Next Phase: The 1960s (Revised Edition), by Thomas K. Finletter (1960).

Defense of the Middle East: Problems of American Policy (Revised Edition), by John C. Campbell (1960).

Communist China and Asia: Challenge to American Policy, by A. Doak Barnett (1960).

France, Troubled Ally: De Gaulle's Heritage and Prospects, by Edgar S. Furniss, Jr. (1960).

The Schuman Plan: A Study in Economic Cooperation, 1950-1959, by William Diebold, Jr. (1959).

Soviet Economic Aid: The New Aid and Trade Policy in Underdeveloped Countries, by Joseph S. Berliner (1958).

Raw Materials: A Study of American Policy, by Percy W. Bidwell (1958).

NATO and the Future of Europe, by Ben T. Moore (1958).

African Economic Development, by William Hance (1958).

India and America: A Study of Their Relations, by Phillips Talbot and S. L. Poplai (1958).

Nuclear Weapons and Foreign Policy, by Henry A. Kissinger (1957).

Moscow-Peking Axis: Strength and Strains, by Howard L. Boorman, Alexander Eckstein, Philip E. Mosely and Benjamin Schwartz (1957).

Russia and America: Dangers and Prospects, by Henry L. Roberts (1956).

Date Due
OCT 24